Architectures of Display

Through an international range of case studies from the 1870s to the present, this volume analyzes strategies of display in department stores and modern retail spaces. Established scholars and emerging researchers working within a range of disciplinary contexts and historiographical traditions shed light on what constitutes modern retail and the ways in which interior designers, architects, and artists have built or transformed their practice in response to the commercial context.

Anca I. Lasc is Assistant Professor of Design History in the History of Art and Design Department at Pratt Institute, Brooklyn, New York.

Patricia Lara-Betancourt is a design historian and research fellow at The Modern Interiors Research Centre, Kingston University, London, UK.

Margaret Maile Petty is Professor and Head of the School of Design in the Creative Industries Faculty at Queensland University of Technology, Brisbane, Australia.

Routledge Research in Interior Design

The Routledge Research in Interior Design series provides the reader with the latest scholarship in the field of interiors. The series publishes research from across the globe and covers areas as diverse as the history and theory of interiors, evidence-based case studies, technology, digital interior design, materials, details, monographs of interior designers, and much more. By making these studies available to the worldwide academic community, the series aims to promote quality interior design research.

For a full list of titles in this series, please visit www.routledge.com/architecture/series/RRINTD

Titles in the Series

Architectures of Display
Department Stores and Modern Retail
Edited by Anca I. Lasc, Patricia Lara-Betancourt, Margaret Maile Petty

Architectures of Display

Department Stores and Modern Retail

Edited by Anca I. Lasc,
Patricia Lara-Betancourt,
Margaret Maile Petty

Routledge
Taylor & Francis Group

LONDON AND NEW YORK

First published 2018
by Routledge
2 Park Square, Milton Park, Abingdon, Oxon OX14 4RN

and by Routledge
711 Third Avenue, New York, NY 10017

Routledge is an imprint of the Taylor & Francis Group, an informa business

© 2018 selection and editorial matter, Anca I. Lasc, Patricia Lara-Betancourt,
Margaret Maile Petty; individual chapters, the contributors.

The right of the editors to be identified as the authors of the editorial material,
and of the authors for their individual chapters, has been asserted in accordance
with sections 77 and 78 of the Copyright, Designs and Patents Act 1988.

British Library Cataloguing-in-Publication Data
A catalogue record for this book is available from the British Library

Library of Congress Cataloging-in-Publication Data
Names: Lasc, Anca I., author. | Lara-Betancourt, Patricia, author. |
Petty, Margaret Maile, author.
Title: Architectures of display : department stores and modern retail /
Anca I. Lasc, Patricia Lara-Betancourt, Margaret Maile Petty.
Description: New York : Routledge, 2017. | Series: Routledge research in
interior design | Includes bibliographical references and index.
Identifiers: LCCN 2017011133 | ISBN 9781472468451 (hardback) |
ISBN 9781315567792 (ebook)
Subjects: LCSH: Store decoration. | Display of merchandize. | Department stores.
Classification: LCC NK2195.S89 L37 2017 | DDC 729–dc23
LC record available at https://lccn.loc.gov/2017011133

ISBN: 978-1-472-46845-1 (hbk)
ISBN: 978-1-315-56779-2 (ebk)

Typeset in Sabon
by Out of House Publishing

Contents

List of figures

Notes on contributors

Ana María Fernández García holds a PhD in Art History (with honours). She specializes in artistic relations between Spain and America with regards to contemporary art (art market and artistic emigration), and she is currently working on decorative arts in Spain. She has been a visiting researcher at the Universities of Buenos Aires, Santiago de Chile, Autonomous University of Mexico, Cambridge, and Kingston (Modern Interiors Research Centre). She has published several books and articles on Spanish art in Argentina, Chile, Cuba, the United States, Ecuador, and the United Kingdom. She was president of the Danae Foundation, curator of the Selgas Falgae Foundation, and co-ordinator of the European Master in Conservation, Preservation and Heritage Management with the Universities of Naples, Lisbon, Athens, Seville, Ripon & York, Paris–the Sorbonne, and Berlin. She has been the principal investigator of several regional, national and European projects. She is the director of *Res Mobilis: International Research Journal*.

Alice Friedman is the Grace Slack McNeil Professor of American Art at Wellesley College, USA, where she has taught since 1979. Professor Friedman is the author of numerous books and articles on gender, sexuality, and the social history of architecture, including *House and Household in Elizabethan England: Wollaton Hall and the Willoughby Family* (University of Chicago Press, 1989), *Women and the Making of the Modern House: A Social and Architectural History* (Abrams, 1998; Yale paperback 2007), and *American Glamour and the Evolution of Modern Architecture* (Yale, 2010). Current projects include a study of Richard Lippold's sculpture and installations, and a special issue of *Interiors: Design, Architecture, Culture* on "Spaces of Faith," which she is co-editing with Professor Anne Massey of Middlesex University, UK.

Emily Gephart teaches the history of American art and visual culture at the School of the Museum of Fine Arts, Boston, USA, affiliated with Tufts University, USA. Her work explores how material objects provided tools through which discoveries about modern psychology, perception, and aesthetics were negotiated; she also examines the interchange between art, commerce, and ecology in the late nineteenth and early twentieth century. Her essay concerning synaesthetic aspects of painter Arthur Davies' murals has appeared in the 2014–2015 issue of *Imago Musicae: The International Journal of Musical Iconography*. Her current book manuscript addresses the dynamic relationship between visual culture and the psychology of dreams at the turn of the twentieth century, and how it changed the way Americans thought about the self and the subconscious.

Beverly K. Grindstaff is Professor of design history at San José State University, USA. Her areas of specialization are critical theory and nineteenth- and twentieth-century art and design. Themes unifying her work include formal theories of aesthetics and the construction of identity through the fine arts, design, popular culture, and the museum. Representative publications include the 2009 article "The origins of unsustainable luxury: becoming 'slaves to objects'," *Design Philosophy Papers* 3, and the 2015 chapter "The Outdoor Kitchen and Twenty-first Century Domesticity" in *Making Suburbia: New Histories of Everyday America*, edited by John Archer, Paul J.P. Sandul, and Katherine Solomonson. Current projects focus on mid-century interior designers and the "dream houses" of early twenty-first-century America.

Susan Haight is currently completing her PhD in Canadian History at Carleton University in Ottawa, Canada. Her research concentrates on the T. Eaton Company's use of model houses and room interiors as marketing devices during the interwar period, arguing that this major Canadian department store created these displays not only to sell goods but also to claim cultural authority as traditional values were transformed by mass consumerism. She received an MA in Victorian Studies from the University of Toronto, Canada in 1982 and subsequently worked in administration and exhibition development at the Royal Ontario Museum and the Canadian Centre for Architecture.

Trevor Keeble is Dean of Creative and Cultural Industries at the University of Portsmouth, UK. He is a graduate of the V&A/RCA MA History of Design program, and was awarded a PhD for his thesis, *The Domestic Moment: Design Taste & Identity in the Late Victorian Interior*, by the Royal College of Art in 2005. He is the co-editor of *Designing the Modern Interior* (Berg, 2008) and *Performance, Fashion and the Modern Interior* (Bloomsbury, 2011), and has contributed essays to a number of recent collections about the history of domestic design and material culture.

Douglas Klahr is Associate Dean of the College of Architecture, Planning and Public Affairs at the University of Texas at Arlington, USA. He received his PhD in the History of Architecture from Brown University, USA. His research interests have focused upon nineteenth- and twentieth-century German architecture, as well as architectural photography, especially stereoscopy. Recent publications include: "Traveling via *Rome through the Stereoscope*: Reality, Memory and Virtual Travel," *Architectural Histories* 13 June 2016, 4(1): 8, pp. 1–14, DOI: http://dx.doi.org/10.5334/ah.185; "Nazi Stereoscopic Photobooks of Vienna and Prague: Geopolitical Propaganda Collides with a Distinctive Visual Medium" in *Paper Cities: Urban Portraits in Photographic Books*, edited by Susana S. Martins and Anne Reverseau (Leuven: Leuven University Press, 2016), 171–190; "Stereoscopic Photography Encounters the Staircase: Traversing Thresholds, Borders and Passages," *Archimaera* 5 'Grenzwertig' Issue (July 2013), 89–97 www.archimaera.de/2012/grenzwertig/stereoscopic_encounters/archimaera005_Klahr.pdf; "The Radically Subversive Narrative of Stereoscopic Photography," *Kunsttexte.de Bild/Wissen/Technik* 'Die Grenzen der Narration im Bild' Issue (April 2013) www.kunsttexte.de/index.php?id=361; and "The Elusive Challenge of Photographing Urban Spaces: Nineteenth Century Berlin as Exemplar," in

Documenting History, Charting Progress, and Exploring the World: Architecture in Nineteenth Century Photographs, edited by Micheline Nilsen (London: Ashgate Press, 2013), 155–171.

Patricia Lara-Betancourt is a design historian and researcher at The Modern Interiors Research Centre, Kingston University, London, UK. Within the field of modern interiors and design history, her research focuses on the themes of modernity, representation and identity. Recent publications include "The Quest for Modernity: A Global/National Approach to a History of Design in Latin America," in *Designing Worlds: National Design Histories in the Age of Globalization* (Berghahn, 2016), "Contesting the Modernity of Domestic Space: Design Reform and the Middle-Class Home, 1890–1914," in *Space and Place: Exploring Critical Issues* (Inter-Disciplinary Press, 2014), and her co-authored chapter, "Latin America 1830–1900," in *History of Design: Decorative Arts and Material Culture, 1400–2000* (Yale University Press, 2013). She is co-editor of *Seductive Discourses: Design Advice for the Home* (*Interiors* – Taylor & Francis – vol. 5, no. 2, July 2014) and of *Performance, Fashion and the Modern Interior: From the Victorians to Today* (Berg 2011).

Anca I. Lasc is Assistant Professor in the History of Art and Design Department at Pratt Institute, Brooklyn, NY. She studies the invention and commercialization of the modern French interior and the development of the professions of interior designer and commercial window dresser. She has been published in *Interiors: Design, Architecture, Culture*, the *Journal of the History of Collections*, and the *Journal of Design History*. Her book, *Designing the French Interior: The Modern Home and Mass Media*, co-edited with Georgina Downey and Mark Taylor, was published by Bloomsbury in 2015 (paperback 2017). A recent volume, *Visualizing the Nineteenth-Century Home: Modern Art and the Decorative Impulse*, was released by Routledge in May 2016, while Dr. Lasc's monograph, *Interior Decorating in Nineteenth-Century France: The Visual Culture of a New Profession*, will be published by Manchester University Press as part of its "Studies in Design and Material Culture" series.

Margaret Maile Petty is Professor and Head of the School of Design in the Creative Industries Faculty at Queensland University of Technology, Australia. Her research broadly investigates the discourse, production, and consumption practices of the modern built environment, with a particular focus on artificial lighting and interiors. She has published broadly in academic journals such as the *JSAH*, *Journal of Design History*, *Home Cultures*, *Interiors*, and *PLAT*, and is co-editor of *Cities of Light: Two Hundred Years of Urban Illumination* (Routledge, 2015) with Sandy Isenstadt and Dietrich Neumann.

Laura McGuire is a US-based architecture and design historian. She is an Assistant Professor in the School of Architecture at the University of Hawaii at Mānoa, USA, where she teaches architectural history and theory. She has also taught in the School of Architecture & Design at Virginia Polytechnic Institute, USA and in the School of Architecture at the University of Texas at Austin, USA. She has a PhD in Architecture from the University of Texas at Austin. Her research has focused on American and Central European architecture and design of the nineteenth and twentieth centuries, and the role of immigrants in twentieth-century

American design culture before World War II. Her essays have appeared in books and journals, including *Endless Kiesler* (Birkhäuser, 2015), *Frederick Kiesler: Theatervisionäre – Architekt – Künstler* (KHM/Brandstätter, 2012), and *Norman Bel Geddes Designs America* (Abrams, 2012). She is currently editing a collection of Frederick Kiesler's unpublished theoretical writings, and completing a book on his architecture and industrial design of the interwar period.

Emily M. Orr is the Assistant Curator of Modern and Contemporary American Design at Cooper Hewitt, Smithsonian Design Museum in New York. She is also a PhD graduate from the History of Design at the Royal College of Art/Victoria & Albert Museum, where her thesis, "Designing Display in the Department Store: Techniques, Technologies, and Professionalization, 1880–1920," explores how visual merchandising advanced as a design profession and an industry in department stores in Chicago, London, and New York at the turn of the twentieth century. From 2009 to 2012 she was the Marcia Brady Tucker Fellow in the American Decorative Arts Department at the Yale University Art Gallery, where she contributed to the collection catalog *A Modern World: American Design from the Yale University Art Gallery, 1920–1950*. She graduated with an MA in Visual Culture: Costume Studies from New York University, USA, where she developed a research interest in contemporary retail architecture.

Kevin C. Robbins is Associate Professor of Modern French Urban and Cultural History, Department of History, Indiana University, Indianapolis, USA. With a PhD from Johns Hopkins University, USA (1991), Robbins currently focuses his research and published professional writing on modern French civic and art history. He is especially interested in radical and anarchist graphic artists revolutionizing the production of mass-circulation, illustrated publications in the print worlds of modern Paris and other European capital cities. His new research encompasses the cultural history of visual satire, irreverent, comic mockeries of authorities in multiple media, and the visual politics of the French Third Republic. Recent publications include peer-reviewed articles on illustrated European, French, and American comic serials in *Ridiculosa* (2012–2013), and book chapters in *The Flâneur Abroad* (2014) and *Visualizing Violence in Francophone Cultures* (2015). Robbins is currently at work on the first major study in English of radical, anarchist illustrated publications in modern Paris, such as the acerbic, satirical *Assiette au beurre*, their enterprising editors, technical production staff, and affiliated radical artists of both French and international origins.

Michael Rossi is an historian of science and medicine at the University of Chicago, USA. His work examines sciences of language and perception in the nineteenth and twentieth centuries, with a particular focus on embodied aesthetics. Past essays have appeared in *Isis*, the *London Review of Books*, *Cabinet*, and *Endeavor*, among others, as well as numerous edited volumes. He is currently completing a manuscript about the history of color science in the United States.

Anna-Sophie Springer is a curator, writer, editor, and co-director of K. Verlag – an independent press exploring the book as a site for exhibition making. Having completed an MA in Contemporary Art Theory from Goldsmiths College, University of London, UK, and an MA in Curatorial Studies from the Hochschule für Grafik und Buchkunst, Leipzig, Germany, her practice merges curatorial, editorial, and artistic interests. She is currently Associate Editor of Publications for the 8th Berlin Biennale; she has previously worked as editor for the pioneering German theory publisher Merve Verlag, before launching K. in 2011. Anna-Sophie is also a member of the HKW's SYNAPSE International Curators' Network where she co-edits intercalations, a new book-as-exhibition series co-published by K. in the framework of the HKW's "Anthropozän Projekt."

Mark Taylor is Professor of Architecture at the University of Newcastle, Australia, and has a PhD in Architecture from the University of Queensland, Australia. Previously he held teaching and research positions at Queensland University of Technology, Victoria University Wellington, New Zealand, and Manchester School of Architecture, UK. Mark is an editorial advisor to *Interiors: Design, Architecture, Culture*, and regularly reviews papers and book manuscripts for international publishers. His writings on the interior have been widely published in journals and book chapters, and are included in *Diagrams of Architecture* (2010), *Performance Fashion and the Modern Interior* (2011), *Domestic Interiors: Representing Homes from the Victorians to the Moderns* (2013), *The Handbook of Interior Design* (2013), and *Oriental Interiors* (2015). He has authored and edited eight books, including *Surface Consciousness* (2003), *Intimus: Interior Design Theory Reader* (2006), *Interior Design and Architecture: Critical and Primary Sources* (2013), and *Designing the French Interior: The Modern Home and Mass Media* (2015). He is currently working on *FLOW: Between Interior and Landscape* (2017), and *A Cultural History of Interiors in the Medieval Age* (2018).

John C. Turpin, PhD, FIDEC, is Professor of interior design and Dean of the School of Art and Design at High Point University, USA. He has spent the last twenty years studying the history of interiors and the interior design profession. His work appears in the *Journal of Interior Design*, the *Journal of Cultural Research in Art Education*, and *In.Form: The Journal of Architecture, Design and Material Culture*, with book chapters in *Intimus: An Interior Design Reader* (2006), *The State of the Interior Design Profession* (2010), *The Handbook of Interior Design* (2015), *The Handbook of Interior Architecture and Design* (2013), and *Gender & Women's Leadership* (2010), *Meanings of Designed Spaces* (2013), and *Domestic Interiors: Representing Homes from the Victorians to the Moderns* (2013). From 2010 to 2014 he served as founding co-editor of *Interiors: Design Architecture Culture*, and he is the current editor-in-chief of the *Journal of Interior Design*. He is a past president of the Interior Design Educators Council (IDEC). Turpin earned a Bachelor of Science degree in interior design from Florida State University, USA, a Master of Science degree in architecture from the University of Cincinnati, USA, and a PhD in design history, theory and criticism from Arizona State University, USA.

Alexa Griffith Winton is Assistant Professor at the Ryerson School of Interior Design in Toronto, Canada. Her work engages the visual and material culture of the last century, with a particular focus on the history and theory of interiors. Her research also addresses issues of craft in the industrial and computer ages, the role of technology in modern domestic design, and the theorization of the domestic interior. Winton's work has been published in numerous scholarly and popular publications, including the *Journal of Design History*, *Dwell*, *Journal of the Archives of American Art*, and the *Journal of Modern Craft*. She edited *Textile Technology and Design:*

From Interior Space to Outer Space with Deborah Schneiderman (Bloomsbury Academic, 2016). She has received research grants from the Graham Foundation, the New York State Council for the Arts, Center for Craft, Creativity and Research, Nordic Culture Point, and the Beverly Willis Architecture Foundation.

Sandra Zalman is Associate Professor of Art History at the University of Houston, USA, where she teaches classes on Surrealism, museums and exhibition history, and modern and contemporary art. She is the author of the book *Consuming Surrealism in American Culture: Dissident Modernism* (Ashgate 2015), which was supported by fellowships from the American Council of Learned Societies and the American Association of University Women. She has also received an Arts Writers Grant from the Andy Warhol Foundation for the Visual Arts. Zalman's research has appeared as feature articles in *Grey Room*, *Art Journal*, *Histoire de l'Art*, *Woman's Art Journal*, and the *Journal of Surrealism in the Americas*. In 2016, she was awarded the University of Houston's Award for Excellence in Research and Scholarship.

Yannis Zavoleas is Senior Lecturer in Architecture at The University of Newcastle, Australia and co-founder of Ctrl_Space Lab in Athens. He approaches digital media as "tools for thought." His research focus is on design methodology and new technologies in relation to twentieth-century architectural discourse. He is the author of *Machine and Network as Structural Models in Architecture* (Futura, 2013 – in Greek), and co-editor of *Surface* (EAAE, 2013). His research outputs are about architecture, theory, technology, media, communications, and art (*Thresholds*, *The International Journal of the Arts in Society*, Biodigital Architecture & Genetics, ASA, CAADRIA, ECAADE); he served on advisory/editorial boards for EAAE, ASA, CAADRIA, CommonGround, AEDES and Next Generation Building; won the Excellence in Research Creative Works award (Faculty of Engineering & Built Environment, The University of Newcastle, 2014), and one competition in interactive storytelling; awarded in two architectural competitions; organized research activities on architectural design, theory and computation (Code AB-USE I&II, Unbuilt, Digital Materiality, EAAE Architectural Theory Group); participated in thirteen architectural exhibitions and three short-film festivals. Dr Zavoleas has studied architecture and media at Massachusetts Institute of Technology (MIT – MSc), USA, University of Los Angeles California (UCLA – MArch), USA, and National Technical University of Athens, Greece (NTUA – PhD, professional degree).

Architectures of display

An introduction

Patricia Lara-Betancourt, Anca I. Lasc and Margaret Maile Petty

In 2014, Saks Fifth Avenue took home the top prize at PAVE's *design:retail* Winning Windows awards for the best holiday windows in New York City (Patino Dec. 4, 2014).[1] Collectively titled "An Enchanted Experience," Saks' windows featured a set of six displays showing costumes from designer collections that honored the history of the store since its beginnings in the "roaring 20s" (Patino Nov. 24, 2014). With hundreds of thousands of viewers a day, the windows of Saks Fifth Avenue had been the center of New York City's holiday attractions for years (Trebay Nov. 28, 2014); and, since the city's population expected no less, "An Enchanted Experience" was introduced to the general public with a "bang" – a dazzling spectacle led by the sidewalk performance of thirty-six dancers from the world-famed dance troupe the Rockettes. The curtains lifted during their performance to reveal the colorful window displays while, as the *Daily Mail* reported, "fireworks were shot from the roof into the sky," a sign that "the holiday season has well and truly begun" (Peppers Nov. 25, 2014). The prize was a small reward for the Saks Fifth Avenue creative team, which, chief marketing and creative officer Mark Briggs revealed, had worked for over a year on the windows (Ibid.). With costs rising into the millions, the windows took months of planning: designers would envision the following year's windows before the current year's had even unwrapped (Adamczyk Nov. 25, 2014).

Art Deco and the roaring 20s were only part of the glamor of Saks' 2014 holiday windows. According to Alicia Adamczyk writing for *Forbes*, "An Enchanted Experience" boasted "LED lights, strobes, up-lights, video projections and music" as well as "a light show on the building's façade – incorporating 71,000 lights," which would run every day and night through the New Year (Ibid.). The Art Deco-inspired settings also served as backdrops to classic fairy tales brought to life within iconic New York City locations. Sleeping Beauty was shown resting in the Belvedere Castle in Central Park. Her suitor and "more than 40, custom-made fairies with electrical wings" tried in vain to wake her from her "slumber," *Vanity Fair* contributor Elise Taylor explained – a slumber that hadn't been caused by a witch but rather by her inability to adjust to the "city that never sleeps" (Taylor Dec. 12, 2014) (Fig. I.1). Snow White, on the other hand, was stranded in Times Square and tempted by the Evil Queen with a poisoned apple cart on Broadway. Against a neon-lit group of posters referencing all the stories featured in Saks' windows, Snow White wondered: "Vendor, vendor on the street, what's the safest thing to eat?" The other displays included a meeting between Rapunzel and King Kong on top of the Empire State Building, Rumpelstiltskin spinning straw into gold at City Hall subway station, Cinderella making her way to Saks

Figure I.1 "An Enchanted Experience: Once Upon a Time in New York… A Central Park Setting for Sleeping Beauty," Holiday window display at Saks Fifth Avenue store on December 25, 2014.
Source: Alexander Image/Shutterstock.com

Fifth Avenue to buy herself a new pair of designer glass slippers, and Little Red Riding Hood meeting the Big Bad Wolf at the Plaza Hotel (Patino Nov. 24, 2014) (Fig. I.2). Comfortably ensconced in the red and green Art Deco milieu of New York City's 1907 Renaissance Revival iconic hotel across Central Park, the Wolf – passing as Red Riding Hood's grandmother – was fashionably attired to match his surroundings. Ignoring the dangers ahead, the girl was impressed by the material culture enveloping her. The window caption read: "Once upon a time in New York … Red Riding Hood gasped, Oh my, what a big suite you have… ."

Mark Briggs and his creative team at Saks Fifth Avenue brought traditional fairy tales to life in the Big Apple. The competition they won, however, points towards the development of similar cultures of display in other metropolitan centers around the world. While recreating New York City landmark locations within the store's windows, the designers questioned the relationship between reality and representation, urban architecture and the worlds of fantasy display, desire and material possessions. They summed up more than a century of innovative techniques of retail display developed in European and North American stores such as Bergdorf Goodman, Tiffany & Company, Saks Fifth Avenue, Bloomingdale's, Macy's and Lord & Taylor that had put department store windows on the map as ever more audacious demonstrations of conspicuous consumption. As varied amazements meant "both to delight window shoppers and to lure them toward the registers inside," show windows occupy a central role in the history of modern retail in general, and of department stores in particular (Trebay Nov. 28, 2014). Together with other modern retail display strategies such

Figure I.2 "An Enchanted Experience: Once Upon a Time in New York… Little Red Riding Hood's Hairy Encounter at The Plaza," Holiday window display at Saks Fifth Avenue store on December 25, 2014.
Source: Alexander Image/Shutterstock.com

as model rooms, constructed interiors, showrooms, and show floor cases, they form the core of the analyses that this volume brings together.

In the mid-nineteenth century, the opening of the first department stores in Europe and North America drove the development of an array of strategies meant to enhance the presentation of merchandize, giving rise to a new era of ever-greater "cathedrals of consumption." From innovative use of materials (glass and iron) and new lighting techniques (electricity) to new technologies of mobility (the elevator) and new spaces for socializing (tea rooms, art galleries, writing rooms, or dressing chambers), nothing was spared that could turn the heads of even the most adamant opponents of consumerism. The store was for display and display made the store. Experimental strategies and techniques of display became more widely implemented and were found in a variety of retail environments, from local mercantile shops to other modern spaces of commercial persuasion, including arcades, boutiques and malls, showrooms and wholesale retailers. Indeed, as the twentieth century unfolded, it seemed that the "cathedrals of consumption" had opened their doors and spread their gospel across the built environment.

Architectures of Display: Department Stores and Modern Retail departs from the premise that the presentation of merchandize cannot be separated from the modern materials and building techniques that have been the preferred focus of architectural and art historians so far. Consequently, it proposes to challenge the traditional hierarchy of materials and to replace brick and mortar, paint and stone with theatrical props, tantalizing fabrics, lighting, wax mannequins and artificial flowers as well as a host of other visual effects focused on capturing and sustaining the viewers' attention, which, together, form a real architecture of display. Engaging with new materials, media, and ideas, the studies collected in this volume illustrate the historical importance of commercial display as an essential component of modern art, design, and architecture, highlighting the capacity of retail design to encapsulate, stylize, and reinterpret culture and its diverse manifestations.

Through a series of case studies analyzing strategies of display in department stores and modern retail spaces from the late-nineteenth century to the start of the twenty-first century, *Architectures of Display* aims to provide a rich array of historical insights of value to design, architectural and art historians. Established scholars and emerging researchers working within a range of disciplinary contexts and historiographical traditions shed light on the core of what constitutes modern retail and the ways in which retail and interior designers, architects and artists have built and transformed their practices in response to the commercial context. Focusing on the mechanisms and methods comprising the architectures of display and such spatial typologies as staged sets, window displays, model rooms/homes and corporate environments, our volume emphasizes the ways in which these displays have transformed and enhanced the retail experience through the decades, as well as the economic, political, and social contexts from which they emerged. These varied retail settings are viewed as sites of modernity, in which professionalization and gender also play a key part.

The volume is structured into three thematic sections titled "Displaying Modernity," "Technologies of Display," and "Contested Identities/Contested Displays." United by the provocation that visual merchandizing and the architectures of display have been instrumental in mediating modernity, technology, and modern design, the collected essays highlight the ways in which retail environments and strategies of display can and do communicate a range of social and cultural values. The aim is to offer an important contribution to the scholarship on retail and interior design as well as to provide a useful introduction to the history of modern retail, visual and material culture, design and architecture. Each section considers the ways in which the display of merchandize gave shape to and dramatized modern retail and the experience of modern life, while also calling attention to the agency of shops and designers in creating settings that expressed public and private identities. A number of correspondences, such as those between retail spaces and art practice, and between retail practices and technological expression and innovation, offer further continuities across and within the thematic sections, thus providing an opportunity for the reader to explore display as a conceptual and disciplinary meeting point.

Architectures of Display offers a cross-cultural, cross-disciplinary overview of the different display typologies and strategies emerging in places of commerce from the nineteenth to the twenty-first century around the world. In recent years, there has been an increased interest in the history of visual merchandizing amongst design and architecture historians. Publications such as Louisa Iarocci's *Visual Merchandising: The Image of Selling* (2013), John Potvin's *The Places and Spaces of Fashion, 1800–2007* (2009), David Vernet and Leontine de Wit's *Boutiques and Other Retail Spaces: The Architecture of Seduction* (2007), Elspeth Brown, Catherine Gudis and Marina Moskowitz's *Cultures of Commerce: Representation and American Business Culture, 1877–1960* (2006), Christoph Grunenberg and Max Hollein's *Shopping: A Century of Art and Consumer Culture* (2003), Johnny Tucker's *Retail Desire: Design, Display and Visual Merchandising* (2003) and Rob

Shields' *Lifestyle Shopping: The Subject of Consumption* (1992) are among the titles that have emerged in the last twenty-five years. Concomitantly, scholars have engaged increasingly with the analysis of commercial displays in department stores as part of a larger field of inquiry concerning the history of modern businesses and retail. Examples include Louisa Iarocci's *The Urban Department Store in America, 1850–1930* (2014), Jan Whitaker's *The Department Store: History, Design, Display* (2011) and Geoffrey Crossick and Serge Jaumain's *Cathedrals of Consumption: The European Department Store, 1850–1939* (1999). Further elaboration of modern retail in relation to contemporary social, cultural, economic, and political developments can be found in historical studies such as Lisa Tiersten's *Marianne in the Market: Envisioning Consumer Society in Fin-de-Siècle France* (2001), Erika Diane Rappaport's *Shopping for Pleasure: Women in the Making of London's West End* (2000), William Leach's *Land of Desire: Merchants, Power, and the Rise of a New American Culture* (1993), Bill Lancaster's *The Department Store: A Social History* (1995) and Michael B. Miller's *The Bon Marché: Bourgeois Culture and the Department Store, 1869–1920* (1981). Applying a historian's lens to the development of retail interiors and commercial displays, with the exception of Crossick's and Jaumain's book mentioned above, these scholars generally address very little of the visual imagery that these very same environments engaged with, responded to, and even engendered. Alternatively, the few books that have studied the plethora of designs that the visual culture of retail has produced, including William L. Bird Jr.'s *Holidays on Display* (2007), François Fauconnet, Brigitte Fitoussi and Karin Léopold's *Les Boutiques à Paris: Vitrines d'architectures* (1997), and Leonard S. Marcus' *The American Store Window* (1978), focus narrowly on a specific time period or geographic locale. The social sciences have similarly shown an interest in consumption, but such studies by and large have not addressed the design of commercial interiors and architecture. The primary aim of this volume, therefore, is to foreground new research investigating how retail places have offered an outlet for the expression of various design ideas, methods, and practices and, thereby, how they have contributed to the formulation of new forms of modern aesthetic experience, as well as art and design typologies. The chapters included in this volume, when taken collectively, demonstrate that the boundaries between art, design, architecture and commercial display are not as fixed, static, or clearly defined as they have been portrayed.

Display has always been an intrinsic part of markets, commerce and retailing but it was in the late nineteenth century when it acquired a preeminent role as a promotional strategy, furthering the economic and social importance of trade, retailing and distribution. In spite of this, current scholarship, although discussing at length the production and consumption of goods, does not address in equal measure the significance of retail and display design in understanding how international exchange and local production led to mass consumption.

Charles Dickens in his humorous *Sketches by Boz* (1836) gave an account of London's everyday life at a time of change. What he described as an "epidemic" and "disease" was nothing less than the sudden transformation of shops and retailing spaces through their adoption of new display practices:

> Six or eight years ago, the epidemic began to display itself among the linen-drapers and haberdashers. The primary symptoms were an inordinate love of

plate-glass, and a passion for gas-lights and gilding. The disease gradually progressed, and at last attained a fearful height. Quiet, dusty old shops in different
parts of town, were pulled down; spacious premises with stuccoed fronts and
gold letters, were erected instead; floors were covered with Turkey carpets; roofs
supported by massive pillars; doors knocked into windows; a dozen squares
of glass into one; one shopman into a dozen; [...] A year or two of comparative tranquillity ensued. Suddenly it burst out again amongst the chemists; [...]
and a great rage for mahogany, varnish, and expensive floor-cloth. Then, the
hosiers were infected, and began to pull down their shop-fronts with frantic
recklessness.

In Dickens' description it is worth noting the rapid dissemination of larger plates
of glass and larger windows for the display of merchandize, and a more theatrical
approach to shop fitting and decoration, effectively changing not just shops, streets
and urban life but shopping and consumption habits, features which would become
more pronounced as the century progressed. There were no department stores in
Britain at the time (with the exception of Bainbridges in Newcastle) but from the
1860s onwards, they would colonize the high streets of all major British cities.

This volume's overarching theme is particularly exemplified by the department
store and other related commercial spaces in Europe and America since the late nineteenth century. Part I, "Displaying Modernity," considers display in the period 1880
to 1950 within the context of modernity, a process understood as inextricably linked
to industrialization and to the profound transformations it unleashed in global commerce, business methods, transport, technology, materials, population growth and
urban expansion. There were never this many shops, and they were never so large,
imposing, or attractive, transforming the streets, the city and urban culture. This focus
on commercial modernity and display examines a type of modernity that privileges
visual spectacle, surfaces and strong sensorial experiences.

Although it cannot be claimed that department stores brought about most of the
innovative business methods and marketing techniques that came to characterize them
(many of these innovations were already in place in the eighteenth century), before
the 1830s most urban shops in Europe used bartering and credit as opposed to fixed
prices, sold mostly one type of merchandize rather than a large variety, and had a slow
turnover given the high cost and prices of stock, instead of the model of high volume
sales at low prices. After the 1830s however, some shops began to change their retailing approach, as illustrated by Dicken's testimony above. Department stores did not
invent modern retail, but their success and large scale of operation came to epitomize
it, as well as modern shopping and consumption. By 1920, these modern methods
were widely established and few could imagine shops and department stores without
large and impressive buildings, a continuous front of large windows on the ground
floor and spectacularly designed displays and interiors with abundant, well-lit, colorful, varied and glamorous merchandize.

Most essays in Part I are concerned with design trends born in Europe, particularly
in England and France (such as Historicism and Art Deco), and with the dissemination
of modern design, be it through the examination of "model rooms" in period styles
(Chapters 1 and 2), the introduction of installment payment in the 1920s (Chapter 3),
the powerful alliance of art and commerce (Chapter 4), the successful promotion
of Art Deco designs for the home (Chapter 5), or the use of Neo-Baroque styling as

design strategy (Chapter 6). All essays address the role that department stores played in the design and dissemination of interior environments, with four of them in particular focusing on domestic interiors (Chapters 1, 2, 3 and 5). In doing so, they also consider such interiors from a merchandize and display strategy perspective. There are three cities running the show in this section (London, Toronto and New York), reflecting the leading role played by major urban centers in supporting retail and display innovations. Main cities in this period underwent an intense type of commercialization with innovations in retailing and mediation causing in turn a profound transformation in the ways of consumption, while spurring along production, industry and finance (Hahn 2009, 2, 155).

The first chapter in Part I, Trevor Keeble's "'A world of furniture:' The making of the late Victorian furniture shop," examines London's furniture and furnishing shops in the last quarter of the nineteenth century. It argues that the growth of middle-class domestic consumption during these years constituted the shop as a contested public interface between the professional interests of furnishing and decoration and the domestic desires of the consuming homemaker. The development of specialist furnishers and retailers catering to a non-elite market offered new goods to new consumers, and the presentation, exhibition and display of these goods in dedicated galleries, spaces and windows became a finely conceived aspect of retailing.

In Chapter 2, Patricia Lara-Betancourt's "Displaying dreams: Model interiors in British department stores, 1890–1914" examines the "model room" as a crucial retailing practice in the late Victorian and Edwardian period, highlighting the correlation between the growth of department stores, the expansion of their furniture and furnishing departments, and the sophistication of display designs and strategies. A prominent example was the construction of realistic and impressive modern domestic interiors, displayed in the store and at national and international exhibitions, in an array of styles and budgets, complete with ceilings, panelled walls, plants and lighting. The essay discusses in particular the craze for the modern "period room" during which traders, decorative artists and consumers consciously chose historical styles and designs to convey the modernity of the home.

Following the theme of the "model home," this time in North America, Susan Haight's essay "Home economies: The T. Eaton Company's Thrift House, 1926–1950" (Chapter 3) uses as case study one of the most important Canadian department stores, which, by 1940, was among the largest in the world. The author examines the role played by Eaton's model house in defining the store's marketing strategy. Known as the "Thrift House," the model and its displays were an integral part of a promotional campaign designed to introduce and inform customers about Eaton's new installment credit service. Together with the Thrift Bureau, the office that drew up individualized household budgets, they constituted a program of public pedagogy intended to teach consumers the principles of wise spending. The author argues that the Thrift House and Bureau helped shape consumers' understanding of modern domesticity while redefining middle-class thrift as sensible consumption. Responding to a democratizing effort, the rationale for the Thrift House was intended to facilitate the ordinary householder purchasing the home of their dreams through the instalment system. This was also the case of the budget "model room" discussed in Chapter 2, in its attempt to bring to the masses the furniture and furnishing styles favored by the well-to-do.

Although the product of individual designers or design teams, the shop and exhibition displays of model rooms and houses discussed in this section were credited to the store with very few exceptions. It is later, in the 1930s and 1940s, when recognized designers and artists are acknowledged as creators of shop windows, interiors and exhibits displayed in the shop, and their names are prominently included in promotional material. There is a move from an emerging professional capacity in interior design and decoration (subsumed in the branded store credentials) in the late nineteenth century towards an established and recognized area of individual professional expertise, as exemplified by Salvador Dalí, William Pahlmann and Dorothy Draper.

In Chapter 4, Sandra Zalman's "The art of window display: Cross-promotion at Bonwit Teller and MoMA" examines New York's Fifth Avenue department store's 1936 windows, designed by prominent contemporary artists. Referring to Dalí's work for the store as a case study, the essay illustrates avant-garde art's liaison with commercial display practices. Not only were Bonwit's surrealist windows given over to avant-garde symbols and strategies, but they also displayed a copy of the catalog for the Surrealism exhibition concurrently on view at the Museum of Modern Art down the street, thus showcasing the imbricate relationship between the worlds of art and commerce. Zalman's examination of the association between Bonwit Teller and MoMA (which would itself feature retail-window designs during the "Modern Art in Your Life" exhibition) demonstrates that these institutions were not in competition over visual culture but in fact recognized that cross-promotion could strengthen their appeal to shared audiences. This chapter resonates well with Alice Friedman's essay in Part III, "The Cultured Corporation: Art, architecture and the postwar office building," where the author further examines the role of art and artists in corporate branding, and the significance of artistic display in the creation and definition of a new type of retail space.

Beverly Grindstaff in Chapter 5, "William Pahlmann and the department store model room, 1937–1942," considers the work of the popular American interior decorator and designer. As head of the Lord & Taylor's department of interior design for five years, Pahlmann's displays and installations ranged from the October 1937 "International Show" to the May 1942 "Pahlmann's Proverbs," with suites appearing in popular media and being quickly and widely imitated by other department stores. His most celebrated was the "Peruvian Show" (Winter 1941), drawing up to 30,000 people per month. Pahlmann was the first to design model rooms for department stores as a semi-permanent display of domestic furnishings and home decorating advice. The author argues that his model rooms boldly revised the department store display and were instrumental in shifting American tastes to new interiors and especially modernist Art Deco forms.

In the sixth and last chapter in Part I, titled "Baroque lines in a modern world: The retail displays of Dorothy Draper," John C. Turpin examines the retail strategies employed by this influential interior designer. Among female decorators, Draper was one of the very few who engaged in retail design. Turpin discusses her redesign of Coty Beauty Salon (1941), a New York store specialized in selling cosmetics. The author argues that at a time when Modernism was a dominant influence, Draper's employment of Historicism in the design of retail spaces was both romantic and strategic, showing how she relied on aesthetic stylings to engage the romantic ideals of the American middle-class housewife, who sought to emulate the upper class. She was effectively redesigning retail space to support women's new roles, and her designs both empowered and indulged the female consumer through addressing her psychological needs.

The theme of historicism examined in Lara-Betancourt's discussion of the "model room" (Chapter 2) is also addressed in Turpin's essay. In both cases, an appeal to history is made in connection to middle-class aspirations. This theme is also connected to the recognized role of the department store in democratizing luxury or a perceived wealthier way of life. As shown in the essays grouped here, modern retail, exemplified in department stores' display and retail practices, had a determining role in shaping, disseminating and communicating modern design. Particularly the show window was a key mediator and communicator, while model interiors constituted a successful retail strategy and pedagogical tool in defining and promoting notions of modern design, modern interiors and modern domesticities.

In Part II, "Technologies of Display," the authors call attention to the influences and impacts of an array of technologies on the development of display design and retail merchandizing practices, as well as concurrent artistic investigations of these same technologies within the retail context, but with the aim of public engagement rather than increased sales figures. Focusing on show windows as a central interface between retail environments and public engagement, this section offers views into the adaptation of artificial lighting and other mechanical innovations as means of increasing the public appeal of displays, particularly when employed by a new generation of display designers and window dressers (Chapters 7 and 8). Similarly, attention is given to the role of these display technologies as utilized in the retail context by avant-garde artists in efforts to democratize both the experience of modern art and the modern department store (Chapters 9 and 10). Providing bookends to the major technological advances that transformed the practices of retail display and customer experience between the nineteenth and twenty-first century, Part II explores the ways in which technologies of both production and consumption have contributed to the design of the retail environment and shaped expectations of customer experience (Chapter 11).

Opening the second thematic section, Chapter 7, Emily M. Orr's "'The Age of Show Windows' in the American department store: Techniques and technologies of attraction at the turn of the twentieth century," provides an evaluation of the onsite construction of displays in American and British stores. It argues that visible technology in the form of lighting effects, revolving stands, and the use of automatons became instant attractions towards the beginning of the twentieth century, show windows thus celebrating both careful handcraftsmanship and mechanical innovation at once. According to Orr, a window dresser would convey the store's up-to-date reputation not only by employing personal skill but also by engaging the aid of technology in order to choreograph continual transformation of the show window's contents.

In Chapter 8, "Drawing power: Show window display design in the USA, 1900s–1930s," Margaret Maile Petty explores the role of electric lighting in defining and advancing new approaches to window display design aimed at communicating consumer messages to the public and enticing customers into the retail environment. Examining the transition of the retail show window from a means of displaying merchandize inventories to a site of theatrical invention, consumer spectacle, and artistic expression, "Drawing power" traces the development of the show window as a frame and context for display design in relation to a number of factors, including the emergence of an independent profession of window display designers, the appropriation of modern stagecraft techniques and technologies, and the influence of the electric industry and the newly defined field of illuminating engineering. Contextualizing electric lighting as a common interest and concern across these parallel forces, as demonstrated in the shared ideas, beliefs, practices, and objectives that shaped both its uses and meanings, this chapter illustrates the importance of this modern and ephemeral technology as both a primary medium of and conduit for modern display design during the first third of the twentieth century in the United States.

Chapter 9, Laura McGuire's "Automatic show windows: Frederick Kiesler's retail technology and American consumer culture," examines the retail work of the Austrian émigré stage and exhibition designer Frederick Kiesler in the late 1920s and early 1930s, arguing that, for this artist, the employment of technological developments was essential to a store's success. In a series of texts on show windows, McGuire explains, Kiesler laid out a vision of stores populated with robotic salespeople, subliminal films, automatic merchandize dispensers, and enormous television screens that would "help him wage aggressive, multi-media campaigns to woo potential buyers." In addition to incorporating innovative technologies and display techniques, Kiesler's proposals for streamlining the shopping experience also promoted his vision that retail spaces could be democratically inclusive.

With "Prop art: Harald Szeemann and the Warenhaus Gebrüder Loeb AG, Bern," Anna-Sophie Springer revisits Szeemann's pioneering curatorial work in the 1960s and 1970s through the examination of an unusual set of engagements involving a provocative renegotiation of the role of the department store and the department store window as sites of both commerical activity and artisitic practice. Bringing new attention to Szeemann's long-standing but little-known relationship with the Swiss department store Warenhaus Gebrüder Loeb AG, Chapter 10 provides fresh insights regarding the idiosyncratic function of spectacle in Szeemann's seminal thematic exhibitions through the exploration of two group installations staged in Loeb AG's display windows, as well as Szeemann's involvement with the department store's props workshop in the realization and fabrication of his famous 1975 Bachelor Machines exhibition.

In Chapter 11, Mark Taylor and Yannis Zavoleas expand the chronological frame of this section, from the nineteenth-century origins of modern retail display to the digital disruptions of twenty-first century technologies and design practices, with their study, "From retail stores to real-time stories: Displaying change in an age of digital manufacturing." Contrasting the first generation of department stores, with their vast collections of merchandize enabling customers to see and purchase prefabricated items displayed in store, to that of contemporary digital retailing largely accessed through online portals and virtual shopping, Taylor and Zavoleas examine the ways in which these technologies are challenging and reshaping the customer experience as well as the architectures of display – both physical and virtual. In parallel, the authors explore the implication of such seismic cultural and technological shifts on the production and consumption of commercial fashion and the role of display in mitigating the transformations in the customer experience as well as in creating new forms of consumer engagement with the retail environment and transactions. From bespoke fabrication to ready-to-wear to mass-customization, Taylor and Zavoleas call attention to the sustained centrality of display in maintaining a connection with consumers and providing a conduit for the customer experience.

The essays in Part III, "Contested Identities/Contested Displays," break down the larger themes of display and consumption to understand not only how display practices have influenced the distribution of goods but also how display itself has consistently responded to social, cultural, political, economic, religious, and gender norms. Sensually stimulating displays aimed to incite consumer desires in a female audience (Chapter 12), taxidermied animal *tableaux* mimicking natural history museum presentations (Chapter 13), lavishly decorated windows eschewing religious associations to gain political support (Chapter 14), corporate merchandizing strategies associating consumer practices with artistic excellence and elite art patronage (Chapter 15), product design, museum displays, and exhibition tours artfully promoting commercial flatware (Chapter 16), and cross-cultural influences paradoxically informing retail displays while simulating a rejection of capitalist consumption (Chapter 17) have formed a contested terrain where the boundaries between right and wrong, good and bad, moral and immoral were consistently dropped.

In "Exotics to erotics: Exploring new frontiers of desire within Parisian department store décors," Kevin C. Robbins studies, through a critical analysis of Émile Zola's novel *The Ladies Paradise* and Félix Valloton's paintings, the effects that the newly built and constantly redecorated nineteenth-century commercial zones exerted on the psyches and social behaviors of urban consumers, especially women. Capitalizing on the mass allure of sensually stimulating store displays that eroticized consumption and incited consumer desires in order to yield higher profits, Robbins argues that the gendered displays promoted by commercial institutions such as Au Bon Marché also provoked a frenzy for store-inspired imagery at the level of paintings and prints, novels, and even plays. The store's innovative display strategies thus informed modern visual culture, taking the nascent gendered debates about proper behaviour and class associations to the public sphere.

On the other hand, Emily Gephart's and Michael Rossi's "Dovetailed displays: Show windows, habitat dioramas, and bird hats" examines the contested nature of early window displays that employed taxidermied animals to enhance consumption. The authors skilfully argue for strong affiliations between the seemingly disparate institutions of the natural history museum and the department store that arose from interrelated strategies of display. While nineteenth-century critics often blamed women and their artistically feathered hats for the loss of bird life, at the further encouragement of commercial institutions, museum curators bore a shared amount of the blame.

In Chapter 14, Douglas Klahr continues the examination of contested identities and displays in his chapter titled "Department stores and their display windows during the prewar Third Reich: Prevailing within a hostile Nazi consumer culture." In Germany, Klahr argues, an anti-*Warenhäuser* (anti-department stores) sentiment had developed since the 1880s. This reached an all-time apogee in the Nazi period, following contemporary identification of department stores with their Jewish owners. Since they were vital to supporting the regime, large-scale retailers were never shut down, but the merchandize they sold and the displays they created were heavily regulated by the Nazi regime. In order to prevail "within a hostile consumer culture" and to differentiate themselves from small shops, *Warenhäuser* created elaborate *tableaux* in their display windows, where goods, although in tone with the ongoing political agenda, were part of a larger narrative. "How to put on a gas mask," "how to care for stockings," or how best to travel thus became favorite themes that ornamented the streets of modern German cities.

In Chapter 15, "The cultured corporation: Art, architecture and the postwar office building," Alice Friedman widens the frame of display architecture, from its confinement within the retail environment to the larger landscape of cultural production and consumption. Examining the twin notions of "corporate identity" and "corporate culture" as core tenets of not only capitalist economic theory but also popular ideology within the industrialized societies of the United States and Western Europe, Friedman illustrates the significance and influence of the corporate context within the history of modern architecture and design, calling special attention to the role of display and conspicuous exhibition strategies in the articulation of corporate spaces. Examining a breadth of techniques and technologies utilized in corporate display and architecture, Friedman contextualizes these spaces against the backdrop of American popular culture, analyzing the efforts of a number of artists and designers who contributed to the translation and display of corporate identities. Lending the prestige and social status of the art world to new, ever-grander corporate projects, these companies leveraged art-world celebrity through such patronage to bolster and redefine the image of American corporations. Opening up the discourse on display architecture through the analysis of such projects from the 1950s and 1960s, "The cultured corporation" offers new ways of understanding the uneasy partnerships art and commerce forged in their making.

Similarly, in Chapter 16 Alexa Griffith Winton investigates an expanded definition of display in the dissemination and popularizing of Modernism among popular audiences in "'Knife/Fork/Spoon:' The Walker Art Center and the design and display of 'Contour' sterling flatware service, 1949–1951." Giving close consideration to the role of the museum in showcasing the possibilities of modern design, Winton analyzes a series of rotating exhibitions utilized in the Walker's national campaign to launch its modern flatware pattern, "Contour." Describing the close relationship between both the design and exhibition of "Contour," Winton suggests that the design of the product line and its promotion through public exhibitions were essential to the modernist project in the United States. Calling attention to the role of American modern art museums during the postwar period in domesticating previously avant-garde notions of design for the American public, this chapter situates the important role of display in these efforts to bring good design to middle-class consumers.

In Chapter 17, "Galerías Preciados (1943–1975): A Spanish cathedral of consumption and its display strategies during the Franco years," Ana María Fernández García analyzes the commercial history of Galerías Preciados starting soon after the Spanish civil war and during Franco's dictatorship at a time of isolation from the international community. She reconstructs the process of the arrival and dissemination of a department store model imported from Havana, Cuba, which, in turn, followed North American retailing practices. She argues that Galerías Preciados adopted this commercial model and developed with it a true mass-consumption society. Taking this store as a paradigm for modern consumerism, the chapter traces developments in window and merchandize display and, in the introduction of new technologies, innovations that would soon be copied by its competitor El Corte Inglés. The store became a symbol of Spain's modernization, and a paradoxical example of the economic achievements of an autocratic and nationalist regime that, on an ideological level, opposed capitalist consumption.

Note

1 The mission of the Planning and Visual Education Partnership (PAVE) is to "support students studying in the field of retail design and planning and visual merchandising through its annual design competitions for college students [...] through projects, seminars, workshops, and the annual fundraising Gala with proceeds dedicated to educational programs and projects benefiting students." See PAVE, www.paveinfo.org/aboutpave/pavemission (accessed March 15, 2016).

References

Adamczyk, Alicia. 2014. "Holiday Window Displays Light Up New York City." *Forbes*, November 25. Accessed March 15, 2016. www.forbes.com/sites/aliciaadamczyk/2014/11/25/holiday-window-displays-light-up-new-york-city/#3a1b9ef2627a.

Bird, William L. Jr. 2007. *Holidays on Display*. Washington D.C. and New York: Smithsonian Institution in association with Princeton Architectural Press.

Brown, Elspeth, Catherine Gudis and Marina Moskowitz, eds. 2006. *Cultures of Commerce: Representation and American Business Culture, 1877–1960*. Hampshire: Palgrave Macmillan.

Crossick, Geofrey and Serge Jaumain, eds. 1999. *Cathedrals of Consumption: The European Department Store, 1850–1939*. Aldershot, UK: Ashgate.

Fauconnet, François, Brigitte Fitoussi and Karin Léopold. 1997. *Les Boutiques à Paris: Vitrines d'architectures*. Paris: Editions du Pavillon de l'Arsenal, Picard.

Grunenberg, Christoph and Max Hollein, eds. 2002. *Shopping: A Century of Art and Consumer Culture*. Hatje Cantz Publishers.

Hahn, H. Hazel. 2009. *Scenes of Parisian Modernity: Culture and Consumption in the Nineteenth Century*. New York: Palgrave Macmillan.

Iarocci, Louisa, ed. 2013. *Visual Merchandising: The Image of Selling*. Burlington, VT: Ashgate.

Lancaster, Bill. 1995. *The Department Store: A Social History*. London and New York: Leicester University Press.

Leach, William. 1993. *Land of Desire: Merchants, Power, and the Rise of a New American Culture*. New York: Pantheon Books.

Marcus, Leonard S. 1978. *The American Store Window*. New York: Whitney Library of Design.

Miller, Michael B. 1981. *The Bon Marché: Bourgeois Culture and the Department Store, 1869–1920*. London: George Allen & Unwin.

Patino, Alexander. 2014. "Fairy Tales in the City: Saks Unveils Its Holiday Windows." *SaksPOV*, November 24. Accessed March 14, 2016. http://sakspov.saksfifthavenue.com/features/saks-holiday-fairy-tale-enchanted-experience-window-unveiling/.

Patino, Alexander. 2014. "Saks Takes Home Design: Retail 'Winning Windows Award.' " *SaksPOV*, December 4. Accessed March 15, 2016. http://sakspov.saksfifthavenue.com/region/nyc-region/pave-gala-winning-windows-award/.

PAVE. n.d. Accessed March 15, 2016. www.paveinfo.org/aboutpave/pavemission.

Peppers, Margot. 2014. "Christmas is officially on its way! The Rockettes perform as Saks Fifth Avenue unveils iconic holiday window display." *Daily Mail*, November 25. Accessed March 14, 2016. www.dailymail.co.uk/femail/article-2848862/Christmas-officially-way-Rockettes-perform-Saks-Fifth-Avenue-unveils-iconic-holiday-window-display.html#ixzz42vRKYAr6.

Potvin, John, ed. 2009. *The Places and Spaces of Fashion, 1800–2007*. New York and Oxon: Routledge.

Rappaport, Erika Diane. 2000. *Shopping for Pleasure: Women in the Making of London's West End*. Princeton, NJ and Oxfordshire, England: Princeton University Press.

Shields, Rob, ed. 1992. *Lifestyle Shopping: The Subject of Consumption*. London and New York: Routledge.

Taylor, Elise. 2014. "A Stroll Through New York's Gorgeous, and Occasionally Trippy, Holiday Windows." *Vanity Fair*, December 12. Accessed March 14, 2016. www.vanityfair.com/style/photos/2014/12/new-york-city-holiday-windows.

Tiersten, Lisa. 2001. *Marianne in the Market: Envisioning Consumer Society in Fin-de-Siècle France*. Berkeley and Los Angeles, US, and London, England: University of California Press.

Trebay, Guy. 2014. "Holiday Window Displays Lure Them Inside, by Dazzling Outside." *New York Times*, November 28. Accessed March 14, 2016. www.nytimes.com/2014/11/30/fashion/holiday-window-displays-lure-them-inside-by-dazzling-outside.html?_r=0.

Tucker, Johnny. 2004. *Retail Desire: Design, Display and Visual Merchandising*. Mies, Switzerland, and Hove, UK: RotoVision.

Vernet, David and Leontine de Wit, eds. 2007. *Boutiques and Other Retail Spaces: The Architecture of Seduction*. New York and Oxon: Routledge.

Whitaker, Jan. 2011. *The Department Store: History, Design, Display*. London and New York: Thames and Hudson.

Part I
Displaying Modernity

1   "A world of furniture"

The making of the late Victorian furniture shop

Trevor Keeble

The final three decades of the nineteenth century saw the development of a specialist house furnishing trade in London's Tottenham Court Road. Though the area had long been home to a diverse range of trades associated with domestic provision and furnishing, the rapid expansion of the retail sector in the later nineteenth century witnessed the development of large-scale, comprehensive retailers catering for all aspects of domestic furnishing design and provision. This chapter considers the rise of the specialist furniture and furnishing retailer during the later decades of the nineteenth century. It argues that furnishers developed to serve a non-elite, "middling" market by offering new goods to new consumers, and that the presentation, exhibition and display of these goods in dedicated galleries, spaces and windows became a finely conceived yet contested aspect of retailing. These new retailers offered an innovative mode for purchasing furniture and furnishings that was formed in distinction to the well-established practices that characterized the earlier years of the nineteenth century. These can be understood to have offered a polarized mode of provision, with highly esteemed house furnishing companies offering a bespoke service to the moneyed elite, the small-scale manufacturers and productions of workshops and journeymen providing for a relatively prosperous middle class, and a substantial trade in secondhand furniture providing for the majority.

Importantly, the innovations of these new retailers owed much to contemporary developments in the retail of other kinds of goods, such as fashions, clothing and smaller domestic items. The development of the department store in the later decades of the nineteenth century represents the most significant contextual influence upon the development of furniture retailers. Yet the influence of the "general" department stores posed a fundamental challenge to the specialist nature of the furniture and furnishing retailer, and this meant that practices and innovations, such as fixed pricing, the ticketing of goods, and advertising, that were taken up more readily for other kinds of goods, were challenged and disputed within the context of furnishing. In this sense, the chapter characterizes the final three decades of the century as a moment of change as furniture retailing practices become established and "formalized." It argues that the growth of middle-class domestic consumption during these years constituted the shop as a contested public interface between the interests of the established furniture and furnishing professions and a developing culture of retailing, and that this tension complicated the nascent opportunities for display and presentation within these new furniture shops.

In a ground-breaking study, Hamish Fraser suggested that the transformation of the distributive trades in this period amounted to a revolution that took many forms. The most apparent of these, he suggested, was the emergence of static shops as the focus of retail trading (Hamish Fraser 1981, 133). The development of defined spaces in which new furniture and furnishings were "retailed," as opposed to produced and sold, was innovative and reflects a dynamic momentum of change that can be seen to have formalized the relationship between manufacturers and distributors, retailers and customers.

The fundamental "respectability" of the furnishing trade, derived from the authority of production and manufacture and established through the personalized and bespoke relationships of patronage and commission, stood in marked contrast to the impersonal culture of "modern" retailing. Whereas until the middle of the century, the customer for furniture and furnishing would have received a highly personalized interaction with a furnisher, dealer or upholsterer, the increasing standardization of "products," rising commercial competition and general expansion of a middle-class market for furniture and furnishing led to a more formalized yet anonymous relationship between the retailer and his customer. Within these shops, the identification of fixed prices, rather than prices based upon "the shopkeeper's judgment of what the customer would bear," regulated trading for both retailer and customer. Meanwhile, the emergence of new strategies of "self-advertisement" such as "window and front of shop displays" provided the retailer with the means to establish and maintain a visible presence and reputation beyond "hearsay" (Hamish Fraser 1981, 133).

While little coherent documentary evidence of actual furniture shops as they were conceived and presented during the nineteenth century survives, their spaces and images proliferated widely throughout the expansive print culture of the time. Evidence drawn from retail and trade journals, catalogs, advertising and ephemera describes changes that configured the shop as a crucial node that linked furniture production, distribution, advertisement and consumption. An uncertain yet nascent coalescence of consumerist representation found also in the international exhibitions, popular and trade magazines, and advice literatures of this time placed the specialist furniture shop within a contested territory in which it had to establish its place. The nature of this contest can be best characterized as the transition of influence from the established realms and practices of furniture production to the nascent commodity and retail cultures ushered in by late-Victorian modernity.[1]

In this sense, the furniture retail space can only be understood within the context of other emergent spaces and practices of commerce at this time. Primarily, these were found in the innovations of the department stores that had developed throughout Western Europe and North America in the final decades of the nineteenth century. The principal difference between the department store and the specialist furniture providers can be seen in their contrasting approaches to range and scope of product lines. Whereas department stores had multiple suppliers who provided them with multiple lines of different goods, within which there was often only limited choice, specialist furniture stores carried a more restricted range of products but offered greater choice within that range. Importantly, the development of this kind of specialist furniture establishment, which also drew upon the longstanding traditions of the bespoke furniture trade that serviced the higher echelons of society, also created a new class of retailer in the form of the "salesman." Just as the specialist furniture shop developed in the space between the department store and the elite, bespoke house furnisher, the furniture salesman occupied a position between the "general" and explicitly commercial character of the sales assistant and the specialist authority of the house furnisher, steeped as he was in the knowledge and traditions of furniture design, manufacture and production. This development and the challenge it posed to the established authority of the furniture and furnishing sector certainly contributed to the contested and uneven development of retailing within this specialist sphere.

The space of the shop

The London furniture and furnishing trade had, until the middle years of the nineteenth century, been a largely disparate one that ranged from the long-established house furnishers and decorators of the city's West End to the smaller scale artisanal producers located in East End areas such as Curtain Road and Bethnal Green (Kirkham 1989). This industry of furniture manufacture and production existed alongside a considerable trade in upholstery, textiles and fittings, which tended to operate in an even more diffuse manner, ranging from the highest quality comprehensive furnishers of the West End through to drapers and small general stores and, more commonly, street markets.

The nature of this development created a highly stratified market for house furniture and furnishing with only the richest portion of society able to avail themselves of the comprehensive services of renowned West End furnishers such as Holland and Son, Gillow, and J.G. Crace & Son. The considerable majority of householders would have furnished their homes via the large secondhand market in furniture with its sidelines in property, appraising and undertaking, and with pieces handed down or inherited from family. Where finances allowed, they might also have purchased individual items from local makers and from the non-specialist general stores, ironmongers, and drapers that were common by the mid-century (Kirkham 1989).

An 1876 description of W. Waines Furnishing Warehouse published in the *Furniture Gazette* testifies to the growth and scale of a furnishing business as it steadily expanded into all aspects of furniture and furnishing. Located in Newington Butts in South London, this business grew from a single shop in 1848 to more than two acres of combined workshop and retail premises. Listing numerous rooms arranged according to different types and styles of furniture, the article notes:

> There are also workshops in which every process of furniture is going on; in one, cabinet and chair makers are busily plying their tools; in others, inlayers and artists are employed in the decorative portions; polishers, couch and chair stuffers and bed and mattress makers; While elsewhere may be heard the unceasing click of sewing machine, and women be seen actively sewing together breadths of carpet and fashioning into shape all sorts of material for curtains.
> (*Furniture Gazette* February 12, 1876, 97)

By the 1870s the "shop" in which furniture was both produced and sold was a fairly commonplace and sometimes substantial feature of many urban districts. While the intention of this innovation was to exploit retail opportunities for makers, the co-location of workshops and retail effectively put production on display. These hybrid spaces came about over time as furniture craftsmen and producers began to more formally arrange a portion of their workshops, usually toward the front of their premises, into spaces in which customers might view, select, or even commission furniture. In this sense, the co-location of furniture production and retail served to reinforce the specialist nature of the retailer, offering the customer" some sense of patronage more commonly associated with the higher end of the trade. Its roots and connections with specialist manufacture and production gave it the authority to "advise" the newly affluent expanding middle classes for whom the opportunity of domestic design and furnishing was now a real possibility and expectation. This is an important characteristic of the furniture shop that differentiated it from many other areas of general trading such as fashions and smaller household goods that were less explicitly associated with cultures of production and manufacture, and were more keenly focused upon convenience and easing the experience of choice and purchase in a less personalized manner (Whitaker 2011, 63).

Of course, furniture shops were not the only, or perhaps even the most, notable form of retail developing and expanding at this time. The second half of the nineteenth century is synonymous with the development of the department store. The history of the department store abounds with tales of single-item sellers who, from the middle of the nineteenth century, moved from market stalls to grand premises in urban and regional locations throughout Britain. While many of the strategies and techniques used to consolidate these great enterprises were also used in the expanding furniture market, the development of the department store is significantly different in that it was projected as a "general" rather than "specialist" provider. The department store tended to reject the notion of specialization in its bid to be a "Universal Provider," as William Whiteley self-styled his store established in Westbourne Grove in 1863. The boastful measure of this universality, that a department store would be able to supply any product or thing requested, serves to confirm that the innovation of this type of store was, in its unencumbered role as retailer, free to distribute any good or production at the request of its clientele.

Given its origin within furniture and furnishing production, the specialist furniture and furnishing shop was unable to operate in such a manner, and had to instead project the authority of its specialism at all times. However, in projecting itself as the legitimate representative of the furniture trades, the specialist shop addressed the aspirational needs of many newly middle-class consumers. In his study *Retail Trading in Britain, 1850–1950*, J.B. Jeffreys argued the importance of choice and individuality for the middle class consumer who, with more time and opportunity than his working class counterpart, "placed greater emphasis on specialization of the merchandizing function, on specialization in buying, selling, display design and advertisement." Those stores, he argued, that went beyond the large-scale economies of standardized articles to offer "a range, a selection and a distinctiveness that could not be matched by other retailers were successful in attracting customers from afar" (Jeffreys 1954, 33). Given this, it is clear why the specialist furnishers that developed during the nineteenth century did so within close proximity to one another. Though they were indeed in competition, their agglomeration as specialist providers within the environs of Tottenham Court Road, with its nearby rail and bus services, in effect mutually enhanced their specialist nature (Edwards 2011). Nevertheless, the close proximity of competitors must have heightened the importance of maintaining an engaging and current display of merchandize to potential customers.

By the mid-1870s James Shoolbred & Co was the largest retailer on the Tottenham Court Road. The expansion and development of this business is typical of many of the large specialist house furnishers of the period. Established initially as a drapery business at 155 Tottenham Court Road in 1817, Shoolbred purchased neighboring properties over a period of fifty years to accommodate expansion into ever more specialist lines of textiles, carpets and furniture (Edwards 2011). From 1874, Shoolbred & Co began to offer items of furniture, which soon developed into a comprehensive and expansive range of products in various styles and prices. Though no records of the actual business transactions exist, an extensive range of furniture is depicted in a lavishly bound and illustrated store catalog of 1876.[2] Without any background in furniture manufacture, Shoolbred established work-shops at its Tottenham Court Road premises and moved into production. However, it has been suggested that it quickly took up a practice known as buying "in the white" (De Falbe 1985, 54). This constituted subcontracting the manufacture of goods to other producers but finishing and labeling the products themselves. While this process allowed the firm to efficiently control supply and production costs, and to respond to customers' needs and requirements, it also meant Shoolbred could legitimately project itself as a manufacturing producer of high quality "branded" goods (De Falbe 1985, 54). This practice typifies a gradual shift away from furniture manufacture and production in Tottenham Court Road as retailers came to understand the greater value of their London premises being turned over entirely to retailing.

This should not, however, suggest that the relatively "new" providers of Tottenham Court Road were understood to offer anything like the quality of product and service that their near neighbors in Oxford and Bond streets provided to their far wealthier clientele. As Clive Edwards has demonstrated, in spite of their desire to project their specialist credentials, the Tottenham Court Road furnishers were often derided within the wider furniture trades of London, with the quality and taste of the products they sold often equated neatly with the quality and taste of their "middling" clientele (2011, 152). This was satirized by E.M. Forster in his 1908 novel, *A Room with a View*. In it, the aesthetic man of taste, Cecil Vyse, surveying the failure of his future mother-in-law's drawing room, noted that it had the "trail of Tottenham Court Road upon it" (Forster 1996, 93). Whether it is the customer of Tottenham Court Road furniture or the character judging her that is the object of Forster's satirical observation, the equation of Tottenham Court Road furniture with the largely uninformed and unschooled tastes of the middle-class customer is unmistakable.

In December 1873 the *Furniture Gazette* published an extended review of the premises and stock of Messrs. Maple & Co entitled "A World of Furniture." Originally established as a draper in the early 1840s, Maple & Co had grown through subsequent purchases of adjoining premises and redevelopments into one of the largest and most comprehensive specialist furniture shops on Tottenham Court Road. Whereas in all discussion of furnishing design and production the journal promoted a reformist agenda based on sound principals and good taste, in its discussion of the furnishing store it presented a democracy of consumption whereby the "gaudy and vulgar, luxurious and elegant, or pleasant and comfortable" might be supplied to any customer according to their particular preference and purse (*Furniture Gazette* December 20 1873, 606). In its commercial complicity with the retailer, the trade journal gave voice to the emergent consumerist ideals of a society organized by the ability to buy at "prices ranging from the lowest consistent with sound workmanship and good material to sums which only the wealthy can afford to pay" (Ibid.).

The premises comprised long, large showrooms that stretched from the store's Tottenham Court Road frontage to its Gower Street façade, where service areas such as storerooms, stables, packing-sheds and workrooms were located. The "furniture packed closely, yet well displayed, from floor to ceiling" was found to be "in every sort of material, from the most cheap and simple to the most costly and elaborately decorated" (Ibid.). The article repeatedly emphasized the extent to which Maple & Co sought the patronage of a broad and varied range of customers. It reiterated the soundness and quality of the objects offered irrespective of their particular price. It also belied a practical sensibility against inappropriately ostentatious furniture, noting that some things "are too great and grand for the ends they serve" (Ibid.).

While the *Furniture Gazette's* review of the Maple & Co showrooms celebrated the multiplicity of objects on view, it revealed the extent to which, at this time, these objects were not presented or classified beyond any simple "production" understanding of cabinetwork, upholstery, carpets or drapery. The review makes no mention of any attempt to display furniture in combination or ensemble. Nevertheless, the mere fact of these objects being included for display within the showrooms represents a statement of commercial judgment on behalf of the retailer at a time when commercial interests were becoming increasingly aware of the reciprocity between retailers and the objects they "chose" to sell. This sentiment was given voice in an early twentieth century catalog of the Kensington High Street firm John Barker & Co, which invited readers to visit the company's furniture showrooms where "it will be found that every recognizable style of furniture is represented" (Barker & Co 1908, 31). This statement, though seemingly rather perfunctory, articulated a subtle context of commercial representation in that it explicitly acknowledged the representational nature of both the catalog and the showroom, and suggested that key to this mode of representation was "recognition:" anything outside the showroom, just like anything beyond the margin of the sales catalog, was neither recognized nor recognizable. This situates both the showroom and catalog within a culture of taste-making more explicitly associated with the conventions of women's fashions, domestic advice, and magazines. In spite of the explicitly masculine culture of the furnishing trades and industry from which specialist furniture retail emerged, the cultural contexts of retail and its feminized arena of "taste" and "style" gradually became central to it commercial character (Cohen 2006, 89–121).

The shop in view

From the 1870s the shop window was increasingly viewed as the principal means of attracting a dealer's or furnisher's customer, and for the draper, outfitter and decorating shop it had particular significance as an important means of demonstrating the taste and judgment of the proprietor (Robertson 1911, 49–66). Claire Walsh has described how historians of the nineteenth century have used the development of the shop window to explain the novelty and innovation of consumer culture in that period. Yet she suggests that the techniques of display and "browsing" have a much longer history and existed in various forms during the eighteenth and nineteenth centuries (Walsh 1999, 61). Walsh usefully argues for a history of retailing based upon continuity and change rather than sudden innovation, and this certainly reflects the lengthy period, and uneven development and take-up of furniture and furnishing display during the final decades of the nineteenth century (1999, 68).

Describing the mission of the shop window as "to tempt," W.B. Robertson advised that variety and change were key to maintaining the attention of prospective customers. In the case of the furniture retailer he suggested quick changes such as a complete bedroom at the beginning of the week and then a dining room at the end of the week (Robertson 1911, 65–6). This more strategic use of the shop window as a means to engage prospective customers suggests that retailers came to understand their power to attract and engage consumers more fully than the more informal and "passive" practices of browsing that had characterized earlier years.

An original feature of the *Furniture Gazette* was its regular column "Out and About." This featured the commentary of an unnamed correspondent who would "take in" the windows, and occasionally the showrooms of the trade. These wanderings invariably focused upon the London trade rooms, although the column did on occasion review premises further afield. These short articles, often little more than a column and a half in length, offered an opportunity to discuss the latest productions of some of the most renowned manufacturers, and were occasionally cause for dispute. One such review lambasted the "dismal sight" presented in the windows of the widely respected Oxford Street firm Jackson and Graham (*Furniture Gazette* February 28, 1874, 212). Dismissed as "but a reflex of that fashion for which the public taste is responsible," the designs on show were described as being within the prevailing "love of black," variations of which "range from mud and wet clay, through cheerful varieties of coke, coal and slate" (Ibid.). While the *Furniture Gazette* would in time come to accept and even celebrate these japanned objects as the height of art furnishing, in 1874 their innovation and apparent fashionability could only be damned.

What is interesting in the commentary, however, is that the objects on display were roundly dismissed as deriving from "public taste" rather than the good sense of the reputable profession, and that this challenge was expressed through the spectacular medium of the window display. It is clear from much of the commentary of the 'Out and About' correspondent that the practice of displaying furniture and furnishing in windows for a spectating public was not in any way agreed upon as a respectable means of conducting business. As the criticism of Jackson and Graham's furniture suggests, the implication of displaying the latest designs in such public and unregulated fashion was in itself bound up with contested notions of novelty and fashion, concepts that the respectable manufacturing trade had historically sought to marginalize as feminine and counter to its authoritative judgment based on experience and sound principles. Nevertheless it is clear from the pages of the *Furniture Gazette* that, over time, the opportunity of the shop window would be discussed more favorably, leading one contributor to suggest that "much may be learnt by those desirous of setting off their interiors to the best effect by the survey of the arrangements carried out in shop windows" (*Furniture Gazette* November 8, 1884, 374).

While the shop window emerged as an important space for the presentation of furniture and furnishings in much the same way that other goods such as fashions and smaller household goods had been presented in department and general stores, its rise was possibly influenced by widespread regulation of streets and thoroughfares in the later decades of the nineteenth century. Historically, furniture dealers had commonly maximized the depth and range of their stock by using the adjacent pavements and walkways to display their products (Fig. 1.1). During 1878, the *Furniture Gazette* reported widely on its readers' opposition to Newington Vestry's imposition

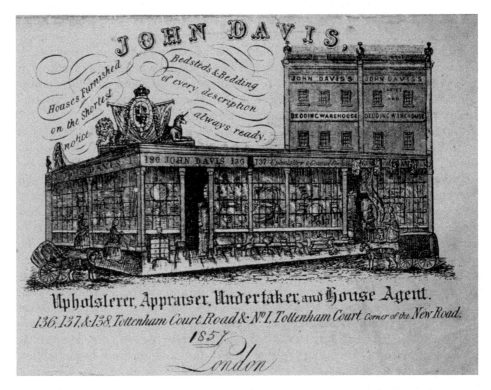

Figure 1.1 A printed trade image of John Davis, Upholsterer, Appraiser, Undertaker and House Agent, 136–138 Tottenham Court Road. (Annotated, 1857).
Source: London Borough of Camden Local Studies and Archives Centre, LCP.942.143

of an order banning them from displaying their goods in such a way. While the immediate impact of this change was that a shop had to reduce stock quite substantially, given that it could no longer displace it to the street during opening hours, in the longer term this ruling imposed a regulation upon the shops that contributed to their formalization.

This only really came about, however, once retailers had the opportunity to redevelop the site of their premises. In 1854, the bedding and bedroom furnisher Heal & Son commissioned the architect James Morant Lockyer to redevelop their Tottenham Court Road site. Though no photographs exist of the interior, which was subsequently extended and remodeled, a photographic view taken in 1855 shows a man and woman looking into the large plate-glass windows that made up its street level façade. The floor-to-ceiling windows set within a cast-iron framework show a variety of items of furniture neatly arranged in presentation to the street. Hung behind these are a number of runs of wallpapers and textiles. Though relatively simple in presentation, the displays are full and formal, and would have undoubtedly offered a spectacular new vista to passers-by.

By the early twentieth century it was widely recognized that advertising, and publicity in general, was the most direct means through which retailers might "represent" themselves to the customer. Inherent to this strategy was the representation not only of the commodities available but also of the physical space of the shop. W.B. Robertson suggested the interrelation between the spectacular aspects of the shop and the representational duty of the advert:

> Some retailers make a practice of having conformity between the window displays and the advertisements in local newspapers. This is good. The window then is the stepping-stone between the newspaper announcement and a visit to the shop. The customer is interested by the printed page, impressed by the window, and inspired by both with a desire to examine more closely and handle the article advertised. The window may be made to supplement the story of the newspaper column, to intensify any interest aroused by reading the weekly sheet, and to this end the articles shown in the one should be written about in the other.
>
> (1911, 63)

Not surprisingly, the trade press went to great lengths to reassure manufacturers and retailers of the suitability of advertising. An article entitled "Tradesmen and Printers Ink" demonstrates how reluctantly businesses embraced the innovations of modern commerce as it suggested that advertising was "like marking the price of goods in your shop-window. Ten years ago it was thought to lower the credit of a man's shop in the estimation of the public, if he "ticketed" his goods, but that mistaken notion has most properly died out" (*Furniture Gazette* July 4, 1874, 686).

The model interior

Touring the wholesale premises of Messrs. Moore and Hunton in 1886, a *Furniture Gazette* correspondent noted that "a number of additional 'interiors' have been fitted up, and thus are typical examples of a dining-room, drawing-room, library, morning-room, bedroom, and various other apartments" (*Furniture Gazette* December 1, 1886, 414). Stressing the remarkable good taste shown in these rooms, and the harmony and symmetry provided by their arrangement, the reviewer emphasized their use as a means of showing off the very latest products and ranges. As a wholesale establishment, these displays were not strictly intended for the consuming householder. However, as the review made clear, the arrangement of items within "interiors" provided the provincial dealer, cabinet-maker or London house furnisher the opportunity to bring his customer to the premises where he would find a large stock of goods "so arranged that the work of selection becomes comparatively easy," the arrangement of the goods within interiors affording the opportunity to judge the "effects" (Ibid.).

The creation of model rooms and interiors within the furnishing store marked the expansion of print practices undertaken in popular magazines and catalogs into three-dimensional form. Since the advent of popular domestic advice literature in the early 1870s, domestic advice books and the many magazines and catalogs they quickly came to influence had long used the "room" or "interior" as the representational mechanism of their work. Indeed, large catalogs featuring lavish illustrations of such rooms and interiors, often commissioned by retailers from renowned architects and designers, became an important mode of representation for the furnishing retailer in the 1870s as companies sought always to expand the opportunity and choice for their customers beyond the physical constraints of their showrooms (James Shoolbred & Co 1876).

Whether in print or three-dimensional form, the innovation of the designed "interior" was its ability to synthesize disparate objects of stock into a single conception that might assist selection, judgment and choice. It offered retailers a model of stylistic arrangement that might lead customers to make multiple purchases, or simply offer them a vision of future possibilities to aspire to. However, the extent to which retailers adopted these practices remains unclear.

As late as 1908, the catalog of John Barker & Co of Kensington High Street made great claims to the innovation of the newly constructed room displays they had created to assist customers in their selection. Although primarily concerned to configure and present the historicist "English" styles that proliferated during the first decade of the twentieth century, the catalog confidently asserted that a visit to the store's new showrooms "will carry with it the conviction that they must be classed among the first of their kind in the metropolis" (Barker & Co 1908, 594). In spite of the uncertainty concerning the development of model 'interior' room settings within retail stores, there is clear evidence that retailers and furniture producers took this approach when exhibiting at international and trade exhibitions.

Heal & Son, the Tottenham Court Road furnisher, presented "A Guest's Room" at the 1900 Paris Exposition. Although primarily a specialist in bedding and bedroom furniture, Heal & Son had by the end of the nineteenth century expanded its range of furniture beyond the bedroom (Goodden 1984). Nevertheless, in its presentation at Paris it chose to reiterate its specialist nature through its display. "A Guest's Room" was designed by Ambrose Heal, craftsman and chairman of the family-run firm, in collaboration with his cousin and friend, the architect Cecil C. Brewer, who would by 1917 remodel Heals & Son's purpose-built mid-nineteenth-century store.

Commemorative publicity materials for "A Guest's Room" show a suite of contemporary oak bedroom furniture, comprising twin bedsteads, wardrobe, toilet table and chairs within a full interior room setting, created to echo the geometric patterned designs of the furniture's inlaid marquetry and hangings (Heal & Sons 1900). Though no doubt created specifically for exhibition at Paris, this display of furniture and furnishings was clearly typical of the objects to be found at the firm's Tottenham Court Road shop. While the use of a room display within the exposition echoes an increasing interest in the "designed" interior within continental decorative arts at this time, and certainly afforded Ambrose Heal the opportunity to characterize his company as one concerned with the progressive ideals often associated with these developments, the model room provides an immediately consumable image of contemporary living, all of which was available – at a price.

Importantly for Heal & Sons, the creation of "A Guest's Room" provided a narrative of the firm's accomplishments. The furniture returned to the London store having been awarded two silver medals at the Paris Exposition, "the only instance of so high an award being made for a display, consisting ... solely of bedroom furniture" (Heal & Sons 1900). In spite of this success, however, there is little evidence to suggest that Heal & Sons used model rooms more widely within their Tottenham Court Road Store. Photographic views taken at that time by the renowned architectural photographer Bedford Lemere show the rooms and galleries of the store were still classified according to items such as bedsteads, or chairs (Heal and Son c.1900). Model rooms were, however, being used elsewhere.

Heelas Sons & Co was a department store to the west of London, in Reading. Originally established in 1854 as a drapery business, the store expanded to sell linen,

One of the Model Rooms.

Figure 1.2 Photographic view of "One of the Model Rooms" exhibited by Heelas Sons &
Co, Reading, c.1895.
Source: Heelas Sons & Co, catalog, John Lewis Partnership Archive. Ref: 194/A/4(1)

silk, carpets and furniture, and in 1890 gained the warrant of his Royal Highness The
Prince of Wales. In 1953, Heelas Sons & Co was brought into the ownership of the
John Lewis Partnership, in whose archives survives a modestly published catalog dat-
ing from the mid-1890s that features a photograph of a model room (Heelas Sons &
Co c.1895) (Fig. 1.2). Presented as "One of the Model Rooms," this three-sided box
room, replete with a fully dressed window, is furnished with a suite of furniture comprising side chairs and a settle, a writing desk, and a freestanding glass curio cabinet.
The draped fireplace and mantel mirror, along with the frilled lace tablecloths and
lampshades, are typical of the period and express a delicate and feminine domesticity
to which many of the store's customers might have aspired. This room was considered
fashionable in the sense of reflecting prevailing tastes of the day without being avant-
garde or cutting edge.

The presentation of model rooms may well have carried greater novelty in a non-
specialist, regional department store, and it is likely that the creation of these rooms
was linked to the store's "decorating department." Such departments became a key
feature of specialist and general furniture retailers alike towards the end of the century, and they offered means by which a shop could offer a "specialist" service to its
customers. As the image of the decorating department in Heelas Sons & Co shows, it
was a dedicated space featuring sample books and runs of wallpapers and carpets, as

Decorating Department.

Interior and exterior House Painting.

Heelas, Ltd. send competent assistants to advise in all matters of decorating, and give Estimates Free of Charge.

The Decorating Showroom.

Figure 1.3 Photographic view of the "Decorating Department" at Heelas Sons & Co, Reading, c.1895.
Source: Heelas Sons & Co, catalog, John Lewis Partnership Archive. Ref: 194/A/4(1)

well as other sample items, such as mirrors, presented against different wall finishes (Heelas Sons & Co c.1895) (Fig. 1.3). Given that bespoke decoration and furnishing was the mainstay of the established, reputable furnishers at the top end of the market, the development of decorating and house furnishing services within primarily retail spaces indicates that retailers understood both the importance of taste-making within the store and the commercial opportunity for "personalizing" their engagement with their customers. In this way, the retail decorating department offered a spectacular and apparently specialist mode of production defined by the newly configured retail sector, and in this sense a mode of specialization through "service" could be presented.

Conclusion

A tension between furniture production and retail characterized the burgeoning furniture trade of the later nineteenth century. This tension marks a significant shift in authority away from long-established furniture manufacturers and producers towards new retail services and industries as exemplified by department stores. Practices such as advertising and display that were becoming increasingly common to other areas of the retail sector remained challenging to a broadly conceived furnishing sector that understood reputation to be achieved only through the production of quality items reflecting professional good judgment and taste. Yet nothing could prevent these products from being drawn into the spectacular web of modern retailing that made them visible to the consumer.

The commercial practice of display – the spectacular presentation of goods – presented challenges to the furniture and furnishing industry in London, which prided itself upon established traditions of quality and workmanship of production. The shift towards visual commodification of furniture, both through display and commercial presentation in catalogs, was contentious on account of broader shifts that were occurring within the furniture industry. These saw a move towards a more fragmented production of objects, in often piecemeal fashion, that were subsequently brought within the developing brand identities of retailers who had increasingly established themselves as retailers rather than manufacturers or producers, or were makers who were steadily moving away from production towards the more financially lucrative realms of retail. To this end, the nascent yet spectacular display cultures of the final decades of the nineteenth century testify, alongside other commercial practices such as standardized products, fixed prices, hire purchase, and the ticketing of goods, to the ascendency of the retailer, and a move away from the established markets of the furniture trade of the mid-nineteenth century.

Notes

1 Issues of gender are implicit to any discussion concerning the development of retail and consumer culture in the final years of the nineteenth century. Historians such as Rappaport (2001) and Sanders (2006) have argued persuasively that the development of urban retailing afforded women opportunities for legitimate public experience as both shoppers and workers in a manner denied to them in earlier years. The perceived "femininity" of this consumer culture, and the ensuing cultural representation of women with it (Lysack 2008), would have only served to compound the masculine perceptions of commerce that characterized the established furnishing trades and industry.
2 Retail and trade catalogs of the nineteenth and early twentieth centuries can be very difficult historical sources as they are often intentionally undated so as to ensure that they can be used for a number of years. The James Shoolbred & Co catalog of 1876 is dated whereas many of the Heal & Son catalogs cited later in this chapter are not and were in use for over a decade.

References

Barker & Co. 1908–9. *Catalogue*. National Art Library. Pressmark: TC.D.6.

De Falbe, S. 1985. "James Shoolbred & Co. Late Victorian Department Store Furniture." MA diss., Royal College of Art.

Cohen, Deborah. 2006. *Household Goods. The British and their Possessions*. London and New Haven: Yale University Press.

Edwards, Clive. 2005. *Turning Houses into Homes: A History of the Retailing and Consumption of Domestic Furnishings*. Aldershot: Ashgate Publishing.

———. 2011. "Tottenham Court Road: The Changing Fortunes of London's Furniture Street, 1850–1950." *The London Journal* 36: 140–160.

Forster, Edward Morgan. 1996. *A Room with a View*. London: Folio Society.

Goodden, Susanna. 1984. *A History of Heals at the Sign of the Fourposter*. London: Lund Humphries

Hamish Fraser, W. 1981. *The Coming of the Mass Markets 1850–1914*. London: Macmillan Press.

Heal & Son. 'A Guest Room' Souvenir Brochure. Archive of Art & Design: Heals Archive Catalogues and Publicity AAD/1978/2/274.

Heal & Son. 1900. Printed ephemera commemorating the exhibition of Heal & Sons' "A Guest's Bedroom" at the Paris Exposition, 1900. Archive of Art & Design: Heals Archive Catalogues and Publicity AAD/1978/2/274.

Heal and Son. 1900. *Catalogue of Bedsteads, Bedding & Bedroom Furniture.* Archive of Art & Design: Heals Archive Catalogues and Publicity AAD/1978/2/274.

Heelas, Sons & Co. 1895. *Catalogue.* John Lewis Partnership Archive. Ref: 194/A/4(1).

James Shoolbred & Co. 1876. *Catalogue.* National Art Library. Pressmark: 25.11.76.

Jeffreys, James B. 1954. *Retail Trading in Britain 1850–1950. A study of trends in retailing with special reference to the development of co-operative, multiple shops and department store methods of trading.* Cambridge: Cambridge University Press.

Kirkham, Pat. 1989. *The London Furniture Trade, 1700–1880.* London: Furniture History Society.

Leach, William. 1993. *Land of Desire: Merchants, Power, and the Rise of a New American Culture.* New York: Pantheon.

Lysack, Krista. 2008. *Come Buy, Come Buy: Shopping and the Culture of Consumption in Victorian Women's Writing.* Athens, OH: Ohio University Press.

Marx, Karl. 1976. *Capital* Vol.1. London: Verso.

Rappaport, Erika Diane. 2001. *Shopping for Pleasure: Women in the Making of London's West End.* Princeton: Princeton University Press.

Robertson, W.B., ed. 1911. *Encyclopedia of Retail Trading.* Harmsworth Business Library Volume VI. London: Educational Books Company Ltd.

Sanders, L. Shapiro. 2006. *Consuming Fantasies. Labor, Leisure and the London Shopgirl, 1880–1920.* Columbus: The Ohio State University Press.

Simmel, Georg. 1991. "The Berlin Trade Exhibition." Translated by Sam Whimster. *Theory, Culture & Society* 8: 122.

Walsh, Claire. 1999. "The Newness of the Department Store: A View from the Eighteenth Century." In *Cathedrals of Consumption: The European Department Store 1850–1939*, edited by Geoffrey Crossick and Serge Jaumain. Aldershot: Ashgate.

Whitaker, Jan. 2011. *The Department Store. History, Design, Display.* London: Thames and Hudson.

2 Displaying dreams

Model interiors in British department stores, 1890–1914

Patricia Lara-Betancourt

Dreams arise from the need to envisage a better future, so not surprisingly the nineteenth century engendered visions of a new world based on the promises of industrialization and technological advancement. In Europe and across the Atlantic in the USA and Canada, the late nineteenth and early twentieth centuries witnessed the emergence of a powerful form of retailing – the department store. It would become one of the most remarkable retail developments of the period. Many such stores grew into economic giants, achieving public company status on the same level as heavy industry, transportation and finance; and through business success many store owners acquired political power and became prominent members of their communities. At the time, department stores and their displays were often described using adjectives such as dazzling, enticing, stunning, sumptuous, mesmerizing and artistic (Zola 2012 (1883)). These adjectives speak of the department store's powerful appeal for millions of people, as this modern type of shop came to represent the best of what progress and modernity signified, introducing consumers to the latest in design, fashion, art and technology. The dream of a better life embodied by department stores was a dream of abundance and beauty housed in buildings resembling palaces and populated with modern goods displayed in irresistible ways through the clever arrangement of glass, mirrors, light, color and interior design.

Shops and their displays were all about awakening desire for new goods and stirring up longings for a beautiful and even luxurious way of life that shoppers could contemplate and vicariously inhabit in shop windows, galleries and model interiors. For the middle-class woman, this modern type of shopping and consumption represented freedom from toil as she was no longer expected to make her own clothes and home furnishings. Being able to visit the stores un-chaperoned also gave her freedom of movement, and instilled in her a sense of empowerment and exhilaration through browsing, selecting, buying (for herself and on behalf of her family) and socializing in public. In Janet Wolff's words, "The establishment of the department store in the 1850s and 1860s provided an important new arena for the legitimate public appearance of middle-class women" (1995, 45). The sheer abundance and enticing display of modern goods also attracted women with the promise of self-affirmation and self-definition through choice and consumption in perfect alignment with notions of class and gender. Many adverts and the images they used reinforced and celebrated the perception of shopping and consumption as a feminine task.

In Britain, the expansion and power of retailing was based on the relentless growth of the urban middle class in these decades, developing with it an interdependent relationship that created and strengthened a culture of consumption targeting the home.

Stores were instrumental in establishing a solid middle class-based consumer culture through responding to, giving shape to, and realizing deeply-held middle-class aspirations. British department stores relied mainly on middle-class demand, which differed from that of the working class. For the latter, demand was strongly linked to low prices while for the middle class, although still concerned with price, choice and quality were more important in that they allowed better expression of individual and nuanced taste. Jose Harris explains that, "the middle-class family was usually much more concerned with immediate consumption than with long-term saving or accumulation of property [...] all contemporary observers agreed that the ethic of conspicuous consumption had soared to a crescendo by the 1900s" (1993, 70). The following words by a middle-class woman and historian remembering the early twentieth century illustrate the delight she found in the consumption of modern things:

> London, now that the reign of Edward VII had begun, became very pleasant [...] those who had not lived before 1914 could have no idea of the perfection to which civilization had attained. Travel by road, rail or sea had become cheap and easy, home life had been brightened by new schemes of architecture, house decoration and gardening, and craftsmanship had achieved a pitch never dreamt of during the Victorian Era. How beautifully things were made in those days! What exquisite furniture, glass and china, what lovely dress materials were to be found in the London shops!
>
> (Webster 1949, 142)

Although traditionally, department stores have been associated with the selling of clothing and fashion, and most of them in Britain and elsewhere started out as draper shops, this chapter focuses on the type of store that specialized in selling furniture and furnishings or turned these into their most prominent departments.[1] At this time, the British furnishing and retailing industry was one of the most dynamic and influential in the world, supplying not only the British market but also its far reaching colonies and many other regions under its commercial influence, including Latin America.

Judging by their size, scale of operations and number of departments, most large house furnishers were effectively department stores, but, at the time, firms and shops did not use that term and preferred to portray themselves as an all-encompassing kind of business, catering for everything related to the home: from selecting and renting a house to decorating, fitting and furnishing it. Departments would merchandize a large variety of furniture in a comprehensive range of styles, and an even bigger variety of wallpaper, curtains, carpets, upholstery, lamps and fireplaces, among many other household articles. As mentioned, most British department stores began life in the 1840s and 1950s in the shape of small draper shops, and went on to grow in a piecemeal manner, expanding greatly during the years 1890 to 1914. By the 1890s, firms occupying a whole block, and five to eight stories, were promoting themselves as house furnishers, manufacturers, furniture designers, upholsterers, decorators, exporters and dealers in antiques. Their ever-growing scope of services included expert advice from store decorators, the preparation of estimates, designs, and decorative schemes, besides other support services such as delivery, removal, storage, lighting, plumbing and heating. In London, such stores included Maple's, Heal's, Shoolbred's, Waring & Gillow's, John Barker's, Hampton & Son's, Oetzmann's, Whiteley's and Harrod's, to name a few of the more prominent (Lara-Betancourt 2008, 1–55). Restricted by building regulations, British department stores were never as large as their Parisian and

American counterparts, but shared with them the same pattern of growth and success based on the adoption of modern business methods. Economies of scale, for example, allowed them to bring costs and prices down while exerting control over production and supply from local and national cabinet makers and manufacturers.

With new and abundant merchandize there was a greater need for novel display techniques. Selling furniture and household goods, compared to drapery and clothes, presented different challenges, which required an innovative merchandizing approach. According to William Leach, between 1895 and 1925 and through a clear aesthetic transformation, there was a revolution in how American department stores displayed and merchandized their wares. Goods were no longer hidden from view but were openly displayed on stands, showcases and glass cabinets, aided by clever lighting and strategically placed mirrors. The whole store attained a theatrical character and the function of color, light and glass became more prominent and spectacular (Leach 1989, 119–120). The importance of the shop window to the department store cannot be overestimated. As the first encounter with potential clients, windows and their displays had the power to encapsulate the shop and symbolize what the goods, store, shopping experience and consumption represented. With the dissemination of the large plate of glass and electric lighting in this period, the shop window was never more effective in its capacity to exert a fascinating hold on shoppers and passers-by through exploiting a sense of the theatrical. Given their enclosing simulated rooms, shop windows became a perfect medium for the setting and display of domestic interiors and for enticing onlookers to enter the shop.

Displaying interiors

As British department stores grew in size, volume of trade, and number of departments, the need for sophisticated display techniques became all important. This chapter examines the "model room" as a specific retailing strategy that became instrumental to the highly successful display, advertising and selling of furniture, furnishings, household goods and decorating services in this period. The "specimen room," as it was called at the time, was a consequence of the massive increase in urban housing in the late nineteenth century. In response to the growing demand for furniture and furnishings, the stores set up realistic-looking domestic interiors, some of them complete with ceiling, panelled walls, dressed windows, furniture and fireplaces. This chapter also discusses the impact of the Antique movement and the craze for the "period room," both of which were instrumental in disseminating historicist styles and popularizing model rooms. A journal article announcing the 1888 Whiteley's catalog referred to the shop in these terms: "Cabinet furniture occupies the premier position, and is first of all set out in charming interiors, showing that Mr William Whiteley is prepared to furnish apartments in any style, from vigorous Renaissance to delicate Louis Seize" (*Cabinet Maker* 1888, 106) (Fig. 2.1). A few years earlier, in 1881, Whiteley's shop windows had surprised and delighted street crowds with a magnificent display of domestic interiors: a Chippendale dining room and a luxurious drawing room in ebonized woods (*Cabinet Maker* 1881, 63). Model rooms proved a quick and effective way of conveying a variety of fashionable period styles, while targeting different budgets ranging from £150 to £750 rooms. In the 1870s, besides placing similar types of furniture and wares together, retailers had begun to arrange their goods in groupings according to related function, and in domestic-type settings replicating the different rooms in the home. As demand increased, firms built large

Figure 2.1 "A Hall in the English Renaissance Style. A page from Mr William Whiteley's
New Illustrated Furnishing Catalogue," *The Cabinet Maker and Art Furnisher*,
1 October 1888.

showrooms for the sole purpose of displaying (rather than storing) their wares to the
utmost advantage. This move required significant additional space and many stores
devoted whole new floors to this end (Lara-Betancourt 2008, 1–55).

The British department store, in terms of its architecture and modes of display,
related to the bazaars and warehouses that first appeared in the late eighteenth century, and to the arcades of the early Victorian years. A most impressive precedent was
the Crystal Palace built for the Great Exhibition of 1851. With its enormous size and
miles of galleries displaying artistic and industrial products from all over the world,
it was seen as the epitome of a grand shop and was described at the time as the greatest bazaar of all. In the following decades, with world fairs taking place every couple
of years from 1855 to 1914, it seemed that department stores and large exhibitions
challenged and inspired each other to develop ingenious architectures of display to
attract the masses. It became common for stores to participate at large national and
international exhibitions, usually displaying domestic room settings and sometimes,
as was the case with the *Daily Mail* Ideal Home Exhibition in London (1908–2009),
setting up complete houses in realistic environments as an imposing way of conveying
the shops', designers' and manufacturers' decorative skills and artistic competence
(Fig. 2.2). Since the 1880s museums, such as South Kensington (V&A), and department stores participating at national and international exhibitions all made a point of

Figure 2.2 "Two Interiors at the Ideal Home Exhibition," *The Cabinet Maker and Complete House Furnisher*, April 16, 1910.

displaying the best historical examples in furniture and furnishing (Waring & Gillow 1906, 5). Sometimes stores recreated historical aristocratic interiors such as the "Room in the British Pavillion by Messrs. Waring [& Gillow]" exhibited in Paris (*The House* 1900, 45), which was a reconstruction of the long gallery at Knole, the celebrated Jacobean country house in Sevenoaks. Retailers' participation was effectively a marketing exercise to entice potential customers to visit the store. In 1908 Hampton & Sons participated in the Decorative Arts Palace of the Franco British Exhibition in London. The firm displayed "specimen rooms" interpreting traditional English styles. One of the exhibits, the "Specimen House in the Colonial Adam Style," was set up in the shop's showrooms after the event.

The practice of setting up model interiors, which had started back in mid-century, became firmly established by the 1890s. In 1874, the Glasgow firm Wylie and Lockhead built show flats to display their furniture, and Kendal Milne in Manchester set up special furniture showrooms complete with fabrics and wallpaper (Lancaster 1995, 53). As early as 1858 Heal's was illustrating its catalogs with professional drawings of domestic rooms showing an assortment of bedroom settings and exemplifying the type of furniture and objects displayed in their showrooms (Heal's Catalogs 1844–1950). "One advertisement accompanying Charles Dickens' Mugby Junction (the part of All the Year Round for Christmas 1866) was devoted to inviting the public to see a series of small rooms showing bedroom suites in their appropriate atmosphere 'so that customers are able to see the effect as it would appear in their own rooms'" (Goodden 1984, 17). By the early 1880s, the use of room illustrations in stores' trade catalogs was disseminating. In its 1896 catalog Heal's included photographs of their showrooms displaying fitted bedrooms (Fig. 2.3).

Store expansion

Between the 1860s and 1914, department stores were constantly expanding in response to their increasing customer base. Stores' growth usually occurred through buying adjoining properties, and rebuilding on a larger scale. New edifices used the latest in materials and building techniques, and incorporated new facilities. Some firms preferred to knock down existing buildings to erect new premises. In June 1906, less than a decade after its founding, Waring & Gillow opened a large and luxurious purpose-built eight-storey shop in Oxford Street in London. The new premises offered eight acres of space (33,500 square meters) housing 150 "specimen rooms" with more than 100 galleries. The brand new building was designed to impress: a 90-foot high atrium covered with a glass dome flooded the interior with light, and shop-front windows formed islands and arcades. Facilities included four elevators, and "a prettily decorated Restaurant and a Ladies' Room where tea may be served" (Waring & Gillow *Souvenir* 1906, 20). The trend for department stores to expand and improve continued after World War I and, in 1917, Heal's new and completely refurbished shop opened exhibiting a "Mansard Flat" furnished in cottage style on the top floor (Fig. 2.4), where clients would find "many charming suggestions and ideas for the equipment of the modern home. They are [...] a delightful suite of rooms planned in the modern spirit of furnishing and decoration" (Heal's advert 1918; see also Goodden 1984, 39 and 41).

Throughout the nineteenth century it was common for buildings to be afflicted by fires. When this happened, business owners took it as an opportunity to rebuild the

BED SITTING ROOM.

Figure 2.3 "Bed Sitting Room," Heal & Son, trade catalog, 1902.

stores to a grander scale and give them unified, impressive façades with large plate-glass windows of long frontage on the ground floor.[2] After the last fire suffered by Whiteley's in the 1890s, its directors planned a grand scale, purpose-built store, which opened on 21 November 1911, occupying a whole block on Queensway, London (Shaw 2006, 1–3). The building incorporated several of the typical elements in department store architecture, all designed to inspire and excite: the corner tower, large expanses of glass, a rotunda/atrium, skylights and a grand staircase. A press advert invited the public to "inspect its beautiful and spacious galleries, its lofty domes, its marble staircases [...] its modern equipment and convenient service" (Whiteley 1911, 4). The most impressive feature of all, however, was the significant increase in display area and the numerous galleries devoted exclusively to specimen rooms.

Affordable dreams

The owner and director of Maple's, Blundell Maple, realized in 1900 that the biggest profits were made not from furnishing hotels or the palaces of the aristocracy, as the store had been doing since the 1870s, but from catering for the growing middle-class

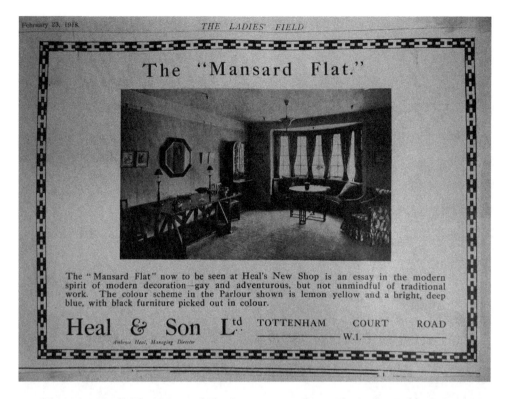

Figure 2.4 Heal's The "Mansard Flat," newspaper advert, *The Ladies Field*, 1918.

market. Accordingly, a substantial part of the 11,250 square feet of showroom space was allocated to specimen one-bedroom flats (Barty-King 1992, 87). This was an important move made by all large department stores and furnishing houses. Besides responding to artistic and aesthetic concerns, the stores made it clear that their high quality designs, although exclusive, were within reach of the ordinary householder. Underscoring the store's marketing strategies was a concerted effort to democratize the dream of a better life, one originally inspired by the taste and wealth of the landed gentry (Lara-Betancourt 2008, 19–55).

According to its 1890s catalog, the showrooms of the Leeds department store Marsh, Jones, Cribb & Co had been thoroughly remodeled, redecorated and supplied with an extensive range of goods. A later catalog explained that "recognizing the demand on the part of the public for Inexpensive and Reliable Furniture, [this firm has] built in their showrooms an eight roomed house, completely furnished, for the moderate sum of £250" (Marsh, Jones, Cribb & Co. c. 1905). Similarly, by the end of the nineteenth century the firm Hampton & Sons of London claimed it could "put a tastefully furnished home within reach of the most modest income." In 1894, the firm issued a lavishly illustrated catalog (printed by the new collotype process) reproducing many "artistic interiors, in various styles." The catalog also explained that Hampton's turnover was so high because the goods the shop offered were very popular: "therefore, the firm was enabled to buy materials in considerable bulk and thus minimise costs for high quality articles." The catalog also explained that all the furniture made in Hampton's own workshops was created with use of "all the latest machinery for preparing the woods and other material," but that every article was "finished by hand by skilled, experienced craftsmen." As was common practice at the time, the brochure included furnishing estimates for houses of different sizes, from an eight-room house at £250 to an eighteen-room house at £2000 (Hampton & Sons 1894, 8–10).

That Waring & Gillow also had the ordinary, middle-class family market firmly in mind is beautifully illustrated in its 1896 "Model House" catalog with photographs of each of the eight rooms displayed in their Manchester shop. The brochure explained: "All who desire to furnish in good taste at a Moderate Outlay should view the MODEL HOUSE by Waring & Gillow [...] Houses completely furnished from £250." Its 1906 London store catalog advertised "a series of five Model Houses ranging from a country cottage at £100, by gradations to £200, £300, £500 and £750" (Waring & Gillow, 16). The stores and catalogs also displayed model interiors for flats, which were becoming popular as an alternative to house accommodation (Fig. 2.5).

PLATE XLII. THE FLAT HALL. *Photographed at Warings.*

Figure 2.5 "The Flat Hall," Waring & Gillow's showroom, trade catalog, c. 1900.

Displaying the "modern period room"

Besides affordability, an additional reason for the widespread popularity of the model room in British department stores relates strongly to the influence of the so-called Antique movement in art and design (1870–1900s), and the craze for the "modern period room" that it helped originate. The movement crystallized partly as a result of the Arts & Crafts group's appreciation and promotion of past English styles and designs from the medieval period up to the eighteenth century. As design historian Stefan Muthesius has pointed out, in fostering a cult of the past and the old, ordinary object, the Antique movement tried to bypass the trade and its commercially-produced modern furniture, which it condemned (Muthesius 1988, 233–36). This was in tune with the design reformers' campaign to discredit and undermine machine-produced merchandize found in shops and department stores. Retailers reacted quickly by becoming dealers in antiques themselves, and by giving rise to a new industry: that of reproducing old models and creating and promoting what they labeled "the modern period room" – that is, a model room representing a particular historical style. Department stores encouraged the antique and period-room craze with their constant commercialization of historical models (Lara-Betancourt 2008, 98–99). Stores, designers and manufacturers treated history and past designs as an inexhaustible source of inspiration, albeit reproduced with modern methods and materials to answer contemporary needs: "to meet the demand for [fireplace] grates in harmony with Georgian schemes of decoration, many of the old patterns have been copied, and the Carron Company have now reproduced a number of the fine old patterns they were manufacturing more than a hundred years ago. These grates are being made, however in bright steel and brass, which does not easily tarnish or get dirty" (Elder-Duncan 1907, 48). Although inspired by the past, period rooms and their furnishings were promoted and sold as modern. The use of historical styles became a popular way of furnishing the modern home in the 1880s through to the 1920s. Not everybody had the means to collect antiques, but department stores shaped and nurtured a much wider audience and market for modern reproductions.

In order to educate the public in the somewhat confusing range of past styles, firms set up model rooms, first and foremost in the shops but also, as mentioned, at national and international exhibitions. In London, most West End department stores created galleries displaying "authentic" arrangements of furniture and furnishings from past centuries. Shoppers gradually became familiar with what must have been a bewildering range of styles, interiors and furniture said to represent past eras. To guide customers, stores recommended the use of sixteenth- and seventeenth-century styles (Elizabethan and Jacobean) as appropriate for the hall, study and dining room. These styles were deemed dignified and their look and decoration were meant to embody masculine values. With heavy and dark-colored furniture, many schemes would also include hunt trophies and armour. In contrast, English and French eighteenth-century styles seemed to agree with a feminine sensibility and were therefore promoted as suitable for the drawing room and best bedroom (Kinchin 1996; Lara-Betancourt 2008, 157–164). English styles from the eighteenth century were labelled in general as Georgian, and more specifically as Chippendale, Adam, Hepplewhite and Sheraton, after the renowned eighteenth-century designers and cabinet makers. Although these representations were not authentic in the sense of replicating a genuine Jacobean room, they took their inspiration from historical spaces and based modern designs on past ones. The popularity of historical styles for domestic interiors throughout the period can obscure the fact that their representation was constantly changing and adapting to modern requirements. The name of the styles did not change but the ways of characterizing them kept varying. Although people became more knowledgeable about the different styles, the way in which producers redesigned, interpreted and recreated them continued to change. What was sold as a Jacobean room before the 1890s could look quite different from the one promoted in the early 1910s. Perhaps inevitably, history was deployed in the service of fashion (Lara-Betancourt 2008, 128–134).

Model rooms were widely represented through photos and drawings in every available printed media, such as trade catalogs, advertising, and articles appearing in newspapers, popular magazines and trade journals. The craze for the modern period room was also supported by the publishing of specialized books on the history of the decorative arts, and manuals on furnishing and decorating. The latter publications exemplified the prolific genre of advice literature, acquiring a fundamental role in disseminating artistic and commercial ideas and designs about the home, together with trends and fashions such as the modern period room. H.J. Jennings, in his book on decoration, *Our Homes and How to Beautify Them*, written on behalf of Waring & Gillow, encouraged householders to use the wide range of good designs that the store had made available to any person with a modest income: "Chintzes, cretonnes, brocades, damasks, tapestries and velvets are now designed in almost every style and are obtainable in every shade of colour" (1902, 96). Jennings explained that "(m) echanical production has made such strides that designs in hangings and upholstery, which were formerly only obtainable by the wealthy, are now within reach of the householder of very moderate means" (Ibid. 114). Many of the book's illustrations were photographs of the shop's showrooms, which had previously also been published in catalogs featuring whole furnished interiors. Showrooms, particularly in the 1890s and 1900s, demonstrated the capacity of the store to create and transform interiors without recourse to architectural permanent structures, thus avoiding the much higher costs involved in the latter (Fig. 2.6). The fundamental message was that, using quality materials and modern production techniques, Waring & Gillow could produce any type of interior of any period to a high standard of workmanship. As the caption to a room illustrated in their trade catalog stated: "This Dining Room is a typical example of Waring's work and well illustrates the possibilities of judiciously applying the quaintness which characterises Old English Woodwork and Decoration to a modern room, without, in any way, sacrificing the necessary conditions of convenience and comfort which are required to-day" (Waring & Gillow c. 1900, 30). The kind of rooms depicted in the book and in catalogs gave prominence to decorative woodwork, showing what could be achieved on walls, doors, floors, ceilings, fireplaces, ingle nooks and fitted bedrooms. Until the 1880s the cost of wood panelling had been high and only the wealthier kind of customer could afford it. So displaying rooms with an abundance of woodwork at an affordable cost was a very attractive proposition for the potential buyer.

The strong grip of history on modern furnishing and decoration is partly explained by the anxiety many people experienced around change and modernization, prompting them to look to the past for reassurance. It seemed that the stronger the wave of modernity and transformation, the bigger the appeal of history and tradition. Furthermore, given historical styles' association with traditional aristocratic homes, to a significant number of middle-class consumers these styles better expressed their

PLATE XXI.   DINING ROOM IN MODERNIZED JACOBEAN.   *Photographed at Warings.*

Figure 2.6 "Dining Room in Modernized Jacobean," *Substantial and Inexpensive Furniture*, Waring & Gillow's trade catalog, c. 1900.

social claims and aspirations. Throughout the nineteenth century, the simultaneous fascination with novelties and historical models gave rise to a paradoxical attitude that sought new things but without totally accepting them looking new.[3]

The paradox of expressing modernity using antiques and past models was reinforced in equal measure by the spheres of art and commerce. In decoration manuals and advice literature, writers tried to ease the tension through the combination of old and new elements, by integrating and framing the new within the context of tradition. A good number of the schemes recommended consisted of old designs reproduced with modern methods, colors and materials, and arranged to evoke period rooms. This apparently harmonious result, however, was in turn compromised by the different meanings people ascribed to history and to those styles representing it, responding to notions of class, gender, nation and their social and symbolic meaning. The Arts and Crafts movement and those involved in reforming commercial design tried to rule out this type of symbolic association in their designs of furniture and furnishings. Reformers aimed for an artistic and moral language in the decorative arts responding mainly to aesthetic and production concerns claiming, for example, that machine-made goods were dishonest. They refused to acknowledge that, for most middle-class people, the task of furnishing and decorating the home was driven more by social and family values than by being faithful to a particular vision of art and architecture. For most people, the latter could be important but only if aligned with the former (Sparke 1995, 50–69; Lara-Betancourt 2008, 96–164).

Retailers and commercial designers, on the other hand, encouraged consumption motivated by the rich social and cultural meanings that belonged to the spheres of gender, class, family, nation and history. In their aim to gain consumers' favor they were more sensitive and non-judgmental of consumers' desires, beliefs, expectations and habits. Furnishing firms understood, for example, the anxiety related to class. An increasing number of people were in the process of acquiring and consolidating their middle-class status. Many were eager to show it and many were haunted by the possibility of slipping back down the social ladder. Displaying what they believed to be the right taste in domestic decoration was a way of assuring their social standing. Historical styles, even when newly reproduced, seemed to answer this need better than others. Attentive and sensitive to consumers' needs and aspirations, retailers supplied and advertised a wide and affordable range of period furniture, furnishings and interiors. Even at the height of Arts and Crafts and Art Nouveau appeal, there was a large number of images and references to historical styles in trade catalogs and advice literature (Collard 2003, 35–48; Lara-Betancourt 2008, 96–108).

Modern notions of gender, family and nation also looked to the past for means of expression. The ambitions were modern but needed to be articulated through history. Gender and family roles were strongly linked to notions of respectability and therefore to class but, within those confines, it was the diversity of historical styles that allowed for the expression of difference and particular gender sensibilities. The sense of nation was exacerbated by external economic competitive factors in the international industrial and commercial arena. Again, in their expression of national allegiance people resorted to history, rediscovering and recreating English and British historical styles in furniture and furnishings. This was at its most evident at international exhibitions where British department stores took model rooms to a new level and where, besides expressing values such as craftsmanship and taste, displays represented the nation to an international audience. Department stores' exhibits aligned with national economic purposes while representing the best in British commercial design and manufacture.

Conclusion

Judging by their continual presence in trade catalogs, model exhibits proved an effective way of luring customers not only to visit the shop but also to place orders for whole schemes, whole suites, or individual items belonging to such schemes. The advantage for clients, according to the brochure, was that by contemplating the beautifully presented model rooms they could easily picture the end result and could judge the effect of assembled items. By virtue of their attractive ensemble, the specimen room enhanced the qualities of the suites of furniture while providing an ideal stage for them. This concentrated form of display acted simultaneously as an instructional guide on how to decorate, including notions of style, color schemes, types of wood, new materials, and fashionable patterns.

Display and model rooms were an effective marketing strategy because they reflected retailers' understanding of the client's needs, desires and ambitions regarding their homes. Specimen rooms simulated the real thing, allowing customers to see what they could realize at home. By walking along the galleries, contemplating the diverse range of rooms, or by walking into one of the show interiors, clients could envisage what it would be like to own them. Store designers, in designing and setting up model rooms, created an environment that was immersive, and, by experiencing it, customers could effortlessly project their fantasies of inhabiting it and could imagine enacting the behaviours and domestic practices associated with it. The display of objects in situ as a selling strategy instilled the desire of ownership or at least the ambition to possess, if not the whole ensemble, a part of it. In assembling diverse elements, designers invested the model room's objects and components with added value and a certain "magic" – that of the unified designed environment where everything came together in a harmonious whole. Even if subsumed in the shop's credentials, this was interior design in action and at its most effective.

Shop designers and cabinet makers were not often acknowledged publicly for their creations, as authorship and credit usually went to the store, reinforcing the brand name. At the time, there was a growing tension between architecture as a long-established profession and the emerging but successful commercial interior designer and interior decorator represented by the store. As discussed earlier, department stores provided a service that promised the transformation of any interior to suit a wide range of historical styles and budgets. Architects criticized this practice, saying that it was dishonest as it could not be considered proper architecture. Design reformers joined the complaint by discrediting machine-made furniture. Together they denounced the use of new materials to resemble something else, such as printed wallpaper made to look like marble, or the use of surface beams applied to ceilings instead of the structural variety. However, department stores' model rooms appeared to customers as accomplished examples of modern interiors in historicist styles, which consumers decidedly favored in their drive to achieve and maintain unquestionable middle-class status.

The model or specimen room as display method was popular and effective because it responded well to the expectations of hundreds of thousands of middle-class customers patronizing the shops. It established strong links between the growth and expansion of department stores and the refining of its modes of display. Model rooms gave stores the opportunity not just to display their goods and wares but to highlight the capabilities of the store in providing the most up-to-date furniture, designs, novelties, materials, colors and styles, and to do it in such a way that a large percentage of the market was able to afford it. This type of temporary architecture was so convincing that it remained a firm display strategy well beyond World War I and into the interwar period, still responding to middle-class ambitions which in turn sustained the stores' continued success.

Notes

1 For discussions of retail historiography see Gareth Shaw, 1992, "The Evolution and Impact of Large-Scale Retailing in Britain," 135–136, and John Benson and Laura Ugolini, 2003, "Introduction: Historians and the Nation of Shopkeepers," 1–24.
2 The reason for frequent fires was linked to an abundance of flammable material, such as textiles and wood, found in shops, workshops and depositories, and to a lack of efficient alarm and security measures.
3 This attitude echoed Ruskin's criticism of "the fatal newness" of furniture and furnishings in William Holman Hunt's painting *The Awakening Conscience*. Quoted in S. Muthesius, *Why do we Buy Old Furniture?*, 233.

References

Aynsley, Jeremy. 2006. "The Modern Period Room: A Contradiction in Terms?" In *The Modern Period Room: The Construction of the Exhibited Interior, 1870–1950*, edited by Penny Sparke, Brenda Martin and Trevor Keeble, 8–30. London and New York: Routledge.

Barty-King, Hugh. 1992. *Maples Fine Furnishers: A Household Name for 150 Years.* London: Quiller Press.

Benson, John and Laura Ugolini. 2003. "Introduction: Historians and the Nation of Shopkeepers." In *A Nation of Shopkeepers: Five Centuries of British Retailing*, edited by John Benson and Laura Ugolini, 1–24. London: I. B. Tauris.

Collard, Frances. 2003. "Historical Revivals, Commercial Enterprise and Public Confusion: Negotiating Taste, 1860–1890." *Journal of Design History* 16: 35–48.

The Cabinet Maker and Art Furnisher. 1888. "Reviews of Trade Literature," October 1.

The Cabinet Maker and Art Furnisher. 1881. "A Glimpse at Whiteley's House Furnishing Department," October 1.

Elder-Duncan, J. H. 1907. *The House Beautiful and Useful: Being Practical Suggestions on Furnishing and Decoration.* London: Cassell and Company.

Goodden, Susanna. 1984. *At the Sign of the Fourposter: A History of Heal's.* London: Heal & Son.

Hampton & Sons. 1894 [1994]. *The Victorian Catalogue of Household Furnishings*, introduction by Stephen Calloway (pages unnumbered). London: Studio Editions. Re-print of Hampton & Sons, trade catalog, *Book of Specimen Interiors and Furniture.*

Hampton & Sons Ltd. (London) 1908. *Hamptons Furnishers and Decorators* (souvenir of the specimen rooms exhibited by Hamptons in the Decorative Arts Palace of the Franco British-Exhibition), trade catalog.

Harris, Jose. 1993. *Private Lives, Public Spirit: Britain 1870–1914.* London: Penguin Books.

Heal's Catalogues 1844–1950. Adam Matthew Publications. Accessed May 2016. www.ampltd. co.uk/digital_guides/heals_catalogues_1844-1950/Contents.aspx

The House: An Artistic Monthly for Those Who Manage and Beautify the Home (1897–1903). 1900. October 6.

Jennings, H. J. 1902. *Our Homes and How to Beautify Them*, 2nd edn. London: Harrison & Sons.

Kinchin, Juliet. 1996. "Interiors: Nineteenth Century Essays on the 'Masculine' and the 'Feminine' Room." In *The Gendered Object*, edited by Pat Kirkham, 12–29. Manchester and New York: Manchester University Press.

Lancaster, Bill. 1995. *The Department Store: A Social History.* London and New York: Leicester University Press.

Lara-Betancourt, Patricia. 2008. "Conflicting Modernities? Arts and Crafts and Commercial Influences in the Decoration of the Middle-Class Home, 1890–1914." PhD diss., Kingston University.

Leach, William. 1989. "Strategists of Display and the Production of Desire." In *Consuming Visions: Accumulation and Display of Goods in America, 1880–1920*, edited by Simon J. Bronner, 99–132. New York and London: Norton on behalf of Winterthur Museum.

Marsh, Jones, Cribb & Co. (Leeds). 1890s. *Home Furnishing*, trade catalog, Leeds.

Marsh, Jones & Cribb Ltd. (Leeds). c. 1905. *Furnishing with Taste and Economy*, trade catalog, Leeds.

Muthesius, Stefan. 1988. "Why Do We Buy Old Furniture? Aspects of the Authentic Antique in Britain 1870–1910." *Art History* 11: 231–254.

O'Neill, Morna. 2007. "Rhetorics of Display: Arts and Crafts and Art Nouveau at the Turin Exhibition of 1902." *The Journal of Design History* 20, 3: 205–225.

Oliver, J. L. 1966. *The Development and Structure of the Furniture Industry.* London: Pergamon Press.

Shaw, Gareth. 1992. "The Evolution and Impact of Large-Scale Retailing in Britain." In *The Evolution of Retail Systems c. 1800–1914*, edited by John Benson and Gareth Shaw, 135–165. Leicester: Leicester University Press.

Shaw, Gareth. 2006. "Whiteley," *Oxford Dictionary of National Biography*, [www.oxforddnb.com/view/article/36870]: 1–3.

Sparke, Penny. 1995. *As Long as It's Pink*. London: Pandora.

Whiteley Advertising. 1911. *The Times*, Tuesday, Nov 21, p. 4, issue 39748, col A.

Waring & Gillow. 1897. *Model House*. Deansgate, Manchester.

Waring & Gillow. 1906. *Souvenir of the Opening of Waring & Gillow's New Building*, June. London.

Webster, Nesta Helen (1876–1960). 1949. *Spacious Days: An Autobiography*. London: Hutchinson & Co. Ltd.

Wolff, Janet. 1995. *Feminine Sentences: Essays on Women and Culture*. Cambridge: Polity Press.

Zola, Emile. 2012 (1883). *The Ladies Paradise*. Trans. with an Introduction and Notes by Brian Nelson. Oxford: Oxford University Press. Oxford World's Classics. Kindle edition.

3   Home economies

The T. Eaton Company's Thrift House, 1926–1950

Susan Haight

In January 1926, Toronto's T. Eaton Company opened a new model house on the main floor of the department store's House Furnishings Building. Known as the Thrift House, the model was a life-sized representation of a two-storey, six-room dwelling with a simplified neo-Georgian exterior similar to those being built in the middle-class suburbs to the north and west of the city center (Fig. 3.1). Sproatt and Rolph, a well-known local architectural firm, designed the structure. Spatial constraints made it necessary to place the lower and upper floors side by side but, confident that this would not compromise the model's aura of domestic realism, Eaton's advertising department claimed that the display was constructed "in such a way that imagination easily carries you up the stairway from one to the other" (Ad 44, *Globe* January 18, 1926) (Fig. 3.2).

At its inception, the Thrift House was an integral part of a promotional campaign designed to inform Torontonians about Eaton's new deferred purchasing plan, an installment credit service that allowed customers to buy certain goods on time terms. The model house was complemented by a Thrift Bureau staffed by trained home economists capable of drawing up individualized household budgets free of charge. Eaton's advertising campaign portrayed the Thrift House and the Thrift Bureau as elements in a program of public pedagogy intended to teach consumers the principles of wise spending. Not coincidentally, wise spending was portrayed as an investment in the material comforts of middle-class domesticity.

By 1926, in-store model houses were no longer a novelty in large North American department stores (Whitaker 2006, 312–315). As early as 1896, Wanamaker's Grand Depot in Philadelphia had displayed a complete model apartment suite (Iarocci 2014, 115–116). In 1908, the store's New York branch installed a 22-room House Palatial that was intended to represent a domestic environment designed for an elite family (Iarocci 2014, 116–122; Leach 1993, 80–81). Eaton's itself created a "model art home" comprising six rooms in 1899, which was advertised as the first of its kind in Canada. The Robert Simpson Company, Eaton's rival for the loyalties of Toronto shoppers, anticipated the Thrift House by introducing its own Budget Bungalow in 1924 as a mechanism for promoting the store's Home Lovers' Club, an installment credit service that had existed since 1915.

Although Eaton's Thrift House was not unique, even in the context of interwar Toronto, it holds interest for business and retail historians as well as historians of retail interiors. The creation of the Thrift House signaled a significant change from the store's previous cash-only policy, tying the model house at the outset to larger

Figure 3.1 Thrift House – main floor, House Furnishings Building, exterior, 1926.
Source: F229-308-0-2043, T. Eaton Company fonds. Eaton's Archives photographic and documentary art subject files, Merchandise-Ont-Toronto-House furnishings-Furniture-Model Homes, B411202 Container B-551

issues surrounding Eaton's corporate identity. The link between the display and the store staff's free advice on household budgeting and interior decorating points to the important role played by public pedagogy as a marketing strategy at Eaton's. This particular display had an unusually long lifespan (from 1926 to 1950) and the alterations made to it over time can be documented to a significant degree, thanks to the minutes of Eaton's House Furnishings Committee (held by the Archives of Ontario, T. Eaton Company Fonds TECF, F229–69). Committee members discussed plans for the redecoration of the Thrift House, and their behind-the-scenes deliberations can be correlated with advertisements publicizing the resulting changes in Toronto newspapers, particularly the *Globe*, a daily aimed at a middle-class readership. Over the years the Thrift House served a variety of corporate objectives including, but not limited to, the sale of furniture and furnishings. At different times it taught Torontonians lessons about financial management, decorating trends, and how to adapt to wartime conditions. The model house also promoted normative values of consumerist domesticity that helped shape ideas of home in Toronto during the first half of the twentieth century.

Figure 3.2 Thrift House – main floor, House Furnishings Building, hallway, 1926.
Source: F229-308-0-2043, T. Eaton Company fonds. Eaton's Archives photographic and documentary art subject files, Merchandise-Ont-Toronto-House furnishings-Furniture-Model Homes, B411202 Container B-551

Introducing installment credit at Eaton's

When it first opened, Eaton's promoted the Thrift House as a didactic exhibit intended to aid Torontonians in achieving a comfortable, tasteful domestic setting while living within their means. However, as the ad introducing the new display shows, financing a middle-class standard of living was becoming more complicated (Fig. 3.3). Rising material expectations coupled with the increasing number of relatively secure, salaried workers in Toronto had made deferred payment plans a respectable method of purchasing durable consumer goods. Thrift was no longer a matter of frugal self-denial; instead, it had been redefined as planned spending aimed at achieving a range

EATON'S DAILY STORE NEWS

The Opening of THRIFT HOUSE

On the Main Floor, House Furnishings Building

Takes Place Tuesday Afternoon at 3.30—On Conclusion of Lecture by Mrs. Seaver of New York

Thrift House Itself--

¶ Delightful little six-room dwelling built from plans by Messrs. Sproatt and Rolph, Architects, Toronto.

¶ Papered, painted and furnished by our interior decorators to show how comfortable and charming Thrift House—or your own house, flat or bungalow—can be made for a sum wholly in keeping with the average, limited income.

¶ A two-story house, upper and lower floors placed side by side in such a way that imagination easily carries you up the stairway from one to the other.

Cupboards, Fireplace, Windows

and doors are located with an eye to convenience and pleasing effect. If you're building in the Spring, Thrift House will give you many hints, architecturally.

People-About-to-Be-Married

have a special claim on Thrift House. A "Thrift Adviser" is ready to talk prices for the furnishing of three, five, and six-roomed flats —or larger houses. She will make lists of what is needed—from furniture to tea cups. No charge for advice or lists of household equipment.

The Budget Idea

COMMONLY associated with public treasuries. Governments base their expenditures on what is in the bag, or, as the French call it—bougette. Household Science applies the budget idea to home management. In 1923 it was spread over the United States by

Messrs. John Wanamaker with
"The Little Home That Budget Built"

set up in brick and plaster in their New York store and furnished in a way to prove the big advantage of buying with thrift and good taste. Linked with this was the Home Budget Service for the instruction of Wanamaker customers in the principles of wise expenditure. With the introduction of our **Deferred Payment Plan**—requiring more thought and adjustment on the part of the customer than does our simpler method of cash payment —**T. EATON C⁰**ₗᵢₘᵢₜₑ𝒹 will boom the budget idea in

Thrift House and Thrift Bureau

Thrift Bureau

HERE are Thrift Advisers whose business is to straighten out the muddle of making ends meet. Or to put a nice, comfortable income in the best shape possible for spending and saving. When you come to consult them there will be utmost privacy in discussion. Just a personal talk with one intimately acquainted with the principles that govern the proper division of incomes. She will point out ways to wise buying and she will

Budget Your Income for You

—give you a working plan suited exactly to your needs, considering all your special preferences and predicaments. She will go deep into detail—of food, clothes, educating the children.

Thrift House and surrounding promenades will be open to the public on Tuesday and following evenings--- for exhibition purposes only

FROM 7 TO 11 O'CLOCK

Through the Courtesy of
John Wanamaker's of New York

MRS. FRANCES SEAVER

Director of the Wanamaker Home Budget Service

Will Give a Lecture in the Concourse in Front of Thrift House on the Subject

"PLAN YOUR SPENDING"

Mrs. Seaver was the originator of this budgeting service which has become so popular as an institution among Wanamaker customers. She is a well-known authority on all matters relating to home economics. She will discuss such questions as:

How to balance income and expenditure.

What proportion of the family means should go to rent, household improvements, holidays, donations, etc.

How to save systematically.

How to buy more wisely and thriftily.

Why it is so helpful and advantageous to plan your spending.

Time of Lecture--2.30 p.m., Tuesday

AFTER THE LECTURE THE FORMAL OPENING OF THRIFT HOUSE WILL TAKE PLACE. THOSE WHO ATTEND THE LECTURE WILL HAVE THE FIRST GLIMPSE OF THE HOUSE.

Your Choice:

THE ECONOMY OF CASH PRICE
OR
DEFERRED PAYMENTS WITH AN EXTRA CHARGE

WITH Cash you expect to buy for less, whether it is a house or goods. Reasonable, because Cash Dealing involves least expenses for the seller. EATON Prices are Cash Prices, based upon the well-known economies of Cash Dealing, which enables us to offer the best values available on the average.

But if you prefer to purchase with Deferred Payments, you can do so in certain lines of merchandise by making arrangements with the PURCHASERS' FINANCE COMPANY, LTD., which has been formed for the purpose and which is located on the Fourth Floor of our House Furnishings Building.

Until further notice, terms of the Purchasers' Finance Company, Ltd., to accredited persons are: On initial purchases totalling $50.00 or more, a minimum cash deposit of 20%, and the remainder, plus the P. F. Co. charge of 7½ thereon, is payable in ten equal monthly payments. On classes of goods where the time set for payment is longer or shorter than ten months, the PURCHASERS' FINANCE CO.'S rate charged would vary also.

The Purchasers' Finance Company Ltd. Office is on the Fourth Floor of our House Furnishings Building, where full particulars may be obtained. In our Semi-annual Sale of Furniture and House Furnishings is presented an unequalled assortment of well-chosen goods, purchased at the favourable prices we get with Quantity Buying, and marked at a profit based on the low cost of Cash Selling.

Examine our Values on either basis---
Cash or Deferred Payments.

STORE HOURS: 8.30 A.M. TO 5 P.M.   SATURDAYS: 8.30 A.M. TO 1 P.M.

ᵀᴴᴱ T. EATON C⁰ₗᵢₘᵢₜₑ𝒹

Figure 3.3 Eaton's Daily Store News: "The Opening of Thrift House," Toronto *Globe*, January 18, 1926: 16. Uploaded: http://catalogue.library.carleton.ca:80/record=b2030589~S9.

of class-appropriate goals. Such planning involved applying modern accounting techniques to the business of the household, which included purchasing decisions based on projected future earnings.

Compared to most major North American department stores, Eaton's was a late-comer in offering installment credit to customers.[1] Internal correspondence reveals soul searching by the store's senior managers prior to the introduction of a deferred purchase plan. To understand their prolonged resistance, one must realize the importance of cash payments to Eaton's corporate culture.

By 1919, the small, dry goods shop Timothy Eaton founded in 1869 had become Canada's largest department store. In addition to its dominance of the Toronto market, the family-owned T. Eaton Company had developed an extensive mail-order business and opened a branch in Winnipeg in 1905. Expansion continued throughout the 1920s with the opening of large stores in Montreal (1925), Regina (1926) and Calgary (1929), and the building of a second Toronto store (1930). From the beginning, Timothy Eaton made it his policy to accept only cash payment for his merchandize. As the business went from strength to strength, institutional advertising frequently ascribed the store's success to the founder's insistence on ready money.

The importance of the policy to the company's self-image is evident in the Golden Jubilee souvenir book Eaton's published in 1919. The section on the store's history portrays Timothy Eaton as a retailing innovator ahead of his time:

> When Mr. Timothy Eaton refused to adopt the charge account and marked his goods in plain figures with one unchangeable price he stood out among his fellow store-keepers in Toronto as an idealist—an oddity. Failure was predicted for his new policy. Who could run a successful store on a "No Credit" basis? It was a wild dream, they said.
>
> ("The Scribe" 1919, 36–37)

Far from being the eccentricity of a wild dreamer, Timothy Eaton's refusal to provide credit reflected standard practices in late nineteenth-century urban retailing.[2] While not original, Eaton's cash-only policy served the company well during its first half century. Financial liquidity gave Eaton's an advantage in bargaining with suppliers, and the savings allowed lower prices and higher turnover (Santink 1990, 63–66). Additionally, the price of Eaton's goods did not have to include the costs of administering charge accounts and absorbing bad debts. Cash dealing also simplified customer relations: credit worthiness was hard to determine in a growing city where shopkeepers no longer knew their clientele.

In the 1920s, however, Toronto's retail landscape was changing. Eaton's main competitor, the Robert Simpson Company, had introduced deferred payment for furniture and household appliances in 1915. Initially offered only during Simpson's semi-annual house furnishings sales, the plan allowed approved customers to buy merchandize on an installment basis while prices were at their lowest. The price of the goods was unaffected by the method of purchase (Ad 5, *Globe* February 13, 1915). In effect, this meant that cash customers helped carry the overhead costs associated with credit services ("Social and Economic Consequences" 1927, 31). Eaton's managers refused to adopt Simpson's pricing policy, considering it unethical in its treatment of cash buyers (T. Eaton Company Fonds TECF, F229-8-0-48, letters, August 17 and October 1, 1925). They continued to adhere to cash-only purchasing, even as they reached out to wealthier segments of Toronto's population and started selling luxury items such as antique furniture and pianos.

As the decade wore on, Eaton's upper management began to worry that this insistence on cash payment was causing the store to lose business in the house furnishings departments. Sales personnel dealing directly with the public blamed sluggish turnover on the company's refusal to provide credit services offered by other retailers, particularly Simpson's (TECF, F229-8-0-48, letter, October 1, 1925). Commercial expediency eventually triumphed, but it was not an easy victory. Correspondence between company president R.Y. Eaton and other members of upper management shows that the discussion about introducing credit – in the form of a deferred payment plan limited to purchases of consumer durables for the home – was also about the morality of different consumer choices (TECF, F229-8-0-48, letter, October 12, 1925). The debate reflected changing social attitudes to debt that legitimized borrowing in order to invest in the family home while continuing to stigmatize using credit to pay for transitory personal pleasures.

Exchanges between R.Y. Eaton and H.M. Tucker, manager of the Winnipeg, Manitoba store, are revealing. A long-time Eaton's employee, Tucker was deeply committed to the cash system. During the World War I years, a booming wheat economy had encouraged Manitoba farmers to go into debt to purchase new equipment. Prices declined disastrously after the war, plunging farmers into serious financial difficulties. This confirmed Tucker's suspicions about credit. Given Winnipeg's dependence on Manitoba's agricultural fortunes, he believed his customers shared his concerns and would see deferred payment as a trap, not a benefit (TECF, Eaton, F229-8-0-48, letter, August 7, 1925).

As Tucker reluctantly acknowledged in the same letter, his resistance to credit was contrary to prevailing trends. Many North American consumers increasingly felt entitled to the higher standard of living made possible by industrial innovations (Calder 1999, 235; Hyman 2011, 36–37). Consumer durables that had been considered luxuries before World War I were redefined as necessities in the 1920s. This was particularly true of automobiles. Their cost had dropped significantly as a result of Fordist production efficiencies, but automobiles remained out of reach for the ordinary consumer. Introducing installment buying made it possible for workers receiving a regular income to obtain a desired commodity. Deferred payment plans for automobiles proved hugely successful as a marketing strategy and retailers of other types of goods began to follow suit. For Tucker, the popularity of deferred payment plans for cars represented a slippery slope: the undisciplined spending habits created by consumer credit would, he believed, inevitably lead to economic disaster.

R.Y. Eaton took a more nuanced approach to the problem. Although he, too, was uncomfortable about abandoning the principle of cash-only transactions, he was equally troubled about the possibility that the store might lose sales and market share, arguing: "If the motor trade alone were to have a monopoly of instalment payments, trade in other lines would be starved. If other lines offer instalment facilities there will be that much less available for motor payments" (TECF, F229-8-0-48, letter, August 11, 1925). Brought up to believe that a penny saved is a penny earned, R.Y. Eaton was aware that a new generation of purchasers had different attitudes. He believed that, given the younger generation's lack of financial responsibility, it was even possible to view deferred payment contracts as a lesser evil than the thoughtless frittering away of money. As he told Tucker in a letter dated August 11, 1925: "If part of the [consumer's] income is ear-marked for payments on useful articles of some enduring value there will be less spent on movies and candies, and thus thrift will be fostered" (TECF, F229-8-0-48).

Installment credit could thus lead to financial discipline. Committing income to payment for household amenities such as comfortable living room furniture would contribute to the broader social good by making individual family members less likely to squander money on transitory pleasures. R.Y. Eaton's argument reflected a shift in the popular definition of thrift that shaped discourse about spending and saving in North America during the early twentieth century. While extravagance was still deplored, spending to achieve a class-appropriate standard of living was encouraged by a spectrum of opinion makers that included reformers as well as retailers (Yarrow 2014). As the number of workers receiving regular salaries increased, using income rather than savings to finance purchases became increasingly acceptable.

By the mid-1920s many analysts of consumer spending believed that installment buying was there to stay (Calder 1999, 235–237). R.Y. Eaton had reluctantly reached the same conclusion. Once the company decided to introduce a deferred payment program, it faced a marketing issue: persuading customers that the new service did not betray the cash-only principle underlying the store's reputation for value and honest dealing. The solution was to transform the introduction of installment credit into a course in financial literacy for Toronto shoppers. The outline of the terms for deferred payment began with a reiteration of the company's mantra proclaiming the advantages of cash. Should customers prefer to pay by installment, they would first have to get credit approval from the Purchasers Finance Company, a subsidiary that Eaton's management had set up to establish some distance between the store and its consumer credit financing agency. If credit was granted, buyers would have to purchase at least $50 worth of goods (later reduced to $25) and pay 20% down. The outstanding balance, together with a 7% carrying fee, would then be paid off at regular intervals over the next ten months. Eaton's advertising argued the 7% fee was justified on the grounds that credit payments involved extra administrative charges for the store. The imposition of the 7% service charge was not only intended to cover Eaton's expenses; it was also a mechanism for getting consumers to think critically about the cost structures that lay behind the prices assigned to goods in department stores such as Simpson's, which did not impose fees for credit.[3] Finally, credit was only available for a limited list of items, virtually all of which were furniture and house furnishings. In this way, Eaton's encouraged investing in middle-class domesticity.[4]

Materializing the new thrift

Blithely ignoring the fact that Eaton's was duplicating Simpson's Budget Bungalow, store ads claimed that the Thrift House was inspired by a marketing strategy pioneered at Wanamaker's, a prestigious New York department store (Ad 44, *Globe* January 18, 1926). Wanamaker's "Little Home that Budget Built" predated both Simpson's and Eaton's displays, having opened in 1923. Possibly influenced by such U.S. civic initiatives as National Thrift Week and the Better Homes movement, Wanamaker's had hired Frances Seaver to not only manage the model house but also to provide free financial advice to customers.[5] The ultimate objective was to sell furniture and furnishings but, in hiring Seaver, Wanamaker's positioned itself as an advocate of carefully-planned spending. While Eaton's did not employ someone with a national profile to manage the Thrift House, the store followed the lead of its New York counterpart by supplementing the display with a "Thrift Advisory Bureau," an office located next to the model house and staffed by women advertised as "expert home economists" capable of drawing up budgets tailored to the needs of individual customers (Ad 38, *Globe* January 22, 1926). As in New York, this service was offered free of charge and with no obligation to buy.

Eaton's promotional campaign bolstered the illusion that the Thrift House was a private domestic space rather than a merchandizing tool:

> Men take off their hats and women drop their shopping manner as they step through the doorway. The atmosphere of Thrift House is so home-like you assume the character of a visitor to a private house. Would any hostess have arranged flowers more charmingly than those daffodils are arranged in the purple glass bowl in the living-room?
>
> (Ad 59, *Globe* January 23, 1926)

Ads described the launch of the Thrift House as a "house warming" that attracted thousands of curious Torontonians. When these "visitors" entered the "stucco house with vari-colored cedar shingle roof, gracious Georgian doorway, painted white, dull green shutters, swinging back from the white window frames," they were confronted with a small, formal hallway containing a false staircase intended to suggest a two-storey house. On one side of this hall lay the living room and sunroom; on the other the dining room and kitchen. A passage from the kitchen led to an imagined second storey containing three bedrooms, a bathroom and a sewing room (TECF, F229–96, *Eaton's News Weekly* 1926). Eaton's claimed the new display was greeted with enthusiasm by shoppers who expressed "every phase of approval from admiration to amazement," with one "smart-looking woman" saying: "I wish I could move right in […] The sight of that linen room makes me hate my stuffy, inconvenient little flat" (Ad 59, *Globe* January 23, 1926).

The home-like aura surrounding the Thrift House was somewhat undercut by the price lists in each room (Fig. 3.4). However jarring, these lists linked the display to the store's message that it could provide good taste on a budget. Over the years, Eaton's had taken steps to establish itself as an authority in all matters pertaining to the world of goods. One important move was the 1910 hiring of Edith Macdonald, a former columnist in the women's pages of the *Toronto News*. Macdonald helped transform the store's advertising in the *Toronto Globe* into a lively news bulletin about the wonders of the Big Store. Writing as "The Scribe," she instituted "You Were Inquiring," an advice column responding to shoppers' queries about subjects ranging from travel wardrobes to wedding etiquette. Interior decoration was a recurring topic, with The Scribe offering suggestions about color schemes, window treatments, and furniture placement. Responding to needs revealed by the column, Eaton's created the Shopping Service: women who would guide shoppers to various departments or, for customers unable to come to the store, make purchases on their behalf. The Thrift Advisers occupied the same middle ground as The Scribe and the Shopping Service, solving consumers' problems by selling them goods.

The price lists in the Thrift House also suggested the class of shoppers the display was primarily designed to serve. The promise that the Thrift Advisers could show Torontonians how to replicate the house was not realistic for many: the cost of

Figure 3.4 Thrift House – main floor, House Furnishings Building, living room, 1926.
Source: F229-308-0-2043, T. Eaton Company fonds. Eaton's Archives photographic and documentary art subject files, Merchandise-Ont-Toronto-House furnishings-Furniture-Model Homes, B411202 Container B-551

decorating and furnishing the house was "less than $2,600" at a time when the average Canadian earned $1,200 a year (Thompson and Seager 1985, 138). The thrifty homemakers Eaton's hoped to attract were firmly ensconced in the middle class. An indicative ad for the Thrift Bureau describing "three imaginary but typical problems" appeared in the *Globe* in April 1926. The incomes involved ranged from $1,500 a year (a business girl planning her wedding) to a family of seven facing the horrors of being reduced from $12,000 to $10,000 a year. Somewhere in the middle was the family of five:

> They had lived comfortably on $6,000, but now the house needs redecorating throughout, and no money exists for the purpose. The Thrift Adviser suggested a family conclave and the Budget plan. It was adopted. Each member of the family agreed to cut down expenses. By the new scale of living – at no privation to any one – a furnishing fund of $65 a month was evolved. This in addition to the regular saving of $70 per month. Result: $780 at the end of the year to rejuvenate the house.
>
> (Ad 57, *Globe* April 21, 1926)

None of the three case studies presented installment credit as a possible solution to financial problems. Unlike Simpson's and many of its other Toronto competitors, Eaton's initially marketed its deferred purchase plan as a service to be granted sparingly, rather than a product to be sold aggressively. The store recognized that, while deferred payment was one way of satisfying the longings aroused by the Thrift House, there were dangers associated with this method of financing. Company managers feared that customers, believing that installment buying was an easy option, would apply for credit only to be denied as a bad risk. Good will would be lost as a result. The Thrift Bureau advisers may have served as a first line of defense, filtering out unsuccessful applications by drawing up realistic budgets. Such budget consultations validated a rational approach to spending that would help reduce the company's exposure to bad debts.

Fittingly, the launch of the Thrift House was timed to coincide with Eaton's semi-annual sale of home furnishings. During the first months of the display's existence the house was redecorated roughly every four weeks. Eaton's ads featured tantalizing descriptions of the marvels that could be achieved "for a sum wholly in keeping with the average, limited income" (Ad 44, *Globe* January 18, 1926). A month after opening, the store boasted that more than 70,000 shoppers had visited the model home (Ad 31, *Globe* February 19, 1926).

Both the House Furnishings Committee minutes and the *Globe* advertisements indicate that, in later years, managers still synchronized the redecoration of the model house to coincide with regular events in the store's merchandizing calendar: the semi-annual sales in January and August, and the new fashion seasons in spring and fall. The pace of change may have slowed, but the display continued to be popular with Torontonians throughout the 1920s.

Usually the new interior decoration schemes for the Thrift House were the work of the women of the Thrift Bureau. Their clientele was different from the wealthier customers who patronized the store's male-dominated Interior Decorating Service. The female Thrift Advisers were knowledgeable but not intimidating. They catered to shoppers of more limited means, who were responsive to Eaton's promise that the house model would show them how to combine good taste and economy. Ads describing the various iterations of the display emphasized practicality as well as attractiveness. It was generally not a venue for startling innovations in décor. Period furniture in the dining room, chintz slipcovers in the living room, and the efficient layout of the kitchen tended to be constant features, made novel by changes in color and pattern. In her book *Household Gods*, historian Deborah Cohen argues that middle-class taste in interior design had become standardized in interwar Britain as a result of "the widespread diffusion of home decoration periodicals and advice manuals" (2006, 188). For similar reasons, the same tendency towards "safety first" in home furnishings arguably characterized many Torontonians. Thus Eaton's Thrift House both responded to and reinforced the conservatism of the local market.

On occasion, though, the Thrift House became the setting for debates about interior design. For the spring opening in 1930, the young matrons of Toronto's Junior League, drawn from the city's social elite, were invited to use the model as the basis for an experiment in taste:

> Does Toronto's younger set like the new idea in decoration? Or does she prefer period treatment? Has she a yearning for antiques? Or does she consider a

compromise more interesting? [...] The collected opinions of the Junior League argue in very different ways that all these schemes are popular – as displayed in the rooms which you are invited to inspect on Monday and during the week.

(Ad 76, *Globe* March 22, 1930)

According to the minutes of the House Furnishings Committee, this promotional event was extremely popular with Toronto shoppers, drawing 21,600 during its first week (TECF, F229–69 April 9, 1930). Customers enjoyed the opportunity to compare and contrast amateur efforts at creating effective domestic settings. The use of the Thrift House for this purpose was appropriate, as ads for the display communicated the message that ordinary housewives could achieve a range of tasteful interiors in collaboration with the store. It was also appropriate that no definite consensus seems to have emerged from this exercise, as Eaton's aimed to serve the full gamut of style preferences on display.

Thrift House in troubled times

In late October 1930, Eaton's moved the company's home furnishings departments to their new home, a few blocks north of the main store complex at Queen and Yonge.[6] The company had built the elegant Art Deco structure, known as Eaton's College Street, with the intent of creating Toronto's most prestigious home furnishings store. While in many ways the new building was aimed at a wealthier class of customer than the downtown store, a new version of the Thrift House was built in a prime location on the main floor in recognition of the continuing importance of middle-class consumers (Fig. 3.5). The basic features of the original were reproduced, but the added height of the College Street store's ceilings made it possible to construct a mezzanine space on the roof to accommodate the offices of the House Furnishings Shopping Service, which included the staff of the Thrift Bureau. Despite such competing attractions as formal period rooms and a significantly more ambitious model house on the fourth and fifth floors, the display retained its interest for shoppers. In February 1932, the House Furnishings Committee noted that 435,163 people had visited the model house in its new setting during the previous year and "a very good response was received from the buying public for the merchandise displayed there" (TECF, F229–69).

For the most part, department store displays were short-lived. Show windows changed rapidly, reflecting the store's dependence on the quick turnover of goods. Life-sized model houses, however, had a different trajectory. Like their real-life counterparts, they represented a significant financial investment and thus were not lightly discarded. Instead, they were subject to an ongoing process of maintenance and renovation not dissimilar to the patterns of upkeep that could be observed in middle-class neighborhoods. Allocating the money necessary to keep house displays fresh and inviting was debated by members of Eaton's House Furnishings Committee, just as it would be by the family budgeting councils advocated by the store's Thrift Advisers. Thrift House staff, like real homeowners, had to adapt to financial and physical constraints. The Depression and, to a greater extent, World War II created additional difficulties.

When Eaton's College Street opened, it was still believed that the economic crisis was temporary. As the Depression continued, however, the store began to advertise aggressively in response to falling sales. Spending on Canadian-made house furnishings

Figure 3.5 Thrift House – main floor, College Street store, exterior, 1930.
Source: F229-308-0-2043, T. Eaton Company fonds. Eaton's Archives photographic and documentary art subject files, Merchandise-Ont-Toronto-House furnishings-Furniture-Model Homes, B411115 Container B-399

was presented as both a civic duty and a chance to take advantage of reduced prices (Ad 34, *Globe* January 1, 1934). But, once the backlog of stock was gone, price inducements were no longer available and, in 1935, Eaton's shifted to selling credit actively, instead of reluctantly providing it to customers unwilling to pay cash (Ad 35, *Globe* March 28, 1935). Conditions were eased: the list of eligible goods was expanded to include the more expensive clothing lines, the required down payment was reduced to 10%, and term lengths became negotiable for larger purchases.

The effects of these changes on the Thrift House were subtle. Eaton's advertisements stopped stressing the Thrift Advisers' expertise in all facets of household budgeting and instead began describing them more narrowly as specialists in economical interior design. The decoration of the house was not redirected toward less expensive merchandize; instead, in early 1935, the store experimented with installing a Budget Arcade of furnished rooms in the basement. This was discontinued after a few months because of fears of increased property taxes, but the concept was not transferred to the Thrift House. The company's aspirations for College Street, together with the prominent position of the display on the main floor, probably precluded a more down-market approach to decoration.

One way in which Eaton's hoped to stimulate demand during the 1930s was by promoting modern furniture design. In 1933, the Thrift House departed from the usual pattern of redecoration by the Thrift Advisers. The task was given to René Cera, who was responsible for merchandize display at College Street. Cera had been originally hired in 1928 as a specialist in modern interior design, which, at the time, meant the style now known as Art Deco (Ad 68, *Globe* September 4, 1929). In 1929, after assessing the Canadian market, he created the House of Today, a model house entirely in the new style that was first featured at the opening of Eaton's Calgary store before being rebuilt on the floor of the Toronto House Furnishings Building. This innovative display, which was accompanied by a suite of small boutiques, was dismantled when house furnishings moved to Eaton's College Street and, unlike the Thrift House, it was not rebuilt in the new location. It seems Torontonians were hesitant to take home this form of modernity, although it proved more popular as a design vocabulary for public spaces such as the 1930 College Street store.

Eaton's and Cera did not give up, however, and in 1933 Thrift House became an object lesson in adapting Art Deco to the needs of a middle-class household. This renewed effort was prompted in part by the style's popularity at the 1933 Chicago World's Fair. The store's furniture ads during the later 1930s suggest that some headway was made in creating a taste for modern design. But period styles continued to dominate the Toronto market. When the Thrift Advisers returned as decorators, they featured the Colonial treatments that were considered particularly appropriate for smaller houses during the interwar years.

Lack of money limited middle-class home renovations in the 1930s. During World War II, the problem became the scarcity of consumer goods as manufacturers redirected production to meet military needs. The Thrift House used these challenges to once again prove its value as a site for imagining middle-class domesticity in Toronto. Advertisements appearing in the mid-1940s portrayed the model house as the home of the fictional Jeffersons, a family deeply involved in the war effort. The Jeffersons' storyline was continued in several more advertisements that detailed the ways in which they adapted their domestic surroundings to meet wartime demands. In a 1943 ad, Torontonians were urged to revisit the Thrift House: "The kind of home that reaches right out and shakes your hand [...] that's every homemaker's dream! And in these days, when you can't make a lot of dramatic changes in your décor, it's the little things that bring the sparkling homey look!" (Ad 43, *Globe* March 22, 1943). In this way, Eaton's Thrift Advisers made a virtue out of wartime necessity. The limited options available to them accurately reflected the situation in the city the store sought to serve.

As discussed in Joy Parr's study of postwar consumerism in Canada, scarcity of domestic goods remained a fact of life in the immediate postwar period (1999). When resources were at last available for the construction of new housing, it became clear that Torontonians' residential expectations had changed significantly since the Thrift House was constructed in 1926 as a representative middle-class dwelling. Efforts were made to update the model house, such as the installation of a picture window in 1946. But the disjunction between the display and Toronto's postwar housing developments in suburbs such as Thorncrest Village was too great (TECF, F229–69, Memo, February 1, 1946). The Thrift House had finally outlived its usefulness: it no longer functioned effectively as a model for Toronto's new homemakers and Eaton's dismantled it in June 1950 (TECF, F229–69, Memo, July 3, 1950). Its replacement was the Aluminum House (later known as the House of Trends), an open-plan bungalow located on the fourth floor of the College Street store (Fig. 3.6). Tellingly, the house included a garage, symbolic of the changes in transportation and lifestyle that made the Thrift House obsolete.

Figure 3.6 Visitors lining up to enter Aluminum House, 1949.
Source: T. Eaton Company fonds, Records of the Eaton's Housefurnishings Merchandise Office, Furnished homes "Aluminum House," B294475 Container 21–69

Conclusion

Visitors to the Thrift House were invited to imagine how modest, affordable changes could make their homes more convenient, comfortable and attractive, rather than to desire radical makeovers. Such goals were more consistent with prevailing patterns of middle-class domestic consumption during the interwar years. In many ways, the display undercut the store's ongoing attempts to tie the consumption of home furnishings to a fashion cycle that privileged novelty through its appeal to the "make do and mend" spirit prevalent among most Toronto homemakers during this period. Furniture was frequently described as a long-term investment, an attitude that militated against frequent replacement with the latest style. Eaton's customers were encouraged to take advantage of the various repair and refurbishment services offered by the store. New slipcovers, curtains and wallpaper could work wonders at moderate cost. The non-threatening women of the Thrift Bureau were at hand to suggest how limited funds could be used to maximum advantage.

When first installed, the Thrift House was associated with a specific corporate objective: the promotion of wise spending that prioritized the comforts and conveniences of a middle-class home. Over time, however, Eaton's personnel used the display to engage shoppers in a number of different ways. In the hands of the Junior League, it became the setting for a group of elite women to demonstrate their taste in public, encouraging others to take on the task of interior decoration. René Cera, Eaton's specialist in modern interior design, used the Thrift House to prove that Art Deco Modernism could meet the needs of the middle class. During World War II, the House represented the ways in which conventional domesticity was reshaped by a national emergency. Throughout its long history as a display, this model house served as a pedagogical tool that reinforced Eaton's authority not just as a tastemaker, but also as a corporate citizen determined to promote a middle-class lifestyle centered on home and family. As a case study, Eaton's Thrift House demonstrates the ways in which retailers could use display architecture to define appropriate consumer desires.

Notes

1 Eaton's was not completely alone: Macy's did not introduce installment credit until 1939. Up to that time, store advertising emphasized the savings associated with cash payment. When Macy's finally gave in and introduced a credit plan, the store also made it clear that interest would be charged to distinguish credit from cash purchases (Calder 1999, 276–277).
2 This was true in Canada and the United States as well as in Great Britain (Santink 1990, 63–64).
3 See also R.Y. Eaton to H.M. Tucker, October 1, 1925, for competition from Simpson's (TECF, F229-8-0-48).
4 Eaton's managers were not content to trust that customers would absorb the messages put forward by the company's advertising about its credit terms. In May 1926, Eaton's announced an essay contest to test whether their pedagogical goals had been achieved. Entrants were to write a response not exceeding two hundred words to the question "Should the buyer who pays Spot Cash be asked to pay as much for an article as the buyer who is given ten months to pay? If so, why? If not, why not?" An independent panel of three judges chose 116 winners, who received prizes totaling $2,000. Winning essays were incorporated into Eaton's *Globe* ads (see, for example, Ad 44, *Globe* July 10, 1926).
5 Both National Thrift Week and the Better Homes movement were widely promoted by government agencies and business organizations in the United States during the 1920s (Yarrow 2014; Hutchison 1986). *Good Furniture Magazine*, a trade journal for furniture retailers and manufacturers that would have been familiar to managers at Eaton's and Wanamaker's, frequently reported favorably on marketing initiatives linked to these campaigns (see, for example, May 1925, 224).
6 As of 1930, Eaton's had two locations in Toronto: a complex of buildings at Queen and Yonge that included factories and stables as well as two retail buildings, the main store and the House Furnishings Building. Eaton's College Street contained retail and office spaces. When the house furnishings departments moved to the new store, the old House Furnishings Building was renamed Eaton's Annex and was stocked with lower-price goods aimed at working-class consumers. The original Thrift House was dismantled, and a new version was built at the College Street store.

References

Ad 5, Display Ads, Toronto *The Globe (1844–1936)*, February 13, 1915.
Ad 31, Display Ads, Toronto *The Globe (1844–1936)*, February 19, 1926.
Ad 34, Display Ads, Toronto *The Globe (1844–1936)*, January 1, 1934.
Ad 35, Display Ads, Toronto *The Globe (1844–1936)*, March 28, 1935.
Ad 38, Display Ads, Toronto *The Globe (1844–1936)*, January 22, 1926.
Ad 43, Display Ads, *Globe and Mail (1936–Current)*, March 22, 1943.
Ad 44, Display Ads, Toronto *The Globe (1844–1936)*, January 18, 1926.

Ad 44, Display Ads, Toronto *The Globe (1844–1936)*, July 10, 1926.

Ad 57, Display Ads, Toronto *The Globe (1844–1936)*, April 21, 1926.

Ad 59, Display Ads, Toronto *The Globe (1844–1936)*, January 23, 1926.

Ad 68, Display Ads, Toronto *The Globe (1844–1936)*, September 4, 1929.

Ad 76, Display Ads, Toronto *The Globe (1844–1936)*, March 22, 1930.

[Toronto *The Globe (1844–1936)* and *Globe and Mail (1936-Current)*, available at: http:// catalogue.library.carleton.ca:80/record=b2030589~S9]

Calder, Lendol. 1999. *Financing the American Dream: A Cultural History of Consumer Credit.* Princeton: Princeton University Press.

Cohen, Deborah. 2006. *Household Gods: The British and Their Possessions.* New Haven: Yale University Press.

Good Furniture Magazine. 1925. May.

Hutchison, Janet. 1986. "The Cure for Domestic Neglect: Better Homes in America: 1922–1935." *Perspectives in Vernacular Architecture* 2: 168–178.

Hyman, Louis. 2011. *Debtor Nation: The History of America in Red Ink.* Princeton and Oxford: Princeton University Press.

Iarocci, Louisa. 2014. *The Urban Department Store in America, 1850–1930.* Burlington, VT: Ashgate.

Leach, William. 1993. *Land of Desire: Merchants, Power and the Rise of a New American Culture.* New York: Vintage Books.

Parr, Joy. 1999. *Domestic Goods: The Material, the Moral and the Economic in the Postwar Years.* Toronto: University of Toronto Press.

Santink, Joy L. 1990. *Timothy Eaton and the Rise of his Department Store.* Toronto: University of Toronto Press.

"Social and Economic Consequences of Buying on the Instalment Plan." 1927. *Annals of the American Academy of Political and Social Sciences*, January: 1–57.

TECF – T. Eaton Company Fonds, F-229, Archives of Ontario:

    F229–8 Eaton's Executive Office general files

    F229-8-0-48 Credit business in Eaton's stores, Deferred Payment Plan:

    Letter, R.Y. Eaton to H.M. Tucker, August 7, 1925

    Letter, R.Y. Eaton to H.M. Tucker, August 11, 1925

    Letter, H.M. Tucker to R.Y. Eaton, August 17, 1925

    Letter, R.Y. Eaton to H.M. Tucker, October 1, 1925

    Letter, R.Y. Eaton to H.M. Tucker, October 12, 1925

    F229–69:

    Eaton's House Furnishings Merchandise Office, House Furnishings Committee Minutes, April 9, 1930 and February 19, 1932

    Thrift House/Faircraft House 1945–6/Thorncrest Village: Memo, Phyllis Stagg to B.W. Smith, February 1, 1946

    Memo, H.B. Haliday, General Office, July 3, 1950

    F229–96:

    Eaton News Weekly, Thrift House Number, January 23, 1926

"The Scribe" (Edith Macdonald). 1919. *Golden Jubilee 1869–1919: A Book to Commemorate the Fiftieth Anniversary of the T. Eaton Co. Limited.* Toronto: The T. Eaton Co. Limited.

Thompson, John Herd and Allen Seager. 1985. *Canada 1922–1939: Decades of Discord.* Toronto: McClelland and Stewart Ltd.

Whitaker, Jan. 2006. *Service and Style: How the American Department Store Fashioned the Middle Class.* New York: St. Martin's Press.

Yarrow, Andrew L. 2014. *Thrift: The History of an American Cultural Movement.* Amherst and Boston: University of Massachusetts Press.

4 The art of window display

Cross-promotion at Bonwit Teller and MoMA

Sandra Zalman

When the Fifth Avenue department store Bonwit Teller took out an advertisement in 1936, it did not showcase alluring models or the latest gowns (Fig. 4.1). Instead, the ad illustrated a disembodied eye and urged shoppers to come to the store – not to see the new merchandize but to see the new window displays, one of which was designed by Surrealist artist Salvador Dalí.[1] Not only were Bonwit's windows given over to Surrealist symbols and strategies, but in the corner of seven of the eight windows was a copy of the catalog for the Surrealism exhibition concurrently on view at the Museum of Modern Art (MoMA) down the street. The relationship between Bonwit Teller and MoMA demonstrated that these institutions were not in competition over visual culture but in fact recognized that cross-promotion could strengthen their appeal to their shared audiences and provide them each with new ones.

Dalí was invited back to Bonwit Teller in 1939 to again design its windows. This time, however, the episode ended in disaster after the store tried to censor the artist's displays and the artistic community shunned Dalí for being a sell-out. Though his reputation as an artist suffered, Dalí's 1930s windows signal a major turning point in the history of window display because of the sensational way they demonstrated both the subversion of legible display techniques and the preservation of a designer's integrity. A decade later, when MoMA celebrated its twentieth anniversary with the exhibition "Modern Art in Your Life," the museum's curators duplicated six full-scale, Surrealist-inspired windows that had originally been created for Fifth Avenue department stores, showcasing the interrelation of fine art and everyday life. But although Dalí had actively participated in introducing Surrealist techniques to American window designers, the curators chose to install only the displays of full-time professional designers (including Gene Moore and Henry Callahan) to illustrate Surrealism's role in commercial display practices. This time the tie-in was even more seamless – window display gained cachet through its installation inside the museum while the museum associated itself with the world beyond its walls. Furthermore, in exhibiting the windows, the museum lent publicity to Saks, Lord & Taylor, and Bonwit Teller, and showed off an array of their merchandize (including neckties and jewelry), conveniently available for purchase again in these stores, just around the corner.

This chapter analyzes Bonwit Teller's Surrealist windows in the winter of 1936, both in the context of evolving window display techniques and in that of the avant-garde visual concepts they demonstrated. It then examines the difficulty of Dalí's second collaboration with Bonwit Teller, the critical fallout from that failure, and MoMA's institutional endorsement of window display as an artistic aspect of modern life. The chapter ultimately argues that the Surrealist window advanced the interests

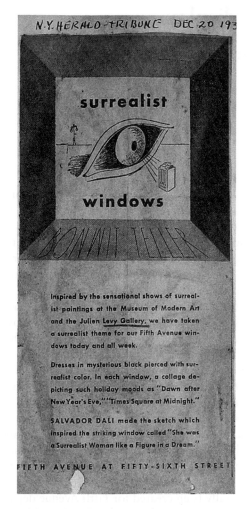

Figure 4.1 Advertisement for Bonwit Teller windows, *New York Herald Tribune*, December 20, 1936.

of art and fashion, the museum and the marketplace, fortifying their shared pursuit of fantastic display.

Art and fashion in Surrealist windows

The ad for the Surrealist-themed windows appeared in the Sunday edition of the *New York Herald Tribune* on December 20, 1936. It was the weekend before Christmas and the windows would be up during the holidays. Then, as now, the Christmas season meant extra pressure on retailers and an increased visibility of consumer culture. An article appearing the same day as the ad noted: "To distract thousands of women bent on Christmas shopping, on the last Saturday before Christmas is not easy. But these eight Bonwit Teller windows stop traffic and evoke hundreds of comments of admiration, amusement or revolt. Never indifference, however" (Hughes 1936).

Figure 4.2 Salvador Dalí, Window at Bonwit Teller, "She was a Surrealist Woman – She Was Like a Figure in a Dream," 1936.
Source: City Museum of New York

Bonwit Teller's display manager, Helen Cole, deployed Surrealism like a secret weapon, installing the windows, with Dalí on hand to consult, in the middle of the night of December 18–19.

Of the eight Surrealist-themed windows, Dalí's window garnered the most press (Fig. 4.2). It also was the most eccentric: Dalí's design flouted recent display trends that advocated foregrounding the merchandize in uncluttered, spare yet dynamic arrangements much like Frederick Kiesler's 1928 window for Saks Fifth Avenue. While Dalí's design did feature a mannequin dressed in a black gown, with accessories including a purse and jewelry, these were among the few items for sale featured in the window. *New York City Retailing* described the rest of the display as "an assortment of junk ranging from whiskey glasses to red hands pushing through walls" (*New York City Retailing* 1936). If *Retailing* did not associate stemware and elongated arms with the high-end fashion of Fifth Avenue, Dalí was nonetheless practicing the Surrealist philosophy of uniting random, everyday objects to evoke beauty through chance interactions. *Women's Wear* assessed Dalí's window as "quite the gayest of all," describing how "hundreds of teaspoons cover the floor; dozens of cocktail glasses hang suspended from a dinner jacket, and red arms, their fingers tipped with white fur nails, reach out from the walls of the case toward the mannequin whose 'head' is one mass of red roses" (*Women's Wear* 1936). Descriptions of Dalí's window reveal the way he used the accumulation of objects to create a total environment that diffused the aesthetic aspects of the merchandize. Instead of concentrating on clothing, another writer describing Dalí's window dwelled on the drama inherent in the tension between the scarlet hands and the black-gowned woman as the hands unsuccessfully stretched to touch her or ply her with gifts. This writer also noted that "on a small table, whose legs are like a human leg and foot, the black base of a telephone rests. Its receiver is a lobster; its dial, a string of pearls. This is Dali at his best" (Hughes 1936). Many critics realized that Dalí's window borrowed heavily from his fine art work (especially his painting *Three Surrealist Women*, and object *Lobster Telephone*, both 1936), but the author's proclamation presciently predicted that Dalí would become best known for his commercial forays – or, perhaps more accurately, for blending his artistic practice with a commercial one. The coverage Dalí received in trade magazines like *New York City Retailing* indeed contributed to this. Dalí and his window made waves in these magazines, whereas the art critical coverage of MoMA's exhibition preferred to address Surrealism's aesthetic worth and cultural relevance.

The other seven Surrealist-inspired windows, far more conventional than Dalí's display, were conceived by professional window designers and executed by Copeland Displays. They showcased mannequins in "mysterious black" dresses, each punctuated with bursts of a different "Surrealist" color – delphinium, canary, gold, white, red, pink and violet. The design of these Surrealist-inspired windows seems to have owed a great debt to Raymond Loewy's famous windows for Macy's in 1919, in which he installed "only a single mannequin in a black evening gown with fur and a few accessories 'scattered' on the floor" (Leach 1989, 114). But these displays were far more spare, and consisted of the mannequins looking at or away from framed Surrealist images propped on easels, so that the Surrealist aspects of the scene were not visually integrated with the fashions on display. These framed collages often included both two- and three-dimensional representations of eyes, women, bottles with cellophane champagne fizz, and even a *New York Times* story on King Edward's abdication. All in all, the images provided a disjointed vision of romance, glamour, desire and altered states (Fig. 4.3).

But Bonwit's windows were more than an appropriation of Surrealist techniques, as they also included reference material. In the corner of each of the windows, except for Dalí's, was the catalog for MoMA's recently opened exhibition "Fantastic Art, Dada, Surrealism." Open at the first page, which had a distinctive Arpian illustration, the title of the show and curator Alfred Barr's name were easily visible. Behind the open catalog was another closed copy, so that the title could be seen twice. In the canary-colored window, in front of these two iterations of the catalog was a page on which some of the more sensational works in the show were reproduced – Meret Oppenheim's *Object (Luncheon in Fur)* (1936), René Magritte's *The False Mirror*

Figure 4.3 Violet Surrealist window at Bonwit Teller, 1936.
Source: City Museum of New York

(1928), and of course Dalí's own *Persistence of Memory* (1931) (Fig. 4.4). In the pink window, the catalog was again shown both open and closed, but the reproduction featured was Man Ray's lips painting, *A l'heure de l'observatoire* (1932). In the white window, the two catalogs were shown without any other reproductions. So, while the campaign foregrounded color with placards naming its windows, the inclusion of the exhibition catalog further bolstered the windows' connection with Surrealism.

That the windows were arranged by color represented another aspect of Surrealism's appeal to retailers. Historian William Leach notes that the words "display" and "colorful" entered the language of retailing in the 1890s and 1920s respectively (Leach 1989, 99–132; Lancaster 1995, 64). Shortly after Bonwit's windows appeared, a "surrealist color card brought out by the Celanese Corp. of America" included "such unusual combinations as orchid, lilac and Bagdad [sic] blue" (*Women's Wear Daily* 1936). Lord & Taylor introduced woolen evening capes "which contrast vivid and pale shades, like Tarantella red with hyacinthine blue, or intense green with faded pink, in the Dali technique" (*Women's Wear Daily* 1936). Advertisers hailed Surrealism for its exotic color, considering that to be one of the prime aspects of its eye-catching ability. The Surrealist windows were instrumental in demonstrating new ways that color could be used disruptively, and that mundane objects could be invested with mystery. Meanwhile, the museum was not unenthusiastic about fostering these

Figure 4.4 Canary Surrealist window at Bonwit Teller, 1936.
Source: City Museum of New York

associations. In some ways, the commercial world had more leeway in experimenting with Surrealism as a practice.

Bonwit Teller was not the first New York department store to play off an exhibition occurring at the Museum of Modern Art. The first occasion was in 1935, when Saks Fifth Avenue created a set of windows to coincide with MoMA's Van Gogh exhibition, which became the museum's most popular show in its then short history. The *New York World Telegram* reminded readers that Bonwit's Surrealism display was just "one more occasion when industry and art joined hands to make John Q. Public art-conscious – and also to sell merchandise" (*World Telegram* 1936). The article went on to describe the way the clothes arranged in the Saks windows matched the colors of the Van Gogh reproductions that were the center of the displays. Saks' strategy of using reproductions of paintings seemed to echo the advice of designer Frederick Kiesler, who had proposed that: "The department store acted as the interpreter for the populace of the new spirit in art. Here was the art gaining acceptance not through slow fostering of its theories and principles in academies and art schools, but simply by planting its creations down in the commercial marts" (Keisler 1930, 66). A writer for *Time* recalled, "Taking a cue from the Museum of Modern Art's highly successful Van Gogh exhibition, Saks hung its windows with splashy Van Gogh reproductions, surrounding them with splashy garments" (*Time* 1940). However, a major difference between the Van Gogh-inspired windows and the Surrealist-influenced ones was that Surrealism was able to function as an adaptable style rather than as a static quotation. It was Surrealism's adaptability that made it so appealing to designers.

While color was featured prominently in both sets of windows, the Surrealist windows did not need "splashy garments" to demonstrate the chicness of the design. The collage images within the frames, towards which mannequins turned, were unique creations in their own right rather than mere reproductions. Though one reviewer referred to them as "impressionistic reproductions of some of his [Dalí's] most famous paintings," they were in fact not traceable to a single artist (Hughes 1936). Nonetheless, Dalí's window in particular provided the best example of translating – even integrating – Surrealism for commercial ends, even though *Retailing* singled out his window as the least commercial of the eight, perhaps simply because it did not showcase the merchandize in a legible way. Instead, Dalí's window not only demonstrated how Surrealism could convey a mood but also suggested how psychological space might be more important than any specific object for sale.

The lack of merchandize on display was a new sign of the power of the department store (Burke and Kober 1946, 63). Surrealism may have been especially alluring because in many ways it thwarted the characteristics of good design that were rapidly becoming standard practice inside the department store. A 1946 handbook on modern store design, for example, proclaimed that modern design should be simple, functional, and practical. However, the authors acknowledged that irregular forms were occasionally necessary for an interesting display (Burke and Kober 1946, 8). MoMA, too, was engaged in promoting good design values such as functionalism and simplicity from the 1930s through the 1950s. Even recent design commentary has noted how Surrealism thwarts the principles of good design (Smith 2009, C25). As an art movement, Surrealism flouted the idea of rational Modernism, and its psychological occupations made it particularly useful as a disruptive strategy to complement modern design. Ironically, Surrealism had not been developed as a primarily visual movement, and many of its theorists were devoted Marxists. However, while Surrealism's official allegiance was to Marxism and the intended overthrow of bourgeois culture, Surrealism also gave that culture some of its most beguiling commercial strategies.

"Amused and annoyed:" The windows' reception

Though window display was an acknowledged mass entertainment, the extra attention that the Surrealist windows garnered was noted in newspapers. According to store management, the Surrealist windows "not only attracted large crowds of passers-by, but also sold far more of the dresses shown than was the case with a more usual form of display" (*Daily Telegraph* 1937). The *New York World Telegram* reported "crowds six deep around Bonwit Teller's windows last week of people wondering what all this attractive madness was about" (*New York World Telegram* 1936). The store window was touted as the most important feature of a store in the 1946 handbook on *Modern Store Design*: "This is the most valuable advertising space any store commands. The 'circulation' of a well-located well-arranged show window is at least equal to a full page of display space in the leading newspaper" (Burke and Kober 1946, 63). For Bonwit Teller, the Surrealist windows offered multi-layered publicity opportunities – the store took out an ad for its windows, the windows advertised for the store, and in addition, the papers promoted the windows as news items.

The following week, Bonwit ran another, more conventional, advertisement to promote its "Fashion Fantasy for New Year's Eve." This time, the ad illustrated fashion sketches of women in dramatic gowns, while the text promised that the "finishing touch" would be "fresh flowers, touched with the zany cloud-cuckoo mood that has set the world talking about the Surrealist art exhibitions and our current Surrealist windows" (*New York Herald Tribune* 1936). Again, Bonwit's copy gave credit to the museum and gallery iterations of Surrealist display while simultaneously foregrounding their own. Scattered amidst the fashion illustrations were a mix of motifs taken from paintings by Dalí and Magritte: drawings of a melted timepiece at five minutes to midnight and a floating eye with a clock face at five minutes past 12, marshaling Dalí's *Persistence of Memory* and Magritte's *The False Mirror* (both in MoMA's collection) to reference the stroke of midnight on New Year's Eve, but perhaps also commenting on the importance in the world of fashion of being *à la mode*.

Dalí's imprimatur also helped Surrealism dominate advertising in the 1930s. Because Surrealism was a contemporary avant-garde movement, it seemed sophisticated to upscale consumers – whether or not they had extensive art history knowledge. That there was a Surrealism show at a midtown art gallery demonstrated Surrealism's contemporary status, while the "Fantastic Art, Dada, Surrealism" exhibition at the Museum of Modern Art spoke to the movement's historical importance. *Women's Wear* cited Surrealism's dual position – between art and life – as giving it extra power: "Definitely one realizes the commercial potentialities of surrealism [...] The use of real objects in the composition of a picture which bewilder the average spectator in the surrealistic art gallery becomes dramatic and tangible coupled with a display of merchandise." The journal *Retailing* reported that Dalí's window, even when not dealing explicitly with merchandize, "both annoyed and amused Bonwit's mink-coat clientele as they paused on the avenue to stare at it" (*Retailing* 1936).

As the "Fantastic Art, Dada, Surrealism" exhibition traveled around the country, so too did the influence of Surrealism on window displays. Calling Bonwit's windows a stunt in the publicity sense, *Retailing* advised its readers: "The stunt is of interest to out-of-town display men because the exhibition [at MoMA] will be sent to San Francisco, Boston, Philadelphia, Milwaukee, Springfield, Mass. and other cities" (*Retailing* 1936). The implication is that the temporary museum exhibition provided the platform for other stores to profit from their own cross-promotional displays. The social historian Jan Whitaker further described how "watered-down Daliesque displays" migrated from New York as agencies provided photographs and descriptions of Bonwit's windows to retailers across the country (Whitaker 2006, 123). Eventually, department stores in at least Boston (Filene's) and Philadelphia (Blum's) installed their own Surrealist windows (Lynes 1973, 146).

Dalí's 1939 window

As Surrealism became a popular and effective marketing tool, designers tamed its more risqué aspects to suit commercial needs. Gene Moore, who was the display director at Bonwit's from 1945 to 1962, recalled: "During the 1930s, when I got my start in window display, the reigning style was surrealism. Few styles could have been better suited to windows, because surrealism has to do with dreams, with unconventional ways of looking at things" (Moore and Hyams 1990, 18). Of course, Moore's interpretation of Surrealism was inflected by its commercial uses, rather than by its psychoanalytic engagement or Marxist undercurrents. When Bonwit Teller commissioned Dalí to once again design its windows, in the Spring of 1939, Dalí seemed set on reminding the New York fashion world that, despite its appropriation by the fashion industry, Surrealism was still an avant-garde pursuit (and, by extension, that he was still an avant-garde artist).

Instead of providing the sophisticated, eye-catching visual production that Surrealism had come to signify in the commercial world, Dalí instead created an installation that foregrounded sex, myth, sensuality, and violence. The windows were themed "Day" (Narcissus) and "Night" (Sleep). Since only a few saw the windows before they were censored and then destroyed, I rely heavily on reported accounts to describe them: "The Narcissus window centered about a fur-lined bathtub filled with water. Three wax arms on floats bobbed in it, each holding up a medieval mirror. The walls of the chamber were upholstered in purple and from various points other mirrors obtruded. [...] A manikin stood by the bath. She was adorned in green feathers and her hair, bright red, was three feet long" (*New York World Telegram* 1939). Another newspaper described this window more explicitly: "Gazing into the tub and the mirrors was a figure clad in a green negligee of feathers" (*New York Herald Tribune* 1939). The Night window, on the other hand, "showed a manikin lying on a black bed. The mattress consisted of flaming coals. At the headpiece loomed the snout of a grumpy old water-buffalo" (*New York World Telegram* 1939). Both windows played with Surrealist motifs of subjective perception, dreaming, and altered states. Their connection to Bonwit Teller's merchandize was tenuous at best, since they failed to feature any fashions available for purchase inside the store.

A central aspect of the conflict generated by the windows revolved around the type of mannequins Dalí had used, even more so than what they were or were not wearing. Dalí worked on the windows through the night before they were unveiled to the public on the morning of March 16. By mid-afternoon that day, Bonwit Teller had received enough complaints from passers-by about the risqué nature of the windows that the store decided to make some alterations: "At 2 p.m. it was decided to change the display, and a more modernistic type of mannequin was placed in the window. Nor was it clad in the feather negligee, but in a tailored suit" (*New York Herald Tribune* 1939). Several reports focused on the replacement of "the old-style dummy with a modernistic model" (*Daily Mirror* 1939). A key part of Dalí's original display was his purposeful selection of a turn-of-the-century style mannequin, made of wax, which was more realistic (and eerie) than the more stylized mannequins in vogue in the late 1930s. One paper described the original mannequin as "ungainly and Victorian, not the least bit type 1939" (*New York World Telegram* 1939). In another demonstration of the replacement mannequin's Modernism, the *New York Journal American* called it "a streamlined model" (*New York Times* 1939). The outmodedness of Dalí's mannequins may have been a gesture to the Surrealist sense of the uncanny, but it also served as a subversion of the fashion industry's obsession with constant currency.

Dalí's windows were short-lived. In an attempt to salvage his original design (and thus his artistic vision), Dalí ended up breaking the window as he struggled with the bathtub. While most reports focused on the fur-lined bathtub that smashed through the Bonwit Teller window (and Dalí's near-decapitation as he tumbled through the shards of glass after the tub), the larger issue was Dalí's loss of creative control over the project. Two and a half hours after Bonwit's employees altered the display, "Dali went to the store at 4:30 p.m. Aghast at what he saw in the window, he stormed inside, saying things angrily in Spanish and French. [...] Dali declared he had been 'hired to do a work of art' and not to have 'my name associated with typical window dressing'" (*New York Herald Tribune* 1939). Through an interpreter, Dalí conveyed that Bonwit's alterations "had changed the display from an artistic creation to a commercial window display" (Ibid.). Although most accounts thought the damage accidental rather than intentional, he was subsequently arrested on charges of malicious mischief; but the store's representatives reduced the charge to disorderly conduct. Even at night court, the issue of artistic merit was central. Dalí's lawyer explained that "Mr. Dali, a recognized leader in a school of art, could not bear to see his work changed" (Ibid.). Magistrate Louis B. Brodsky, "a discerning appraiser of art and manners, suspended the sentence" but Dalí did not walk away from the incident unscathed (*New York World Telegram* 1939).

The publicity that followed the event further undermined Dalí's artistic reputation, even as it cemented his place in the history of window display. The *New York Times* called Dalí's reaction "a rampage," while the *New York Sun* headline proclaimed that the artist had proceeded "Through the Window to Fame" (McBride 1939). Of course, Dalí was already famous as an artist, but not yet for celebrity-style antics. When Dalí later wrote about the incident, he accused the management at Bonwit Teller of altering his display because it was "too successful; [...] there had been a constant crowd gathered around them which blocked the traffic" (Dalí 1942, 374). Given the natural bias of the author, the veracity of Dalí's statement is unclear. While Dalí continued to receive positive publicity for his influence on window display, his reputation as an artist suffered from what was widely perceived by the art press to have been a publicity stunt, one ironically generated from Dalí's attempt to maintain artistic control.

Again, the Bonwit windows had been timed to coincide with an exhibition of artwork, this time a solo show at the Julien Levy gallery. *Newsweek* noted that in addition to Dalí's $1000 fee for the windows, he received front-page publicity for his upcoming gallery show (*Newsweek* 1939, 27). When the show of Dalí's paintings opened less than a week later at the Julien Levy gallery, the exhibition almost sold out, with lines of interested viewers winding around the corner, waiting to get into the gallery (Bird 1939). And just as the Bonwit scandal garnered more attention for the exhibition at Levy's gallery, the gallery show, in turn, was presented as a tie-in to Dalí's next project, an amusement at the New York World's Fair of the same year called "Dream of Venus." On the façade of the amusement display, plaster arms would stretch out in all directions, never quite reaching the Venus of their dreams. That project, which cemented Dalí's position as a commercial artist, drew on the same themes as his Bonwit window – playing with mirrors and reflections, sleeping and dreaming, and especially the water motif of his Day window.

While Dalí found his reputation as an artist threatened by his involvement with commercial display, his windows for Bonwit Teller can be credited with assuring the success of Surrealist techniques in window display, a practice that continued energetically through the 1940s and which is still seen today. For example, the following year, the Marshall Field's department store opted to bypass the artist in favor of the technique: "For fresh display inspiration, to dramatize the new series of decorator colors, Marshall Field & Co. went to the Surrealistic school, and here are the striking results! Objects arranged in the Dali manner cleverly build up various schemes" (*Retailing* 1940). In his account of the development of the American store window, Leonard Marcus cites Dalí's 1939 venture with Bonwit Teller as a pivotal turning point because the installation made explicit the function of store windows to arouse a new kind of desire (fed by envy and vanity) that could ostensibly be satisfied by the possession of material objects (Marcus 1978, 32–33). While this was not new to Dalí, nor to store display, the fact remains that Dalí's windows were innovative. Their real innovation, however, may have been their ardent disassociation from the material objects for sale. Indeed, several accounts of display techniques cite Dalí specifically or Surrealism more generally for influencing the course of American window design. Gene Moore said of the 1939 windows: "It was quite a mess, but those windows put Dali on the map" (Moore and Hyams 1990, 18). More recently, Tony Morgan, head of visual merchandizing at the Fashion Academy in London, wrote in his 2008 book on contemporary display: "In the 1930s, the surrealist artist Salvador Dalí can be credited with setting the American creative criteria in window display" (Morgan 2008, 14). While not a historian, Morgan's generalization speaks to the impact Dalí still has on professional designers.

As Surrealism infiltrated commercial design, display professionals continued strengthening their associations with art. Designer Tom Lee regularly drew inspiration from New York galleries, particularly the Julien Levy Gallery (probably because it specialized in Surrealist art). Indeed, Lee's 1938 "Trompe l'Oeil" window design included a placard informing viewers of the ongoing show at Levy's gallery. Further, Lee was also Bonwit Teller's display director in 1939 when Dalí made his second, notorious foray into window design. In 1950, a book claiming to be one of the first on the history of American window display featured Gene Moore, Bonwit Teller's display director at the time, citing Dalí's window designs as an example of the artistic development of contemporary window display. Calling display "three-dimensional painting," Moore concluded that much was owed to modern painters (Moore 1950, 7). The main focus of the book was to advocate for window display as an art form and the window displayman as a blend of artist and showman. And yet in 1950, Moore conceded that the "field" of window display – that is, treating display as a profession – was "so young that even this book covers only a period of about ten years" (Moore 1950, 5). For those who strove to elevate window display as an aesthetic endeavor, Surrealism proved to be integral.

Completing the circle: Window display at the museum

Just as department stores had previously provided tie-ins for museum exhibitions, museums also saw opportunity in promoting department store wares. In 1934, MoMA had shown industrial objects in its galleries in the exhibition "Machine Art," while exhibition series like "Useful Household Objects under $5" (1938) had encouraged museum-goers to be discerning shoppers by displaying retail objects that emphasized "good" design. Later, this initiative would be formalized through the annual "Good Design" shows of 1950–1955, in which household products were displayed at MoMA in the winter and made available for purchase at the Merchandise Mart later the following year (Riley and Eigen 1994). All of MoMA's design shows foregrounded stylistic qualities to direct consumers toward objects of formal clarity and function. And just as MoMA showed functional, "well-designed" consumer items, the department stores occasionally showed fine art. But if Dalí was not unique in uniting modern art with commodity culture, his pliable brand of mesmerizing confusion ran counter to more pedagogically-minded displays of commodities both within the museum and on the streets outside.

In making the case for the importance of window display in American culture, Gene Moore cited MoMA's anniversary exhibition to demonstrate that "Even so august an institution as the Museum of Modern Art saw fit to devote considerable space to window display in a recent exhibition" (Moore 1950, 5). That exhibition was MoMA's twentieth anniversary show, "Modern Art in Your Life" (1949) (Fig. 4.5). By that time, Surrealism had become an accepted part of commercial culture, even as its status as a contemporary avant-garde movement was supplanted by the burgeoning New York School. For its twentieth anniversary, MoMA's curators wanted to make the case that "modern art is an intrinsic part of modern living," and so they showcased pots and pans, a lazy Susan and tubes of toothpaste. Embodying MoMA's original mission in many respects, "Modern Art in Your Life" aimed to encourage the accessibility of modern art through its influences on daily life, exhibiting painting and sculpture in conjunction (though not side by side) with commercial culture.

Window display featured prominently in the Surrealism section of the exhibition, where Surrealism's influence over the psychology of commodity culture was foregrounded. Through a curtain flanked by figurative paintings by Dalí and Yves Tanguy, the viewer entered a room painted entirely in black. Inside, René d'Harnoncourt had installed six full-scale recreations of Fifth Avenue department store windows

Figure 4.5 "Modern Art in Your Life" installation photograph, Museum of Modern Art, 1949.
Source: Museum of Modern Art

theatrically lit by spotlights. The plate-glass windows featured mannequins draped in bizarre configurations of merchandize – ties, hats, furs, and feathers – in stark contrast to the functional applications of abstract art to furniture design and architecture. Choosing not to recreate Dalí's designs but those originally done by professional window dressers, MoMA maintained a tenuous division between art and commerce, even though the six recreated windows from Bonwit, Lord & Taylor, and Saks Fifth Avenue had nonetheless been influenced by Dalí's commercial work.

While the art community felt that Dalí had compromised his reputation through his commercial work, MoMA's catalog made the case that Surrealism "contradicts usual habits of seeing and accepted ways of 'good' design. It is in this sense that surrealism is 'inartistic' and gradually becomes 'artistic' " (Goldwater 1949, 34). For MoMA, Surrealism illustrated the way "good" design could be usefully – even artistically – subverted. Surrealism brought an uncomfortable but seamless interaction between modern art and mass culture, in part because it lent a powerful strategy to commodity culture's perpetuation.

"Modern Art in Your Life" acknowledged and displayed the close, yet complicated, relationship between the visual imagery of avant-garde and commercial culture. Surrealism opened up new possibilities for window display, and window display (along with advertising in general) expanded the audience for Surrealism. As a visual strategy, Surrealism was perhaps even more effective in the window of a department store than it was in the museum. Art historically, it proved difficult to categorize: as a style, it was both abstract and figurative, automatic and academic, visual and literary; as culture, it shifted between high and low, transcendent and absurd, avant-garde and kitsch. But it was this very versatility that made Surrealism effective as a marketing tool. The cultural capital of modern art was transferable and dynamic; the department store and the museum were hardly at cross-purposes and were perhaps even codependent.

Note

1 The correct spelling of "Dalí" has been used throughout the text; however, to remain truthful to the original sources, "Dali" has been used when other authors have referred to the artist as such.

References

"A Dali Dream Come True." 1939. *Newsweek*, March 27: 27.
"Art: Art for Window-Shoppers." 1940. *Time*, August 5.
"Art Changed, Dali Goes on Rampage in Store, Crashes Through Window Into Arms of Law." 1939. *New York Times*, March 17: 1.
"Bathtub Bests Surrealist Dali in 5th Ave. Showwindow Bout." 1939. *Daily Mirror*, March 17.
Bird, Paul. 1939. "The Fortnight in New York." *Art Digest*.
Bonwit Teller Advertisement. 1936. *New York Herald Tribune*, December 27.
Burke, Gene and Edgar Kober. 1946. *Modern Store Design*. Los Angeles: Institute of Product Research.
Dalí, Salvador. 1942. *The Secret Life of Salvador Dalí*. Translated by Haakon M. Chevalier. New York: Dial Press.
"Dali, Surrealist, Has a Nightmare While Wide Awake." 1939. *New York World Telegram*, March 17.

"Dali Comes Out Store Window With a Bathtub." 1939. *New York Herald Tribune*, March 17.

"Dali's Headache." 1939. *New York Journal American*, March 17.

"Dealing with Dali." 1936. *Women's Wear Daily*, December 15.

"Displays at Field's Go Surrealistic." 1940. *Retailing*, April 29.

Eigen, Edward and Terence Riley. 1994. "Between the Museum and the Marketplace, Selling Good Design." In *The Museum of Modern Art at Mid-Century: At Home and Abroad*. New York: Museum of Modern Art, distributed by H. N. Abrams.

"Fifth Avenue Crowd Stops to View Dalí Window." 1936. *New York World Telegram*, December 26.

Goldwater, Robert. 1949. *Modern Art in Your Life*. New York: Museum of Modern Art.

Hughes, Alice. 1936. "Dali Does a Surrealist Shop Window." *New York American*, December 20.

Kiesler, Frederick. 1930. *Contemporary Art Applied to the Store and Its Display*. New York: Brentano's.

Lancaster, Bill. 1995. *The Department Store: A Social History*. New York: Leicester University Press.

Leydenfrost, Robert J. 1950. *Window Display*. Cornwall, NY: Architectural Book Publishing Co, published by Cornwall Press.

Leach, William. 1989. "Strategists of Display and the Production of Desire." *Consuming Visions: Accumulation and Display of Goods in America 1880–1920*, edited by Simon J. Bronner. New York: Norton.

Lynes, Russell. 1973. *Good Old Modern: An Intimate Portrait of the Museum of Modern Art*. New York: Atheneum.

McBride, Henry. 1939. "Through the Window to Fame." *New York Sun*, March 25.

Moore, Gene. 1950. "Foreword." In *Window Display*. Cornwall, NY: Architectural Book Publishing Co, published by Cornwall Press.

Moore, Gene and Jay Hyams. 1990. *My Time at Tiffany's*. New York: St. Martin's Press.

Morgan, Tony. 2008. *Visual Merchandising: Window and In-Store Displays for Retail*. London: Lawrence King Publishing.

"Newest Art Sensation Inspires Bonwit's To Do 'Surrealist' Windows." 1936. *New York City Retailing*, December 25.

"'She was a Surrealist Woman – Like a Figure in a Dream,' The New Art in Show Window Display." 1937. *The Daily Telegraph*, January 9.

Smith, Roberta. 2009. "The Ordinary as Object of Desire: Review of *What Was Good Design?: MoMA's Message 1944–56*." *New York Times*, June 4.

"Surrealism Inspires Newest Window Displays at Bonwit Teller." 1936. *Women's Wear*, December 21.

"Surrealist Colors Offer Fresh Ideas for Negilgee [sic] Promotions." 1936. *Women's Wear Daily*, December 31.

Whitaker, Jan. 2006. *Service and Style: How the American Department Store Fashioned the Middle Class*. New York: St. Martin's Press.

5 William Pahlmann and the department store model room, 1937–1942

Beverly K. Grindstaff

In 1987, the *New York Times* marked the passing of William Pahlmann (born 1900) with a generous admiration of the interior decorator's distinctive style and many innovations. What came to be called Pahlmann's "eclectic look" (he preferred "modern Baroque") was an individualistic approach that embraced sectional units, oversized lamps, splashy drapery prints, fur and leather floor coverings, and yards of taffeta used as window treatments. It freely blended styles and periods such that a living room might include Louis XVI armchairs, a long, low contemporary sofa, and a seventeenth-century bronze Tibetan Buddha (Krebs 1987). He introduced groundbreaking color palettes (one brief calls for a "shocking" amount of color) and blond Swedish Modern styles to an American public long-committed to dark wood reproduction furniture (Loring 2000, 212–215). Accounts of Pahlmann's long career describe his work as extravagant, luxurious, chic, outrageous, cluttered, and theatrical (O'Brien 1964; Smith 1987; Krebs 1987; Loring 1999); indeed, one may argue that his success hinged on a liberal exercise of exacting training and good taste that kept the entire endeavor refreshingly and unexpectedly elegant.

Pahlmann is also acknowledged as innovator of the American department store model room as a semi-permanent display of residential furnishings and home decorating advice. His scrapbooks document ten themed and fully realized series of model rooms he designed from 1937 through 1942 while head of the department of interior design at Lord & Taylor, the Manhattan Fifth Avenue department store (WPP, Series 9, Box OS 1–2). These Depression-era displays presented credible multi-room homes, typically organized with one wall opening into a central aisle, such as the three-room "penthouse" and the three-room "apartment" of the summer 1941 "Wedding of American Art and American Décor" display ("American Art," 54–55). Themes ranged from the "International Show" (fall 1937) to "Pahlmann's Proverbs" (summer 1942). The most celebrated, the "Peruvian Show" (winter 1941), drew up to 30,000 people a month, so many that police were frequently called to help maintain order (Smith 1987, 158). Each was informed by the decorator's unorthodox combination of antique and modern furniture, mirrored surfaces, rich textiles, bold and highly saturated color, and *objets* precious and novel to create an effect at once luxurious and unexpected. In a typed essay dated June 29, 1948 and intended for the Parsons School of Design Alumni Bulletin, Pahlmann wrote of his years at Lord & Taylor, "where it was possible to splash around color, architecture, and design at will. I knew only too well I was an extremely lucky person to have the backing of that organization and practically a *carte blanche* attitude from the powers that be" (WPP,

Figure 5.1 "International Show" (October 1937), Pahlmann's first suite of model rooms
      for Lord & Taylor, New York.
Source: William Pahlmann Papers, Hagley Museum and Library

Series 1, Box 60). Introduced in the fall of 1937, Pahlmann's approach to the model
room received immediate media coverage and was just as quickly appropriated by
competing Manhattan department stores.

The first of Pahlmann's increasingly complex themed display rooms was the
"International Show," which opened in October 1937 (Figs. 5.1 and 5.2). It debuted
what would become the much-copied Lord & Taylor format: a series of architecturally realized and interconnected rooms with painted and papered walls, typically with
a single wall open in the manner of a stage set; plastered ceilings; windows (occasionally backlit for enhanced realism); electric lighting; and floor treatments, all installed
in a space that originally housed salesrooms for musical instruments. Its October 7
media launch was overseen by Dorothy Shaver, Lord & Taylor's visionary first vice
president and fashion director. Newspapers announced the following day:

> A preview of a series of rooms featuring a collection of antique furniture and
> art accessories, creating a new trend in decoration, was given yesterday after-
> noon on the seventh floor of Lord & Taylor's store…. The exhibit was designed
> and executed by William Pahlmann, head of the interior decorating staff of the
> store, who recently returned from Europe. The seven rooms have an international

Figure 5.2 "International Show" (October 1937).
Source: William Pahlmann Papers, Hagley Museum and Library

flavor, with antiques from Norway, Sweden and Denmark, as well as France and England. They are shown under modern treatment of fabric and color.

("Art Furnishings Shown" 1937)

The seven "rooms" combined Louis XVI furniture with European and Scandinavian antique furnishings in Art Deco-inspired settings. Gone was American retail's prior focus on a single period style. Also absent was the prevailing presentation of chairs, sofas, beds and case goods in homogenous rows, a format that reflected the typically specialized output of individual furniture manufacturers (Alex Mitchell, interview by author). At pre-1937 Lord & Taylor, display took the form of "rows and rows of sofas and chairs […] and then you had dining room tables. There was no room set up with dining-room chairs like people would live with," according to Jack Connor, Pahlmann's long-time business associate (WPP, Interview, 1989, Collection Case File 2188). In their stead were designed ensembles demonstrating the livable potential of furnishings available in the store. Acknowledging but fundamentally differing from precedents, including street-level window displays and short-term expositions, Pahlmann's spaces presented customers not so much with goods for purchase as with decorating suggestions born of his own formal education and professional practice in interior decorating.

It is clear Pahlmann referred to European equivalents in staging the "International Show;" indeed, their use heightened the desired cosmopolitanism of his display. But, as design historian Judith Gura explains, "The displays in Europe (like those Peter Behrens did for Tietz Department Store) were essentially just arrangements of matched suites of furniture. Pahlmann used the Lord & Taylor rooms not merely to merchandize the furniture, but to suggest ideas and introduce new design concepts to the store's customers." Referring to Pahlmann's innovation, she adds:

> [They] were not merely furniture displays; they were actual design projects, each planned around a specific theme. In my prior research I did not find anything like them done in America before his work at Lord & Taylor – only museums and trade fairs had done anything remotely similar, and his were part of an ongoing program, changed throughout the year.[1]
>
> (Gura)

Consumer excitement generated by the "International Show" quickly led to widespread emulation of its format and the immersive, experiential encounters with store services and merchandize it offered potential consumers. Within the month, model rooms appeared on the furniture sales floors of competing Manhattan department stores. Periodicals from November 1937 demonstrate the rapidity with which Pahlmann's concept was appropriated. For example, advertisements in *House & Garden* announced the new W. & J. Sloane Smaller Homes Shop, with 11 rooms, "each the size of a room in an average house," executed in harmonious colors and carefully selected pieces as proof of Sloane's quality and distinction (34); meanwhile, B. Altman & Company reinstalled and elaborated on its earlier, short-lived Progress House exhibit as a season-long demonstration of a "delightful home" for present-day living (8e). Editors of *House Beautiful* summarized the new display mode in a December 1937 issue ("Contemporary Versions"). "There is no revolution," they noted, "but there is progress." They continued:

> In the past you bought your table, had it sent home and took your chances that it would look well in an actual room. Now you may see it in relationship to other furniture in a proper background [...] You want traditional furniture, adapted to the modern demands of comfort and set in rooms which are bound together by imaginative, subtle color schemes (of which more next month), by sound architectural details, and by fabrics which are, first of all, pleasant to live with. As such [these rooms] are a valuable document, a portrait of the contemporary background. They are warm and human, not abstract or pretentious, and the ideas embodied in them are eminently practical.
>
> ("Contemporary Versions," 44)

Importantly, the practicality assigned to the model room was resonant with the "related arts" emphases introduced in 1920s and 1930s home economics courses in American high schools and college. Girls and young women in these vocational courses studied the applied arts as related to their future consumer choices. According to design historian Carma Gorman, these courses taught women to perform formal analysis and exercise good taste, to develop a "'scientific,' assessing gaze and attitude," and apply design principles to problems of the domestic household. They constituted, in Gorman's analysis, a government-sanctioned consumer education (2000, 47). This growing national cohort of women was prepared to appreciate the model room as both the realization of instructional training and, in a certain sense, the continuation of photo-illustrations in leading related arts textbooks. Harriet and Vetta Goldstein's *Art in Every Day Life* (1925), for example, used 285 illustrations, many of them photographs demonstrating how to dress a table or mantel, select appropriate draperies, hang mirrors and artwork, or create optimal furniture arrangements within a given room.[2] Most importantly, what Gorman identifies as consumer education allowed women to recognize the model room as an extension and demonstration of their own formal training. Within eighteen months of the "International Show," Pahlmann-style model rooms appeared in department stores in every sizeable city in the United States ("Furniture for Modern Living" 1939, 42).

"Good taste now dominates the mass market"

Pahlmann had arrived at Lord & Taylor in 1936 as a trained interior decorator with his own shop and prominent clientele. He had been prompted by the harsh economic climate of the 1930s to join other similarly qualified men in seeking employment with magazines, manufacturers, and department stores. This infusion of "creative energy into the mass fields had amazing results," noted a 1939 editorial in *Life* ("Furniture for Modern Living," 42). Pahlmann had come to decorating through a 48-part *Arts & Decoration* correspondence course he undertook in his twenties while still in San Antonio, Texas. In 1927, he entered the interior decorating program at the New York School of Fine and Applied Art (renamed Parsons School of Design in 1940) and supported two years of study by performing in Broadway musical choruses and, later, working as an assistant stage manager (Gura 2008, 66). His close familiarity with strategic theatrical effects informed much of his commercial work. Students in professional interior design programs such as that offered by the New York School of Fine and Applied Art spent a year mastering the basics of form, color and composition of architecture and furniture design, and two years measuring, sketching, and creating detailed renderings and technical drawings of museum period rooms and their furnishings (Merwood-Salisbury 2011, 116). Pahlmann excelled in the program, and in 1929 was awarded a scholarship that allowed two final years of study at the school's Paris branch. The Paris program was notable for instruction based on examples of fine decorating found in the houses of wealthy aristocrats. Students focused on translating traditional French styles for upper-middle-class American consumers, in the process frequently integrating modern elements into period styles in what came to be known as the "Parsons look" (Merwood-Salisbury 2011, 116). In addition, Pahlmann was hosted in Paris by Josephine and William Seton Henry, a prominent, old-moneyed American couple who introduced the tall, charming and photogenic Pahlmann to the American expatriate community and East Coast socialites who would become his first important clients. In 1931, Pahlmann returned to New York and opened his own practice. His first commission was for his former hosts' eighteenth-century Pennsylvania estate, Pen Ryn; other clients included Mrs William Paley, wife of the founder of CBS (Smith 1987, 157–158). Obliged by the circumstances of the

Depression, Pahlmann had a short stint with the B. Altman department store before being hired by Lord & Taylor in 1936 to provide decorating services for private clients and oversee in-store merchandize displays.

Pahlmann's talents quickly came to define the Lord & Taylor interior decorating services. His arrival at the department store came shortly after a lavishly photo-illustrated account of his extensive work at the Seton Henrys' colonial-era Pennsylvania estate appeared in the February 1936 issue of *Country Life*. It was Pahlmann's first media coverage and the article makes clear the depth of his training and illuminates the creation of his later model rooms. Pen Ryn was established in 1744 by a distinguished Philadelphia family, and subsequently underwent four major architectural additions that Pahlmann removed, replaced, or integrated into a symmetrical plan anchored by the original home. His project extended into the 125-acre grounds, which he organized with bricked terraces, esplanades that connected house to river, and hedge-lined driveways. A large swimming pool was installed "with bath houses in Mayan design, curiously harmonious with the dignity of the Colonial house" (Yarnall 1936, 21). Pahlmann's interiors integrated the Henrys' Aubusson rugs and Flemish tapestries, collections of Sèvres and Dresden china, Neoclassical paintings, and heirloom furniture in styles including Duncan Phyfe, Louis XVI, Directoire, Empire and English Regency into rooms with sunburst mirrors, lamps with rock crystal-block bases, and heavy, unlined taffeta drapery (Fig. 5.3). "With an unfailing eye for unity of style and general feeling, Mr. Pahlmann has made it impossible to tell where one era began and another ended," the article noted of interior and exterior alike (Yarnall

Figure 5.3 Pahlmann's design and decoration for the 1796 salon at Pen Ryn.
Source: The William Carroll Pahlmann Archive, Texas A&M

1936, 21). In a summary that would come to describe Pahlmann's department-store work, *Country Life* added:

> The mere listing of the different types and nationalities of furniture and accessories makes it evident that to create the impression of harmony which is the paramount feeling of the room, there must have been a presiding genius of extraordinary taste. It was, of course, Mr. Pahlmann [...] who made just this contribution to the house because it was formerly a conglomeration of everyone's ideas and fancies.
>
> (Yarnall 1936, 23)

One of Pahlmann's most significant decorating commissions at Lord & Taylor came soon after his hiring. Mrs Pauline Rogers sought decoration for a library in the Port of Missing Men, the lavish 1,400-acre Southampton estate built by the son of Standard Oil magnate, Henry Huddleston Rogers. Previously Eleanor Brown, the Parsons-trained decorator, known for her translations of traditional interiors for an affluent American clientele, had echoed the estate's Colonial Revival architecture with Early American furniture accented with Renaissance frescoes, exotic wrought-iron work, and rare eighteenth-century tiles (Gura 2008, 61). The effect was at once formal and imbued with an air of comfort, and *Architectural Record* deemed it "splendidly dramatic" (Petrow 2004, 93). Much as Pahlmann would do the following year in the "International Show," his library brought a style well suited for a client accustomed to exacting fine period interiors and capable of appreciating the wit and challenge of his pronouncedly anachronistic combinations. Queen Anne, Louis XIV and modern armchairs were arranged amid glass-topped rectangular tables sporting skirts with embellished hems, a daring *en suite* anchored by a room-sized white shag rug. A coffee table fashioned from a massive disk of polished granite set atop a thick columnar pedestal served as counterpoint to a pair of fine Georgian desks flanking the main entrance. Pahlmann described the completed library as "designed in the grand manner," and his annotations on photographs documenting the project recorded:

> Fine walnut upholstery paneling is a distinguishing feature. Room is mellowed by the warmth and beauty of old leather books. Sofa is upholstered in satin stripe. Table behind it has a mirror top, felt skirt with kick-pleats to the floor. The room has several conversation groupings and a small French desk for writing letters [...] Accessories here are all fine and the atmosphere is one of great elegance.
>
> (WPP, Series 9, Box 1, Book 2)

Where the *Country Life* article announced Pahlmann's arrival as a decorator, the Rogers commission validated the continuation of his services through the Lord & Taylor decorating department. Both piqued interest in his merchandize display work. An intermediary phase of the coming model room was Pahlmann's November 1936 installation of 20 different window treatments in variations on the Baroque, English Regency, Georgian and other period styles. The *New York Times* covered the showroom display, identifying Pahlmann by name and stating that his work demonstrated "how new ideas and textiles can be adapted to period styles" or made to create original "sophisticated modern effects in which buttons and leather belts become decorative motifs" (Storey 1936, 14). An accompanying photograph showed a typical treatment built around a tall "window" inserted into a free-standing, 8×8 foot wall, framed with dark taffeta drapes and flanked by sconces. A dressing table centered directly in front sported a valance and cornice of the same heavy fabric, and a large mirror on its mirrored top, propped against the window, enhanced the reflective surfaces. Only the exposed edges of the wall drew attention to the artifice of the setting. An important precursor of Pahlmann's model rooms, the installation as a whole demonstrated both refreshingly updated period styles and immediately accessible decorating options.

Why Lord & Taylor? Important precedents

Multiple factors made Lord & Taylor a logical site for Pahlmann's innovative model rooms. First was the visual in-store merchandizing strategies Lord & Taylor had long employed to garner attention and boost sales. As explained in corporate promotional materials, "the public's first definite consciousness of what it wanted was inspired by the sight of a satisfying article. Demand and supply were simultaneous" (Lord & Taylor c. 1925, 57). By the 1910s, window display managers throughout America were showing goods in comprehensive settings that suggested their use (Benson 1986, 102). So important was display to Lord & Taylor that the elegant Starrett & van Vleck Italian Renaissance-style building it had occupied since 1914 was planned with special attention to show windows. A "cleverly contrived mechanical device" allowed street-level displays to be lowered to the basement and, in a matter of minutes, replaced with new displays. Another full set of show windows appeared on the second floor, and "a dressed window [was] raised to fill the space of the main entrance" when the store closed (*Architectural Criticism* 1914, 77). Accounts from 1938 demonstrate the efficacy of window displays. For example, an elaborate promotion for National Spring Millinery Week so effectively spurred consumer desire that it generated the headline, "Display Lifts Hat Sales; Nine Windows Bring 39% Gain for Lord & Taylor." This was despite an overall decrease of East Coast retail sales of 8 to 20 percent in the same period (*New York Times* 1938, 23). In the unseasonably warm November of 1938, Dorothy Shaver countered 70-degree temperatures with an especially inventive blizzard staged with blowers, acid-treated cornflakes, and recordings of howling winds. The kinetic promotion spurred winter clothing sales even though the sole items in the windows were signs reading: "It's coming!" and "Sooner or later!" ("Snowstorm in Store" 1938, F 9).

Dorothy Shaver, whose lifelong career at Lord & Taylor began in the early 1920s, was herself an important figure in American retailing. An avid promoter of American fashion and design, in 1937 Shaver was elected first vice president under new president Walter Hoving. In 1945, she became the first woman president of a major American retail establishment, serving as president of Lord & Taylor until her death in 1959 (Taves 1943, 141–151). In 1928, Shaver presented an important predecessor of the department store's model room. "The French Decorative: An Exposition of Modern French Decorative Art" ran at Lord & Taylor from February 29 through March 17 and served to introduce its customers to the International Exposition of Modern Decorative and Industrial Arts, held in Paris in 1925. The original exhibition, best known for introducing the Art Deco style to a mass audience in the United States, was part of the larger French promotion of trade through international fairs, and furniture. Home furnishings in particular benefited from three annual large-scale exhibitions that each ran for up to three months to provide "an extensive survey of the application of new ideas, not only to objects seeking primarily artistic quality, but also to those serving the ordinary purposes of everyday life and work" ("The Promotion of French Trade" 1925, 818).

The "French Decorative" was part of a larger collaboration between the Metropolitan Museum of Art and leading New York department stores that generated a series of short-term but high-profile exhibitions between 1925 and 1932. As early as 1913 the Metropolitan Museum had collaborated with Macy's to promote period furniture, and held "twice-weekly classes on the history of furnishings and decorative arts for buyers, designers, and sales people from Macy's, Lord & Taylor, James McCreery and Company, Bonwit Teller, and Best & Company" (Davidson and Friedman 2007, 171). Among those in attendance was Walter Hoving, who, while vice president at Macy's (1932–1936), had refined his taste through four years of night classes in painting, textile design, antique silver, and furniture. Hoving would later serve as president of Lord & Taylor from 1936 to 1946 (Hoogenboom 2000). Coursework was not for executives alone. Starting in 1914, Lord & Taylor sales employee training included New York University coursework "in retail merchandising, interior decorating, and color and design at the store's expense" (*History of Lord and Taylor* c. 1925, 55–56). Much of this instruction took place in the classrooms, conference rooms, and library on the store's eleventh floor, a space wholly "devoted to the development of our organization and of the individual of which it is composed" (*History of Lord and Taylor* c. 1925, 60).

The most recent of such collaborations with the Metropolitan Museum had been the R.H. Macy and Company "Exposition of Art in Trade," held May 2–7, 1927, and the first to feature European and American decorative arts (Miller 1990, 9). Opening comments by museum president Robert de Forest noted the increasing presence of industrial and applied art in principal American art museums, and drew attention to "the last great Paris art exhibition" of industrial art and its partial staging in Parisian department stores ("Accessions and Notes" 1927, 180). De Forest concluded: "Our great department stores [...] exert an even wider influence than our own art museums. They not only show, but they circulate – they give the opportunity not only of seeing but of buying, taking away, and bringing into the home" (180). The "French Decorative" marked the next Lord & Taylor collaboration with the Metropolitan Museum. Installed in the department store, this exhibit presented artwork by Picasso, Braque, Laurencin, Dufy and Derain; furniture, rugs, fabrics, silver and glassware; and contemporary residential furnishings by Ruhlmann, Jourdain, Sue et Mare, and other leading French designers. Notably, the collaborative exhibit also featured "five fully realized American rooms that continued Shaver's dedication to American designers and high-quality Modernist design." Extended twice to become a 32-day exhibit, the "French Decorative" was attended by over 300,000 visitors. So strong was the lure of the furnishings in its exhibit rooms that virtually all pieces sold in multiple copies (Davidson and Friedman 2007, 172).

A glowing summary of the temporary exhibit and its value as a retail device was given by Lewis Mumford in the March 1928 *New Republic*. "The exhibition of modern French decorative art at Lord and Taylor's has breadth, sweep, élan," wrote Mumford, adding,

> The space has been generously disposed: the furniture and textiles are arranged in rooms and alcoves: and the large room that contains the glass, silverware, stoneware, sculpture, *is in itself a contribution to what a modern room in a museum*

might be. It is a very good show indeed, for it gives a sense of the unity and interdependence of all the arts: but one can scarcely see the spectacle because of the spectators. They have come in thousands to this exhibit. They come: they look: they handle: they purr: they admire: they are shocked: they are delighted. *One notes the women putting themselves in the midst of these rooms and wondering if they could live in them ....* The ladies pause!

(Mumford 1928, 154) [*emphasis* added]

The review followed de Forest's words in expressing the department store as a new form of museum, and consumer desire as a near-palpable wave of delight in response to carefully designed spaces suggesting not so much décor as the possibilities of a future life. Lord & Taylor plans for a follow-up American exhibition were critically disrupted by the stock market crash of 1929 and, with the exception of short-term exhibits, were not revisited until the Depression began to lift in 1937, allowing the "International Show" to take place.

Mumford's comparison to the modern museum period room is apt. The Lord & Taylor exhibit, like Pahlmann's later model rooms, drew on the format, which enjoyed a "remarkable growth in interest" in 1920s and 1930s America (Storey 1930, 16). The appropriation was ingenious: the original carried significant cultural signifiers of value, and invoking it within the department store helped transform mass-produced goods into industrial art. Historically arranged museum gallery spaces showcased artworks in approximations of their original settings, and offered a means of educating the public and inculcating taste in manufactured goods. In the 1927 assessment of Dr. Charles R. Richards, then director of the American Associations of Museums, the period room is ideally suited to retail collaborations fostered by the Metropolitan Museum. "If our public is to enjoy and gain in appreciation and if our designers are to be inspired by the achievements of the past, it will be first of all through the careful assemble and display of objects representing a common quality of design brought into artistic relationship," he noted, adding that for laymen, the random display of "great numbers of similar objects, even of beautiful objects, [...] is of questionable worth" ("An Endorsement," 5). Richards' observation that objects and images gain value, coherency and meaning through contextualization was resonant with related arts curricula, and helped explain the reception and operations of model rooms.

Pahlmann's post-1937 rooms

In July 1939, department store model rooms in Manhattan were still new enough to merit regular coverage in the popular press: they were acknowledged as sources of entertainment for "visiting firemen and home-town boys and girls alike" (*House & Garden* July 1939, 38). Macy's "Forward House" and W. & J. Sloane's eight-room "House of Years" were among those singled out as "high spots" of a summer best known for the World's Fair, then taking place in nearby Flushing Meadows. Competition between department stores demanded high-stakes inventiveness. Pahlmann responded with "Excitement into Summer Decor" (opened May 1939), six fully realized model rooms heralded for décor spanning "the sentimental to dashing sophistication." Two additional shadowboxes, or full-scale partial rooms intended strictly as visual displays, proposed a contemporary drawing room and cocktail corner (Fig. 5.4). The themed display both engaged and countered the efficient practicality of the World's

Figure 5.4 "The home of tomorrow moves in new directions," Pahlmann's cocktail corner shadowbox from "Excitement into Summer Décor" (Summer 1939) for Lord & Taylor, New York, Photograph by Hans Van Nes.
Source: William Pahlmann Papers, Hagley Museum and Library

Fair exhibition, "Town of Tomorrow." Colored plate glass defined walls and revealed illusionary gardens set inside window openings; some rooms had furniture that rotated or sank into the floor at the touch of a button (See "Rooms of Tomorrow" 1939, L 32).

Even here, however, Pahlmann delivered more than promotional novelty. His model rooms satisfied as demonstrations of individualism, even when pushed to conspicuous, often daring extremes. Professional photographs in the decorator's scrapbooks, many from magazine shoots, preserve displays of dining sets, upholstered pieces and case goods set in mocked-up dining-, living- and bedrooms defined by parquet floors, slat blinds and recessed lighting. Pahlmann continually and successfully raised the stakes of visual appeal in retail display. The unique accents he used included an eighteenth-century porcelain stove; matched pairs of grand pianos; leather rugs; an expansive mural depicting the Villa Hadrian in "Fantasy, Dramatic Rooms" (opened October 1938); seventeenth-century Venetian "Blackamoor" figures and a massive chandelier containing a birdcage that housed a stuffed peacock in "Pahlmann Predicts" (September 1940) (Fig. 5.5); John Stuart Curry paintings in "American Art and Décor" (April 1941);

Figure 5.5 "Pahlmann Predicts" (September 1940) model room for Lord & Taylor, New York, Photograph by Hans Van Nes.
Source: William Pahlmann Papers, Hagley Museum and Library

and a collection of pre-Columbian Moche vessels and South American folk art, which he acquired on a Lord & Taylor-sponsored buying expedition to Peru, in "Peruvian Show" (November 1941). Whether engaged as a tactile, physical surround, or merely visually through widely circulated media photographs, Pahlmann's work provided more than comprehensive ensembles for each new season. It gave vivid form to the individualization promoted by figures ranging from Elsie de Wolfe, whose *House in Good Taste* urged women to "feel free to use modern prints and Chinese porcelains and willow chairs and anything that fits into your home," (1913, 268) to Dorothy Draper, who promoted a design sensibility best summarized as "a zest for life" in works such as *Decorating is Fun!* (1939). Even Emily Post's doctrinaire *The Personality of a House* (1930) spoke to the necessity of charm and variety in one's interiors. "The house that does not express the individuality of its owner," wrote Post, "is like a dress shown on a wax figure" (3). If one substitutes the dress in this analogy with a chair displayed simply on a showroom floor, one can easily see the immediate appeal of the alternative introduced by William Pahlmann – namely the model room as a fully realized environment within the department store home furnishings display.

Pahlmann's work at Lord & Taylor ended in 1942 when he entered the United States Army Air Corps (later renamed the United States Army Air Forces) as a volunteer. In

1946, he returned to Manhattan to form William Pahlmann Associates. His highly successful postwar interior design firm offered residential and commercial services, and its clientele included Bonwit Teller and Tiffany & Company (both under the direction of Walter Hoving), the Hotel Pierre and New York Hilton, and restaurants ranging from the Forum of the Twelve Caesars to the Four Seasons in the Seagram Building. His syndicated column, "A Matter of Taste," ran in national newspapers from 1962 to 1973. While he did not resume his inventive work in model rooms, the significance of his approach to interior design became a matter of fact. "Except for Miss de Wolfe, no one has influenced American home decoration more than Mr. Pahlmann," noted the *New York Times* when Pahlmann won the 1964 Elsie de Wolfe Award from the New York Chapter of the American Institute of Interior Designers (O'Brien 1964, 58). Moreover, the Pahlmann-style model room assumed an authority on par with self-help books and columns on interior decorating. John Gerald, head of B. Altman's decorating department from 1935 to 1945, and later vice president of W. J. Sloane, recalled in a 1958 interview that, until the end of World War II, model rooms functioned as designer "tips" and set trends, supplanting privately contracted decorators (Reif 1958, L 20). This applied even to the fanciful displays favored at Lord & Taylor. "Because department stores set popular standards in interior decoration," declared the *Architectural Forum*, "and because Pahlmann quickly developed a style which managed to be both spectacular and inoffensive, he has probably cut as wide a swathe across the American home as any other designer you could name" ("Stores with Personality" 1947, 15). Pahlmann's mastery of the "Parsons look" coupled with his bold engagement with the model room format constituted, as *House Beautiful* had stated in late 1937, not a revolution but rather a deeply satisfying progress in how home furnishings were presented to consumers.

Notes

1 Personal communication. Judith Gura has several publications on Pahlmann and his private commissions. She has generously allowed use of her unpublished research on Pahlmann's Lord & Taylor model rooms in this chapter.
2 The Goldstein sisters were themselves graduates of the New York School of Fine and Applied Art, and had studied under the direction of Frank Alvah Parsons (Gorman 2000, 48).

References

"Accessions and Notes." 1927. *Metropolitan Museum of Art Bulletin* 22, 6: 178–181.
"American Art and William Pahlmann." 1941. *Interiors*, May.
"An Endorsement." 1927–1928. *Bulletin of the Pennsylvania Museum* 23, 117: 3–9.
"Architectural Criticism." 1914. *Architecture* 29, 4: 77–79.
"Art Furnishings Shown: Store Exhibits Rooms Decorated With Antiques From Europe." 1937. *New York Times*, October 8: L 46.
Benson, Susan Porter. 1986. *Counter Cultures: Saleswomen, Managers, and Customers in American Department Stores, 1890–1940*. Urbana and Chicago: University of Illinois Press.
"Contemporary Versions." 1937. *House Beautiful* 79, December 12: 43–49.
Davidson, Gail S., and Marilyn Friedman. 2007. *Studies in the Decorative Arts* 14, 2: 170–73.
de Wolfe, Elsie. *The House in Good Taste*. [1911] 1913. New York: The Century Co.
"Furniture for Modern Living: Good Taste at Low Prices Now Dominates Mass Market." 1939. *Life* 7, 5, July 31: 42–49.

Goldstein, Harriet Irene and Vetta Goldstein. 1925. *Art in Every Day Life*. New York: The Macmillan Co.

Gorman, Carma R. 2000. "'An Educated Demand:' The Implications of *Art in Every Day Life* for American Industrial Design, 1925–1950." *Design Issues* 16, 3: 45–66.

Gura, Judith. 2008. *New York Interior Design, 1935–1985*, vol. I. New York: Acanthus Press.

The History of Lord and Taylor, 1826–1926: One Hundred Years of Building for Tomorrow. [c. 1926]. New York: Guinn Co., Inc. Facsimile reproduction reprinted by The B. Earl Puckett Fund for Retail Education, Inc.

Hoogenboom, Olive. 2000. "Hoving, Walter." <www.anb.org>. *American National Biography* Online. Copyright American Council of Learned Societies. Published by Oxford University Press.

Krebs, Albin. 1987. "William C. Pahlmann, Decorator Known for Eclectic Designs, Dies." *New York Times*, December 11. Accessed February 20, 2016. www.nytimes.com/1987/11/11/obituaries/william-c-pahlmann-decorator-known-for-eclectic-designs-dies.html.

Loring, John. 2000. "William Pahlmann: Shaking Up Interiors with a Surprisingly Diverse Vision." *Architectural Digest* 57, January: 212–215.

Merwood-Salisbury, Joanna. 2011. "Interior Design as Environmental Design: The Parsons Program in the 1960s." In *After Taste: Expanded Practice in Interior Design*, edited by Kent Kleinman, Joanna Merwood-Salisbury, and Lois Weinthal, 110–129. New York: Princeton Architectural Press.

"Midsummer in Manhattan." 1939. *House & Garden* 76, July: 38–41.

Miller, R. Craig. 1990. *Modern Design in The Metropolitan Museum of Art, 1890–1990*. New York: Harry N. Abrams, Inc., Publishers.

Mitchell, Alex (industry historian and creative director of Baker Furniture). 2013. Interview by author, July 2, Tomales, California.

Mumford, Lewis. 1928. "Modernist Furniture." *New Republic*, March 20: 154.

"Display Lifts Hat Sales; Nine Windows Bring 39% Gain for Lord & Taylor." 1938. *New York Times,* March 12: 23.

O'Brien, George. 1964. "The 'Eclectic Look.'" *New York Times Magazine*, March 1: 58–59.

Petrow, Steven. 2004. *The Lost Hamptons*. New York: Arcadia Publishing.

Post, Emily. 1930. *The Personality of a House: The Blue Book of Home Design and Decoration*. New York: Funk & Wagnalls Company.

"The Promotion of French Trade through Exhibitions and Fairs." 1925. *Journal of the Royal Society of Arts* 73, 3791: 816–819.

Reif, Rita. 1958. "Decorating Expert Aims To Lure Young Couples." *New York Times*, September 19: L 20.

"See 'Rooms of Tomorrow'; 500 Attend Preview Showing the Latest Trends in Furnishings." 1939. *New York Times*, May 16: L 32.

Smith, C. Ray. 1987. *Interior Design in 20th-Century America: A History*. New York: Harper & Row, Publishers.

"Snowstorm in Store: Lord & Taylor Stops Crowds With Realistic Displays." 1938. *New York Times*, November 13: F 9.

"Stores with Personality: What makes a woman buy?" 1947. *Architectural Forum* 86: 15–16.

Storey, Walter Rendell. 1930. "Period Furnishings for Modern Rooms; The Decorator Is Strongly Influenced by Georgian And Colonial Styles." *New York Times Magazine*, February 9: 16.

———. 1936. "Murals Seen As One With Their Settings; In a Current Exhibition Unity of Subject and Technique Receives Special Emphasis." *New York Times Section Magazine*, November 1: 14.

Taves, Isabella. 1943. *Successful Women and how they Attained Success*. New York: E. P. Dutton & Company, Inc.

The William Carroll Pahlmann Archive. Texas A&M University College of Architecture Technical Reference Center, College Station, Texas 77843.

William Pahlmann Papers (WPP). Accession 2388. Manuscripts and Archives Department, Hagley Museum and Library, Wilmington, Delaware 19807.

(WPP) Interview with Jack Connor by Gayle Gibson, December 6, 1989, p. 11. Collection Case File 2188, William Pahlmann and Associates Records.

(WPP) Lord & Taylor. Series 9, Client Photo Presentation Books, Box OS 1–2, Books 1 and 2.

(WPP) William Pahlmann, autobiographical essay for Parsons School of Design Alumni Bulletin (29 June 1948), 4pp. Series 1, Box 60, Folder "Parsons School, 1948, 1957–59."

Yarnall, Sophia. 1936. "Pen Ryn on the Delaware: The Historic Residence of Mr. and Mrs. Seton Henry." *Country Life (Country Life in America)* 69, 4: 22–26, 64.

6 Baroque lines in a modern world

The retail displays of Dorothy Draper

John C. Turpin

Dorothy Tuckerman Draper (1888–1969) was a mid-twentieth-century American interior decorator and designer who reached national notoriety by the end of her career, despite not having received any formal training in interior design.[1] This was not entirely unusual, as a number of early women decorators crafted their "good taste" into a successful career. Such was the case of Elsie de Wolfe (1865–1950), Frances Elkins (1888–1953), Nancy Lancaster (1897–1994), and Sister Parish (1910–1994), to name a few. Many decorators ventured into the commercial sector as they applied their understanding of the residential environment to hotels and restaurants – spaces with familiar functions like eating, sleeping and entertaining. Draper, however, was one of the very few who engaged in retail design and received recognition for her work.[2]

The majority of Draper's professional portfolio in the 1920s and 1930s consisted of private residences, restaurants, apartment buildings (particularly lobbies and other public spaces), and hotels. In 1940 she was presented her first opportunity to design a retail space, the Coty Beauty Salon (1941) located in Rockefeller Center in New York City. The salon's primary purpose was the selling of Coty cosmetics – from perfumes to lipsticks, soap to powders. The store included display units for merchandize and counters with mirrors where women could test the products. Treatment rooms on the second floor provided a space for customers to receive facials and professional application of the products. The finished Salon interior received great praise. *Interior Design and Decoration* (September 1941) featured it on the cover and Emerich Nicholson (1945) included it in his book, *Contemporary Shops in the United States*. Nicholson's self-defined selection process included "an understanding of contemporary American merchandising problems, originality and freshness of design, success from both the merchants' and consumers' point of view, and a contribution to the field of commercial architecture" (11). Draper's inclusion was notable for two reasons. First, she was one of very few women included in the selection, and the only interior designer – all the other women were trained as industrial designers (Elsie Krummek Crawford, Freda Diamond, Virginia Connor, Virginia Hamill). Second, her interiors and displays differed noticeably from the other selected projects. While the vast majority demonstrated the popularity of streamline Modernism, Draper utilized bold historic references from the Baroque period. In this chapter, I will argue that, at a time when Modernism was a dominant influence, Draper's employment of historicism in the design of retail spaces was both romantic and strategic.

Draper's exposure to historical design began in her childhood. Until the age of 23, she lived in the fashionable community of Tuxedo Park, New York. Her love of historicist design originated with her parents, who had built and lived in four homes in this exclusive community. Draper's parents, Paul and Susan Tuckerman, commissioned James Lord Brown (1858–1902) to complete the first two homes in the Tudor and Queen Anne styles, respectively. The third was completed in 1899 and boasted a distinct Richardsonian Romanesque-inspired façade. This was the last of the three homes Draper would inhabit as a child. She articulated her appreciation for her surroundings in the dedication of her book, *Decorating is Fun!* (1939):

> To
> *My Mother and Father*
> Susan and Paul Tuckerman
> *The best amateur planners I know, who after more than fifty years*
> *of married life, secretly long to build still another house*
> *and to whom plans and decorations*
> *are an unending fascination, delight and challenge,*
> *this little book is dedicated with love,*
> *gratitude and admiration.*

Draper carried this appreciation for historicist interiors into her professional career, believing that everyone should be surrounded by beautiful spaces, which she equated to the interiors of her childhood (Varney 1988).

From a strategic standpoint, I suggest that Draper relied on her aesthetic stylings to engage the romantic ideals of the American middle-class housewife who sought to emulate the upper class (Sparke 1995; Crane 2000, 16). "The goal at the end of the rainbow was ownership of property on an ascending scale of expense: first, clothing and cosmetics […] then a car, a house" (Baritz 1989, 106). By surrounding consumers in an interior with connotations of the upper class, Draper tapped into their desire for social progress, which encouraged them to value her spaces more than those of her competitors, who tended to focus on Modernist stylings as a representation of the latest fashionable trend. She articulated this strategy in an interview with Frances McMullen in regards to her work on apartment buildings:

> It involves little things, from the sort of hardware and window trim to the size of servant's rooms and the decoration of the entrance. It may even be a question of the doorman's uniform. These are the things that give the building atmosphere, that make people want to live there rather than somewhere else
>
> (1930, 26).

Draper transferred this idea of atmosphere in relation to class to her retail spaces in order to influence the consumer's decision-making process.

Little has been written about Draper's retail strategies. Following her death in 1969, her name fell out of the nation's consciousness, even though her firm continued her work under Carleton Varney (b. 1939), current president of Dorothy Draper & Company. Varney's 1988 biography of his former boss, *The Draper Touch: The High Style and High Life of Dorothy Draper*, laid the foundation for future research. Along with *In the Pink: Dorothy Draper, America's Most Fabulous Decorator* (Varney 2006), this text exposed the public to a substantive portion of Draper's archives between 1930 and 1960. Scholars began exploring Draper's life and career, focusing on a variety of aspects. Mitchell Owens (2005) analyzed Draper's work relative to the hotel industry within the context of her own career. Blossom and Turpin (2008) used

Draper as one of three case studies to discuss the social, familial, and economic risks early female decorators accepted as they pursued their professional careers. In several journal articles Turpin has also critically examined Draper's relationship with the middle class (2000, 2003a, 2008), and how her designs were a form of social criticism as it related to class (2003b). In an exploratory study he also analyzed her products (written and physical) and why they were deemed successful (2015). None of the current research, however, provides an in-depth examination of Draper's work in the retail sector, particularly her unique styling of retail displays. This chapter analyzes her work within the context of retail design during the early 1940s and argues that her use of historicism was a means of influencing consumers' decision-making process by appealing to their desire to emulate the upper class.

Becoming a merchandizer

Dorothy Draper led the life of a typical nineteenth-century upper-class female with all of its trappings, expectations and obligations (Varney 1988). Nannies and governesses raised her at home, while her mother taught her important lessons regarding taste and etiquette. She married George "Dan" Draper (1880–1959) in 1912, leaving her childhood home in Tuxedo Park for Manhattan. She entertained regularly, as was expected for her gender and station in society. As Martha Coman noted in a *New York Times* article on May 13, 1925, guests at her parties praised the decoration of her house – but this was not the catalyst for her professional career. An informal lunch with a friend, who was frustrated with the process of selecting an architect for a new home, gave Draper an idea that turned into her first business venture (McMullen 1930). In 1925, Draper created the Architectural Clearing House, a business that matched clients with the appropriate architect based primarily on stylistic preferences (Towne 1925). Draper soon inserted herself into the design process, where she became "almost like a member of the architect's firm during the process of building and construction" (Towne 1925, 42). She began accepting high-profile projects as the sole decorator all over Manhattan, including the National Junior League Headquarters (1928), Sherry's Restaurant (1930), and the Carlyle Hotel (1930). Draper outgrew the Architectural Clearing House and opened Dorothy Draper, Inc. in 1930 (Varney 1988). She clarified her new mission in an article that same year: "We are style consultants. We aim to do the same thing for apartment buildings that the more familiar sort of stylist does for department store stock" (McMullen 1930). It was at this moment that Draper first referenced her awareness of merchandizing as an important part of her firm's services. By 1937, she was using the term "merchandizing" as a way to describe her company's philosophy when it came to the design of commercial projects (Roe 1937). During her interview with journalist Evelyn Roe, Draper used her most famous project to date, the Hampshire House in New York City (1937), as an example of her approach. She stated that merchandizing a space required that all components of an interior, from furniture arrangements to the smallest detail (eg color of the letterhead), should support the purpose of the space. Draper equated merchandizing with consistent styling, a combination of ideas that eventually led to the concept of branding.

Draper's big break arrived in 1934 when she accepted a contract to renovate the Sutton Place Tenement Apartments, a block of deteriorated mid-nineteenth-century

New York row houses. Its neglected condition meant the property was not able to yield enough money to pay the taxes. With a sturdy structure already in place, Draper went to work. She painted the exterior a glossy black with dead-white trim, stripped doorways of ornament to present a simple yet elegant entrance, and transformed the fire escapes into picturesque faux balconies. Brilliantly colored doors in watermelon pink and citron yellow brought the exterior to life. Upon completion, the apartments were filled and the rent quadrupled. *Business Week* (1936) and the *Christian Science Monitor* (Roe 1937) praised her accomplishments from a financial standpoint, and Janet Flanner confirmed in her article that "real estate agents and builders knew of her abilities to return a profit on large-scale public projects" (1941, 90). They recognized her work as an excellent return on investment.

Draper received a number of high-profile commissions following the success of Sutton Place Tenement Apartments, including the Hampshire House (New York City, 1937), Terrace Club at the New York World's Fair (1939), the Arrowhead Springs Resort (San Bernardino, California, 1939), and the Mayflower Hotel (Washington, DC, 1940). In each of these instances, Draper offered full interior services that included everything from selection and coordination of furniture and materials to full graphics packages that covered the designs of menus, matchbooks and soap wrappers. Referencing her company's scope of service for her newest project, the Quitandinha Hotel in Brazil (1946), she stated that "when we package a hotel, we put in everything necessary for its perfect functioning – the livery of the doormen, the caps of the maids, the furniture, the interior architecture; even the notepaper" (Fisher 1942, 8). Up until this point in her career, all of Draper's projects revolved around interiors that functioned in much the same way as domestic spaces. It was not until July 9, 1941 that Draper unveiled her first commission that required something quite different – that is, the display and selling of products.

Coty Beauty Salon, New York City

Located at the corner of Fifth Avenue and Rockefeller Center Promenade, the Coty Beauty Salon was part of a growing French presence in midtown Manhattan. The store was situated in *La Maison Française* or The French House (1932), one of the many buildings in the Rockefeller Center complex. Its purpose was to showcase French and Francophone culture. Coty, Inc. was one of France's notable exports, and it was perhaps not a surprise that the company, then headed by Léon Cotnareanu, moved its store from just a block down the street to this new, prestigious location.

François Coty (born Joseph Marie François Sportuno, 1874–1934) established his first American store in 1910 at 714 Fifth Avenue in New York City. He commissioned René Lalique (1860–1945) to design the interior and a three-story work of art to replace a part of the façade (Barille and Tahara 1996). Coty became involved with the creation of perfumes when he worked for a pharmacist who sold his own concoctions. He produced his first fragrance, Cologne Coty, shortly thereafter. According to an article in *The New Yorker*, Coty's olfactory nerve – a requirement for a fine perfumer – was "marvelously talented and acute" (Flanner 1930). He used this talent to serve middle-class women – his primary customer – even though the upper class frequently commissioned him to create unique products for their personal consumption

Figure 6.1 First floor of Coty Beauty Salon designed by Dorothy Draper & Company,
New York City, 1941, with permission from Dorothy Draper & Company, Inc.
Source: Dorothy Draper Archives. Loose leaf. New York: Dorothy Draper & Company

(Barille and Tahara 1996, 158). Coty's business strategy revealed his desire to reach a
large audience:

> Give a woman the best product to be made, market it in the perfect flask, beauti-
> ful in its simplicity yet impeccable in its taste, ask a reasonable price for it, and
> you will witness the birth of a business the size of which the world has never seen.
> (Toledano and Coty 2009, 100)

The available space for Coty to rent at the *La Française Maison* consisted of two
storeys. The first floor (Fig. 6.1) included the display and selling of merchandize (eg
perfumes, lipsticks, powders) and a waiting area, while the upper floor consisted
mainly of treatment rooms and a service counter to try on products. Upon entering the
space, customers were likely lured to the rear of the store where a Baroque-inspired
wall display sat on axis with the front door. Draper turned to Lester Grundy (1914–
1985), an influential staff member in the development of Draper's style, for the design
(Owens 2005). As an art historian with a "curator's depth of knowledge," his passion

for the eighteenth century and the work of Grinling-Gibbons' Baroque wood carvings inspired him to produce with great ease the large scrollwork Draper frequently integrated into her designs (Varney 1988, 117). The firm worked with the Cinquinni family, a well-known group of Italian-American craftsmen located in Brooklyn, for the execution of Grundy's designs (Owens 2005). Although Draper relied on specialists to help her visions come to fruition, she was a fully committed and engaged supervisor: all decisions needed to be approved by her, as evidenced by the countless number of archival documents that bore her initials, comments and edits.[3]

The stark white, custom built-in display (Fig. 6.2) ran the full height of the nine-foot pale blue wall. The soft, curving edges of the scrolls topped with a gentle swag anchored by a shell created a capsule-shaped opening. Each of the four glass shelves provided a surface for three unique samples of perfume. Bottles sat next to their corresponding packaging so that consumers could easily interact with the product. Draper and her team crowned the composition with two gracious, well-proportioned

Figure 6.2 Custom display designed by Dorothy Draper and Ted Grundy and executed by the Cinquinni family in the Coty Beauty Salon, New York City, 1941.

Source: Reprinted with permission from Dorothy Draper & Company

c-scrolls. The lower portions of the scrolls curved inward to create a visual base while the top burst into a plume of leaves. A seven-armed candelabrum provided decorative light. The framed mirror reflected the light fixture and completed its anticipated radial composition. The mirror that backed the display area doubled the reflected light produced by all the glass surfaces. In an attempt to transition more smoothly with the wall, Grundy designed the case with beveled corners that included two additional sets of candelabras on each side.

Draper and Grundy presented the bold, deeply-carved baroque gestures, which were visually softened by the white painted plaster, in a dramatic scale more appropriately proportioned for a much larger space. The scale of the display would have consumed the customers' visual field as they examined the product. The mirrored back likely drew the women even closer to the display as they became aware of their reflection – a common response in women who have been taught to be "concerned" about their appearance (Fox 1997). With the soft glow from the candelabras, Draper had essentially created an intimate space within a larger space that acted much like a magnificent vanity in a palatial home. By doing so, Draper connected an experience with the product to the customer's value system (perceptions of social status) that would have likely influenced their decision to purchase (Pine and Gilmore, 1999).

Another craftsperson whose work was prominent on the first floor was Alice Willits Donaldson (1885–1961). According to her obituary in the *New York Times*, she studied at the Cincinnati Art Academy and the Pennsylvania Museum of Industrial Arts in Philadelphia, and worked as an artist, designer and illustrator. At the beginning of her career she painted covers and illustrations for *Country Life, Children's Vogue, Delineator, House Beautiful* and the *Saturday Evening Post*. She then moved into the decorative arts, designing fabrics, wallpapers, ceramics and rugs (*New York Times* 1961). Her artwork at the Coty Beauty Salon decorated the counters and shadow boxes on the right hand of the store (Fig. 6.3) and the screens flanking the seating area on the left. Donaldson was also responsible for the large hand-painted bouquets on the sides of the first floor counter displays that welcomed customers entering the store. The simple geometry and flat surfaces of the cabinets ensured that her work would be the emphasis of the piece. A smaller running motif framed the glassed front of the floor units as well as the edges and frames of the shadow boxes that hung on the wall directly behind. The floor- and wall-mounted display cases were box forms with modestly curved, scalloped interior edges to create a visual frame for the merchandize. Donaldson painted her artwork on black paper, which was then laminated to the piece and given a glossy finish. The press referred to this treatment as "plasdecor," a portmanteau of "plastic" and "decoration."

According to Dorothy Draper & Company's press release (1941) on the design of the Coty interior, "the display cases on the main floor – usually so unimaginative and stereotyped a part of any commercial scheme – have been turned into priceless frames for Coty products." Draper clearly intended to offer designs normally associated with luxury and the upper class. In addition, her inclusion of Donaldson's work offered a contrast to the otherwise white Neo-Baroque displays and bannister, and the soft blue walls. Draper concentrated her most intense use of color in order to frame the employee and create a differently scaled experience for the consumer as they peered into the case, much as they would into a jewelry box. The protection of the merchandize behind glass elevated its status to something precious that must be safeguarded, as did the custom styling of the display.

Figure 6.3 Custom displays painted by Alice Willits Donaldson in the Coty Beauty Salon,
New York City, 1941.
Source: Reprinted with permission from Dorothy Draper & Company

Dorothy Draper, Inc. was a logical choice for this commission. After World War I,
the new consumer "was willing to believe, just enough, that purchases of fashionable
goods could bring her status, success, and at least a measure of happiness" (Whitaker
2006, 39). Though François Coty died before this project was even conceived, he
and Draper recognized these traits and had similar views when it came to the experience of the customer. Coty's strategy was to seduce his customer with the kind of
enticements usually reserved for the very rich (Barille and Tahara 1996, 158). Draper
wanted to create "a place for people to come and feel elevated in the presence of great
beauty, where the senses could look and feel and absorb the meaning of a quality of
life" (Varney 1988, xiv–xv). Both Coty and Draper embraced the "democratization of
luxury," a concept the department store had begun to boast in the 1880s (Lancaster
1995; Masset 2010). Draper's preferred method to achieve this goal was to employ

a design language inspired by the eighteenth-century aristocratic palaces of Europe (Turpin 2003b).

By 1910, Tuxedo Park was an architectural display of grand homes in all manner of styles (eg Shingle Style, Georgian, Jacobean, Queen Anne) by some of the most prestigious firms (Sonne, Hempel and Bleeker 2007). Draper also traveled extensively in Europe as a child and continued to do so as an adult, which, according to her entry in the 1941 edition of *Current Biography,* "augmented and enriched her own background and natural good taste" (90). Draper recognized the effect of her traditional upbringing surrounded by interiors of "pleasant good taste" (Roe 1937, 6). She carried these experiences into her professional career.

However, Draper was by no means a purist when it came to history. Objects, historical or contemporary, were simply artifacts to be manipulated to suit her purposes. In a 1957 televised interview on *Person to Person* with Edward R. Murrow, Draper discussed the work she had carried out on a family heirloom, an eighteenth-century Dutch cabinet with dark lacquered wood and floral motifs (a striking resemblance to Donaldson's ornamentation). Draper explained that she had cut the doors in half so that they could open like bi-fold doors. They collapsed on themselves, reducing the physical space required when open and revealing the contents within. During her interview with Murrow she stated: "We have no respect for whether things are old or not, we just cut anything we want if it looks better." Draper's sentiment, "looks better," was her qualifier for good design. She frequently simplified it for the American consumer by saying, "If it looks right, it is right" (Flanner 1941, 85). Albeit incredibly vague, Draper's design philosophy emphasized the quality of the interior experience regardless of whether she focused on private or commercial spaces.

Articles in shelter magazines re-emphasized that customers preferred shopping in an attractive, pleasant atmosphere ("Interior Design an Economic Asset" 1941; Parker 1940). Store design and display techniques that aimed at affecting consumer behavior in positive ways became known as "atmospherics," a term coined by Philip Kotler (1973). This is still considered a key factor in the success of retail stores (Yeh and Hsieh 2015). The challenge for designers was identifying what they thought the consumers deemed attractive and pleasant when creating these atmospheres.

Draper's distinct nod toward historicism ran counter to the prevailing modern, streamlined stylings of the 1930s and 1940s. Richard Longstreth noted that "the department store became the place where large numbers of people were introduced to modernist design in the late 1920s" (2010, 37). This originated from a merchandizing strategy that equated the store's Modernism (in design and selection of products) to its perception as a trendsetter in fashion (Longstreth 2010, 37). The participation of high-profile designers like Norman Bel Geddes and Raymond Loewy raised the profile of retail design and made it an acceptable vehicle for experimentation in the emerging modern style (Iarocci 2013, 5). The absence of decorative elements not only celebrated the advancements of the machine age, but also suited Depression budgets because they were less expensive to produce (Whitaker 2011, 125).

Emerich Nicholson's *Contemporary Shops in the United States* made the point regarding design styling visually. In his introduction, he referred to the streamlining that was occurring throughout the 1930s; however, he admitted that since his publication lacked an "analysis of trends, methods of display, the whys, the wherefores and don'ts in merchandising, it [was] best that the photographs of the stores [...] tell their own story" (Nicholson 1945, 13). Of the almost 100 stores featured in the book, only four – besides

Draper's Coty Beauty Salon – offered a suggestion of historicism. A women's specialty shop in Greensboro, North Carolina, by Otto Zenke (1904–1984), showed a Baroque molding surrounding a large portal. T.H. Robsjohn-Gibbings (1905–1976) included a modern interpretation of Rococo-inspired metal furnishings for John Frederics in New York (1940) that emphasized line more than form. A gold-finished hat stand wrought in the shape of flowers sat atop a round, glass-top table with cabriole-inspired legs. Finally, the May Company Wilshire in Los Angeles, California included timid Baroque details over doors and as light fixtures in the millinery section and women's shoe salon, respectively. But none of them committed to the same degree of historicism as Draper and only one utilized it in the actual display of merchandize.

Draper's bold use of historicism was far more effective in creating a romanticized atmosphere for middle-class consumers who looked up the social ladder with hope. She connected their values and aspirations with a product through the mediation of historically-inspired imagery. The continued interest in historicism was evident in the many decorating books like Emily Post's *The Personality of House* (1930), Mary Roberts' *Inside 100 Homes* (1936), Gladys Miller's *Decoratively Speaking* (1939), and Dorothy Draper's *Decorating is Fun!* (1939) that continued to promote the decoration of homes in historic styles – just like those found in the mansions of the upper class.

Conspicuously, all of the spaces that did rely on historical references carried products specifically for women. They likely used a strategy similar to that of interior designer Tom Douglas for Saks Fifth Avenue (*Interior Design and Decoration* 1940), who referenced Empire style sources in the Millinery Salon and a silver leaf Baroque fireplace surround on the Custom-Made Gown floor. He noted that these were specialty stores for "patrons of taste who appreciate – and desire – quality of design lavished upon their surroundings even while shopping" ("Plastics Utilized in Store Interiors" 1940, 32). This was not a new concept. According to Claire Masset (2010, 14), William Whiteley (1831–1907), founder of Whiteley's Department Store in London, was one of the first retailers to recognize that sumptuous displays were as important as the products. Draper's application suggested that a market persisted for customers who valued the detail of historical styles and the implied exclusivity and service that came with it. In fact, this was a common tactic for Draper. Turpin has argued that her decision to use palatial-scaled European ornamentation went beyond aesthetic considerations and was a form of social critique (2003b). Draper rejected the notion that upper-class women were the sole purveyors of taste in *Decorating Is Fun!* (1939), and mocked high society's restrictive rules of etiquette in *Entertaining Is Fun!* (1941). Throughout her career, in her projects and media communications, Draper empowered the middle-class woman, centering her as a source of taste and deserving of beautiful interiors.

All the other projects selected by Nicholson presented far less applied ornamentation in the interiors and on the display units. In his article "Store Design," American architect Morris Lapidus (1902–2001) gives one reason that may have motivated this approach: "Merchandise is the best decorative motif the architect can use" (*Architectural Record* 1941, 129). Store after store in Nicholson's *Contemporary Shops* featured geometrically derived architectural planes with smooth surfaces – and perhaps an interesting pattern or color – as a backdrop to showcase the merchandize in the store. For example, Rebajes jewelry shop on Fifth Avenue in New York City consisted of walls veneered in light oak when not covered in mirrors. According to Nicholson, the dominant feature was a 30-foot-long suspended serpentine counter.

The base, square in section, lacked any ornamentation other than the rhythm of the drawer pulls that led to the hidden, but easily accessible stock – a strategy championed by Morris Ketchum (1904–1984), a respected designer of retail spaces during the 1940s. A mirrored glass top provided the surface for the various small products. Another glass shelf of the same serpentine shape floated approximately 15 inches above the objects. Here, jewelry items were presented by the salesperson at a level at which the customer could inspect the item more closely and even try it on. The various shapes of the products brought the store to life. They shone and sparkled under directed lighting. The repetitive planes of wood veneer fell into the background as the shopper was drawn to the counter.

Many designers approached the display of products in a similar fashion. Ketchum provided a display cabinet for Wallach's men's store in Brooklyn that was very similar in form to the one decorated by Donaldson for the Coty Beauty Salon. Both had a glass front and top, but instead of the bursting floral designs, Ketchum offered a light wood veneer for the display of two hats, a tie and a pair of gloves. Whether shadow boxes anchored to the wall, or counters that negotiated the location of the customer and salesperson, display units in the form of cabinetry were predominantly simple geometric forms sheathed in a veneer with glass casings – simple frames to contrast with the more decorative object. However, Draper's designs "worked" just as well. Her Baroque frames announced a small product from a substantial distance. She quickly drew the customer through the store via her orchestration of light and texture. As customers walked by the counter, Donaldson's robust florals drew their eye and encouraged them to peer into the precious case that had been given so much attention.

In a 1941 article appearing in the *New York Times* ("New Salon Open in Air of Splendor"), a member of the press described the interior of the Coty Beauty Salon as a "jewel-box," which was likely met with great satisfaction by Draper. She valued the experience of shopping, how the space felt. Her press release for the grand opening emphasized this point and revealed the reasoning behind the color palette:

> Blue – the color of hope [...] With red – the exciting factor that stirs a woman to the bottom of her soul and her purse. Mirror for its glitter and gayety [sic]. Baroque plasterwork like frozen music. Black lacquer, enriched with mother of pearl and huge flowers in natural color, to provide an exotic note. And textures everywhere so rich and sleek and eye-satisfying that they spell luxury plus.
>
> (Varney 2006, 96)

Mention of the product was conspicuously absent. She and her team focused on describing the environment and relating it to human emotions: hope, desire, and happiness. By placing the consumer in this mood, the interior and all of its components would sell the cosmetics. Recent research has validated this approach, suggesting that if the physical attributes of a product (or in this instance the design of the interior and its components) yielded a positive psychosocial response from consumers, then the experience supported what they valued and the consumer left satisfied (Reynolds and Olson, 2001; Turpin 2015). Draper articulated this idea when discussing the success of the Sutton Place Tenement Apartments: "People coming into a building can tell whether it is successful. Successful in its equipment, its operation, its prestige. Such success permeates all the details" (Roe 1937, 6). Draper understood the collective effect of a well-orchestrated and strategically-designed interior as a means to create an atmosphere or experience. Perhaps more importantly, she knew of its power as a way to influence consumers.

In 1941, the National Cash Register Company published a series of booklets to assist those wanting to start a business. One titled *Better Retailing* focused on display selling. Their first paragraph recognized that merchandize display was "a powerful factor in selling." They went on to state: "A good display (1) places goods where customers can see them; (2) creates desire; (3) entices customers to stop and examine articles; (4) reminds customers of goods they would forget; and (5) acts as a silent salesman" (107). Creating desire and giving an inanimate object the role of salesperson were perhaps two of the most difficult goals to achieve. However, for Draper, they were a driving force: the environment sold the product. Overall, while her approach was unconventional for the time, Draper demonstrated an effective understanding of retail merchandizing.

Conclusion

During the early part of the twentieth century, historically inspired commercial spaces were common. With the gradual influence of Modernism, department stores began equating the style of the interiors with trendsetting fashions. Draper, however, relied on the romanticism of the past to create atmospheres that supported the aspirations of the middle class, which were traditionally connected to the design language of the elite's grandiose homes. By attaching an experience with a product, Draper intended to influence the decision-making process of the consumer.

Draper used her Neo-Baroque scrollwork to great effect throughout the late 1930s and 1940s (including one other retail space, Kerr's Department Store in Oklahoma City, 1944), and it eventually became her trademark style. Nicholson's selection and inclusion of the Coty Beauty Salon in his book placed Draper in a sea of Modernists. A similar situation occurred in Burke and Kober's *Modern Store Design: A Practical Study of the Influence of Store Style on Modern Merchandising* (1946). One picture stands out among the countless illustrations of streamlined interiors: a pencil rendering of a predominantly modern architectural shell showing Baroque scrollwork above the counter, displays and doors. The caption reads: "Modern baroque with flowing lines can be a welcome relief from straight line modern" (69). It was in this need for "relief" that Draper forged a unique and successful design for the Coty Beauty Salon – the interior was strategically romantic.

Notes

1 A 1960 survey by the Center for Research in Marketing indicated that more American housewives knew Draper than the likes of industrial designer George Nelson and furniture designer T.H. Robsjohn-Gibbings (Varney 2006, 27).

2 Other women participated in the design of retail spaces, but they were trained industrial designers, such as Elsie Krummek Crawford (1913–1999), who attended Parsons School of Design, and Freda Diamond (1905–1998), who attended the Women's Art School of the Cooper Union.

3 The Draper Archives are a series of scrapbooks located on a shelf at Dorothy Draper & Company in New York City. They have yet to be cataloged in an official manner. The archives were scanned by the author for his personal research in the summer of 1998.

References

Barille, Elizabeth and Keiichi Tahara. 1996. *Coty: Parfumeur and Visionary.* Paris: Editions Assouline.

Baritz, Lauren. 1989. *The Good Life: The Meaning of Success for the American Middle Class.* New York: Alfred A. Knopf.

Blossom, Nancy and John Turpin. 2008. "Risk as a Window to Agency: A Case Study of Three Decorators." *Journal of Interior Design* 34: 1–13.

Burke, Gene and Edgar Kober. 1946. *Modern Store Design: A Practical Study of the Influence of Store Style on Modern Merchandising.* Los Angeles, CA: Institute of Product Research.

"Re-Styled Buildings." 1936. *Business Week*, September: 34.

Coman, Martha. 1925. "Woman of Society Works as Expert Consultant on Houses." *New York Times*, May 13.

Crane, Diana. 2000. *Fashion and Its Social Agendas: Class, Gender, and Identity in Clothing.* Chicago: University of Chicago Press.

"Dorothy Draper." 1941. *Current Biography*: 237–238.

Dorothy Draper & Company. 1941. *Press Release: Coty Beauty Salon*, loose leaf. Dorothy Draper Archives, New York.

Draper, Dorothy. 1939. *Decorating Is Fun!* New York: Doubleday, Doran & Company, Inc.

Fisher, Barbara F. Scott. 1942. "Dorothy Draper, Designer, Ties Up Her Hotel Decorations All in One Package." *Christian Science Monitor*, October 28: C10.

Flanner, Janet. 1930. "Perfume and Politics." *The New Yorker*, May 3. Accessed November 15, 2015. www.newyorker.com/magazine/1930/05/03/perfume-and-politics.

Flanner, Janet. 1941. "The Amazing Career of Dorothy Draper." *Harper's Bazaar*, January: 89–90.

Fox, Kate. 1997. "Mirror, Mirror: A Summary of Research Finding on Body Image." *Social Issues Research Center*. Accessed December 11, 2015. www.sirc.org/publik/mirror.html.

Iarocci, Louisa. 2013. "Introduction: The Image of Visual Merchandising." In *Visual Merchandising: The Image of Selling*, edited by Louisa Iarocci, 1–15. Farnham, UK: Ashgate Publishing Limited.

Interior Design and Decoration. 1941. Cover, September.

"Interior Design an Economic Asset." 1941. *Interior Design and Decoration*, March: 42–44.

Kotler, Phillip. 1973. "Atmospherics as a Marketing Tool." *Journal of Retailing* 49: 48–59.

Lancaster, Bill. 1995. *The Department Store: A Social History.* London: Leicester University Press.

Lapidus, Morris. 1941. "Store Design: A Merchandising Problem." *Architectural Record*, February: 113–136.

Longstreth, Richard. 2010. *The American Department Store Transformed, 1920–1960.* New Haven: Yale University Press.

Masset, Claire. 2010. *Department Stores.* Oxford: Shire Publications.

McMullen, Frances. 1930. "Mrs. Draper, Home Stylist." *Woman's Journal*, March: 16–17.

Miller, Gladys. 1939. *Decoratively Speaking: The Essentials and Principles of Interior Decoration.* New York: Doubleday, Doran & Company.

Murrow, Edward R. 1957. Interview with Dorothy Draper. *Person to Person with Edward R. Murrow.* CBS. May. Videocassette.

National Cash Register Company. 1941. *Better Retailing: A Handbook for Merchants.* Dayton, OH: Merchants Service, NCRC.

"New Salon Open in Air of Splendor." 1941. *New York Times*, July 10.

Nicholson, Emerich. 1945. *Contemporary Shops in the United States.* New York: Architectural Book Publishing Co., Inc.

"Obituary: Alice Willits Donaldson." 1961. *New York Times*, November 14.

Owens, Mitchell. 2005. "Living Large: The Brash, Bodacious Hotels of Dorothy Draper." *The Journal of Decorative and Propaganda Arts* 25: 254–287.

Parker, Neel. 1940. "Interiors for Commerce." *Interior Design and Decoration*, June: 46-[49].

Pine, Joseph and James Gilmore. 1999. *The Experience Economy: Work Is Theater & Every Business a Stage*. Boston: Harvard Business School Press.

"Plastics Utilized in Store Interiors." 1940. *Interior Design and Decoration*, February: 32.

Post, Emily. 1930. *The Personality of a House: The Blue Book of Home Design and Decoration*. New York: Funk & Wagnalls Company.

Reynolds, Thomas and Jerry Olson. 2001. *Understanding Consumer Decision Making: The Means-End Approach to Marketing and Advertising Strategy*. Mahwah, NJ: L. Erlbaum.

Roberts, Mary. 1936. *Inside 100 Homes*. New York: Robert McBride & Company.

Roe, Evelyn. 1937. "Giving 'Style' to Real Estate." *Christian Science Monitor*, August 25: 6.

Sonne, Christian, Chiu Yin Hempel and James Bleeker. 2007. *Tuxedo Park: The Historic Houses*. Tuxedo Park, NY: Tuxedo Park Historical Society.

Sparke, Penny. 1995. *As Long as It's Pink: The Sexual Politics of Space*. London: Harper Collins Publishers.

Toledano, Roulhac and Elizabeth Coty. 2009. *François Coty: Fragrance, Power, Money*. Gretna, LA: Pelican Publishing Company.

Towne, Charles. 1925. "A New Service for Those about to Build." *Country Life*, November: 42.

Turpin, John. 2000. "The Doors of Dorothy Draper: Vestiges of Victorian Manners with a Middle Class Sensibility." *In.Form: The Journal of Architecture, Design & Material Culture* 1: 8–15.

Turpin, John. 2003a. "Domestic Doyennes: Purveyors of Atmospheres Spoken and Visual." *In.Form: The Journal of Architecture, Design & Material Culture* 3: 42–54.

Turpin, John. 2003b. "Interior Space: A Site for Social Criticism." *Journal of Cultural Research in Art Education* 21: 107–118.

Turpin, John. 2008. "The Life and Work of Dorothy Draper: A Study in Class Value and Success." PhD diss., Arizona State University.

Turpin, John. 2015. "Dorothy Draper and the American Housewife: A Study of Class Values and Success." In *The Handbook of Interior Design*, edited by Nancy Blossom and Jo Ann Thompson, 29–45. New York: John Wiley & Sons.

Varney, Carleton. 1988. *The Draper Touch: The High Life and High Style of Dorothy Draper*. New York: Prentice Hall.

Varney, Carleton. 2006. *In the Pink: Dorothy Draper, America's Most Fabulous Decorator*. New York: Pointed Leaf Press.

Whitaker, Jan. 2011. *The Department Store: History, Design, Display*. London: Thames and Hudson.

Whitaker, Jan. 2006. *Service and Style: How the American Department Store Fashioned the Middle Class*. New York: St. Martin's Press.

Yeh, Tsu-Ming and Pei-Ling Hsieh. 2015. "Measuring Brand Equity of Cosmetic Chain Stores by Hybrid Multiple Criteria Decision Making Methods." *International Journal of Services and Operations Management* 21: 27–49.

Part II
Technologies of Display

7 "The Age of Show Windows" in the American department store

Techniques and technologies of attraction at the turn of the twentieth century

Emily M. Orr

From the late nineteenth century, show windows in leading American department stores became progressively sophisticated due to the imaginative techniques of their designers, the organizational framework of supportive fixtures, and the dynamism of modern technologies. In addition to revealing new products to the public, these window displays also showcased the skills and tools of the developing window dressing profession. Men dominated this new field due to the physical labor and unconventional hours that it demanded. While at first the terms "window trimmer" or, more often, "window dresser" defined this role, by 1915 the more authoritative term "displayman" came into wider use to reflect the professional's greater responsibility in the store's visual merchandizing scheme, of which the window continued to be a leading component (*New York Times* August 1, 1915, 86).

As the department store advanced at the turn of the twentieth century in New York and Chicago, the display staff choreographed a creative and continually evolving presentation of goods to earn consumers' praise and investment. In 1897, L. Frank Baum founded *The Show Window*, the first American periodical entirely devoted to merchandize display. With work experience in theatre and the dry goods trade, Baum recognized the potential of dramatic display and aimed to elevate the window dressing field and to provide practical instruction. In *The Show Window*'s November 1897 issue he advised:

> This is the age of show windows. The up-to-date merchant realizes that his window is his best advertisement, and therefore persistently strives to make it as beautiful and attractive as possible [...] and in this age of sharp competition, the contention is who shall be able to present the brightest and most attractive display of goods that may wile the passer-by into his store.
>
> (*The Show Window* November 1897, 17)

Consumers actively assessed a store's quality and personality based firstly on an evaluation of the window dresser's work from the sidewalk. Steady competition among stores pushed new display ideas forward in order to turn passers-by into purchasers.

In drawing attention to the development of the window dressing profession and the visual appeal and selling capacity of display in the American department store, this chapter will build on the pioneering scholarship of William Leach (1993), the illustrated window display compilation by Leonard Marcus (1978), and the more recent research of William Bird (2007) and Louisa Iarocci (2013). These works have discussed and pictured the show window largely in its stage of completion. The following chapter will expand on this existing scholarship by tracing the behind-the-scenes construction process of the window arrangement and arguing that consumers' fascination with the display's assembly and technology was crucial to its success as a modern promotional strategy.

Methods of merchandize presentation popular in the mid-nineteenth century often overwhelmed passers-by with material variety and profusion. The trade periodical *Merchants Record and Show Window* communicated the belief, commonly held by 1920, that "the heavily trimmed stocky window [...] merely dazzles, and bewilders the observer leaving no definite idea" (Davis 1920, 86). In a configuration where goods filled the window top to bottom, the consumer could decipher neither the displayman's skill nor the store's character. In the years approaching 1900, merchandizing methods had become more precise and consumer attention expanded beyond the commodities to the window dressers' manual expertise and the new technologies at work in their display. For instance, consumers perceived the execution of an ambitious layout or the presence of mechanization as evidence of a modern store that was accordingly worthy of their patronage. Frequent reconfiguration of the window's contents built a continually responsive consumer market that was alert to the method of presentation. As author William Nelson Taft suggested in *The Handbook of Window Display*:

> The majority of people who pass a store window do so every day and, if they are brought to realize that there is something new to be seen, it would not be long before they formed the habit of stopping to look at the window regularly, instead of waiting until they had a special item in mind.
>
> (Taft 1926, 36)

The diverse work of the window dressers conditioned the public's curiosity and established the window as a site deserving of focused attention.

While this chapter will concentrate on the American window dresser, it is important to note that the growth of the profession was international in nature and that displaymen traveled abroad to gain new ideas. For instance, in February of 1898, *The Show Window* sent a correspondent "to photograph the window decorations of all the European capitals" (*The Show Window* February 1898, 85). In 1914, the merchandize manager of Selfridges visited Lord & Taylor in New York (*Merchants Record and Show Window* July 1914, 28). An American journalist pronounced in 1920 that, "Other countries may dress windows, but Americans make Window Displays" (*Merchants Record and Show Window*, August 1920, 86). This research will crucially build upon this argument and explore how the American displayman's process of making in Chicago and New York distinguished his practice. This chapter's emphasis on these two cities at the turn of the twentieth century yields examination of show windows as well-funded sites of active design production.

Important studies of the American department store, including those by Susan Porter Benson and Jan Whitaker, have largely focused on the saleswomen and the profusion of goods that these women sold to the public (Benson 1986; Whitaker 2006; Whitaker 2011). Here, I will offer an alternative orientation towards the department store dealing with the "non-selling" staff, or the displaymen, and will explore those goods in the window that were not for sale: the fixtures and technologies invented specifically to enhance commercial display. I will begin by describing the architectural framework for the window as well as the professional development and role of the display staff in shaping this new advertising space. Drawing on examples from guidebooks, trade literature, and reports in the popular press, an evaluation of the fabrication of the window display will prove how the public perceived the show window as a celebration of both careful handcraftsmanship and mechanical innovation.

View from the sidewalk

Didactic literature on display touted the show window as "the merchant's closest connecting link with the public" (Terry 1882, 11) and advised that it should aim to halt consumers' rhythms of walking and looking as they moved through crowded streets (Fig. 7.1). The corner of State and Madison Streets in Chicago was known as "the busiest corner in the world" as it was shared by Mandel Brothers, Carson Pirie Scott and the Boston Store and thus dominated by those stores' show windows (*Souvenir of Chicago in Colors* 1908, 57). Expanses of plate glass delineated the department store at street level. The windows registered the energy on the streets and reflected contemporary events while at the same time focusing the attention of the crowd inward and onto the store's merchandize. This storefront space was built and then designed for an audience.

The position and size of show windows became priorities and symbolized progress in the construction of a department store. The ideal was to obtain an "island site,"

Figure 7.1 People looking into a Marshall Field & Co. department store window, 1910.
Source: Courtesy Chicago History Museum, DN-0008625; Chicago Daily News

an entire city block with entrances and plate glass on all sides (Dennis 2008, 302). As of 1902, Marshall Field's had achieved this with a total of 65 windows around all four sides of their building (Twyman 1954, 152). When Lord & Taylor built a new "business palace" of iron and glass on the corner of Broadway and Twentieth street in New York in 1870, the press reported that, "Among the first things which attract attention, are the plate glass windows on Broadway, eight in number, each one seven feet wide and sixteen feet in height," with the additional detail that "the corner on Broadway and Twentieth street is cut off diagonally, giving an excellent opportunity for a show window looking toward the North-east" (*Christian Union* October 1870, 2).[1]

Stores reinforced the significance of their windows by featuring them in illustrated advertisements, and including statistics on their quantity and quality in promotional literature. Consumers thus became acquainted with the scale and appearance of the storefront through the store's publicity; then the display decorated the façade and further helped the consumer to identify one store from the next. Advice in the 1921 guidebook *Selling Service with the Goods* proves the importance of display for store recognition:

> Never change the window display on Monday or Tuesday. Experience has shown that many people who see show windows Saturday evening and Sundays very often go out on Monday or Tuesday to buy something that attracted them when seen. If the windows are changed, they may be unable to locate the store, and hence a sale is lost. Thursday or Friday is a better day to change the windows.
>
> (Woodward and Fredericks 1921, 128)

This advice detects not only consumers' close attention to window arrangements but also their use of display style as a memory aid to organize their shopping experience. The displays served as signposts to aid pedestrian shoppers' navigation of urban shopping districts.

Growth of a new profession

In 1902 *New York Times* reported that "of the mechanical, routine workers there is large supply" to help the department store operate at a vast scale, while the specialist employees working in display roles were few. The journalist identified that, "While there is room in every department of the stores and retail houses generally for talent and knowledge, a lack of properly equipped workers is felt in the spheres of window dressing, decorating of interiors, card-sign painting, and advertisement writing" (*New York Times* 1902, 29). Although the role of sales assistant had long been attainable through an established training program, the field of display required a new hybrid understanding of art and commerce, whose prerequisites were just beginning to be defined. But by the turn of the century, those working in display distinguished themselves in the store's complex operation and were acknowledged as particularly valuable to a store's advertising and monetary success.

Window dressing earned recognition as a vocation due to the development of professional organizations, an education system comprised of both in-store training and independent schools and classes, and a literature of its own in which window dressers documented and shared their skills.[2] In 1898, L. Frank Baum formed the National Association of Window Trimmers, which became the International Association of Displaymen in 1914. The organization's first annual meeting was held in Chicago in August 1898 and, by 1900, it had members in almost every American state (Sherman 1900, 10). Guidebooks outlined the strategies and construction techniques necessary for eye-catching assemblages behind glass that would earn these men ascendancy and sizeable compensation within the department store structure. Many of the authors of these texts, including Frank L. Carr and Herman Frankenthal, were well-known inside the industry through their leadership roles and delivery of public lectures, but their names were not more widely recognized or publicized.

The window dresser's primary tasks were to amplify the presentation approaches for routine objects as well as to develop creative ways to introduce new goods. Everyday commodities such as handkerchiefs and spools of thread became building blocks for images of geometric patterns, flowers, bridges, and more, as will be described later. Unconventionality was imperative to the display's appeal. Author George Cole explained that the consumer's "attention must be secured first by some feature with which he is *unfamiliar*" (Cole 1892, 473).

The window's advertising advantage lay in its directness and ability to offer "an object lesson which conveys at one glance more ideas than many columns of a newspaper description" (Cole 1892, 469). The show window trained consumers to examine merchandize visually and without the aid of a salesman; instead, the work of the window dresser, the display itself, facilitated the sale. Endowed with this agency, the show window was considered the "most formidable equipped salesman of the store's selling force" (*Merchants Record and Show Window* July 1920, 37). By 1920, *Merchants Record and Show Window* reported that "frequently do merchants estimate window sales, or sales influenced by displays in show windows, at better than 60 percent, as many merchants have no hesitancy in crediting 75 or 80 percent of total business to the influence of goods displays" (*Merchants Record and Show Window* July 1920, 19).

Show window assembly

As John Wanamaker stated, "There is an outer life of the store with which the public is made familiar by daily contact, and there is an inner life of which the public has scarcely any conception, yet which deserves to be noted as indicating the higher plane to which modern merchandising is advancing" (Wanamaker 1899). In addition to the preparation and shipping of packages, the bookkeeping and mail-order managing, the building of the show window display accounted for an important act of labor concealed within the department store. While many of the goods that consumers encountered on the sales floor were alienated from their place of manufacture, their reconfiguration and transformation into commodities on display occurred on site. This work of the window dresser was dynamic and diverse and required physical strength in addition to an artistic eye. As *The Show Window* advised, "To be worthy of the splendid title, 'professional window trimmer,' I think one ought to master the following trades: architect, carpenter, electrician, plumber, sign writer and scenic painter" (Rompel 1899, 87).

In a section on the window dresser's "property room and workshop," the 1905 textbook *Miscellaneous Merchandise* advised:

> As much of the work as possible should be done in sections, which are fitted and trimmed in the shop and then put together at the place of display, thus minimizing the amount of work that must be done where the business of selling is being carried on [...] By this method elaborate decorations appear and disappear in a night, much to the bewilderment and interest of the general public, thus adding considerable impressiveness and consequent advertising value to the decorations.
>
> (International Textbook Company 1905, 18–20)

The constant invention and reinvention of the window display was the show window's greatest attraction and, at the same time, its greatest logistical challenge. Holidays and sales and store openings offered many possible pretexts for changeover that cultivated a reliable consumer market. Window dressers' calendars filled with as many as weekly holidays appeared in guidebooks and periodicals (*The Show Window* January 1899, 52).

The quickened pace of merchandizing prompted the development of technical devices to facilitate the swift changeover of window display. Patented systems of pulleys and platforms were invented to smooth the assembly of the display in the basement and its subsequent upward movement to ground level. H. Hunter's "Show Window Construction" (Fig. 7.2) was one such advanced system. In his patent description, Hunter cited the current challenges faced by the window dresser, including "limited space" to do the assembly work at storefront level and "loss of the window" if the dressing was done behind blinds or curtains during the day (Hunter 1902). In order to overcome these issues, Hunter's invention moved the entire contents of the show window via a "fixture-carrying floor" that rested on a platform that could be raised and lowered from the basement. A description of the 1914 opening of Lord & Taylor in New York included mention of such show windows "constructed with movable floors" that "can be lowered to the mezzanine basement and rolled off on tracks" (*New York Times* February 25, 1914, 6). The popular press's attention to these construction details suggests a fascination with this "inner life" of the store that significantly drew consumers' attention towards the production process of display.

Not all stores, however, could afford expensive and efficient mechanical systems that hid the assembly action from public view. When it was necessary to assemble the window display during the day, "open window dressing" could serve as good advertisement for business. As window dresser A.W. Jungblut described in *The Show Window* in 1899:

> As soon as I have the construction plans laid and the window looking neat and clean, I remove the curtains and begin the work of arranging the goods. All passers by are interested, and it not infrequently happens that the very goods I am using are in demand [...] there is a natural curiosity as to what will be done next, and goods unfolded and artistically arranged in view of the passers by, attract more than ordinary attention.
>
> (Jungblut August 1899, 77)

No. 709,985.

H. HUNTER.
SHOW WINDOW CONSTRUCTION.
(Application filed Nov. 4, 1901.)

Patented Sept. 30, 1902.

(No Model.)

2 Sheets—Sheet 1.

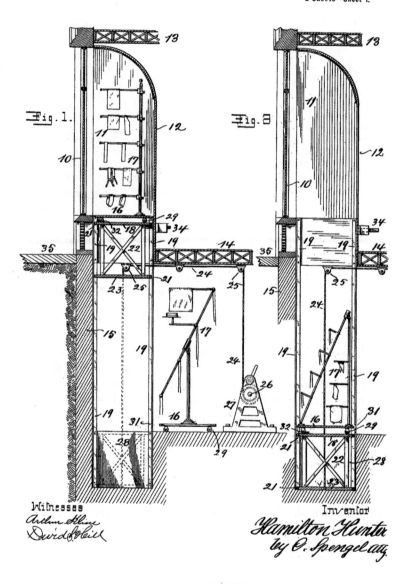

Figure 7.2 Hamilton Hunter, "Show Window Construction," U.S. Patent No. 709, 985, filed November 4, 1901, issued September 30, 1902.
Source: Courtesy US Patent and Trademark Office

WIDE-AWAKE WINDOW DRESSING—DRY GOODS ECONOMIST.—p. 316.

Figure 7.3 "Norwich Nickel and Brass Works 'Perfection Fixtures' for All Departments,"
in Frank L. Carr, *The Wide-Awake Window Dresser* (New York: Dry Goods
Economist, 1894), 316.
Source: Courtesy Winterthur Library: Printed Book and Periodical Collection

In this case, the show window's formation became public entertainment. Passers-by
would have gained an appreciation for the manual skills of the window dresser as
well as the time, creativity, and specialist tools necessary to compose the final product.

A supportive undercarriage of fixtures often helped to determine the display's
arrangement and made it possible to fill the window's entire dimensions. For instance,
in Figure 7.1, tall, flexible stands hold white goods in a tree-like formation in the
foreground and, in the far window, racks bring order to rows of diamond-shaped
handkerchiefs. Manufacturers such as Norwich Nickel & Brass Works (Fig. 7.3)
devised fixtures specifically suited for commodity categories. When, in 1889, the New
York newspaper *The Evening World* visited the window dressing department of J.
Lichtenstein & Sons, their description featured examples of the window dresser's
myriad tools and accessories:

> There is a work-room in the depths of the sub-cellar, where the carpenters build
> all sorts of devices – mechanical, automatic, and otherwise. There are forms,
> frames, pedestals, racks, lattices, arbors, wire work, wheels, balls, cones, cubes,
> hexagons, and what not; and here the 'bottom idea' of the window artist begins
> to take form.
>
> *(The Evening World* December 13, 1889, 5)

Shopfitting firms advertised that the savvy use of their products to create this "bottom
idea" could be directly responsible for increased sales. For instance, in a July 1920

advertisement, Hugh Lyons & Company boasted: "Make your windows business builders [...] Concentrate the attention of shoppers on particular groups. Hugh Lyons fixtures will help to make your windows more profitable – make buyers out of passersby" (*Merchants Record and Show Window* July 1920, 2). Fixtures made the window display more readable for the consumer while also offering the opportunity for more complex but still organized arrangements.

Artistic handcraftsmanship

Accomplished window dressers had a command of textile properties to best style the vast stock of department stores' dry goods by hand and in conjunction with fixtures. As *The Show Window* pointed out, "The simple display of a blot of goods is an advertisement, but a weak one. How much more effective that same piece of goods would become if spread out, or draped, or made into some shape that would mean something, create a mental picture, and leave an impression on the memory" (*The Show Window* August 1898, 67). Window display guidebooks were often organized by textile type, implying that textiles should be handled and arranged appropriately to suit their properties.[3] Cotton goods, the most pliable of textiles, could be easily folded and layered into assemblages. One textbook clarified that, "Perhaps no other article of merchandize is capable of a greater variety of decorative folds, forms, or designs than the handkerchief" (International Correspondence Schools 1903, 1). The textbook proceeded to illustrate step-by-step folding instructions for fan folds, triangular puffs, leaf folds, and many more iterations (Fig. 7.4). A strong illustration of the visual impact of such handkerchief folding techniques can be seen in Mr. E. Katz's work in the window of the leading Brooklyn department store Abraham & Straus (Fig. 7.5). This display's ambitious design won it a reproduction in L. Frank Baum's *The Art of Decorating Dry Goods Windows and Interiors* in 1900 (Baum 1900, 87).

In December of 1889, the New York newspaper *The Evening World* ran a window display contest that attracted the participation of the city's greatest dry goods stores. Under the headline "Art In Window-Dressing: How the Famous Displays in Show Windows are Designed: Talks with Men at the Head of the Profession," the article pictured six named window dressers with brief descriptions of their gold medal-worthy windows (*The Evening World* 1889, 5). The windows' descriptions prove a direct link between prescription and practice in window dressing since these men chose display designs prominently featured in contemporary guidebooks. The first winner mentioned was Sam J. Besthoff of J. Lichtenstein & Sons, with his "fourteen plate-glass windows, with more than one hundred and fifty feet frontage" where "the goods [handkerchiefs] are deftly arranged into the form of plants and flowers" (Cole 1892, 334). Patrick H. McMahon at Simpson, Crawford & Simpson planned a handkerchief arrangement of "over one thousand dozen fine handkerchiefs [...] arranged in gothic arches." The article went on to describe how "Mr. McMahon's forte is in producing artistic effects with merchandise alone, unaided by lay figures or mechanical devices." The author also pointed out that McMahon's "Brooklyn Bridge" composed of spools and textiles, and his "Capitol at Washington" built out of linens and towelings were famous the previous winter (Cole 1892, 530).

While spools, towelings and handkerchiefs may not seem like the most eye-catching merchandize to fill a window, the window dresser turned these familiar wares into something unfamiliar: he used standard stock to form plants and flowers, gothic

Figure 7.4 Handkerchief folding instructions, in *A Textbook on Mercantile Decoration* (Scranton, PA: International Textbook Company, 1903), Section 28, 27, figs. 48 and 49.
Source: Courtesy Hagley Museum and Library

arches, the Brooklyn Bridge, or Washington's Capitol building. Although made by hand, these dramatic displays can be interpreted as commenting on industrialization. They expressed the same symbolism of abundance as the crop art and commodity pictures created at contemporaneous world's fairs (Simpson 2012, 85–111). For instance, retail expert Nathaniel C. Fowler Jr suggested that handkerchiefs could be "built into pillars, arranged in cones, or an immense heap of handkerchiefs can be shown [...] to represent bulk, as characteristic of the size of the handkerchief business" (Fowler 1893, 430). The multitude of handkerchiefs communicated the strength of the textile industry, and the department store's command of global trade since many of the handkerchiefs were likely imported.[4] These contests positioned the window display as a symbol of progress, exemplifying the reputation of the retail establishment. Such competitions also notably showcased the hand skills of the window dressers and their clever use of fixtures, thus feeding consumer interest in how the displays were fabricated.

Further, many female shoppers arrived at the show window with a personal knowledge of textile properties and clothing construction and therefore would have admired the display staff's adept handling of fabric. When selling piece goods, window dressers

Figure 7.5 Abraham & Straus storefront, c. 1895.
Source: Early Brooklyn and Long Island Photograph Collection, ARC 201, Brooklyn Historical Society

imitated the work of the dressmaker. In addition to the use of a mannequin or dress form, they carefully draped textiles over plinths and blocks so as to give an idea of how the fabric would fall on the body. The material was borrowed from the textile departments and it was expected that it be returned unharmed. One window dresser elaborated on his textile "trials" for the *New York Tribune* in 1910: "The saleswoman hands me a roll of silk and tells me she wants a princess dress, a seven-gored skirt, or any old thing, and I must produce the desired effect without even cutting the goods" (Donehower 1910, 14). Patented formulas were developed to aid the draper in producing pleasing visual effects while preserving the dry goods stock. For instance, R.F. Downey's "Method and Apparatus for Draping Dummies from an Uncut Length of Cloth" (patented April 30, 1912) instructed the window dresser in how to drape an uncut length of cloth upon a dummy to produce the effect of a completed garment or suit (Downey 1912). The window dresser used these particular draping techniques to make a sale while simultaneously encouraging shoppers' recognition of his bespoke craftsmanship.

Mechanisms and movement

While Patrick H. McMahon at Simpson, Crawford & Simpson proudly worked "unaided by ... mechanical devices," by the turn of the twentieth century, window displays were increasingly animated with motorized components that stimulated consumer enthusiasm. Rotating stands and revolving mannequins created a kinetic environment for otherwise static objects, while mechanical animals and figures added animation to display scenes. In 1899, The Window Motor Co. advertised that "by the occasional use of something that is full of life and motion, the particular window where it is seen will be well fixed in the minds of the people and the ordinary display will receive their attention because they are constantly looking for something new" (*The Show Window* January 1899, 56). As this advertisement suggests, even the singular use of a motor impressed upon a consumer that the window was worth returning to again.

The use of up-to-date technology earned a store a position of prominence in public opinion. Ehrich Brothers' presentation of a three-ring Dolls' Circus in 1881 was likely the earliest use of an animated window by a New York City department store (Bird 2007, 23). In 1883 Macy's added "mechanical fascination" to their Christmas windows, using steam power to turn dolls and toys into "moving figures" (Schmidt 1995, 161). By 1925, Macy's mechanical experiments had advanced to a "fantastical animated spectacle" made up of "twenty-six stirring scenes with hundreds of marionette actors in a continuous performance" (*New York Evening Journal,* November 25, 1925) that played on a six-minute loop.

Rotating display devices afforded the practical benefit of being able to show merchandize in the round. In 1876, A. Fischer patented a "Revolving Show Stand" with a rotating bottom tier "partly for steadying the rotation of the stand, and partly to attract the attention of passers-by to the mechanism and to the contents of the show-window" (Fischer 1876). Here the patent copy spells out an awareness of public fascination with visible mechanics and movement. The motor was not encased in the device but left exposed so that the public could watch it at work.

Mechanization's largest draw was built upon the mystery of its operation. As Charles Tracy observed, people "will always stop to examine anything that moves" and "will enjoy studying out the mechanism or wondering how the effect has been obtained" (Tracy 1909, 101). The popular mechanical animals by the New York display studio of Messmore and Damon, founded in 1917, stupefied the public when they appeared in department store windows and at world's fairs (Fig. 7.6). In 1927, *Cas Logic: A Magazine of Enlightenment and Progress* reported:

> Here you will find Christmas department store traffic and sidewalk shoppers knotted about a huge elephant, who sways his great bulk from one foot to another, lifts his giant trunk into the air, flaps his ears and switches his tail; a lion who bares his teeth, rolls his eyes and emits fierce roars; and reindeer, who toss their antlered ears, prance and jingle their sleigh bells. And the audience, fascinated and awed, is wondering orally 'what makes the thing work, anyway'?
> (*Cas Logic: A Magazine of Enlightenment and Progress* December 1927, 7)

As this description suggests, mechanical windows successfully drew crowds who were curious about the operation of their visual effects. But, in order to operate as a successful advertisement, the window had to meet its primary goal of selling goods. As L. Frank Baum advised, "It is very true that life or motion in a window attracts more attention than anything else. But judgment must be exercised as to what degree and class of animation you employ." He urged that attention must be

Figure 7.6 Harold G. Messmore demonstrating animated papier-mâché figures in his firm's showroom, c. 1925.
Source: William L. Bird Holidays on Display Collection, Archives Center, National Museum of American History, Smithsonian Institution

attracted "to some purpose;" in other words, to secure a sale (*The Show Window* November 1897, 25).

Conclusion

Department store show windows promoted rapid technological and stylistic change that signaled new attitudes towards the significance and necessity of ephemeral display for a successful retail business. The temporary nature of the overall visual arrangement aimed to match the rapid turnover of many of the individual wares on offer. In order to transform passers-by into consumers, to turn the "desire to possess" into the "will to have," the window dresser had at his disposal an increasing number of published methods and newly invented tools (*Merchants Record and Show Window* July 1920, 37). The more frequent the displays, the more the opportunities for the window dresser to execute fresh designs, experiment with technologies, and earn a reputation for himself and for his business. As such, the show window was a dynamic site of production in which window dressers rearticulated goods and experimented with modern devices. At the turn of the twentieth century consumers became increasingly attuned to the production value of the window display, evaluating the construction and visual impact of one store's show window presentation against another. The originality and complexity of this visual advertisement, as well as the skill and technology that made it possible, persuaded customers to not only purchase merchandize but to marvel at how that merchandize was presented and promoted.

Notes

1 The creative use of the ample space in this corner window earned it recognition and illustration in guidebooks for years to come (Taft 1926, 194–95, 246).
2 Wanamaker founded an internal Commercial Institute as a "business academy or preparatory school," as well as the American University of Trade and Applied Commerce that helped adult employees in the "knowledge and skill of their store occupations" (Purinton 1920, 416).
3 "Silks, arranged in puff form, make a finer display than in any other manner. Brocaded silks and velvets of medium and large pattern show handsomely in long cornucopia shape" was the guidance in "Window Dressing" (*The Chicago Dry Goods Reporter* 1886, 2).
4 For instance, "At Field's you may see handkerchiefs that have fluttered down from all over the world, in thousands of styles. We send several buyers abroad every year just for handkerchiefs. From France they bring a myriad of exquisite novelties. From Ireland [...] they take the output of an entire factory, made to our designs" (*Chicago Daily Tribune* October 11, 1927).

References

"Animated Windows." 1897. *The Show Window*, November: 25.
"Art In Window-Dressing." 1889. *The Evening World*, December 13: 5.
Baum, L. Frank. 1900. *The Art of Decorating Dry Goods Windows and Interiors*. Chicago: Show Window Pub. Co.
Benson, Susan P. 1986. *Counter Cultures: Saleswomen, Managers, and Customers in American Department Stores, 1890–1940*. Urbana: University of Illinois Press.
Bird, William L. 2007. *Holidays on Display*. Washington, D.C.: Smithsonian Institution, National Museum of American History.
Cole, George S. 1892. *A Complete Dictionary of Dry Goods and History of Silk, Cotton, Linen, Wool and Other Fibrous Substances...* Chicago: W.B. Conkey Co.
Davis, O. Wallace. 1920. "The Merchant's Magic Mirrors." *Merchants Record and Show Window*, August: 86.
Dennis, Richard. 2008. *Cities in Modernity: Representations and Productions of Metropolitan Space, 1840–1930*. Cambridge: Cambridge University Press.
Donehower, E. 1910. "A Window Dresser's Trials." *New-York Tribune*, January 23: 14.
Downey, R.F. 1912. "Method and Apparatus for Draping Dummies from an Uncut Length of Cloth," U.S. Patent 1,024, 927, April 30.
"Drapes for Convention Delegates." 1920. *Merchants Record and Show Window*, August: 62–63.
"Even So Simple a Thing as a Handkerchief." 1927. *Chicago Daily Tribune*, October 11. Federated Department Stores' records of Marshall Field & Company, Chicago History Museum, Scrapbook 1852–1928 (14189).
Fischer, A. 1876. "Revolving Show Stand," U.S. Patent 184, 362, November 14.
Fowler, Nathaniel C. 1893. *Building Business: An Illustrated Manual for Aggressive Business Men*. Boston: The Trade Co.

"The Greatest Selling Factor." *Merchants Record and Show Window*, July 1920: 19.

"The Hidden Machinery of a Big Department Store." 1911. *New York Times*, November 12, SM3.

Hugh Lyons & Company Advertisement. 1920. *Merchants Record and Show Window*, July: 2.

Hunter, H. 1902. "Show Window Construction," U.S. Patent No. 709, 985, September 30.

"Hunting Big Game for Christmas." 1927. *Cas Logic: A Magazine of Enlightenment and Progress*, December: 7. Messmore & Damon Company Records, 1892–1998, Archives Center, Smithsonian National Museum of American History. Gift of Pamela Messmore Tobiason (Box 6, Folder 4).

Iarocci, Louisa. 2013. *Visual Merchandising: The Image of Selling*. Burlington, VT: Ashgate.

International Textbook Company. 1903. *A Textbook on Mercantile Decoration*. Scranton, PA: International Textbook Co.

———. 1905. *Miscellaneous Merchandise; Decorations; Collection of Artistic Displays; Illumination and Motion in Displays; Fixtures and Useful Information; Ideas for Window Decorations*. Scranton, PA: International Textbook Co.

Jungblut, A.W. 1899. "Open Window Trimming A Good Advertisement for Your Firm." *The Show Window*, August: 77.

Leach, William. 1993. *Land of Desire: Merchants, Power, and the Rise of a New American Culture*. New York: Pantheon Books.

"Lord and Taylor Opening." 1914. *New York Times*, February 25: 6.

"Macy's Big Christmas Parade" Advertisement. 1925. *New York Evening Journal*, November 25. Messmore & Damon Company Records, 1892–1998, Archives Center, Smithsonian National Museum of American History. Gift of Pamela Messmore Tobiason (Box 6, Folder 4).

Marcus, Leonard. 1978. *The American Store Window*. New York: Whitney Library of Design.

"Marshall Field and Company." 1902. *Chicago Dry Goods Reporter*, October 11. Federated Department Stores' records of Marshall Field & Company, Chicago History Museum, 03052 (24).

"Modern Interiors." 1898. *The Show Window*, August: 67.

"The New Building of Lord and Taylor." 1870. *Christian Union* (Reprint from the *New-York Tribune*), October 1: 2 and 13.

"New School for Store Workers." 1902. *New York Times*, October 5: 29.

"No More 'Window Trimmers.'" 1915. *New York Times*, August 1: 86.

"Notes from New York." 1914. *Merchants Record and Show Window*, July: 28.

"Notion and Novelty Windows." 1920. *Merchants Record and Show Window*, July: 37.

"Our European Correspondent." 1898. *The Show Window*, February: 85.

"Pictorial Value of Window Display." 1920. *Merchants Record and Show Window*, August: 86.

Purinton, Edward Earle. 1920. "Master Workshops of America: The Store with the Right Idea." *The Independent*, June: 19–26, 388–89 and 412–417.

Rompel, John G. 1899. "The Trimmer of Today." *The Show Window*, August: 87.

Schmidt, Leigh Eric. 1995. *Consumer Rites: The Buying & Selling of American Holidays*. Princeton, N.J.: Princeton University Press.

Sherman, Sidney A. 1900. "Advertising in the United States." *Publications of the American Statistical Association* 7, 52: 1–44.

"The Show Window." 1897. *The Show Window*, November: 17.

Simpson, Pamela H. 2012. *Corn Palaces and Butter Queens: A History of Crop Art and Dairy Sculpture*. Minneapolis: University of Minnesota Press.

Siry, Joseph. 1988. *Carson Pirie Scott: Louis Sullivan and the Chicago Department Store*. Chicago: University of Chicago Press.

Souvenir of Chicago in Colors. 1908. Chicago: V.O. Hammon Pub. Co.

Taft, William Nelson. 1926. *The Handbook of Window Display*. New York: McGraw-Hill Book Company, Inc.

Terry, Samuel Hough. 1882. *How to Keep a Store: Embodying the conclusions of thirty years' experience in merchandizing*. New York: Fowler & Wells.

"The Trimmer's Calendar." 1899. *The Show Window*, January: 52.

Tracy, Charles A. 1909. *The Art of Decorating Show Windows and Interiors: A Complete Manual of Window Trimming*. Chicago: The Merchants Record Company.

Twyman, Robert W. 1954. *History of Marshall Field & Co., 1852–1906*. Philadelphia: University of Pennsylvania Press.

Wanamaker, John. 1899. *Annals of the Wanamaker System: Its Origin, Its Principles, Its Methods, and Its Development in This & Other Cities*. Philadelphia: The Company.

Whitaker, Jan. 2006. *Service and Style: How the American Department Store Fashioned the Middle Class*. New York: St. Martin's Press.

———. 2011. *The Department Store: History, Design, Display*. London: Thames & Hudson.

"Window Dressing in Big Stores: An Art Which Enlists Services of Men of Taste." 1902. *New York Times*, October 19: 27.

The Window Motor Co. 1899. Advertisement. *The Show Window*, January: 56.

"Women Window Dressers." 1898. *The Show Window*, April: 151.

Woodward, Warren Olmstead and George A. Fredericks. 1921. *Selling Service with the Goods*. New York: James A. McCann Co.

8 Drawing power

Show window display design in the USA, 1900s–1930s

Margaret Maile Petty

Introduction: Merchandizing with light

As a primary means of communicating consumer messages to the public and enticing customers into the retail environment, the show window became the focus of attention in the United States in the late nineteenth century, reaching a peak of interest during the 1920s and 1930s. In this period the show window transitioned from a means of displaying merchandize inventories to a site of theatrical invention, consumer spectacle, and artistic expression. The development of the show window as a frame and stage for display design was driven by a number of factors, including the emergence of an independent profession of window display designers, the appropriation of modern stagecraft techniques and technologies, and focused attention on show window lighting from the electric industry and the newly defined field of illuminating engineering. While the history of the development of show window display design in the USA necessarily embraces all of these factors and others, this chapter gives pride of place to electric lighting, bringing it to the fore as both a medium of and conduit for modern design. Although arguably one of the most important technologies of modern display design, electric light is all but absent in contemporary scholarship. Addressing this omission without marginalizing other key factors, this chapter positions electric light as an important point of connection between the disparate forces shaping the development of modern display design methods, between window displays and consumers, and between the avant-garde and the masses. Looking broadly at the "drawing power" of electric light, this chapter explores the ideas, beliefs, practices, and objectives that shaped both its uses and meanings, arguing for its significance within the history of modern architectures and cultures of display in the USA during the first third of the twentieth century.

Widely heralded as a powerful and flexible tool to communicate the character and quality of the business and goods on display, to attract and focus viewer attention, and, most importantly, to transform passers-by into customers, electric lighting was a central technology in the development of show window display design. Among the many benefits attributed to electric lighting from very early on was its capacity to capture and direct consumer interest, making it a particularly attractive technology for savvy retailers. Discussion of the importance of integrating electric lighting into retail window displays, and advice regarding the use of new techniques and applications was prominent in both popular and trade media throughout the 1920s and 1930s, when interest in show window design was surging more generally. At this time, individuals leading reform efforts focused on the modernization of theater and scenic design were similarly exploring the expressive and emotive potential of electric lighting, helping to drive new theories and approaches to its use. Likewise architects and artists seeking to define Modernism within the American context also took great interest in electric lighting as a medium and mechanism for creating new architectures of light ("Lighting by Design" 1934; Cheney and Cheney 1936, 199–201). Nowhere was such enthusiasm more prevalent than in the retail sector, which eagerly embraced the breadth of these influences.

By the 1920s, the use of electric lighting in retail display strategies was already being linked to greatly improved customer "drawing power" and increased sales. Writing for *Nation's Business* in 1925, Roy Palmer summarized the findings of a number of studies investigating the positive financial effects of better and increased electric lighting in retail environments. He suggested its widespread adoption could have national significance:

> When the true value of good store lighting begins to be appreciated the thousands of poorly lighted stores will be bathed in an abundance of soft, diffuse light. The retailer, like the industrial executive will then realize the influence of light upon the business of the nation.
>
> (Palmer 1925, 42)

Albeit with more obvious self-interest, General Electric similarly advised its retail customers in 1926:

> The shop window is too full of profit-producing possibilities for the employment of light as a subordinate item. It must be an integral part of the display, as without it display is useless [...] It is a magnetic force in the sales-endeavor more important than the display on which it is focused.
>
> ("The GeCoRay System" 1926, n.p.)

The general rule of thumb was that the more lighting applied, the greater the sales. As early as the 1920s, electric light was popularly associated with modern, scientific approaches to merchandizing and retail display design, and with quantitative and qualitative results. Alongside growing recognition of electric light as a powerful and highly controllable merchandizing tool was simultaneous and equal interest in the emotive and expressive potential of light, which fueled experimentation with lighting techniques adapted from theater stagecraft to show window illumination. Across both popular and industry discourse from the period, one finds a commercially motivated synthesis of scientific and theatrical approaches to electric lighting in the formation of new approaches to retail and show window display merchandizing. Exploring both threads – their intersections as well as their divergences – this chapter demonstrates the formative role of electric illumination in both the theories and methods of show window display design coincident with the emergence of a "culture of desire" in the USA during the first third of the twentieth century (Leach 1993).

The origins of the profession of show window display design

To appreciate the rapid transformation of retail and show window display design between the turn of the century and the 1930s, and the formative role of electric lighting in the modernization of merchandizing practices in the USA, it is helpful

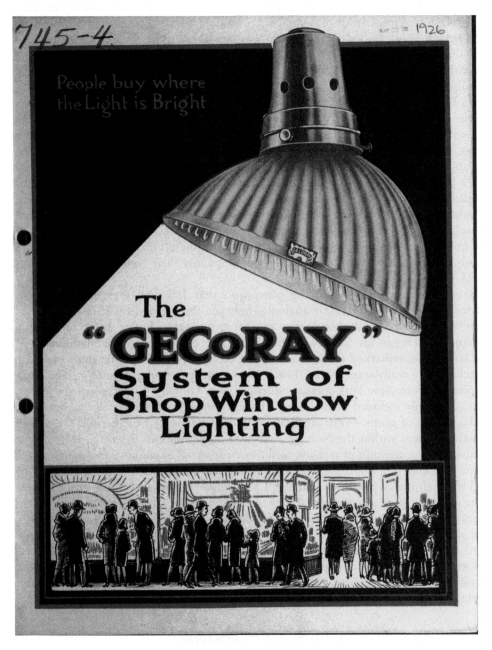

Figure 8.1 Advertisement for "The GeCoRay System of Shop Window Lighting," 1926 (London: The General Electric Co., LTD).

to look briefly at the core principles of retail display design as set forth by the first generation of American display designers. Among the discipline's early innovators was Lyman Frank Baum, better known as the author of the classic children's story *The Wizard of Oz*. Baum contributed much to the establishment and development of the culture and profession of American retail display design. In addition to starting the discipline's first professional journal, *The Show Window*, which began circulation in 1897, Baum also founded the National Association of Window Trimmers in 1898. Before beginning his career in display design, however, Baum had spent a number of years working in the theater, writing, producing, and performing in his own plays. These early experiences were important influences on the development of his approach to window display design, and therefore that of the discipline. In the 1899 publication *The Art of Decorating Dry Goods Windows and Interiors* Baum scolded merchants who allowed goods to just "sit there," suggesting instead that they should make every effort to bring their merchandize to life, like actors on the stage (Leach 1993, 55–61). Throughout his many publications, Baum repeatedly stressed the importance of showmanship in any merchandizing effort, arguing that how the goods were presented to the public directly impacted their "selling" power (Leach 1993, 60).

Baum's contemporaries and the generation that followed him offered similar advice, and by the early 1900s analogies between theater and retail display design were a familiar trope. Arthur Fraser, another turn-of-the-century American display designer, who began his career with the Chicago department store Marshall Field's in the late 1890s, remarked of his work during this period: "We would dramatize our merchandise – really stage work" (Leach 1993, 69). Fraser, who claimed to take great inspiration from New York stage productions, was known for his theatrical displays that commonly included painted scenic backgrounds, furniture, lifelike mannequins and a variety of props – very much like popular stage sets of the period. The scenic design practices within the New York theater community in the early 1900s were focused on the creation of realistic scenic environments to support a visual and aesthetic harmony – in the realist tradition – between the dramatic content of the play and the performers. Fraser was among a progressive group of window dressers who were adapting such stagecraft practices to show window display design in the early years of the twentieth century. The expanding architecture of the show window in this period further encouraged such experimentation, as store windows were deepened and widened, taking on a more prominent role within American retail districts. Taking advantage of the confluence of these factors, Fraser quickly became known for arresting displays that presented consumer goods within message-oriented, stage-like settings aimed at triggering consumer desire (Leach 1993, 69).

The introduction of electric light and the emergence of illuminating engineering

Shortly after the turn of the twentieth century, at roughly the same time as Fraser was becoming well known for his window displays, the young discipline of illuminating engineering turned its attention to show window lighting. A nascent industry, electric lighting had only become feasible as a source of predictable illumination less than 30 years earlier. Even after Thomas Edison's incandescent light bulb was patented in 1879, there was still the necessary matter of determining how these lights would be powered and from where, resulting in a fierce battle between Edison, George Westinghouse, and others to secure the best advantage in terms of the distribution of electric power and light (Friedel, Israel, and Finn 1986; Jonnes 2004). It would take until the turn of the century for these fundamental issues to be resolved, after which a highly competitive commercial environment quickly took shape for all those invested or engaged in the distribution, sale, planning and use of artificial illumination. Out of this turmoil also emerged a group of like-minded professionals from a range of backgrounds, including electrical engineering, manufacturing, local utilities, and government, who came together to support "the advancement and dissemination of theoretical and practical knowledge of the Science and Art of Illumination" (DiLaura 2006, 19). This group formally organized in 1906 as the Illuminating Engineering Society (IES), dedicating its efforts to nurturing the young discipline, providing a forum for the discussion, and supporting the development of new research, theories, and applications of electric lighting – one area of which was show window illumination (DiLaura 2006, 89).

Lessons of the stage: Show window displays lit for profit

As highly visible spaces ripe for experimentation, show windows provided illuminating engineers with an opportunity to bring together the art and science of lighting. In terms of lighting technology, during the first two decades of the century illuminating engineers were exploring both gas and electric light applications and effects, and it was far from given that electric light would replace gas. But regardless of what type of illumination was being employed, enthusiasm for its impact on the show window was consistently high. As Leon Gaster, editor of the British journal *Illuminating Engineer,* observed in 1909: "There is, perhaps, scarcely any field where the principles of illuminating engineering can be more profitably employed" (Gaster 1909, 867). Gaster lamented the persistence of poor lighting in show windows despite such financial and economic promise, and in particular the alarmingly frequent instances of glare that had the unfortunate effect of blinding passers-by. Such glare, caused by the use of unshielded light sources, was exacerbated by the popular but false belief that the brighter the light, the greater the power of its attraction. As Gaster described:

> The use of bright lights has been defended on the ground that it is necessary to be lavish in this respect to attract customers. Excessive glare may, indeed attract the eye involuntarily, but it is questionable whether anything is gained thereby, as the observer naturally tends to advert his gaze from anything actually distressing.
>
> (Gaster 1909, 868)

In summary, Gaster offered readers some simple advice, calling attention to the benefits of successfully integrating theatrical lighting techniques and the usefulness of such strategies in avoiding unwanted, detrimental glare: "The most successful methods of shop lighting seem to be those in which the lessons of the stage are taken to heart, abundant light being shed upon the goods while the actual sources themselves are screened from the eye of the observer" (Gaster 1909, 875). Proposing modern scenic design techniques as models for good display illumination, Gaster called upon an emerging but growing discourse closely tying the framed proscenium-like space of the show window to that of the modern stage.

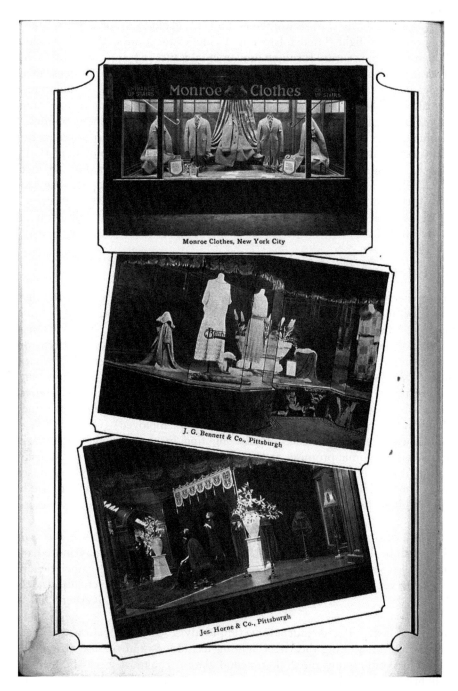

Figure 8.2 Show window design and lighting in keeping with the notion of the "stage," as illustrated in "Show Window Lighting," 1924 (Pittsburgh, PA: Pittsburgh Reflector Company).

Source: Accessed March 3, 2017, https://archive.org/details/ShowWindowLighting

Pointing to a number of American shop windows as exemplars of new retail display techniques, Gaster proposed that in the USA "a tasteful shop-window" was one "devoted to novel and specially interesting goods, so that passers-by may come to regard its contents, not as a catalog, but as a summary of the most recent developments." Popular sentiment, he argued, was turning against the more traditional approach to show window design wherein the display was regarded as an inventory, as complete as possible, of all goods in stock. In such a scenario, he explained, it was expected that a potential customer would pause on the street in order to "make up his mind what he wants by inspection of the window, enter and ask for this article." This approach crowded the window display area, making effective lighting all but impossible to achieve. However, by editing the display and focusing the lighting on select goods of particular interest or visual pleasure, retailers could aim to draw passers-by into their establishments regardless of whether or not they intended to buy a particular object in the window. Rather, the curious passer-by whose interest had been stimulated by the attractively designed and lit display would enter the shop willingly and would "be prepared to entertain suggestions and assistance from the shopman on the subject of what he needs" (Gaster 1909, 876).

While the successful displays described and illustrated in Gaster's article all utilized gas lighting technology, within in a few years electric lighting would eclipse such flame-based illumination sources. When electric lighting was first introduced in the late 1870s, gas lighting was an established and widespread illumination technology with more than a hundred years of development. After the turn of the century, electric light quickly gained popularity as the electric industry relentless exerted pressure through its growing control of the market (Nye 1999; Reich 1992). In these years, the rapid infrastructural development of electricity distribution networks facilitated the quick cannibalization of much of the existing market for gas illumination. Enthusiastic speculation about the potential of electric light and praise for its particular properties and characteristics grew simultaneously. J.G. Henninger captured this excitement in the 1912 *Transactions of the Illuminating Engineering Society*, suggesting the potential electric of light for display: "With the inception of the incandescent lamp there opened a hitherto unrealized, perchance unthought field, both of illumination and display" (Henninger 1912, 178–211). Noting the fortuitousness of the development of electric lighting in relationship to the burgeoning consumer culture of American cities, Henninger linked new approaches to display illumination to an increasing visual literacy among the public in regards to reading the retail environment. He proposed that passers-by could easily judge both the quality of a store and the goods on display based solely upon the aesthetic appearance, merchandize arrangement, and illumination of the show window.

Calling upon the example of jewelers' windows, Henninger described how their displays frequently were dressed with careful attention to background materials, spare arrangements, and sufficiently bright but well-diffused lighting. A window so arranged and illuminated, he reported, gave an overall impression of quality. On the other hand, he described an alternative approach wherein merchants put as many items into the show window as possible, "piled closely together," and illuminated under a "blaze of light." The general effect of the latter, he argued, suggested to passers-by that the store was "open for business with big value for little money." In both scenarios, the merchants were able to communicate to potential customers clearly and readily the character and quality of the store and its merchandize through artificial lighting strategies.

In Henninger's article and other contemporary sources, the drawing power of the show window and its capacity to communicate such value structures was directly correlated to the design and illumination of the display. So convinced of this relationship and the clarity with which such strategies communicated to potential customers, Henninger posited that, "Never before in the history of commerce has the show window occupied the place of prominence that it occupies today" (Henninger 1912, 210).

All too often, however, merchants aimed for maximum efficiency with minimal cost when determining show window illumination solutions. Proposing what he believed a more holistic and profitable strategy, Henninger advised store managers to approach the design and illumination of show windows with the outlook of a theatrical stage director. If the aim was to turn passers-by into customers, then the visual *effect* of the total design was of greatest importance – not the efficiency of the lighting. He wrote:

> Show windows are built for the express purpose of impressing upon prospective customers the value of the wares on display [...] If the stage manager bothered himself a great deal about the amount of energy required for a certain scenic effect, he would probably have few "effects," but he realizes that the "effect" is the all important thing, not the energy he uses to get that effect.
>
> (Henninger 1912, 197)

Offering an example of a show window with just such a superior effect, he described the lighting system of a Cleveland retailer. Flanking outwards towards the street, the show windows created a welcoming "v" that converged at the store's entrance. In keeping with the displays techniques of "quality" stores, the show windows were dressed with a sparing use of merchandize, suggesting superior goods and inviting passers-by to take a closer look. Such inspection was facilitated by bright, softly diffused light emitted from the luminous panels that formed the ceiling plane of the show windows. The luminous ceiling of each window was comprised of individual panels, behind each of which was a recessed rectangular cavity painted flat white and containing a 40-watt frosted tungsten lamp. Seen from the sidewalk, the panels appeared as a flush, continuous luminous surface and provided flattering, glare-free, shadowless light for the goods on display (Henninger 1912, 196). Such novel applications of electric light were also being explored by others outside of the retail context, most notably the Swiss stagecraft designer Adolphe Appia's use of a similar architecturally integrated lighting effects in the *Festspielhaus* constructed for the German garden city of Hellerau near Dresden in 1911–1912. Here Appia created an entirely luminous volume, using back-lit walls and ceiling as a means of creating a visually and spatially unified context for dramatic performance and experience (DeMichelis 1990).

The economy and psychology of light and color in show window displays

The rapid innovation of electric lighting applications in the first two decades of the twentieth century was fueled by the electric industry's investment in research and development. In this period, lighting applications for display illumination formed a core area of research at the Edison Lamp Works in Nela Park, General Electric's industrial campus located outside of Cleveland, Ohio. Established in 1913 following the consolidation of the National Electric Lamp Company with General Electric, the 40-acre campus housed GE's research facilities and lamp works. Matthew Luckiesh, Director of the Nela Park Lighting Research Laboratory and a respected voice on new applications of electric light, published the handbook *Light and Color in Advertising and Merchandising* in 1923, including recommendations regarding "The Show-window," "Displays," and "Stores" (Luckiesh 1923). In keeping with other advocates of modern electric lighting for show windows, Luckiesh stressed the enormous financial potential of the show window for retailers. Unlike other advertising mediums, he argued, the show window presented passersby with "the finger-print of the store," communicating the "atmosphere" of the shop and offering the "welcoming hand of the merchandiser" (1923, 151). Drawing upon evidence from "extensive investigations," Luckiesh asserted that sales increases had been found to follow greater intensities of illumination within show windows (1923, 154–155). He attributed these gains to the relative "drawing power" of the show window, arguing that they could be correlated precisely with the intensity of illumination. Calculating the annual lighting costs and predicted profits based on the drawing power factor, Luckiesh proposed that an annual expenditure of $70 for electric lighting could result in approximately $15,000 in profits (1923, 155–156).

Beyond the bottom line, Luckiesh also described the aesthetic potential of electric lighting for show window design, outlining several principles fundamental to any successful installation. First among his recommendations was the concealment of light sources, a factor of particular significance given the popular association of indirect lighting with quality goods and retailers. As he reasoned, "The progress toward concealing light-sources has been so great that at the present time the mark of a quality store is generally the absence of glaring light-sources." In addition, he recommended adapting powerful spotlights, reflectors, and other lighting applications from the theater for display illumination, suggesting that, "the expressiveness of light can be utilized as effectively [for the retail display] as it is on the theatrical stage." With flourish Luckiesh summarized: "All the expressiveness, impressiveness, and symbolism, in fact, all the possibilities of the psychology of light and color are available at the present time to the display-man through the aid of modern lighting equipment" (1923, 159–169).

In describing the show window as a "miniature stage" and advising the implementation of a host of theatrical lighting effects, Luckiesh was building upon the core principles of display design set forth by the first generation of American window dressers at the turn of the twentieth century, particularly in terms of dramatizing commercial messages (Leach 1993, 39–69). Drawing upon the much greater range of effects and visual conditions possible with modern electric illumination, Luckiesh encouraged the development of lighting strategies and techniques borrowed from theater. At this time, stagecraft reformers such as Appia in Europe, Edward Gordon Craig in England, and Robert Edmond Jones in the USA were exploring the capacity of electric light to visually link disparate objects in a given composition while psychically drawing the viewer into the scene. Directing both the visual and dramatic apperception of the viewer was central to their efforts, and the ideas and techniques they advanced quickly influenced allied design disciplines such as retail and show window design. In period discourse addressing window display design, modern stagecraft techniques were frequently invoked and held up as equally useful for the retail environment. The show window, like the stage, needed to successfully convey an idea, a mood, or relationships between things convincingly to passers-by who, like theater-goers, were held at a distance from the production.

The popular press focused more closely on the siren-like potential of show windows when illuminated with modern electric lighting. An article appearing in the *San Francisco Chronicle* in 1920, authored under the delightful pseudonym "Lady Electra", described the display window as a critical first point of contact for retail businesses: "Just as surely as people are judged by appearances and by first impressions, so are the personalities of stores and shops impressed upon their perspective customer through the show window" (Electra 1920). Describing the benefits of utilizing a range of "artistic" effects in display design, Lady Electra proposed that the invisibility of the source of such artistry made it all the more convincing and engaging for passers-by:

> Lighting plays a most important part in the artistic effects gained by display artists [...] because it is mostly out of sight, it is unnoticed by a large number of people who do not take the effort to analyze the ways and means of gaining the pleasing effects.
>
> (Electra 1920)

Lady Electra also described in some detail a number of lighting techniques that had proven effective in window displays, including mirrored troughs set just beyond the line of sight, the use of angled reflectors to distribute and diffuse lighting, and colored lighting to enhance contrasts. She also stressed that such lighting techniques should not be used solely for the evening hours. Because of the increasingly larger expanses of glass enclosing show windows, powerful electric lighting was necessary to counter daylight reflections on the spectral surface of the glass plate, which otherwise would obscure the view of the goods on display. When properly illuminated with electric light, such as to control reflections, minimize glare, and highlight the goods on display, Electra stated that well-designed show window displays could communicate a variety of characteristics such as "reliability, permanence, and dignity" or "dainty charm." Urging businesses to invest in good lighting, she argued that the "extra expense is more than compensated for in the artistic effect and correct impression of the character of the establishment which the man in the street gains from the window displays"(Electra 1920). In this simple proposition, the retailer having communicated the right impression was rewarded with new consumer business. Lady Electra justified these claims by offering anecdotal accounts of several retailers that experienced dramatic increases in sales after updating their show window displays with new or expanded electric lighting applications.

Such advice and information was disseminated across a variety of media in the 1920s. A few months after Lady Electra's column, *The Hartford Courant* published a short article reporting on a talk about new retail and window display lighting techniques. A.L. Powell, an illuminating engineer at the Edison Lamp Works, had given the talk, and the event was reportedly well attended by both "electricians and merchants" ("Mr. Powell Tells of Illumination" 1920). Offering a range of practical information and technical advice about the types of lamps suitable for different kinds of retail environments, Powell singled out window display lighting as of "great importance," suggesting that the use of colored lighting applications would become increasingly essential for successful retailers. Calling upon the familiar analogy between the show window and the theatrical stage, Powell cast display designers in an important role: "The window is a miniature stage, and the display man is the stage manager" ("Mr. Powell Tells of Illumination" 1920).

Modern art for the masses

While such advice linking retail show window design to theatrical stage craft was common in this period, the influence of Modernism was similarly prominent within display design. Walter Rendell Storey, reporting in 1928 for the *New York Times*, described a range of new, modern show window displays produced by New York City's leading department stores (Friedman 2003). Storey began by reminding readers that the primary role of the show window was "to evoke in the mind of the passer-by attention-arresting thoughts, and then to present suggestive and informing messages, emphasizing the worth of the objects arranged on view" (1928). While this objective had driven the design of show window displays since their inception, Storey suggested that it was the means through which these messages were being conveyed that was changing under the influence of Modernism. He described the use of a range of "distorted geometrical forms, painted surfaces, and metal accents" to evoke specific associations with the machine age, writing: "Suitcases and sports costumes have backgrounds symbolizing this age of the automobile, the great steamship, the railway train, the winging plane." Indicative of the formal ambiguity of many elements of these displays, Storey claimed difficulty in articulating some of the abstract forms utilized for his readers, "because even well-known geometric symbols have been distorted and deformed to make a foil for milady's furs or frocks." Such Cubist-inspired elements were further supplemented by "backgrounds that decoratively suggest the forms and materials of engineering, architecture and machinery." Finally harmonizing this modern scene, the display designers utilized electric lighting applications adapted from the theater, achieving a "subtle dramatization of form and color" through a range of lighting effects (Storey 1928). Furthermore, display designers in the late teens and early 1920s were in step with contemporary stagecraft practices in their rejection of painted scenery in favor of stylized and abstracted modern settings that incorporated new materials, geometric motifs, and specialized lighting applications and focused effects.

Featuring "strange forms," new materials, and dramatic visual effects, modern window displays provided retailers with more than just shock value to stop pedestrians in their tracks. Such installations, Storey argued, had a way of "suggesting to the passer-by that the goods shown are up to date." The modern backgrounds, props, materials and lighting conveyed a message of glamorous modernity. As Storey noted, "The shop window is creating a new form of art expression before our eyes" (1928). Austrian émigré Frederick Kiesler and Donald Deskey, the two designers whose work was featured in Storey's article, were closely associated with the popularization of the machine age modernism in the United States during this period. While both of these men were active in several areas during the later 1920s and 1930s, including interior design, exhibition design, and industrial design, Kiesler in particular demonstrated an unusual interest in commercial display design, as Laura McGuire explores more fully in her chapter in this volume and in related studies (McGuire 2007, 45–78).

One of his more prominent commissions from the period, Kiesler's show window display designs for the Saks Fifth Avenue department store in New York City were published in a five-page article in *Architectural Record* in September of 1930. The feature was primarily comprised of photographs of Kiesler's shop windows, closely cropped such as to appear as individual stage-like settings with no external context except for the small Saks & Company plaque located on the bottom mullion of the window and the slimmest suggestion of the full-height curtains framing the windows. The only text accompanying the article – which was essentially a photo essay – besides the credit caption was a pragmatic statement of purpose: "Window display contributes to the selling of merchandise. Goods and the architectural setting are coordinated, illustrating the close tie-up between selling and display" ("Shop Window Displays" 1930, 215–219). The show window displays illustrated in the article featured characteristic modern elements such as flat backgrounds, a notable absence of decorative patterning, dramatic angular elements, geometric forms, and minimal clutter. Each window featured a single mannequin – reduced to a torso and select accessories, such as a handbag and a pair of shoes – and a lightly articulated side table, desk, or object upon which merchandize might be placed. Kiesler added interest and depth to these otherwise flat spaces and backgrounds with the arrangement of highlights and shadows. Spot lit from above, Kiesler's headless mannequins appeared to advance towards the viewer as progressively deepening shadows emphasized and dramatized this effect.

In *Contemporary Art Applied to the Store and its Display*, published the same year as the *Architectural Record* feature, Kiesler argued for the potential of display design to serve as a medium for synthesizing modern art, technology, and stagecraft within a context highly accessible for the masses, suggesting that it held great promise both as an agent for increased sales as well as for the dissemination of modern art. Throughout the book's four parts and twenty chapters, electric lighting appears as a key consideration, forming the primary subject of two chapters. Describing the role of lighting in effective display design, Kiesler wrote: "The display manager has to paint the picture for the public. His canvas is space, his pigments merchandise and decoration, his brushes, light and shadow" (Kiesler 1930, 102).

Describing specific lighting effects well-suited to window display design, Kiesler proposed a number of innovative applications, including lighting concealed in window borders to create "aura frames" that brought attention to the goods on display and formed "attractive rhythms of light" along the facade of the building. He also described other novel applications to "focus attention on the entrance or the windows," such as the use of glass panels inset into the sidewalk and illuminated from below" (Kiesler 1930, 103). Anticipating the rapid development of commercial lighting technologies, he predicted that, "with the immense increase in the use of lighting effects which is a certainty of the show window of the future, the ceiling inherits a more important role: that of concealer for equipment, flood light systems, reflector attachments, etc." More than just masking lighting hardware, he proposed that the ceiling itself could also be utilized as a lighting control. Essentially describing a luminous ceiling like that used nearly two decades earlier in the Cleveland show windows described by Henninger, Kiesler suggested employing "Viscoloid, glass or transparent materials" for the ceiling so as to produce "an even light diffuse over the entire display" (1930, 109).

Echoing Luckiesh and others, Kiesler made the connection to avant-garde stagecraft design explicit in his recommendations for window displays: "Looking through the glass into the show window is really like looking at the stage – with this difference: the actors, in art terms, are speaking plastics in motion, whereas the merchandise is a silent, static object." In order to "dramatize" the merchandize, Kiesler proposed the use of cubical, three-dimensional masses that "permitted a greater play of light and shadow and afforded to the audience an entirely new feeling of space and volume" (1930, 110). His most extraordinary recommendation was for the use of moveable, semi-opaque panels, either with back lighting or projected lighting from the front, to produce a "color organ upon which to compose and execute [...] symphonies of light decoration." Wary of the potential of diluting the commercial message, however, Kiesler warned that the combined effect of such techniques presented a "very real danger" of distracting attention away from the merchandize, thereby usurping the primary aim of the show window (1930, 118).

Prophesying the future display window as a fusion of an automat and the theater, Kiesler argued that a personalizable design would create a closer connection between the consumer and the merchandize on display. The future "kinetic widow" display, as Kiesler described, would not only allow passers-by to "open and close windows at will," but also to "throw a stronger light at a given spot, should that be wanted" (1930, 110). Drawing together the techniques of display design and theater stagecraft, he suggested that "direct contact between such a display stage and the passerby has been anticipated by the newest stage direction where contact between actor and audience is sought" (Kiesler 1930, 110). Kiesler, who was involved with avant-garde theater and stage design throughout the 1920s and 1930s, had a keen understanding of the principles of the new stagecraft. His belief in the effectiveness of electric light as a unifying and communicative agent, able to minimize the division between actor and audience or commodities and consumers, was shared across these disciplines.

Conclusion: A creative synthesis

As a space and typology defined by spectacle, intended first and foremost as a means of attracting potential customers and communicating tailored commercial messages, the illumination of show windows performed several important roles: maintaining the transparency of the glass; establishing a visual hierarchy within the display; emphasizing or enhancing colors, textures, and forms; providing atmosphere; communicating the character of the store and the value of the goods on display; and, most importantly, eliciting consumer desire. In terms of experimentation, innovation, and popularization of new electric lighting technologies and applications in the USA, few if any periods in the history of electrification can match the 1920s and 1930s; certainly this is true in regards to the illumination of retail window displays. Multiple factors contributed to the growing prominence of electric light and the rapid development of innovative effects in this period, including the influence of Modernism and the introduction of new architectural forms, materials, and principles, and experimentation with new modes and forms of aesthetic expression in the creative arts. Such efforts were greatly aided by the cross-over between disciplines by key individuals, and fueled by the increasing demands of the United States' consumer-centric culture.

Electric lighting was well suited to both the ideology and aesthetics of Modernism in all its variations. In Modernist rhetoric and practice, electric lighting was largely transformed from a functional utility of visual acuity to a conduit for effects – emotive, atmospheric, architectural, and spatial. In these ways, electric light played a central role in the aestheticization of the built environment as well as in the renegotiation of the relationship between actor and audience, or object and subject, during the interwar period. The blurring of distinctions between lighting applications for the theater, residential interiors, exhibition design, and merchandize display is indicative of the broad enthusiasm for a particularly stylized visual environment in the USA. As the American consumer marketplace expanded, developing new sectors, products to sell, and consumers to convert, the aesthetic of desire needed constant innovation and amplification. The era's artists, designers, and engineers were quick to appreciate this opportunity, utilizing a broad and flexible palette afforded by electric light to experiment, explore, and enhance the architectures of display.

References

Cheney, Sheldon and Martha Cheney. 1936. *Art and the Machine.* New York: Whittlesey House.

DeMichelis, Marco. 1990. "Modernity and Reform: Heinrich Tessenow and the Institut Dalcroze at Hellerau." *Perspecta* 26: 143–170.

DiLaura, David L. 2006. *A History of Light and Lighting: In Celebration of the Centenary of the Illuminating Engineering Society of North America.* Illuminating Engineering Society of North America.

Electra, Lady. 1920. "Light Effects of Store Windows Aid Business Man." *San Francisco Chronicle*, May 9, F4.

Friedel, Robert D., Paul Israel, and Bernard S. Finn. 1986. *Edison's Electric Light: Biography of an Invention.* New Brunswick, N.J.: Rutgers University Press.

Friedman, Marilyn. 2003. *Selling Good Design: Promoting the Early Modern Interior.* New York: Rizzoli International Publications.

Jonnes, Jill. 2004. *Empires of Light: Edison, Tesla, Westinghouse, and the Race to Electrify the World.* New York: Random House Trade Paperbacks.

Gaster, Leon. 1909. "Modern methods of Artificial Illumination." *Journal of the Royal Society of Arts*, 107, 2964: 867–889.

"The GeCoRay System of Shop Window Lighting." 1926. London: The General Electric Co., LTD.

Henninger, J. G. 1912. "Show Window Lighting." *Transactions of the Illuminating Engineering Society* 7: 178–211. Accessed July 27, 2017: https://archive.org/stream/illuminatingengi07illu#page/178/mode/2up

Kiesler, Frederick. 1930. *Contemporary Art Applied to the Store and its Display.* New York: Brentano's.

Leach, William. 1993. *Land of Desire: Merchants, Power, and the Rise of a New American Culture.* New York: Pantheon Books.

"Lighting by Design." 1934. *Arts & Decoration* 42: 14–19.

Luckiesh, Matthew. 1923. *Light and Color in Advertising and Merchandising.* New York: D. Van Nostrand Company.

McGuire, M. Laura. 2007. "A Movie House in Space and Time: Frederick Kiesler's Film Arts Guild Cinema, New York, 1929." *Studies in the Decorative Arts* 14, 2: 45–78.

"Mr. Powell Tells of Illumination: store lighting is subject of engineer from Edison." 1920. *The Hartford Courant* 16, September 20.

Nye, David. 1999. *Consuming Power: A Social History of American Energies.* Cambridge, MA: MIT Press.

Palmer, Roy A. 1925. "Light—Citizen and Salesman." *Nations Business* 10: 42.

Reich, Leonard S. 1992. "Lighting the Path to Profit: GE's Control of the Electric Lamp Industry, 1892–1941." *Business History Review* 2: 305–334.

"Shop Window Displays: Saks and Company, New York City." 1930. *Architectural Record*, September: 215–219.

Storey, Walter Rendell. 1928. "New Modes Capture our Shop Windows." *New York Times*, April 29, SM9.

9 Automatic show windows

Frederick Kiesler's retail technology and American consumer culture

Laura McGuire

In the late 1920s, the Austrian émigré stage and exhibition designer Frederick Kiesler focused his attention on show window design and on theorizing the future of American department store display architecture. In 1930, several years after his arrival in New York City, he published an instructional book on modern retail display, *Contemporary Art Applied to the Store and Its Display*. In this text and in other essays on show windows, Kiesler laid out a vision of stores populated with robotic salespeople, subliminal films, automatic merchandize dispensers, and enormous television screens to wage aggressive, multimedia campaigns to woo potential buyers. He predicted that display managers would use these elements to create highly orchestrated environments in which shoppers would be left to contemplate their own desires by virtue of gadgetry and automation. The most poignant aspect of Kiesler's writings was his elucidation of the tension created by individual participatory experiences within a fully mechanized mass culture. His proposals for mechanical window and interior displays that would streamline the shopping experience promoted a vision that retail spaces could be democratically inclusive. Yet Kiesler also acknowledged that for certain retail clientele, exclusivity was a selling point. Consequently, he suggested theatrical lighting and staging concepts that would dramatize product individuality. Spotlights and sparsely decorated window sets emphasized the visual and physical separation between the spectator and the merchandize. His ideas for futuristic and theatrical retail display attempted to mediate a triad of raw individual desires, increasingly prevalent retail efforts to elicit predictable consumer responses, and the ultimately homogenizing effect of growing mass consumerism in the United States.

Kiesler had arrived in New York in 1926 as the designer and curator of the "International Theater Exposition," an important exhibition of avant-garde theatrical design at New York's Steinway Building. He soon transferred his expertise to the world of retail. At the Steinway, he had a significant hand in bringing renderings of International Constructivist and Futurist stage designs to an American audience. These had been mounted on an unorthodox system of rectilinear wooden scaffolds and pedestals meant to encourage visitor circulation and interaction with the works on display. Kiesler's arrival in New York was timely, as the popularity of a variety of modern display styles was increasing in the United States in the wake of the 1925 Paris Exposition of Modern Industrial and Decorative Arts. In May of 1927, Macy's department store sponsored the "Exposition of Art in Trade" in collaboration with the Metropolitan Museum of Art, one of the first shows in the United States devoted to contemporary industrial design and decoration. In the following months, Wanamaker and Lord & Taylor would emulate Macy's exposition with their own shows of new decorative fashions (Friedman 2003, 21–41; Frankl 2013, 84–85). The trend quickly developed into a source of promotional competition between rival stores as they attempted to capture consumer attention with daring forms of contemporary art and design, drawing not only on the modernized Classical arrangements and zig-zagging lines of popular French Art Deco, but eventually on the stripped, rectilinear forms of Constructivism and *Neue Sachlichkeit* functionalism (Schleif 2004, 131–149). As the decade waned, the surge towards modern art in retail display design grew more powerful. Seven separate articles in the January 1929 issue of *Display World* heralded designs with bold geometrical backgrounds, asymmetrical arrangements, abstracted mannequins, minimalist display furniture, and dramatic lighting as the future of the American show window, with guiding dispatches on cutting-edge European trends, including the 1928 "Window Display Exhibition" in Leipzig, Germany (*Display World* 1929, 3–4, 7, 10–11, 18, 20–21, 35–36, 42, 80).

After his "International Theater Exposition," Kiesler had remained largely unemployed until 1928, when Saks Fifth Avenue hired him to design their fourteen windows at the corner of 49th Street and Fifth Avenue (McGuire 2014, 129). The catalyst for this commission was most likely his colleague, the furniture designer Paul T. Frankl, a close friend of Saks' owner, Adam Gimbel (Long 2007, 83). Show window design was a new medium for Kiesler, but it was a natural evolution from his earlier work as a stage and exhibition designer in Berlin, Vienna, and Paris from 1923 to 1925. His stage designs for Karel Čapek's *R.U.R.* and B.F. Wedekind's *Francesca*, his installations for the 1924 Vienna "International Exhibition of New Theater Technique," and his "City in Space" display fixture for the 1925 Paris Exposition of Modern Industrial and Decorative Arts, had drawn from a variety of Modernist idioms, including Expressionism, Neoplasticism, and Russian Constructivism (McGuire 2014, 38–64). Kiesler's windows for Saks were similarly eclectic, and in the spirit of New Stagecraft ideas he envisioned them as flexible stage settings with simple furnishings that could be easily reconfigured to suit the display needs of any promotion. Backdrops of large geometrical panels joined several windows into an expanding composition across multiple panes (Fig. 9.1). Other windows appeared more contained, using dark backgrounds inset with simple mounted shadow boxes for framing individual items. One composition for ladies' dresses featured zig-zag ornamentation derived from popular modern idioms he had seen in Paris. His display furniture was decidedly restrained and evoked trends in German Modernist furniture design, with tables and pedestals comprised of horizontal profiles, dark woods, and simple forms of tubes and circles cut from metal and glass. He selected small numbers of items for each window and set them against mostly monochromatic backgrounds. In apparent contrast to the aesthetics of inclusion and interaction that had guided his efforts in theater, his minimalist arrangements of spotlit objects in a world of floating shapes behind a prominent frame and thick plate glass evoked exclusion and preciousness (McGuire 2014, 129–130).

One of the most arresting windows of the set featured a single black velvet coat and pair of gloves draped over a red-cushioned chair. (Fig. 9.2) Gray-colored back and side panels were sliced with dramatic angles and highlighted with reflective materials, recalling the Expressionist settings in Robert Wiene's film *The Cabinet of Dr. Caligari* (1920). Careful illumination and the relaxed forms of the coat and gloves on the red chair oriented most of the visual interest. In other windows, he used glass and metal cutouts as background embellishments to increase the play of

Figure 9.1 Frederick Kiesler, Display window for Saks Fifth Avenue, New York, 1928.
Source: Austrian Frederick and Lillian Kiesler Private Foundation, Vienna

depth and light around the merchandize. He also experimented with freely curving forms in polished aluminum. Backgrounds jutted outward towards the glass and then deftly receded out of the frame. This visual dynamism demarcated the onlooker's physical separation from the display scene while simultaneously focusing attention on the scene. The influential trade newspaper *Women's Wear Daily* praised the stage-like quality of his designs, noting that his settings created an illusion of depth that thrust the merchandize "into greater relief," like actors upon a stage (*Women's Wear Daily* 1928).

Kiesler's Saks designs were a relative novelty in the New York window design landscape. A handful of designers, such as Norman Bel Geddes, had already begun experimenting with using modern art styles and concepts in show windows. Bel Geddes' first 1928 windows for Franklin Simon captured simplicity and theatricality by reducing the number of different items on display and using color and lighting contrasts to emphasize details. However, Bel Geddes' early designs still relied on the kind of pictorial representation and realistic scenography that Kiesler's Saks windows would eschew (Kiesler 1930, 134). Kiesler kept abreast of display developments in France and Central Europe, and collected photographs of contemporary show window and shopfront designs. The formal simplicity of his windows may have had precedent in recent developments in German display design, such as Lily Reich and Mies van der Rohe's Silk and Velvet Café display of 1927. In his *Contemporary Art Applied to the Store and Its Display*, Kiesler would publish work by students at the Reimann School in Berlin, who were also producing novel displays with asymmetrical compositions and theatrical lighting. Reimann students frequently used the products themselves as

Figure 9.2 Frederick Kiesler, Display window for Saks Fifth Avenue, New York, 1928.
Source: Austrian Frederick and Lillian Kiesler Private Foundation, Vienna

the basis of the display architecture, in a kind of Constructivism composed of consumer goods (Schleif 2004, 44–46; Suga 2006, 140). Both Kiesler and students at the Reimann School drew on modern art and theater for their inspiration, and Kiesler's Saks windows were engaging compositions that demonstrated his mature understanding of stagecraft and audience response. His expanding and contracting backdrops and manipulations of light, shadow, and material lent a playful untouchability to the pricey fashions behind the vitrine – a persuasive technique for piquing consumer desire.

Hoping to capitalize on his commission, Kiesler spent much of 1928 and 1929 writing a book on retail display design, *The Modern Show Window and Storefront*. He conceived of the text as a practical guide to window design and storefront architecture that emphasized the use of modern art aesthetics as a sales strategy. An advance prospectus promised that it would offer comprehensive information on the contemporary arts and how they could be incorporated into a variety of display contexts for business. Renamed *Contemporary Art Applied to the Store and Its Display,* and released for mail-order in April 1930, the book was a vivid compendium of suggestions for retail managers, from the practical to the far-fetched. Kiesler articulated a pseudo-scientific system for display design that would have predictable psychological effects on potential buyers. His suggestions, he wrote, would fuse "the skill of the scientist, the engineer and the artist" to elicit "increased sales through display methods which exercise calculated psychological effects on customers," thereby harnessing "the principles of psychology to the wheels of industry" (Kiesler 1929). Kiesler left the precise nature of these principles unaddressed in the text, but his library and research materials evidence his longstanding interest in physiological psychology, among other approaches to understanding the human mind and behavior.

The first step in realizing such scientifically engineered displays would be to accept efficiency and economy as the basis of all modern design practice. Emphasizing that merchandize should be foregrounded over the display architecture itself, he suggested that display fixtures should be created in uncomplicated shapes using glass, metal, bakelite, machine-cut wood, and other industrially produced materials. He also recommended that techniques derived from progressive stage architecture be adapted to show windows, including mechanical revolving displays and settings on tracks with trapdoors in the floor that would allow new displays to be hoisted into position or hidden from view. These quick changes would help market merchandize to the various types of customers that frequented stores at different times during the day, without the added expense of a large staff of window dressers (Kiesler 1930, 101–106). The most economical tool of the contemporary retail designer was electric light, the flexibility of which window designers had recognized since the turn of the twentieth century (Schleif 2004, 32). Kiesler advocated concealed illumination, spotlighting particular objects, and "painting" with colored light. He also suggested that color schemes might have important psychological effects on purchase decisions (Kiesler 1930, 87). Lighting could be used architecturally around the frames of windows to project their effects into the street, and glass sidewalks illuminated from below could break the street's repetitive cadence and focus attention on displays and entrances (Kiesler 1930, 102–103, 116, 120).

Show windows might further capture visual attention if designers avoided compositional strategies of static symmetry with a single, central focus. Rather, it was *asymmetry* which was at the heart of "practically every modern creation in the arts" (Kiesler 1930, 107). To this end, Kiesler suggested that designers create visual rhythms by expanding or contracting sidewalls and ceilings at different angles, and by positioning merchandize in unexpected areas throughout the display. The suggestion of movement (or even actual kinesis via mechanically moving displays) would "direct the eye straight to the point you wish it directed" (Kiesler 1930, 106–107). His recent scenic and theater architecture designs (which had included film projection, dynamic spiral forms, rotating stages, and mechanically synchronized displays of music and lighting) emphasized kinetic moments of sustained connection between theatrical action and the consuming audience, and he seemed eager to transfer these ideas to the retail world. Theatrical methods of manipulating mental attention might also prove of tremendous practical value in marketing merchandize (McGuire 2014, 38–64, 89–91).

Contemporary Art Applied to the Store and Its Display also schooled readers on the basic principles of recent European avant-garde painting, sculpture, theater, and architecture. Pointing to these principles, Kiesler described how art, lighting, photographs, and machine reproduction might be utilized in display windows in order to attract and sustain consumer attention. He recommended that the design of backdrop patterns be drawn from the work of such artists as Theo van Doesburg, Hans Arp, and Fernand Léger, among others. Otherwise, the contemporary show window designer might use complete reproductions of recent avant-garde paintings or large photographic prints of local scenes of urban life. Invoking the spirit of Dada for American display practitioners, he suggested "composite" layered collage backgrounds comprised of all of these visual elements with unexpected cutout reveals (Kiesler 1930, 114–115). Kiesler also drew on his deep commitment to internationalism in art and architecture, devoting the first part of the book to the utopian virtues of the De Stijl movement, and abstraction. He presented his own renderings of storefronts and tubular steel furniture as characteristic examples for other window designers to emulate. These storefront drawings emphasized staggered volumes that would project into the physical or visual paths of passersby, placing objects in relief in three dimensions (Fig. 9.3). In setback plans for foyers, in which windows were stepped and angled inward toward the doorway, he pointed out that the storefront could also function as a semi-interior and manipulate consumer movements. Dazzled by the receding displays, unsuspecting shoppers would be funneled through a menagerie of glass, lights, and merchandize, and sucked unwittingly into the recessed front door (Kiesler 1930, 81, 102). With its emphasis on the intersections of mechanical efficiency, psychology, stagecraft, and retail display, Kiesler's idiosyncratic book did as much to show the diversity of his thoughts on art and design as to provide practical advice for the store display manager.

In the most radical, latter sections of the book, Kiesler laid bare his fascination with technology and gadgetry in the service of commerce. A project for a "Department Store on Fifth Avenue" was a massive, climate-controlled cubic volume, whose flat exterior walls and cantilevered floors would be composed entirely of a double layer of dark, opaque sheet glass, similar in principle to Le Corbusier's earlier concept for using a double-glazed "neutral wall" to circulate conditioned air (Kiesler 1930, 56; Braham 2005, 1, 3; Braham 1998, 10–11) (Fig. 9.4). The only breaks in the crystalline block would be the street-level window displays, which would form an uninterrupted band around the building, leading customers to the front door from all sides. A second architectural design was set on five large columns housing elevator shafts (Kiesler 1930, 57, 97). In order to entice shoppers to board the elevator and be lifted speedily to the wares housed above, the surface of each structural column was sheathed in glass to become a display window itself. In both of these cases, the street-level architecture was transformed into merchandize windows, while the rest of the building was reduced to a mute and monochromatic surface. Such a radical reformulation of the department store window had little precedent; related forms would not substantially infiltrate the American architectural vocabulary until after World War II (Longstreth 2010, 132–33, 154–158).

The show windows of these future department stores would be designed to promote more direct interaction with merchandize in order to stimulate desire. In contrast to his windows for Saks, Kiesler's proposals in *Contemporary Art Applied to the Store and Its Display* emphasized inclusiveness and interaction rather than exclusive

Figure 9.3 Frederick Kiesler, Illustration of a storefront, *Contemporary Art Applied to the Store and Its Display* (1930).

walls of glass. In the spirit of the popular automat, windows would be equipped with pushbutton systems that would allow a shopper to select merchandize to move it closer for scrutiny, shine lights on it for better visibility, reveal prices, hear recorded information, and then deposit money for direct purchase.[1] By offering a taste of ownership through a laboratory-like procedure of inspection, desire might be piqued even if the item's price rendered it inaccessible in reality. Moreover, furtive purchases could be made by depositing money into a machine without the hassle of registers, the writing out of sales slips, and waiting for wrapping and bagging. By fostering direct contact between passers-by and merchandize, Kiesler's machine automation would democratize shopping and diminish consumer alienation by allowing easier access to goods.

Enhancing his strategy to retain the shopper in a state of desirous contemplation, "sales robots" appearing on screens at sales counters inside the store would provide

Figure 9.4 Frederick Kiesler, Project for a department store on Fifth Avenue, c. 1928, *Contemporary Art Applied to the Store and Its Display* (1930).

information about products and reduce the need for retail clerks. Predicting the rise of the television commercial ten years in advance, Kiesler explained that robot sales films might give rise to a "special film industry [...] to produce motion pictures for promoting merchandise," or show films that appeared to be entertainment, but "with a subtle sales message." Retailers might "develop a steady store audience" by screening "films of the origin and history of merchandise. Fashion news. Daily events. A talking newspaper. Scientific productions. Even straight entertainment", giving merchandizers an opportunity to create "an institutional campaign on a larger scale" (Kiesler 1930, 120).

By 1930, the practical connection between film technology and retail was already entrenched. Fashion newsreels had become a genre popular in cinemas throughout the teens and the 1920s, but film was increasingly a part of the physical environment outside of the commercial theater. The 1923 introduction of 16mm film, coupled with the rise of home film screening, spurred the integration of film technology into the design of interior architectural spaces (Hanssen 2009, 107; Wasson 2009, 4). The urban department store had become a key point for the distribution of visual technology for domestic consumption. Parisian department stores had been screening films since the early 1900s, and, by the late 1920s, American stores like Macy's and Gimbel's had even integrated film rental libraries within their photography counters so that customers could rent or purchase films to watch in the privacy of their own living rooms (Wasson 2009, 7–8; Schwartz 1997, 178). Kiesler's idea to use merchandize films in store display followed naturally from the existent presence of film in some urban stores.

Kiesler's characterization of shoppers as an audience acknowledged that the recent media of radio and film had irrevocably dislocated his former area of expertise – the stage theater – from a position of dominance in American cultural life. To this end, he envisioned the department store as a modern entertainment venue akin to the cinema, but one that would rely even more heavily on the new medium of television. Kiesler believed that the adaptability of television could answer advertising and promotion problems inexpensively, and he predicted that the eventual "perfection of television, whose functionings will embrace and fuse all the dramatic arts through mechanical means" would be the next logical development in the design of show windows" (Kiesler 1930, 112–113). Although a degree of dynamism could be emphasized through asymmetrical composition and moving mechanical platforms, moving images captured the pace of contemporary life with more authenticity and persuasive power.

As suggested earlier, Kiesler's interest in television was timely. Just two years before he wrote *Contemporary Art*, journalists had gathered to witness the first public demonstration of long distance television in the United States (*Literary Digest* 1927, 7). He speculated that televised images could be transmitted across plate-glass screens on a building's surface, flashing fashion information to potential consumers. In a monumentalization of the modern technological age, show windows could act as points of reception in a vast ocean of signals being transmitted across the airwaves, and broadcasting organizations could offer syndicated architectural "tele-decoration services" to all retailers (Kiesler 1930, 120–121). His vision of a network of department stores linked by television broadcasts followed immediately on the heels of the national mania for radio. The number of radio sets in American homes had more than tripled in the four years since Kiesler's arrival in the United States, and the increase coincided with the establishment of 90 new radio stations over the same period (Field 2006, 4–1027).

Yet Kiesler's interest in new media was more oriented towards architecture itself. In a 1931 essay published in *Advertising Arts* magazine, he explored how television show windows could be used to fully reconceptualize department store typologies. Reiterating the show window television screen plan from his book, he now called for the total elimination of the conventional exterior display window. Because of heavy street crowds and automobile traffic, shoppers' visual connectivity with external displays was like an "electric circuit" that had been shorted out. Television screens would replace the exterior show windows, which would then be "inverted" to the inside perimeter of the store (Fig. 9.5). The number of entrance doorways would be increased along otherwise opaque walls, which would create a strong visual division from regular street traffic. The interior sales floor would be arranged in a series of wide avenues around display cases and sales counters, and the inverted show windows would flank elevators, displaying merchandize available on the sales floors above. Within this protected consumer space, window shoppers could relax, "unmolested" by roving pedestrians outside (Kiesler 1931, 37). They would also not be "bothered by sales people", who would be carefully "confined by their counters to the center of the store." Moreover, his store would provide chairs for lounging, music, and refreshments, while simultaneously emphasizing "privacy" and "individuality" (Kiesler, "Window Shopping," 1941).

Figure 9.5 Frederick Kiesler, Department store with television screens, c. 1930, ink and photo reproductions on board.
Source: Austrian Frederick and Lillian Kiesler Private Foundation, Vienna

The juxtaposition of external television screens with an internally focused arrangement for the sales area expressed his acute awareness of how architecture could be used to mediate sensation. A dynamic exterior of television screens would magnify the commotion of hurrying street crowds. Yet at the same time, television was a remotely produced medium that ultimately isolated the onlooker with his or her own thoughts. The interior show windows emphasized a more leisurely pace and made it possible for patrons to shop alone in quiet contemplation. Consumption in Kiesler's hypothesized department store would become an introverted experience in which the individual could assert his or her own desires within the landscape of retail products and services. The physical structure and operation of the building would recede into the background, overshadowed by the key moments of encounter between consumers and their coveted objects. Although in its preliminary stages, the concept was typologically akin to the shopping mall that would be inaugurated some 25 years later.

Kiesler's automated, technological vision for the future of shopping was symptomatic of recent developments in American culture. Writing on the importance of technology to life in twentieth-century American history, historian Walter Leuchtenberg called the first two decades of the twentieth century in the USA a "second industrial revolution" and a period in which the collective American mind was decidedly oriented towards the idea that the products of technology and applied social science would eventually meet the vast majority of daily human needs and desires (Leuchtenberg 1958, 178–179, 221–222; May 1956, 408; Douglas 1995, 187–193). Advancements in manufacturing, electrification, commercial product availability, and rising standards of living seemed to bear this out: from 1900 to 1929, manufacturing output climbed 264% and industrial production as a whole nearly doubled from 1921 to 1929 (Leuchtenberg 1958, 179). Whereas in 1912 only 16% of the population had electric lights at home, that number had jumped to 63% by 1927 (U.S. Department of Commerce 1929, 275). This enormous growth in production and electrification foregrounded machines in American life with a remarkable rapidity, and modern technology in its myriad forms – from radio to affordable automobiles and home appliances – became available for personal use seemingly overnight. The presence of these industrially manufactured products transformed American visual and material environments on all scales.

Kiesler's ideas also linked with a growing discourse among many American designers that a union of technology and commerce might offer a solution to the social problems of the Great Depression. In the early years of the downturn, the centrality of mechanization to American self-conception and future outlooks played a role in design discourses in New York City. For example, the concept of "consumer engineering", developed by New York designers Roy Sheldon and Egmont Arens in their 1932 book of the same name, suggested that the fundamental solution to American economic woes was to dramatically increase consumption of commercial products through improvements in fashionable styling and manufacturing (Sheldon and Arens 1932). Using pseudo-scientific rhetoric to describe their proposal to engineer America into a nation of consumers, Sheldon and Arens argued that designers could help the country buy itself out of the Depression. Another of Kiesler's friends, the theater and architecture critic Sheldon Cheney, proposed an even more utopian view of a future run by machines in his 1930 *The New World Architecture*: "There will ultimately be machine-developed energy to solve all men's work problems, with no more labor than is involved in passing control. The elements themselves will be tamed, weather tempered, transportation becomes effortless, cleanliness universal, the works of intellectual and of the artistic faculties will be transported instantaneously to all" (Cheney 1930, 75). Complimenting Cheney's premonitions of a utopian machine age, the pages of the 1931 *Annual of American Design*, produced by the American Union of Decorative Artists and Craftsmen, were filled with pronouncements that the future of architecture, interior design, and product styling lay with machine production and the ability of the designer to deftly merge beauty with technical efficiency (American Union of Decorative Artists and Craftsmen 1931).

Kiesler's concepts for automatic retail environments ostensibly increased the consumer's agency to navigate within his or her own private sphere of shopping and buying activities. But not everyone was convinced that mechanization was a panacea.

Critics like Lewis Mumford warned of cultural debasement through standardization, and the growing genre of science fiction reflected public anxiety about the potential subordination of humans to machines (Mumford 1931, 10; Fanning 2010, 253). But Kiesler was enthusiastic that the use of new technology in shopping would massage individual aspirations and promote psychological excitement.

Although Kiesler's basic goal – promoting technology in design in order to improve individual service – was relatively clear cut, his ultimate goals in *Contemporary Art* were more ambiguous. By opening the text with a pointed call for international Modernism and following it with sales advice for the store display manager, he simultaneously seemed to advocate both commercialism and utopianism. His implicit message was that, by meeting the routine needs of the retailer, Modernism would also pave the way for social progress: the "language" of the Modernist store window "appeals to everybody and has proved to be the most successful Esperanto for promoting merchandise," he contended. At the same time, he proposed the development of an egalitarian, floating city that would "invent new life [...] make possible the diversity of private life and the freedom of the masses," and in which "streets of huddled cubes will be resolved into free living and working areas" (Kiesler 1930, 9, 48–49). Kiesler took the conflicted position that the use of modern art practices in commerce would somehow offset the more unpleasant aspects of consumer capitalism by improving the shopping experience for all. He sought resolution between retailers' predatory attempts to stimulate imitation of aspirational fashion and his own idealist attitude that individuals could defy the standardizing forces of a technological sales apparatus by harnessing that same apparatus to live more efficiently and privately. His position strikes the contemporary reader as naïve at best. At worst, it comes across as an attempt to manipulate customers with glowing images and glittering gizmos into impulsively dropping their hard-earned money into selling machines in order to be united with the latest desirable (and probably unnecessary) fashions on the other side of the glass.

Yet for Kiesler, the resolution of this tension, between consumer manipulation and the maintenance of individual autonomy, lay in the effective design of the department store and show windows themselves. By building interactive access to products and services into the architecture of the retail environment, Kiesler felt that technology could break through the exclusionary glass of the show window, grant immediate visual access to fashion information from across the globe, and give consumers the freedom to exercise their own power – as well as mechanical and electrical power at their fingertips – in their shopping choices. Today's internet shopping – the contemporary apex of the private shopping experience in which products are shipped to our doors with the click of a mouse and without the physical encumbrances of travel to stores and interaction with shop clerks – is a profound distillation of the type of consumption that Kiesler's automatic department store predicted.

Kiesler's heroic tone throughout *Contemporary Art Applied to the Store and Its Display* represented an exceptionally uncritical position on consumerism for someone of his socialist political sympathies during the 1920s and 1930s. A subtle but lingering uncertainty about the broad ethical implications of his own recommendations tinged the generally positive tone of his text. While he contended that there was no form of Modernism that could not advantageously be applied to commerce (even the more extreme forms of Dadaism, for example), he wondered whether such uses would actually benefit artists. It was a question that clearly disturbed him and that he could not answer (Kiesler 1930, 115). He continued to grapple with his ambivalence about window design well into 1931. In an unpublished draft of "Window Shopping in 1941," titled "Merchandise that Puts You on the Spot, Some Notes on Show Windows" and probably written in April or May of 1931, he lamented the effects of retailers' visual bombardment on the already over-taxed nerves of the urban pedestrian:

> Swarming morning crowds; impetuous lines in lunch rooms. That weary hour before dinner. Our evenings, after the theatre, have you watched the throng moving like a black stream, coherent one to the other? A single mass of emigrants in the land of sorrows and unloved labor (habit convicted labor) gazing straight into the million lights of advertising with eyes that no longer react.
>
> (Kiesler, "Merchandise that Puts You on the Spot")

The only way to attract anyone's attention anymore, he wrote acerbically, would be to create a centrally organized jury of merchants to inspect the attire of people on the street. Those whose clothes were found lacking would be compelled into stockrooms supplying standardized uniforms: "That would be modern, truly modern, not modernistic. Speed. Co-operation. Efficiency," he remarked sarcastically (Kiesler, "Merchandise that Puts You on the Spot"). In May 1931, he gave an interview to Lewis Sherwin of the *New York Evening Post* in which he explained that all his recent work on retail display had "threatened" him with "having to spend the rest of his career designing show windows," which "he emphatically and promptly declined" (Sherwin 1931). He would not accept another retail commission until 1933, when he undertook the interior design for the Modernage Furniture Company store and built the "Space House," a model home showroom to showcase Modernage's products (McGuire 2014, 209–252). Approximately one year later, he completed the storefront redesign for a small shoe store in Buffalo, New York for the brother of his close friend, Sidney Janis (*Buffalo Courier-Express* 1935). But his interest in retail design appears to have ceased after completing these projects.

The vigor with which Kiesler had initially delved into the medium of show windows can mostly be explained by his wider goal to promote his vision of technologically efficient Modernism to an American audience. As design historian Jeffrey Meikle has noted, prominent designers of the 1930s attempted to balance commercial goals of efficiency and increased sales with raising the bar for aesthetic standards nationally (Meikle 1985, 15). Collectively, they viewed the various form languages of modern design and mass production as civilizing forces in America. After the 1929 stock market crash, designers writing for *Advertising Arts* magazine made idealistic assertions that integrating the virtues of avant-garde modern art into consumer products would improve both living and working conditions (Stote 1930, 52; Horwitt 1930, 8). *Advertising Arts* contributors overwhelmingly judged the redefinition of aesthetic beauty as something that resulted from the machine-finished edge, and believed the rationalized symbol to be a core feature of ongoing social and economic progress in the twentieth century. Designer Walter Dorwin Teague, for example, declared that, although some might despise the machine age, it was inescapable that "every one of us is a machinist of one sort or another," and that by virtue of their scientific accuracy, machines had taught us the "beauty of precision, of exact relationships, of rhythmical proportions" (Teague 1930, 21). The only way forward was to explore the possible ways that technology could benefit design and consumerism in all their aspects.

It is therefore most productive to understand Kiesler's writings on show window design within the context that awareness of the negative aspects of mass consumerism was, at the time, still nascent. Large-scale institutional strategies for consumer manipulation in the retail environment were a relatively recent phenomenon, and the goal of popularizing modern design through contemporary technology may have outweighed any less savory, capitalist aspects of the process. As a means, subtle strategies to inspire desire and consumerism ultimately justified the ends: Kiesler may have genuinely believed that if people were able to buy and take home objects presented with a refined or mechanical aesthetic, their lives would be automatically improved through the emancipatory powers of efficiency. Seen through this lens, his joining of the utopian dimensions of modern art and technology with retail display design loses some of its strangeness.

Note

1 Automats were food vending machines that became popular in Europe and the United States around the turn of the twentieth century. By the 1920s, automat shops included seating areas like conventional restaurants.

References

American Union of Decorative Artists and Craftsmen. 1931. *Annual of American Design*. New York: Ives Washburn.

Braham, William. March 1998. "A Physiology of Building: Reptilian, Canine, Monstrous." In *Proceedings of the 86th ACSA Annual Meeting and Technology Conference*, 9–13. Cleveland, OH. Washington, DC: Association of Collegiate Schools of Architecture.

Braham, William. 2005. "Active Glass Walls: A Typological and Historical Account." Paper presented at the American Institute of Architects Convention, Las Vegas, NV.

Cheney, Sheldon. 1930. *The New World Architecture*. New York: Longmans, Green and Co.

"Cite Recent Store Leases, Improvements." 1935. *Buffalo Courier-Express*, June 6.

Display World clipping. 1929. Clippings scrapbook, Austrian Frederick and Lillian Kiesler Private Foundation, Vienna, Austria, January.

Douglas, Ann. 1995. *Terrible Honesty: Mongrel Manhattan in the 1920s*. New York: Farrar, Straus and Giroux.

Fanning Jr., William J. 2010. "The Historical Death Ray and Science Fiction in the 1920s and 1930s." *Science Fiction Studies* 37, 2: 253–274.

Field, Alexander J. 2006. Table Dg117–130, "Radio and television—stations, sets produced, and households with sets: 1921–2000. *Historical Statistics of the United States, Millenial Edition On Line*, edited by Susan B. Carter, Scott Sigmund Gartner, Michael R. Haines, Alan L. Olmstead, Richard Sutch, and Gavin Wright, Series Dg117–130, 4–1027. Cambridge: Cambridge University Press.

Frankl, Paul T. 2013. *Paul T. Frankl: Autobiography*. Edited by Christopher Long and Aurora McClain. Los Angeles: DoppelHouse Press.

Frederick Kiesler Archive. Box_PHO_20, Designinnenraumgestaltung. Austrian and Lillian Kiesler Private Foundation, Vienna, Austria.

Friedman, Marilyn F. 2003. *Selling Good Design: Promoting the Early Modern Interior*. New York: Rizzoli.

Hanssen, Eirik Frisvold. 2009. "Symptoms of Desire: Colour, Costume, and Commodities in Fashion Newsreels of the 1910s and 1920." *Film History* 21, 2: 107–121.

Horwitt, Nathan George. 1930. "The Coffers of Taste, Where Fortunes Lie." *Advertising Arts*, April 2: 8.

Kiesler, Frederick. 1929. *The Modern Show Window and Store Front*. New York: Brentano's.

Kiesler, Frederick. 1930. *Contemporary Art Applied to the Store and Its Display*. New York: Brentano's.

Kiesler, Frederick. Undated manuscript. "Window Shopping 1941," TXT_6008/0, Austrian Frederick and Lillian Kiesler Private Foundation, Vienna, Austria.

Kiesler, Frederick. Undated manuscript. "Merchandise that Puts You on the Spot, Some Notes on Show Windows," TXT_181/1, Austrian Frederick and Lillian Kiesler Private Foundation, Vienna, Austria.

Kiesler, Frederick. 1931. "Window Shopping in 1941." *Advertising Arts*, September: 37–41.

Leach, William. 1993. *Land of Desire: Merchants, Power, and the Rise of a New American Culture*. New York: Vintage Books.

Leuchtenberg, Walter E. 1993. *The Perils of Prosperity 1914–1932* (1958), 2nd ed. Chicago: University of Chicago Press.

Long, Christopher. 2007. *Paul T. Frankl and Modern American Design*. New Haven: Yale University Press.

Longstreth, Richard. 2010. *The American Department Store Transformed, 1920–1960*. New Haven: Yale University Press.

May, Henry F. 1956. "Shifting Perspectives on the 1920's." *The Mississippi Valley Historical Review* 43, 3: 405–427.

McGuire, Laura. 2014. "Space Within—Frederick Kiesler and the Architecture of an Idea." PhD diss., University of Texas at Austin.

Meikle, Jeffrey L. 1985. "American Design History: A Bibliography of Sources and Interpretation." *American Studies International* 23, 1: 3–40.

Mumford, Lewis. 1931. "Culture and Machine Art." *Annual of American Design*, 9–10. New York: Ives Washburn.

Norman Bel Geddes Collection. Photo Box 2, Folder 134.2. Harry Ransom Center, Austin, Texas.

Schleif, Nina. 2004. *Schaufenster Kunst, Berlin und New York*. Köln: Böhlau.

Schwartz, Vanessa. 1997. *Spectacular Realities: Early Mass Culture in Fin-de-Siècle Paris*. Berkeley: University of California Press.

Sheldon, Roy and Egmont Arens. 1932. *Consumer Engineering: A New Technique for Prosperity*. New York: Harper.

Sherwin, Louis. 1931. "Kiesler, Heretic-Architect Builds for Comfort of Man." *New York Evening Post*, May 13.

Stote, Amos. 1930. "The Latin Quarter Goes Commercial." *Advertising Arts*, January 8: 52.

Suga, Yasuko. "Modernism, Commercialism and Display Design in Britain: The Reimann School and Studios of Industrial and Commercial Art." *Journal of Design History* 19, 2: 137–54.

Teague, Walter Dorwin. 1930. "Designing for Machines." *Advertising Arts*, April 2: 19–23.

"Television Makes Its Bow." 1927. *Literary Digest*, April 23: 7.

Untitled article. 1928. *Women's Wear Daily*, March 24.

U.S. Department of Commerce. 1929. *Commerce Yearbook for 1928*. Washington D.C.: U.S. Government Printing Office.

Wasson, Haidee. 2009. "Electric Homes! Automatic Movies! Efficient Entertainment!: 16mm and Cinema's Domestication in the 1920s." *Cinema Journal* 48, 4: 1–21.

10 Prop art

Harald Szeemann and the Warenhaus Gebrüder Loeb AG, Bern

Anna-Sophie Springer

"One of the most important features of contemporary art making is its being public [*Öffentlichsein*]" (Szeemann 1969, 709). So wrote the curator Harald Szeemann (1933–2005) in a short essay about an exhibition he organized in 1969 for the display windows of the department store Warenhaus Gebrüder Loeb AG in Bern, Switzerland. Beginning in the 1950s, Szeemann spent five decades developing large-scale, highly theatrical group exhibitions whose themes were often based on extensive research. With his legacy of "egomaniacal one-man productions" as a young theatre director in the 1950s, Szeemann brought to his work as a curator an understanding of the effective staging of cultural events, and it was his special quality as an exhibition maker to always find new contexts for where and how to make art public (Birnbaum 2005; Szeemann 2007a, 14). Today, alongside such figures as Lucy Lippard or Seth Siegelaub working in North America, he is considered a pioneer of the contemporary role of the independent curator – wherein the curator is an organizer of art events with authorial power regarding the production of meaning, rather than a conservator of culture in the service of history, the institution, and the artist. Szeemann accomplished this shift by revolutionising the concept of the exhibition itself, simultaneously casting himself as one of the exhibition's "key protagonists" (Birnbaum 2005). In the heated debate about the relationship between the artist and the curator, his innovative decisions were capable of inspiring both intense protests and sincere appreciation among his audiences and the people he worked with (Bishop 2007; Bismarck 2011; Mackert 2005; O'Neill 2012).

This essay focuses on Szeemann's work through an unusual set of engagements involving a refashioning of the role of the department store and its window. His long-standing but sparsely addressed relationship with the department store Warenhaus Gebrüder Loeb AG, Bern, Switzerland serves as a prism through which to discuss the idiosyncratic function of spectacle in Szeemann's seminal thematic exhibitions – first by discussing two group exhibitions staged in the store's display windows, and then by examining the complex role of an installation Szeemann custom-ordered from Loeb AG's props workshop when preparing his famous "Bachelor Machines" exhibition. Since 1938, the store's director, Victor Loeb (1910–1974), an art collector and board member of Kunsthalle Bern, had been an important patron during Szeemann's progressive years at the institution (1961–69), and their mutual encounter is reflected in the inclusion of artworks by the contemporary avant-garde in Loeb's collection, whose purchase Szeemann often encouraged.[1] Besides curating two exhibitions in the windows of Loeb's department store in 1969 and 1971, an even more interesting connection exists to Szeemann's unique role as commissioning designer of individual pieces. In 1975, Szeemann used the workshops of the Gebrüder Loeb AG to order the fabrication of a three-dimensional rendering of the execution machine from Kafka's *Penal Colony* for his touring exhibition *"Junggesellenmaschinen"* (Bachelor Machines). Materialized by the facilities that normally built the props for commercial retail displays, this non-original artwork makes tangible the tension between art, theatricality, and creative authorship so crucial to Szeemann's groundbreaking curatorial oeuvre. While the two display window exhibitions serve as case studies for Szeemann's broad approach to possible exhibition spaces and experimental understanding of the public role of art, the discussion of the so-called "Harrow" in the second part of the essay uniquely illustrates the intricacies and development of his curatorial methodology as an intellectual project.

Pour vendre votre vaiselle: Artists as decorators at Gebrüder Loeb AG, 1969

Since 1961, Szeemann had been the director of a Kunsthalle, in Bern, without its own permanent collection. Hence he recognized a necessity for new approaches to exhibiting – both to keep up internationally and, being a young man himself, because he identified with a younger public open for experimentation (Obrist 2011, 83). With a background as a theatre director, he therefore embraced the opportunity to steer the exhibition away from fidelity to art historical categories and the individual fame of the solo exhibition towards the "thematic exhibition," with its wide variety of artifacts and art brought together in exploration and support of a certain idea formulated by the curator. In the spring of 1969 an opportunity arose to interrogate the limits of art, advertising, and commerce while exploring the mundane retail display as an alternative exhibition space to the white cube of the art gallery. Szeemann collaborated with Victor Loeb to produce an exhibition mounted in the Gebrüder Loeb AG's long *Schaufensterfront* [display window front].

The department store Warenhaus Gebrüder Loeb AG had opened in Bern in March 1899, emerging from a Jewish family history in retail across Switzerland and southwest Germany. Still existing today under the name Loeb AG, the store is located at the prominent Spitalgasse and Bahnhofsplatz address, just across from the Hauptbahnhof, towards the historic *Altstadt* [old town] and not far from where, in September 1881, the brothers David, Julius, Luis, and Eduard Loeb had opened a smaller textile business at Spitalgasse 32. As is the case with shops and department stores worldwide, the architecture and interior design of Warenhaus Gebrüder Loeb AG's display windows played an important role. The original building, erected in 1899 and designed by Bern architect Eduard Rybi, kept up with contemporary international currents of retail architecture and boasted an unusual, even controversial display window façade with large glass panes across three full storeys on one side of the building. In 1913, the expanded business received a new but more traditional sandstone façade designed by architect Albert Gerster (Biland 2011). While the display windows on the upper floors disappeared, the ground floor now included an arched colonnade with a panorama of large display windows in a wind-shielded walkway, which would become the store's signature aesthetic interface to the city. By the late sixties this colonnade had been extended in both directions, wrapping around the street corner at Bubenbergplatz. Functioning as an unusually long vitrine, these new windows were regularly used as showcases for display scenographies that went beyond the traditional exposition of a store's product palette.

One such example are the *Länderausstellungen* [Country exhibitions], a series of shop window exhibitions mounted from 1963 well into the 1990s that was realized by Loeb's designers and themed by the cultures and products of different countries (Knuchel, Szeemann, Loeb 1995). In 1967, the store was already trying out new publicity strategies by collaborating more directly with artists, the first being Balthasar Burkardt and Otto Tschumi (Szeemann 1995, 5). This resonated with Szeemann, who was also looking for new ways to explore art as both aesthetic project and socio-economic product. Victor Loeb and Szeemann knew each other through the Kunsthalle, where Loeb's engagement as board member, art collector, and patron had been crucial. The idea to partner for a contemporary art exhibition in the store's display windows was born; it opened in April 1969 under the straightforward title "*Bekannte Berner Künstler haben unsere Schaufenster gestaltet*" [Well-known artists decorated our display windows]. Running concurrently with Szeemann's controversial exhibition at the Kunsthalle, "Live in Your Head: When Attitudes Become Form" (Kunsthalle Bern, 22 March to 27 April 1969), the exhibition in the store included a small group exhibition in the Tea Room of the *Warenhaus*. Fifteen local protagonists of conceptual and kinetic art, Surrealism, and painting were invited to participate. For Szeemann, developing an art exhibition in Loeb's display windows offered an opportunity to actively question the boundaries between art on the one hand, and commerce and advertising on the other.

The result was a much-lauded show for which the artists – an exclusively male group – were each asked to propose an *idea* for a window display design. As would be customary practice in the context of the advertising industry, and in resonance with the emerging practice of conceptual art, these concepts were then realized by Loeb's decorators in their props workshop. The manager of this undertaking was Peter Knuchel (1928–2012), who functioned for three decades (until 1993) as Loeb's display art director, spearheading most of the company's creative projects (Szeemann 1969, 710; Gebr. Loeb AG Bern 1969).

In the realm of conceptual art, such game-like, rule-based and serial setups are typical. One contemporaneous example is independent curator Seth Siegelaub's "Xerox Book" (1968) in New York, only a year earlier, in which each artist was invited to fill 25 pages of a book with a visual series produced using a Xerox photocopying machine (Siegelaub 1968). In case of the 1969 Loeb exhibition, the common condition was to select and implicate into the installation a product or range of products from one of the store's sales departments. The outcome was a diverse set of 15 showcases. Selected goods were arranged as readymades – such as in Herbert Distel's food-themed work using 5,000 eggs, or the Alfred Hofkunst installation that arranged women's underwear around a mousetrap. Other times, objects were transformed into other materials – as in the work of J.F. Schnyder, for example, where cleaning products and utensils were cut and morphed into a Surrealist flower field. The overall strongest response was achieved by the most well-known artist in the group, Jean Tinguely, who presented a machine that systematically shattered dishware sold by Loeb. A humorous provocation, this work is cited in nearly every newspaper review of the show, including headlines such as: "*Pour vendre votre vaisselle CASSEZ-LA EN PUBLIC!*" [If you want to sell your dishware you should destroy it in public!] (Anonymous 1969).

The department store display window: A very brief art history

Szeemann had long understood that art practice kept changing. With artists increasingly outsourcing their projects to manufacturing specialists, he realized that traditional museums, as well as the traditional artist's studio, were struggling to accommodate the interests and urgencies of a new generation of artists. In Szeemann's words, this more recent, idea-based, fabricated art as staged in his exhibition *"Bekannte Berner Künstler,"* "increasingly implicates working methods from outside the realm of art; the finished product thus also requires methods of dissemination that go beyond art" (Szeemann 1969, 709). Just as Siegelaub's publication explored mass-production and the book as an alternative art gallery, Szeemann said the artistic projects in the department store's display windows turned the store's glass front into a "museum in the city" (Szeemann 1969, 710).

While showing artworks in department store windows might have been an unusual strategy in Bern at the time, Szeemann likely would have been aware of the international history of artistic engagement with the mechanism of the shop window, both in its role as a visual device for framing and staging aesthetic compositions as well as a socioeconomic phenomenon of encouraging various commercial desires and fashions. A few examples precede the 1969 project at Warenhaus Gebrüder Loeb AG: in Europe, the photographer Eugène Atget documented shop windows in Paris streets as early as 1912 – the same year in which German expressionist painter August Macke created *Großes helles Schaufenster* [Large Bright Shop Window] (1912), followed by other shop window motifs in his paintings *Modegeschäft* [Fashion Shop] (1913) and *Hutladen* [Hat Shop] (1914); in the early 1920s, Otto Dix, Otto Griebel, and Paul Klee further explored window displays in their paintings; even Marcel Duchamp's famous *Large Glass* (1915–23) – which would become central in Szeemann's later curatorial work – was also partly based on the artist's fascination with a particular shop window he had seen in 1913 (Schleif 2004, 188). Translucent and pictorial at the same time, Duchamp's artwork has been described as an "extraordinary shop-window [...] a brilliant synthesis of the 'outside world' and the inside world of the imagination" (Schleif 2004, 190).

But artists had not only engaged with the shop window culture from an external perspective. Especially in New York, several department stores had been hiring artists as signature window decorators since the early twentieth century. In 1928, for instance, Saks Fifth Avenue commissioned the Austrian-American architect, artist, and theatre designer Frederick Kiesler to develop a series of unconventional presentations that then informed his influential book *Contemporary Art Applied to the Store And Its Display*, which is explored in more detail in Laura McGuire's chapter "Automatic show windows: Frederick Kiesler's retail technology and American consumer culture" in this volume (Kiesler, 1930). When the Museum of Modern Art (MoMA) in New York City presented the exhibition "Fantastic Art, Dada, Surrealism" in 1936, Surrealist aesthetics were made visible in the city through an additional display: Salvador Dalí's designs for the windows of the department store Bonwit Teller, also on Fifth Avenue, as evidenced in Sandra Zalman's chapter. Sometimes the contrasting display scenarios of the museum vitrine and the commercial shop window were explored in museum exhibitions themselves (Schleif 2004), most notably in 1949, when MoMA presented the exhibition "Modern Art in Your Life" on modern art and contemporary design organized by René d'Harnoncourt and Robert Goldwater (MoMA 1949; Schleif 2004, 258–60). This exhibition included gallery recreations of eight exemplary views of shop window displays, which were interspersed with Surrealist paintings by Dalí and Yves Tanguy in order to emphasize the possible dialogues between high and applied art. The emerging Pop Art would continue to push this dialogue further by challenging the distinctions between fine art, advertising, and the commodity. It is thus hardly surprising that central protagonists of the genre such as Jasper Johns, Robert Rauschenberg, and Andy Warhol frequently accepted hired work as window decorators in their early careers. All of these practices had contributed to shaping the conventions of art and its presentation when Szeemann replaced the museum vitrine and art gallery with the shop window of the Loeb AG in Bern in 1969.

Double reflections: The Gebrüder Loeb AG windows as street and museum, 1971

By 1970, Szeemann was further pursuing his interest in the relationship between art and the city by researching and planning an ambitious, five-part exhibition on the cultural history of "the street" to be shown at the Van Abbemuseum in Eindhoven. But due to his appointment as curator of the next *Documenta* – a large-scale exhibition presented every five years in Kassel, Germany, since 1955 – Szeemann ultimately could not finish the Eindhoven project. What he did accomplish in May 1971, however, was a "preview" to the more comprehensive exhibition realized in 1972 in the Netherlands by his collaborator Jean Leering.[2] Organized in four thematic parts – *Topologie der Straße / Straße als gesellschaftlicher Aktionsraum / Element der urbanen Struktur / Straße als technisches, ästhetisches Objekt* [Typology of the street; The street as a space for social action; The street as element of urban structure; The street as technological and aesthetic object] – *"Die Straße: Schaufensterausstellung"* [The Street: Display Window Exhibition] was the second of Szeemann's store window exhibitions at Gebrüder Loeb AG. In contrast to the previous focus of *"Bekannte Berner Künstler"* on the interior reality of the department store, this new show highlighted the windows in their role as interface to the outside. "Life" and "art" were to merge in this display, which brought together a ballet of static and kinetic figures, street cleaning machinery, mailboxes, road signs, street lights, and traffic signals. These intermingled with the motion of Bern street activities that reflected on the glass of the window panes. The project allowed Szeemann to push art further away from the stasis of the museum and towards its potential character as social action and environment, as he described in the exhibition statement:

> The museum has ceased to be the destination of their [artists'] desires. Many artists today contribute actively to the design of their environment. The city is the aim they have their sights on. Their objects are often intended for the Street, their ideas require to be tested in everyday life.
>
> (Szeemann 2007c, 310)

In 1969, Szeemann had been pleased that the store window exhibition "was a tremendous success for both sides, as both the store and the artists were able to advertise on their own behalf" (Szeemann 1969, 710). In the context of *"Die Straße,"* he alluded to the entanglement of commerce, urbanism, and art in even more explicit (albeit presumably tongue-in-cheek) terms by claiming the exhibition as an example of a public business opportunity worthy of a "central advertising fund" in favor of artists, designers, planners, and filmmakers (Szeemann 2007c, 310). However, it is not clear precisely which artists participated in the second display window spectacle. The project nevertheless remains an interesting early case study for Szeemann's unique feel for choosing non-white-cube locations for public art. As he argued, the display window exhibitions were a "brilliant" means to introduce art and artistic actions to an audience that would not necessarily visit a museum (Szeemann 1969, 710).

Museum obsessions: Harald Szeemann as independent curator

Szeemann's ongoing interest in themed exhibitions is thereafter reflected in his decision to give his *Documenta 5* (1972) its own title: "Questioning Reality: Image World Today." According to scholar Beatrice von Bismarck, this made him the "first Documenta curator in history [...] to set an overarching theme, thereby providing guidelines to which the invited artists had to subordinate themselves" (2007, 33). Expanding the authority of the curator to "exhibition *auteur*" caused a wave of protest exemplified in a telegram signed by a group of American artists, among them Carl Andre, Hans Haacke, Sol LeWitt, Robert Smithson, and Donald Judd, the last of whom withdrew his participation, calling Szeemann's work "show business at its worst" – a targeted complaint given the theatricality of Szeemann's curatorial style (Judd (1973) 2005, 209). Placed inside *Documenta 5*'s catalog itself, Daniel Buren wrote that "Harald Szeemann [...] exhibits (the works) staging himself (in front of the critics)" and that the "works presented are carefully chosen dots of color in the tableau" of the exhibition (Buren 1972, 17, 29).[3] The remarks of Judd and Buren highlight how much controversy was stirred up by Szeemann's transformation of the curator's role in relation to artistic autonomy.[4] While other curators of the late sixties and early seventies pushed the boundaries of the exhibition and curatorial practice, as with Lippard's "Number Shows" (1969–74), Szeemann's approach stands out in its explicit intellectual affinity to the *Gesamtkunstwerk* as well as a type of exhibition maker today referred to as "curator-artist."[5]

Szeemann's liberation from museum administrative and classificatory responsibilities had intensified in the aftermath of his seminal exhibition, "Live in Your Head: When Attitudes Become Form" (1969), when he had resigned from his post as Kunsthalle director to become an "independent curator" and founded the one-man enterprise *Agentur für Geistige Gastarbeit* [Agency for Spiritual Guest Work]. Following the motto *"Besitz durch freie Aktionen ersetzen"* [Replace ownership with free actions] and using a *"SELBST STEMPEL"* [self stamp] to manifest his personal presence on the printed matter of his communication, Szeemann henceforth exclusively curated temporary, mostly large-scale exhibitions. While in 1979 he rather modestly purported that the interpretation of his work as art "must be left to others because this [...] isn't a self-imposed prefix," in retrospect, it is arguable that his individual exhibitions together delineate a carefully crafted path underpinned by interrelated concepts concerned with the idea of creative subjectivity (Szeemann 1981b, 120). This is most strongly reflected in his own coinage of paradigmatic leitmotifs such as "individual mythologies" and the "Museum of Obsessions," as well as his recurring preoccupation with the "bachelor machines" and ultimately the *Gesamtkunstwerk* – the total work of art by a single, omnipotent creator (Szeemann 1981b, 119–20).[6]

Prop art: Szeemann's Kafka made by Gebrüder Loeb AG

To achieve his ambitious shows, Szeemann sometimes acted as commissioning designer of individual pieces that did not yet exist or had ceased to exist. This was the case with both the "Bachelor Machines" and the *"Gesamtkunstwerk"* exhibitions, for which Szeemann hired craftsmen to build full-scale renderings of works from art history and literature. The status of these displays was therefore complicated. One such example is a three-dimensional "replica" of the execution machine, or "harrow", from Kafka's *Penal Colony* (1914, 1919) that Szeemann had fabricated in 1975 for "Bachelor Machines," by Werner Huck (design) and Paul Gysin (painting) from the workshops of the Gebrüder Loeb AG. Getting the company's support was not an anomaly but, on the contrary, goes back to the longstanding friendship and professional relationship between Loeb and Szeemann described previously. Materialized in the workshops that would normally build the props for commercial retail displays, the so-called "Harrow" – now fabricated for the real world outside using metal, plexiglas, various hoses, cotton, and batteries – was meant to "visualize" the myth of the "bachelor machines" as appropriated from Michel Carrouges by Szeemann (Carrouges 1975). For Szeemann, these machines stood for "the omnipotence of eroticism and its negation, for death and immortality, for torture and Disneyland" (Szeemann 1975, 7). In the German magazine *Der Spiegel*, one critic affirmed the Harrow's monumentality, even calling it "the most authentic" installation in the show. And this, in spite of the Harrow's unusual origin:

> *Primus inter pares*, the organizer himself enters into the circle of creators. Szeemann defends the retrospective as a means to "express" how one – that is, really, he himself – "sees the things" – thus, as a prototype of a new, subjective category of the exhibition [...]. In order to build it [the execution machine], the exhibition maker Szeemann, having been obsessed with this for so many years, was needed first. The Kafka-piece – which is the only construction from the realm of literature and which Szeemann himself produced together with craftsmen – is not only oppressively monumental but also the most authentic one in the show [...]. After having been constructed by the Bern department store Loeb, this monster can now be admired in the Swiss capital.
>
> (Hohmeyer 1975, 90–91)

Szeemann "recycled" the Harrow for other, later, exhibitions such as "Austria in a Net of Roses" (MAK, Vienna 1996). In reference to Szeemann's French publication *Écrire les expositions*, Tobia Bezzola makes the following remark about Szeemann's habit of re-contextualizing works for different exhibition themes: "An item like Kafka's machine functions like a paragraph which can be inserted in one or another text, or even as a footnote in a quite different context" (Aubart 2007, 61). The original Loeb Harrow still exists today, reminding us of a revolutionary approach to exhibition-making and new cultures of display. Most recently, it was exhibited in 2012 at

New York's New Museum in an exhibition entitled "Ghosts in the Machine," curated by Massimiliano Gioni and Gary Carrion-Murayari. The differing communication about the object in the context of this exhibition reflects the complicated discourse around the distinction of artist versus curator. In the official literature for "Ghosts in the Machine," the Harrow's provenance was described as "Unattributed" and merely "[r]ealized [...] in collaboration with Harald Szeemann" – the same phrasing as in the catalog to the original "Bachelor Machines" exhibition. In a personal interview, however, Gioni stated more freely that he was particularly interested in the object because of its status as an "artwork born out of the desire to see it" (Fiske 2012, n.p.). Due to its unconventional and ambiguous provenance, the Harrow remains stuck in the space between artwork and prop. For Szeemann, who was not focused on traditional roles and the ontology of artworks, what mattered was that something existed for the exhibition – regardless of how it was produced or by whom. As he would say: "I have an idea [...] I take on the job of making the idea a reality. The Agency devises the keyword and the overall plan and assigns the development of the concept to me" (Szeemann 1975, 11; Pinaroli 2007, 68).

A few years after "Bachelor Machines," on the occasion of the *"Gesamtkunstwerk"* exhibition, Szeemann commissioned the set designer Peter Bisegger to reconstruct Kurt Schwitter's *Merzbau* or *Cathedral of Erotic Misery* (1937) on the basis of photographs from 1933.[7] Highlighting the similarities between theatre directing, prop manufacturing, and exhibition making, by designing, producing, and incorporating non-original artworks into his shows, Szeemann staged objects as an aesthetic experience rather than as original works of art, treating them more as signs to be used than as objects with an aura.[8] Both the Harrow and the *Merzbau* are exemplary illustrations of one of the ways in which Szeemann operated. In an interview from 1972 about *Documenta 5* he stated: "The work of art is autonomous. But it can be experienced in various ways: as information, for connection" (Lebeer and Thwaites 2007, 132). If art is treated as information, constructing a narrative through the composition of fragments can be seen as a work of art in itself.

Expanding the canon: A monument for the curator

Together, Szeemann's more than 200 exhibitions for *Documenta*, the Venice Biennale, and various international museums and events such as the two early Loeb *Schaufensterausstellungen* [display window exhibitions] can be understood as works within a larger oeuvre concerned with art's utopian promises. The utopia of the *Gesamtkunstwerk* provided for Szeemann the theatrical mega-structure within which to "connect everything" in the intense atmosphere of creative subjectivity. Contrasting the curator and the artist in a reflection on the "thematic exhibition," Szeemann explains:

> The exhibition organizer [...] has more and more become the administrator of the idea of the *Gesamtkunstwerk*, which the artists have given up more and more as a result of the social necessity of a division of labour and specialisation. A lot of what defines the artist, ranging from the autonomy of the work ... to the utopian demand of production [...], has been passed on to the Kunsthalle director or exhibition organizer.
>
> (Szeemann 1981a, 23)

As a "homeless" guest worker without a host institution, Szeemann realized his temporary exhibitions in many different places (often in industrial or less conventional exhibition spaces). He unified his shows within his one speculative *Gesamtkunstwerk*: the "Museum of Obsessions" – a "place where fragile things and new connections can be tested; like the mind, it is the place where a never static sum of speculations, nourished from various sources, struggle for visualisation" (Szeemann 1981c, 125).

In the 1970s, Harald Szeemann's curatorial methodologies triggered huge controversies, but today his legacy as transformative agent, researcher and author has been canonized. In 2007, the Fondazione Monte Verità in Ascona, Switzerland acquired five percent of Szeemann's archive for the "recovery, cataloguing and exploitation of materials [...] relating to the history of Monte Verità and different artistic, literary, philosophical and spiritual movements connected to it" (Monte Verità 2016a). Connected to this institution is also the Museum Complex Monte Verità, which includes the Casa Anatta with Szeemann's permanently installed exhibition "*Le mammelle della verità*" (1978–1981). Recently closed for refurbishment, the institution's website describes the following treatment of Szeemann's work:

> [The] exhibition is being treated as an artistic installation. It is therefore being reassembled with the utmost respect for the original intentions of the curator, while adhering to the principles of cultural heritage conservation.
>
> (Monte Verità 2016b)

The description continues by mentioning the careful cataloguing process of the 875 objects in the exhibition, and announces an additional educational exhibition *about* Szeemann. The German version of the web announcement goes even further by stating that the exhibition will be literally restored as a "*Gesamtkunstwerk*" (Monte Verità 2016c). This indicates that, more than 35 years after its inception, what was once intended as an "alternative archaeological exhibition" by a curator who challenged the institutional conventions of the profession, has not only become an object of cultural history, itself subject to preservationist care, but has ultimately been elevated to the status of "original intentions" – coming into its own as art exhibited in the museum (Kneubühler 1981, 188; Szeemann 1981a, 26). Reopened to the public in May 2017, after an eight-year renovation phase, Szeemann's curatorial composition in the Casa Anatta has been appropriated as one element in a larger educational framework about the region of Ascona, thus itself being not only re-mediated by a contemporary exhibition project but made into a "dot of color" for applying a new layer to the "tableau" of curatorial interpretation and making of new meaning.

Adding to the growing literature about Harald Szeemann's important curatorial legacy, this essay focused on three instances in which the Swiss curator engaged with the display culture and infrastructure of a company outside of the artworld: the Bern department store Warenhaus Gebrüder Loeb AG. While two art exhibitions in the shop windows connected the store to a history of artistic collaborations fostered by fancy stores in Paris, Berlin, and New York in the early twentieth century, the manufacturing of a fictional object from the realm of literature, custom-ordered by Szeemann for his exhibitions from the store's props workshop, uniquely embodies the unorthodox process of establishing a distinctive curatorial position that remains vitally debated to this day.

Acknowledgements

The author would like to thank the editors of this volume, Margaret Maile Petty, Patricia Lara-Betancourt, and Anca I. Lasc, for their generous engagement and patience throughout the process of completing this piece. Further thanks to Charles Stankievech for his friendship, ongoing dialog about artistic subjectivity and curatorial practice, and the careful attention in particular to my thinking about the exhibition-maker Harald Szeemann while writing this essay. Thank you also to Steve Rowell for visiting the Szeemann Archive at the Getty Research Archive in Los Angeles on my behalf in early 2015.

Notes

1 In a commemoration speech in 1975, Szeemann described Victor Loeb not only as a philan-
thropist and important patron of the Bern art scene, but also as his personal friend (Szeemann
(1975) 2007b, 264). Today, the so-called Anne-Marie and Victor Loeb Foundation (founded
in 1970) is part of the Kunstmuseum Bern: www.kunstmuseumbern.ch/en/service/about-us/
foundations/the-anne-marie-and-victor-loeb-foundation-101.html (accessed 14 July 2015).
2 Under the title *"De Straat, vorm van samenleven"* [The Street: Ways of Living Together], the
Van Abbemuseum would still hold the exhibition curated by Jean Leering in 1972.
3 Unless otherwise specified, all quotes were translated by the author.
4 Besides the telegram, the artists published a letter in the *Frankfurter Allgemeine Zeitung* of
12 May 1972 (reproduced in Glasmeier and Stengel 2005, 259).
5 I have previously made a comparison between Szeemann's ambition towards the curatorial
Gesamtkunstwerk to artist Donald Judd's work in Marfa, Texas (Springer and Stankievech
2013).
6 Michel Carrouges is the author of the 1954 essay "Les Machines Célibataires," a study
on structural similarities between a series of fantastical machines, from the realms of art
and literature, invented by figures such as Alfred Jarry, Raymond Roussel, Edgar A. Poe,
Jules Vernes, and Marcel Duchamp. Szeemann's exhibition "Junggesellenmaschinen" was
profoundly influenced by this essay and took Duchamp's *Large Glass* as a central point of
departure.
7 With an additional copy for travelling exhibitions, the reconstructed assemblage of Schwitter's
Merzbau is nowadays on permanent view at the Sprengel Museum, Hannover.
8 Cf. Szeemann on curating exhibitions (Obrist 2011, 82): "The intensity of the work made me
realize this was my medium. It gives you the same rhythm as in theatre, only you don't have
to be on stage constantly."

References

Anonymous. 1969. "Pour vendre votre vailselle CASSEZ-LA EN PUBLIC!" *Journal d'Yverdoun*,
April 24.
Aubart, François and Fabien Pinaroli. 2007. "Interview with Tobia Bezzola." In *Harald
Szeemann: Individual Methodology*, edited by Florence Derieux, 58–62. Zurich: JRP Ringier
Kunstverlag Ag; Grenoble: Le Magasin; New York: Distributed by D.A.P.
Biland, Anne-Marie. 2011. "Warenhäuser in der Stadt Bern: Ein Beitrag zur lokal gefärbten
Warenhaus-Architektur kurz vor und nach 1900." *bauforschungonline.ch* 06: 10–15.
Bezzola, Tobia and Roman Kurzmeyer, eds. 2007. *Harald Szeemann with by through because
towards despite: Catalogue of All Exhibitions 1957–2005.* Vienna/New York: Springer.
Birnbaum, Daniel. 2005. "When Attitude Becomes Form: Daniel Birnbaum on Harald Szeemann."
Artforum International, 22 June. Accessed February 28, 2016. www.thefreelibrary.com/_/
print/PrintArticle.aspx?id=133644326

Bishop, Claire. 2007. "What is a Curator?" *Idea: art+society* 26: 12–21. Accessed February 28, 2016. http://oncurating.org/index.php/issue-9.html#.VtRg6YwrIy4.

Bismarck, Beatrice von. 2007. "Unfounded Exhibiting: Policies of Artistic Curating." In *The Artist As...*, edited by Museum Moderner Kunst Stiftung Ludwig Wien and Matthias Michalka, 33–47. Vienna: MUMOK.

———. 2011. "Curatorial Criticality: On the Role of Freelance Curators in the Field of Contemporary Art." *oncurating.org* 09: 19–23.

Buren, Daniel. 1972. "Exposition d'une exposition – Ausstellung einer Ausstellung." In *Documenta 5* catalog, edited by Harald Szeemann, 29. Kassel: Verlag Documenta.

Carrouges, Michel. 1975. "Directions for Use." In *Le Macchine Celibi – The Bachelor Machines*, edited by Harald Szeemann, 21–74. New York: Rizzoli.

Derieux, Florence, ed. 2007. *Harald Szeemann: Individual Methodology*. Zürich: Ringier Kunstverlag.

Exhibition catalog. 1949. *Modern Art in Your Life*. New York: Museum of Modern Art.

Fiske, Courtney. 2012. "Raising Spirits: Q+A with Massimiliano Gioni." *Art in America*, 16 August. Accessed February 28, 2016. www.artinamericamagazine.com/news-opinion/conversations/2012-08-16/massimiliano-gioni-ghosts-in-the-machine.

Gebr. Loeb AG Bern. 1969. "Bei Loeb: Kunst im Schaufenster." *Für unsere Mitarbeiter: Hauszeitschrift, der Gebr. Loeb AG Bern*. Year 39.

Glasmeier, Michael, Barbara Heinrich, and Karin Stengel, eds. 2005. *50 Jahre / 50 Years Documenta 1955–2005*. Göttingen: Steidl.

Judd, Donald. 2005. "Complaints: part II." In *Complete Writings 1959–1979*, edited by Donald Judd, 207–11. Halifax: The Press of the Nova Scotia College of Art and Design.

Gebr. Loeb AG Bern. 1969. *Für unsere Mitarbeiter: Hauszeitschrift*. Year 39.

Herrschaft, Felicia. 2004. "Gespräch mit Harald Szeemann: 29. Februar 2004." *Felicia Herrschaft*, February 29. Accessed February 28, 2016. www.fehe.org/index.php?id=237.

Hohmeyer, Jürgen. 1975. "Entkleidung zu Lust und Tod: Spiegel-Redakteur Jürgen Hohmeyer über die Berner Ausstellung 'Junggesellenmaschinen.'" *Der Spiegel*, July 14: 90–91.

Kiesler, Frederick. 1930. *Contemporary Art Applied to the Store and its Display*. New York: Brentano.

Kneubühler, Theo. 1981. "Monte Verita – Berg der Wahrheit." In *Museum der Obsessionen von/über/zu/mit Harald Szeemann*, edited by Harald Szeemann, 177–192. Berlin: Merve Verlag.

Knuchel, Peter R., Harald Szeemann, and François Loeb, eds. 1995. *30 Jahre Loeb Schaufenster*. Bern: Ott Verlag.

Lebeer, Irmeline and John Anthony Thwaites. 2007. "Interviews with Harald Szeemann." In *Harald Szeemann: Individual Methodology*, edited by Florence Derieux, 130–133. Zürich: Ringier Kunstverlag

Mackert, Gabriele. 2005. "At Home in Contradictions: Harald Szeemann's Documenta." In *Archive in Motion: 50 Years Documenta 1955–2005*, edited by Michael Glasmeier and Karin Stengel, 253–61. Göttingen: Steidl.

Millet, Catherine. 1985. "Gespräch mit Catherine Millet." In *Individuelle Mythologien*, edited by Harald Szeemann, 231–252. Berlin: Merve Verlag.

Monte Verità. 2016a. "Fondo Harald Szeemann." Accessed February 29, 2016. www.monteverita.org/en/92/fondo-harald-szeemann.aspx.

Monte Verità. 2016b. "Museum Complex." Accessed February 29, 2016. www.monteverita.org/en/32/museum-complex.aspx.

Müller, Hans-Joachim. 2007. *Harald Szeemann: Exhibition Maker*. Ostfildern: Hatje Cantz.

Obrist, Hans Ulrich. 2011. "Interview with Harald Szeemann." In *A Brief History of Curating*, edited by Hans Ulrich Obrist, 80–100. Zürich: JRP/Ringier.

O'Neill, Paul. 2012. *The Culture of Curating and the Curating of Culture*. Cambridge, Mass.: The MIT Press.

Pinaroli, Fabien. 2007. "The Agency for Intellectual Guest Labor." In *Harald Szeemann: Individual Methodology*, edited by Florence Derieux, 63–71. Zürich: Ringier Kunstverlag.

Schleif, Nina. 2004. *Schaufensterkunst: Berlin und New York*. Cologne: Böhlau Verlag.

Springer, Anna-Sophie and Charles Stankievech. 2013. "The Complete Complex: Marfa, Texas as Donald Judd's *Gesamtkunstwerk*." Paper presented at the 12th International Bauhaus-Kolloquium, Universität-Weimar, April 4–7.

Szeemann, Harald. 1969. "Neue Wege der Kunstpräsentierung." *Werk* 10, 56, October: 709–12.

———. 1975. "Junggesellenmaschinen." In *Junggesellenmaschinen*, edited by Harald Szeemann, 5–14. Bern: Kunsthalle Bern.

———. 1981a. "Oh du fröhliches, oh du seliges Ausstellen." In *Museum der Obsessionen von/über/zu/mit Harald Szeemann*, edited by Harald Szeemann, 23–30. Berlin: Merve Verlag.

———. 1981b. "Agentur für Geistige Gastarbeit im Dienste der Vision eines Museums der Obsessionen." In *Museum der Obsessionen von/über/zu/mit Harald Szeemann*, edited by Harald Szeemann, 107–124. Berlin: Merve Verlag.

———. 1981c. Museum der Obsessionen." In *Museum der Obsessionen von/über/zu/mit Harald Szeemann*, edited by Harald Szeemann, 125–136. Berlin: Merve Verlag.

———. 2007a. "with by through because towards despite." In *Harald Szeemann with by through because towards despite: Catalogue of All Exhibitions 1957–2005*, edited by Tobia Bezzola and Roman Kurzmeyer, 13–32. Vienna/New York: Springer.

———. 2007b. "Victor Loeb, A Patron of The Arts." In *Harald Szeemann with by through because towards despite: Catalogue of All Exhibitions 1957–2005*, edited by Tobia Bezzola and Roman Kurzmeyer, 264–265. Vienna/New York: Springer. Originally read in 1975 as Szeemann's commemoration speech for Victor Loeb.

———. 2007c. "Die Strasse: Schaufensterausstellung." In *Harald Szeemann with by through because towards despite: Catalogue of All Exhibitions 1957–2005*, edited by Tobia Bezzola and Roman Kurzmeyer, 310. Vienna/New York: Springer. Originally published as Szeemann's statement for the exhibition in 1971.

———. 2007d. "Annex Documents." In *Harald Szeemann: Individual Methodology*, edited by Florence Derieux, 72–76. Zürich: Ringier Kunstverlag.

11 From retail stores to real-time stories

Displaying change in an age of digital manufacturing

Mark Taylor and Yannis Zavoleas

In the late nineteenth century the opening of department stores in the US and Europe afforded the opportunity for customers to choose from a range of products enticingly presented for their consumption. From perfumes to household goods, products were carefully organized to enhance the experience of browsing. Among the many items was clothing, which was exhibited using mannequins showcasing the latest fashions to be worn in the modern metropolis. To accommodate customer demand, and to increase profits, many stores provided ready-made attire alongside traditional customized tailoring. The difference was that, while fashions were historically intended only for the elite and involved hundreds of master craftsmen making bespoke clothing, the ready-mades were shaped from a range of sizes in order that they be available to more people.

Within this modern system, bespoke fabrication remained an elegant alternative, usually at some additional cost, and reminiscent of traditional customized tailoring where an individual item was made from templates, or designed from scratch. Under this paradigm, an outfit was fabricated to the customer's specifications and included particular finishes, surface treatments, and shapes, but was likely to require some physical interaction between tailor and client. In both situations customers were enticed to purchase through appealing product display as much as reputation. Alongside in-store retailing, clothing was also displayed through magazines, such as the nineteenth-century British women's periodical *The Queen*, which showed a range of images and offered advice on where and how to make purchases. Catalogs also offered a means by which ready-to-wear items could be seen, purchased and delivered to one's residence. In the US, the Montgomery Ward Company issued the first mail-order catalog in 1872, but the most widely distributed catalog was issued by Sears, Roebuck and Company in 1896 (Drowne and Huber 2004, 100). Many catalogs, including British-based Grattan, are still in business, offering various items for purchase through a range of payment methods.

However, a century later, the emergence of digital retailing has begun to challenge and change the customer experience. Although internet retailing began in the 1990s, the downturn in the economy saw many dot-com companies go bust; as a consequence, second generation companies employ a more economic sales model. Data suggests that e-retailing has grown alongside social media, supported by targeting brands and products to users. In the UK, companies such as Amazon and Argos lead the way, but fashion retailers Zara, Boohoo, Boden, ASOS and Very have all seen significant growth ("Top 100 Online Retailers in the UK" 2013). While not all digital retailing enables the consumer to interfere with the garment's design, those that do present choices of material and design that are normally applicable only to bespoke fabrication.

Displaying change in the department store

In department and clothing stores, particular arrangements of apparel display a moment of "fashion thinking," which comprises both aesthetic trends and material usage. This chapter is not so much concerned with how individual items are arranged but addresses the broader issue of the display of social and cultural change. We focus on the introduction of clothing arrangements made possible through digital technologies and contemporary manufacturing processes that display an emergent trend in the digital bespoke clothing market, enabled by online portals and 3D digital manufacturing. This is not simply an aesthetic concern but is more profound; in order to contextualize this, the essay unpacks some of the issues surrounding the understanding and manufacturing of mass-customized attire.

To explore this shift, this chapter traces how new media and digital manufacturing are gradually changing the retail experience, and how methods of digital clothing fabrication have brought about change through a kind of customized tailoring adapted to online platforms, but with more customer engagement in the actual design. In part, the chapter is prompted by two things: firstly, by an image of the traditional tailoring section from Selfridges department store in London at the turn of the century (Fig. 11.1); secondly, by an account of the recent introduction of a 3D body scanning pod into the store's apparel section in the early 2000s. Following this initial placement of a Bodymetrics pod in Selfridges, another one was introduced into Bloomingdale's

Figure 11.1 Tailoring section of Selfridges department store.
Source: © Look and Learn / Peter Jackson Collection

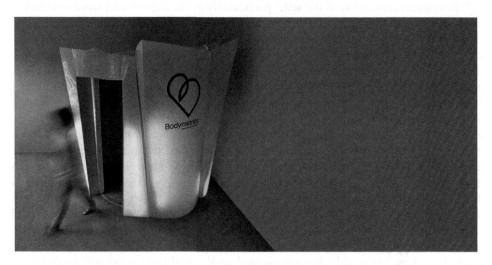

Figure 11.2 Bodymetrics Pod, image reprinted with permission Bodymetrics.

store in Palo Alto, California (Fig. 11.2). This is not to suggest that only Selfridges was active in these areas. Rather, these two images provide bookends for the discussion of how new techniques and processes are displayed, particularly through personalized wear in an age of digital technology.

Many web-based formats for presenting garments tend to link visual images with textual information that leads to a processing system for purchase and dispatch under the guise of "making shopping easier." Many online clothing retail sites promote personalization through choices of materials, colors and design that provide a degree of individuality at no additional cost. The shift to individuality is increasingly displayed through advertising and marketing, cultivating an idea about retailing with reference to "mass-customization" rather than mass-production, the latter of which has traditionally involved technology to make many repeatable products at a lower cost.

To assist an understanding of mass-customization in the digital age, it is useful to be reminded of how the architect and furniture designer Bernard Cache describes an object (a suit, jacket, vase, and so on) as being a dynamic system rather than a fixed representation (1995). Cache's work is relevant in this context as it recognizes how the relationship between surface and volume leads to non-standard modes of production, or what we might call the mass-customized product. Cache uses the concept of *objectile* to outline how objects are no longer defined as fixed entities but exist in a state of constant transformation (1995, ix). He suggests that an object might be approached through parametric relations, in the sense that each part of an object can be described relative to its association with other parts: if one part is changed, the other part is automatically changed as well. This means that an object can be altered, or customized, in real time leading to varied outputs for the same cost – a production model that is applicable to objects of any kind, including retail clothing.

In effect, the proposed model assumes design and manufacturing of clothes as processes of interaction with the customer, and, as such, these may now be integrated with the dynamic activities of viewing, examining, trying on and purchasing. Such activities also implicate this form of consumption in what Stuart and Elizabeth Ewen describe as "the commercialization of the self," particularly as the department store operates as a cultural primer, showing its customers how they should dress and furnish their home (Ewen and Ewen 1982, 215). Michael Miller also observes how the department store contributes to consumer practice rather than just reflecting existing cultural states, thereby giving embodiment to a way of life and ways of production (1981, 182). But, as Miller, Jackson, Thrift, Holbrook and Rowlands note, "consumption was cast adrift from production," particularly through Bordieu and De Certeau, for whom consumption theory tended to emphasize "dynamic and flexible consumer 'tactics' " (1998, 3). However, objects such as customized clothing embody and extend social relations (the relations between an object and its use) in new directions. Hence, in some digital retailing, the display of customized and/or real-time attire is made alongside its mode of production. Although still in very early stages, research initiatives through TU Delft-based Mesh Lingerie are using 3D body scans of prospective customers in order to produce custom-fitting 3D designs, and Pringle of Scotland incorporated laser-sintered nylon fabric into garments used for its Autumn/Winter 2014 collection that were shown at London Fashion Week (Despa 2015). With currently available technology, it is foreseeable that customized and/or real-time attire will probably be made alongside its modes of retail production: for example, a 3D-printed garment purchased from a store or web site could be fabricated within the store, or printed at home, or assembled for immediate distribution through web-based platforms. The challenge for the store is how to display this to its customers.

Retailing and manufacturing

In 1909, Selfridges Department Store opened on Oxford Street, London. Conceived by the self-made American retailing entrepreneur H. Gordon Selfridge, this elegantly decorated commercial environment presented a message that "even large-scale stores were free of mass market taint [and shoppers] would find an abundance of authentic and exclusive objects, not to be confused with the mass produced goods available elsewhere" (Outka 2005, 312). Although the aim was to promote an exclusive range of products personalized to each visitor, this message also contained its own contradictions in that the store "simultaneously invoked the modern pleasures of the mass market: the goods were available to all" (Outka 2005, 314). At Selfridges, for example, the shop window displays, products and the interior space were presented as exclusive and refined, according to Outka, "existing in a purified cultural location outside conventional markers of commerce" (2005, 314). Clever advertising implied that the goods at Selfridges were "one-of-a-kind objects, in direct contrast with the mass-produced goods available at lesser stores" (Outka 2005, 314).

To assist this process of presenting items as exclusive, Selfridges and similar department stores developed a commercial culture that, according to Mica Nava, reflected a cosmopolitanism that was "part of a wider structure of attitude, part of a more general embrace of the modern" (Nava 2002, 4). Support for this broader world view, she argues, was apparent in "the store's promotion of the modern and modernist cultures and products associated with foreign art and popular entertainment forms" (Nava 2002, 4). In contrast to existing conservative attitudes, Selfridges' engagement with the "new" indicated that exotic objects already loaded with cultural meaning were not to be viewed as mere artefacts of the past, but were profoundly individual and displayed a forward-thinking attitude.

Presented this way, a department store filled with ready-made clothing must have seemed very different to any late nineteenth-century shopper more used to ordering "custom" clothing from milliners and tailors. Sufficient products for the department store were only made possible as late nineteenth-century mass-production and standardization began to separate the clothing trade into the pre-industrial practice of made-to-measure and the emerging ready-made market (Levitt 1991). Shoppers could find ready-made clothing on the premises, which, as Margaret Wray writes, was made as a means of occupying their staff when demand for the bespoke was low. These stores and individual retail shopkeepers "began to make rather simpler garments for sale ready-made" (Lemire 2009, 252). Although they were employed on a permanent but exploitative basis with long hours and low pay, Elizabeth Wilson observes that young women "did all kinds of work, from altera-tions of ready-made clothing bought in the store to dressmaking from scratch" (1985, 77). Social historian Bill Lancaster also confirms that in the late nineteenth century, many department store owners began manufacturing, and "clothing was an obvious area [...] with virtually all stores employing workers to make up and adjust clothing [...] in their own workrooms" (1995, 114). UK department stores such as Lewis's (Liverpool) and Bainbridge (Leeds) manufactured clothing, shoes and boots in their own factories outside the store, a practice that helped increase profits alongside the new managerialism practices that were being adopted.

In post-Second World War Europe, many department stores chased after working-class income from prosperous council house tenants. For example, stores in Britain such as Harrods and Browns of Chester took over stores in other cities, and altered their environment and shopping strategy to help working-class customers feel more at ease. Counters were removed and replaced with self-service, and, with the advent of television, stores used this media to advertise their traditional January sales to a broader audience. By the mid-1950s many stores were selling mix-and-match cloth-ing, which enabled customers to wear completely coordinated ensembles.

The emergence of youth culture and the teenager as a social phenomenon, begin-ning in the postwar period, presented another problem for mass retailing. To cap-ture this market, Selfridges launched the Miss Selfridge stores in 1966, and in 1967 Harrods opened their in-house store Way In, both representing the young fashion section of the parent company. Moreover, by the 1970s, a cultural style change across the apparel market altered the way products were presented and promoted (Lancaster 1995, 198). Lancaster illustrates this through the short-lived Biba store that presented an innovative merchandizing policy of "theming a wide variety of items from belts to baked beans," a concept that pre-dates stores such as Next by over a decade (1995, 198). In 1974, Biba moved into the seven-storey building that once housed Derry & Toms department store. There it continued its policy of one display per product, illustrated by the giant baked bean tin can to house baked beans in the food hall, and coat stands used to hang a range of clothing. Windows were blacked out to help retain the shop's Art Deco image, and were never used to display products.

This narrative on twentieth-century retail stores suggests most clothing was pur-chased "as sold." More recently, since the advent of online retailing and automated manufacturing through digital platforms, practices related to customized ready-to-wear tailoring have found room to evolve. This is primarily due to the diminishing additional costs commonly involved in product discrepancy or personalization. As is presented next, the emergence of online retailing is beginning to change the economic equation between mass-produced identical garments and individualized ones, as much as it is changing the role of the store and the manner in which products are presented with reference to their respective manufacturing processes.

Digital retailing

With the advent of online shopping, the concept of retailing has extended beyond its physical setting and, as a consequence, the in-store experience is taking a new direction. Brian Kalms argues that, "The role of the store is shifting to become a showroom where consumers come to examine products and experience brand values without necessarily making a purchase" (2014). This suggests that, while retailing may occur digitally, the physical store will need to provide value-enhancing convenience, innovation and service. For example, stores such as Burberry's now offer soft seating, mirror-sized touch-screen displays and Apple iPads in order to give access to Burberry's full collection displayed online. The intention is to engage shoppers with the online environment while in the physical shop, in order to enhance their understanding of online retail and encourage web purchasing when away from the store. To complete the experience, a large LED screen shows Burberry videos and presents "retailing as theatre" (Niemeier, Zocchi and Catena 2013). Sports manufacturer Adidas has incorporated "Social Mirrors" in the changing rooms of their NEO stores. These full-size flat screens are both mirror and camera, enabling the shopper to take a snap and post it on social media to get friends to comment (Hunstig 2012). These enhancements, and the use of free wifi, are aimed at further personalizing the retail experience, suggesting that store goods are conceived from the start to reflect the customers' exclusive lifestyle even when displayed and sold online. To accentuate this aspect, the store can identify a returning client and offer promotions and additional services with a view to continued custom (Hunstig 2012).

Amplifying the possibilities of a product through promotion of lifestyle associations via both physical and online retailing is an adaptation of an existing phenomenon of emerging digital platforms. Promotion of retail has commonly strived towards merging merchandize to acceptable social standards, in turn prompting their transformation. Since the 1880s, advertising has moved from "selling" a product to intensifying the excitement inherent in it and tending to "endow the goods with transformative messages and associations that the goods did not objectively possess" (Leach 1984, 327). Retailing therefore has become much more than a transaction and, by linking it to an emotional "sensory experience," customers will continue to interact with products through sight and touch, and "experience a brand's lifestyle and values" (Niemeier, Zocchi and Catena 2013). Parallel to this, McKinsey's iConsumer Survey 2010 indicates that people who bought online after visiting a physical store went to the store because "they either 'wanted to touch, feel, test the item' or [...] to 'compare products'" (Niemeier, Zocchi and Catena 2013). The inference is that people were reluctant to buy products online that they could not first see or try on, but after physically experiencing them in the store, the resistances and the limitations of the digital retail setting were subdued.

An important factor of such a turning of the market audience to gradually embrace online retailing is that processes related to the digital experience have also been promoted in the physical store setting. In 2004, the London-based company Bodymetrics installed the first body scanner in Selfridges department store, and three years later placed one in Bloomingdale's Palo Alto location in California, USA (McGlaun 2012). This system, like the Me-ality and Styku scanners, uses scanning technologies to record the human body in detail and produce an accurate, digitized version of the body shape so that clients can either select clothes that might fit or have a pattern made to order (Jopson 2012). Other systems, such as that introduced into Nordstrom stores, use touchscreen computers to enable shoppers to select a body type and enter measurements in order to display various styles and cuts on a rotating, computer-generated figure (Klara 2015). This system of overlaying clothing on an avatar is also used for online purchasing as the simulation can offer some indication of how the clothing might fit the body. Jopson observes that scanners placed in high-value retail stores and shopping malls are currently being used by several denim jeans manufacturers such as Gap to enable shoppers to better match body shape and size to products. He suggests that body scanners will appear in many retail stores worldwide in the next few years, and by using a plugin device attached into a gaming console such as Xbox, it will also be possible to scan one's body from home (Jopson 2012). Rather than merely enhancing the experience of shopping, the placement of hi-tech equipment in retail stores ranging from high-value to popular brands is intended to acquaint customers with digital concepts and practices, and integrate them with those previously seen as being exclusive to the in-store experience.

This shift in the process of capturing, measuring and manipulating the body through digital technology has consequences on the manufacture and display of apparel (Gill 2015). One change is in the individualization offered by online shopping, while the other concerns the process of digital fabrication and the opportunities afforded by mass-customization, thus linking the retail experience with personalization and participation through real and virtual interfaces.

Digitizing the body in retail stores

Digital manufacturing promises more alignment with customers' preferences and is increasingly used in the medical and engineering disciplines as much as it is in design areas such as jewelry, furniture, and architecture. Clothing retail has also seen rapid development in a similar direction, hence the modes of display are beginning to consider and include this new technology as part of the shopping experience. Changes involve how a clothing product may be defined from conception to manufacture through a series of binary instructions set in response to anthropometric data measured directly from the customer's body.

Capturing body data via scanning technology and transferring this to manufacturing is very different from traditional analogue routines. Common practices for customized clothing required the skilled master tailor to physically measure customers by laying palms on their shoulders, feeling the shape of their sides, and "learning the customer's 'form' in order to model to that particular body a particular suit of clothes" (Zakim 2003, 70). Since the early 1820s the new technology of drafting systems has enabled a more commercial and economic means of production (Zakim 2003, 86). At the heart of some systems was the tailor's ability to use proportions and extrapolate sizings from one or a few measurements to create the desired pattern, while others were based on direct measurement to create an anthropometric mapping of the body (Geršak 2013; Ashdown 2007).

One practical constraint with fitting clothes to the body is shape difference (Apeagyei et al. 2007; Otieno et al. 2005). Most data has been obtained from surveys that tended to be quite narrow and which often excluded ethnic diversity, changes to stature and weight as people aged, as well as a broad range of body types. While fashion designers still tend to use tall, thin models to display and promote their garments, this body type represents a small fraction of the population. The cost of obtaining anthropometric garment sizing data is still based on standardized body measurements that produce a minimum number of sizes for the majority of the population. The reinforcement of this system can be found in many examples since the late nineteenth century and into the twentieth century. For example, a 1940s school education manual designed to assist teaching schoolgirls both etiquette and dressmaking presented a "body rectangle" that documented the structural lines of the body (Baxter and Latzke 1949, 20). Measured from the head to the floor the rectangle is divided into horizontal lines (hem, hips, waistline, bustline and chestline) that "resemble the chart given by many pattern companies for taking body measurements" (Baxter and Latzke 1949, 360) (Fig. 11.3).

The recent interest in redefining clothing relative to digitally taken body measurements may be explained as an answer to the limitations of analogue anthropometry, along with the recurring aim for customized apparel. The application of digital techniques in defining the garment and the customer's body shape assumes that the design model is a flexible mold, formed and reformed according to a set of exact functions, and also that by altering these functions the model can very quickly generate different outcomes. In this process, new software techniques and digital procedures are used to describe repeatable operations applied onto the same model, this time enabling sophisticated variations. As a result, the body and the cloth may be viewed as a paired system in transformation in which the body sets the dynamic standards for the cloth to follow. The design is the template model, or the formula expressed in the digital file. Data about the body, such as size and movement, along with other characteristics of color, temperature, environmental requirements, and fabric, set the active parameters of production in the form of a totalizing equation. The design model and these parameters, when brought together under numerically controlled, automated processes, produce unique variable outputs that describe the production chain of non-standard, or mass-customized, manufacturing.

Due to their innovative outlook and appeal, elements and equipment assisting this process have left the backroom and entered the showroom, symbolizing both full customization and extended novelty. This digital advent is somewhat reminiscent of the way traditional customized tailoring often displayed new sewing machinery technology alongside fabric in an effort to announce expertise, quality, and commitment to high-quality, individualized products. In a similar manner, digital body scanners introduced into department stores provide a means to accurately register the customer's body shape and provide more reliable data measurements to interact with a variety of designs. The full body scanners currently available use laser-based technology, or infrared sensors (similar to those developed for computer gaming) installed around the inside edge of the scanner. The customer enters and stands still as the scanner maps the body by applying hundreds of measurements and contours and, in just a few seconds, saves this information to a personal database (McGlaun 2012) (Fig. 11.4). The digitized body is then ready to wear any virtual design garment

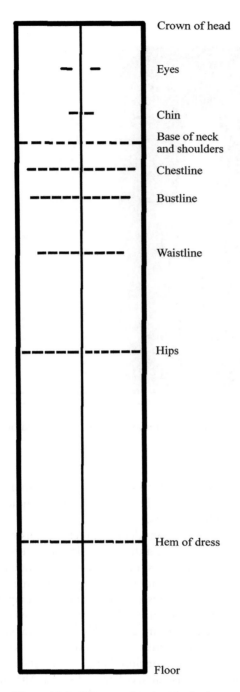

Crown of head

Eyes

Chin

Base of neck
and shoulders

Chestline

Bustline

Waistline

Hips

Hem of dress

Floor

Figure 11.3   Diagram showing the basic structural lines of the figure, redrawn from Baxter
and Latzke, *Today's Clothing*, 1949.

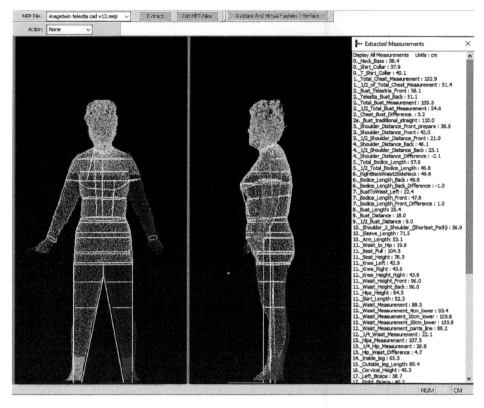

Figure 11.4 Body scan image showing how automated measurements are defined on the system.

Source: Image reprinted with permission from [TC]² Labs

adapted to its own individual shape. The overall process signifies a new ritual for shoppers to become actively involved in customizing the garment of their choice in settings traditionally reserved for ready-made products.

However enticing this experience appears, it faces considerable practical constraints when merging with existing standards. For example, although digital scanners can capture individual data to be matched to clothing sizes, one problem for retailers is that the products on display are still limited to around 15 sizes. To overcome this, the New York menswear store Acustom Apparel scans the body and then employs "proprietary software that creates custom-tailored patterns" that are sent overseas for fabrication and direct distribution to the client (Klara 2015). Using a digital scanner, more than 200,000 data points are collected to create a 3D body model, which, together with clothing fit preferences, is fed into an algorithm that generates the clothing patterns with any individual preferences such as cuffs, collar, and so on. Although the considerable wait time could be inconvenient, the certainty that a garment will fit the client's body, and has a degree of individuality, offers what might be termed "digital bespoke." Such processes, and related technologies such as body scanners and projection equipment, will gradually integrate with existing routines for shopping, and may eventually lead to a redefinition of retail space. As a consequence, space in a traditional retail store reserved for ready-to-wear stock, and related furniture such as racks and shelves, may be reduced to a minimum.

The mass-customized as mass-produced

Alongside developments in body scanning is the emergence of financially viable 3D printers capable of customized production. Advances in materials research now provide the ability to alter a design relative to material properties. While the construction and garment industry have been slower to take up this technology, it has been used more widely in jewelry and shoe design, where the design is relatively independent from the constraints and complexities of the human body. However, the introduction of 3D printing in the clothing industry could revolutionize garment sizing, product development, and mass-production, particularly as it could enable start-up labels to produce small orders and easily customize their designs to suit clients' needs (Fisher 2013). These new customer-centric strategies integrate 3D body scanning, 3D visualizing, and 3D printing techniques to support automatic pattern alterations that are based not only on human body measurements but also on the fabric's dynamic behavior and material characteristics. As such, mass-produced clothing can be individualized through digital technologies and incorporated into the apparel design-manufacturing-retailing chain (Qin, Lagoudakis, Kang and Cheng 2008).

For the customer operating in the digital-age retail environment, fashions are increasingly presented through digital media and, in the case of Australia-based XYZ Workshop, designs are now available for download. Anyone with a 3D printer can "customize and create their own clothing" (Stone 2014) before manufacturing it in their own home. What this means for the retailer and customer is that, increasingly, retail stores will advertise products (in both digital and analogue formats) but, more importantly, they will display the processes by which particular designs can be made, modified and adapted to the customer's body requirements and design preferences. The customer's experience is not limited to catalogs and in-store merchandize but is a blended experience in which products are selected, tested on an avatar, adapted, and printed at home. In effect, the customer is no longer purchasing a physical artefact but is buying a digital file and paying their own material and manufacturing costs.

Incorporating technology

This chapter shares the view that introducing these new technologies into existing retail activities and spaces will have profound implications for the way we understand and accept products. For example, since most people are familiar with body scanners from airports and other locations necessitating anti-terrorist technology, there is a sense that this kind of technological innovation is primarily designed with security in mind and as a result it may not fit within the retail sector. However, even early versions of the Bodymetrics scanners were designed with less emphasis on security and more on enabling use by people unfamiliar with the technology. While they may look like alien objects, they nevertheless display a technologically savvy proposition for the future. Photographer Peter Samuels described the Bodymetrics pod as a "glowing orb like variation to Woody Allen's orgasmatron," a description that reflects the independent unit being lit from the inside and pulsing with different colors (2012). The Australia-based company mPort is currently installing their mPod scanner in several

Westfield shopping centers. Although more conventional in appearance, these rounded rectangular units have a white laminate and timber finish to offer a somewhat familiar representation of modern commercial architecture. They are more photo-booth than future-booth. However, factors such as functional efficiency, tested reliability, ease of use and cost lowering are critical before these technologies are fully accepted as part of the retail environment and experience and are included into the architecture of display next to cash registers, fitting rooms, mirrors, mannequins, clothes rails, and so on.

Aside from any of the sociocultural complexities related to accepting new technologies into the contemporary setting, this chapter suggests that is only a matter of time before these changes will become standard, and therefore it has attempted to forge a new framing for the display of the modern and the new, relative to their associated production practices. On reflection, it is reasonable to predict that the emphasis on customization and off-shore or at-home manufacturing will result in the need for much more limited stock, since manufacturing and distribution will occur elsewhere. Bodymetrics founder Suran Goonatilake argues that this change offers gains for both customer and retailer, with the former obtaining a personalized product that fits his or her body (Shah 2007). The retailer, on the other hand, will require much less stock, if any at all, and will receive payment prior to manufacture. Others have argued that it will lead to fewer returns as clothing should be a good "fit" for the body.

As these technologies are being developed and utilized in the retail sector, it is becoming clearer that digital display is an extension to existing retail practices. It has transformed these practices from static display systems to ones redefined to supplement, support and respond to the inherent limitations of their digital counterpart. The result of this collaboration is the emergence of spaces that display hybrid experiences, part catalog, lifestyle promotion, customized clothing, and manufacturing. Moreover, the digital technologies of body scanning and 3D printing promise the masses a revival of customized clothing that, for more than a century, has been compromised by ready-made garments. To some extent, mass-customization has been pulled through the twentieth century, seemingly reversing any association with economic models based upon the automated reproduction of self-similar objects. Technologies related to mass-customization are introduced into the retail experience, enabling what Cache would call the production of non-standard objects that, as an alternative to traditional tailoring, are developed digitally in real-time simulation platforms. This includes data from the customer's body, selection of the design and materials from a range of options available in the database to define a digital prototype, which is then adjusted to body shape and movement through the use of appropriate software, and finally printed as a 3D prototype.

In Dutch designer Iris van Halpern's terms, these technologies are currently at an experimental stage, and it will not be long before "we see the clothing we wear today produced with this technology" (Voltage by Deezen 2013). And because it is such a different way of manufacturing, it resists the traditional forms of body measurement and manufacturing that extrapolated pattern sizes from a limited set of body measurements, and instead maps each individual body.

The degree that the technological advancements addressed in this chapter engage with the experience of retail shopping reflects a store's ability to accommodate a shift in its marketing practice. Display that revolves around a few samples and an interactive website suggests there will be less stock and more emphasis on product customization. This includes the selection of the design, the fabric, the color, as well as fitting, projection, refining, manufacturing, and final delivery.

The desire by clothing stores to present their goods as exclusive and individual can, through digital manufacturing, now be realized in a manner that more closely reflects this position. However, like the nineteenth-century products capturing the spirit of modernity, the store is again capitalizing on the emergence of new technologies and fabrication trends in an effort to appear forward-thinking. Moreover, these changes still assume that the department store is a version of popular entertainment similar to that proffered at the beginning of the twentieth century, but this time it is made through the customer's personalized involvement in decisions related to his/her individualized needs. This endeavor aims to merge the benefits of mass-production with those of customization, which, due to the current technological advancements, now seems possible.

References

Apeagyei, Phoebe R. 2008. "Significance of Body Image among Female UK Fashion Consumers: The Cult of Size Zero, the Skinny Trend." *Journal of Fashion Design, Technology and Education* 1, 1: 3–11.

Apeagyei, Phoebe R., Rose Otieno, and David Tyler. 2007. "Ethical Issues and Methodological Considerations in Researching Body Cathexis for Fashion Products." *Journal of Fashion Marketing and Management* 11, 3: 332–348.

Ashdown, Susan. 2007. *Sizing in Clothing: Developing Effective Sizing Systems for Ready-to-Wear Clothing*. Cambridge: Woodhead Publishing.

Baxter, Laura and Alpha Latzke. 1949. *Today's Clothing*. Chicago and New York: J. B. Lippincott.

Cache, Bernard. 1995. *Earth Moves: The Furnishing of Territories*. Cambridge, Mass.: MIT Press.

Despa, Horia. 2015. "3D Printed Clothes is the Next Big Thing in Fashion." *Softpedia*. September 10. Accessed December 29, 2015. http://news.softpedia.com/news/3d-printed-clothes-is-the-next-big-thing-in-fasion-491412.shtml.

Drowne, Kathleen and Patrick Huber. 2004. *American Popular Culture through History: The 1920s*. Westport: Greenwood Press.

Ewen, Stuart and Elizabeth Ewen. 1982. *Channels of Desire: Mass Images and the Shaping of American Consciousness*. New York: McGraw-Hill.

Fisher, Alice. 2013. "3D-Printed Fashion: Off the Printer, Rather Than off the Peg." *The Guardian*, October 15. Accessed February 20, 2015. www.theguardian.com/technology/2013/oct/15/3d-printed-fashion-couture-catwalk.

Flaherty, Joseph. 2014. "This Dress is Made From 3D Printed Plastic but Flows like Fabric." *Wired*, September 12. Accessed August 25 2015. www.wired.com/2014/12/dress-made-3-d-printed-plastic-flows-like-fabric/.

Faust, Marie-Eve, Serge Carrier and Pierre Baptist. 2006. "Variations in Canadian Women's Ready-to-Wear Standard Sizes." *Journal of Fashion Marketing and Management: An International Journal* 10, 1: 71–83.

Geršak, Jelka. 2013. *Design of Clothing Manufacturing Processes: A Systematic Approach to Planning, Scheduling and Control*. Cambridge: Woodhead Publishing Ltd.

Gill, Simeon. 2015. "A Review of Research and Innovation in Garment Sizing, Prototyping and Fitting." *Textile Progress* 47, 1: 1–85.

Hunstig, Maria. 2012. "Adidas Neo Sets up Ten Stores in Germany." *Sportswear International*, February 16. Accessed August 25, 2015. www.sportswearnet.com/businessnews/pages/protected/ADIDAS-NEO-SETS-UP-TEN-STORES-IN-GERMANY_4991.html.

Jopson, Barney. 2012. "Cloth Shops Prepare for Body Scanning." *Financial Times*, September 14. Accessed February 20, 2015. www.ft.com/intl/cms/s/0/fb0ef6e2-fa0c-11e1-9f6a-00144feabdc0.html?siteedition=intl#axzz3TC9Oah4n.

Kalms, Brian, ed. 2014. *Re-Thinking Retail in the Digital Era*. London: LID Publishing.

Klara, Robert. 2015. "Could 3-D Body Scanners Help You Find the Perfect Pair of Jeans?" *Adweek*, May 4. Accessed August 25, 2015. www.adweek.com/news/technology/could-3-d-body-scanners-help-you-find-perfect-pair-jeans-164427.

Leach, William R. 1984. "Transformations in a Culture of Consumption: Women and Department Stores, 1890–1925." *The Journal of American History* 71, 2: 319–342.

Lemire, Beverly. 2009. "Developing Consumerism and the Ready-made Clothing Trade in Britain, 1750–1800," in *Fashion: Critical and Primary Sources* (vol 2), edited by Peter McNeil, 241-265. Oxford and New York: Berg.

Levitt, Sarah. 1991. "Cheap Mass-Produced Men's Clothing in the Nineteenth and Early Twentieth Centuries." *Textile History* 22, 2: 179–192.

McGlaun, Shane. 2012. "Bloomingdale's and Bodymetrics Team up for Open Body Sizing Pod." *SlashGear*, August 10. Accessed February 20, 2015. www.slashgear.com/bloomingdales-and-bodymetrics-team-up-for-open-body-sizing-pod-10242503/.

Miller, Daniel, Peter Jackson, Nigel Thrift, Beverly Holbrook and Michael Rowlands. 1998. *Shopping, Place and Identity*. London: Routledge.

Miller, Michael. 1981. *The Bon Marché: Bourgeois Culture and the Department Store, 1869–1920*. Princeton: Princeton University Press.

Nava, Mica. 2002. "Cosmopolitan Modernity Everyday Imaginaries and the Register of Difference." *Theory, Culture & Society* 19, 1–2: 81–99.

Niemeier, Stefan, Andrea Zocchi and Marco Catena. 2013. *Reshaping Retail: Why Technology is Transforming the Industry and How to Win in the New Consumer Driven World*. Chichester: John Wiley.

Outka, Elizabeth. 2005. "Crossing the Great Divides: Selfridges, Modernity, and the Commodified Authentic." *Modernism/modernity* 12, 2: 311–332.

Otieno, Rose, Chris Harrow and Gaynor Lea-Greenwood. 2005. "The Unhappy Shopper, a Retail Experience: Exploring Fashion, Fit and Affordability." *International Journal of Retail and Distribution Management* 33, 4: 298–309.

Qin, Sheng F., Emmanouil Lagoudakis, Q.P. Kang and Kai Cheng. 2008. "Customer-Centric Strategy for E-Manufacturing in Apparel Industry." *Applied Mechanics and Materials*, vols. 10–12. Switzerland: Trans Tech Publications.

Samuels, Peter. 2012. "Bodymetrics – the Science of Fit." *Peter Samuels*, December 18. Accessed August 25, 2015. http://blog.petersamuels.com/?p=1022.

Shah, Dhiram. 2007. "Bodymetrics Bespoke Jeans-scan and get Customized Clothing." *Newlaunches*, January 17. Accessed August 25, 2015. http://newlaunches.com/archives/bodymetrics_bespoke_jeansscan_and_get_customized_clothing.php.

Stone, Madeline. 2014. "3D-Printed Dresses Are Radically Changing the Meaning of Haute Couture." *Business Insider Australia*, August 29. Accessed February 25, 2015. www.businessinsider.com.au/3d-printed-fashion-2014–8?op=1#dutch-designer-iris-van-herpen-was-one-of-the-first-to-use-3d-printing-techniques-in-fashion-starting-in-2010-with-her-crystallization-collection-in-january-2013-she-debuted-this-intricate-lace-like-dress-that-was-created-with-a-laser-printing-technique-by-belgian-company-materialise-1.

"Top 100 Online Retailers in the UK 2013." 2013. *Digital Strategy Consulting*, June 24. Accessed August 25, 2015. www.digitalstrategyconsulting.com/intelligence/2013/06/top_100_online_retailers_in_the_uk_2013.php.

Ulanoff, Lance. 2014. "Nervous System's Dress Breaks the Mold for 3D Printed Fashion." *Mashable Australia*, December 10. Accessed February 25, 2015. http://mashable.com/2014/12/09/softer-3d-printed-dress/.

"Voltage by Iris van Herpen with Neri Oxman and Juila Loerner." 2013. *Dezeen*, January 22. Accessed February 20, 2015. www.dezeen.com/2013/01/22/voltage-3d-printed-clothes-by-iris-van-herpen-with-neri-oxman-and-julia-koerne/.

Wilson, Elizabeth. 1985. *Adorned in Dreams: Fashion and Modernity*. Berkley: University of California Press.

Zakim Michael. 2003. *Ready-Made Democracy: A History of Men's Dress in the American Republic, 1760–1860*. Chicago: University of Chicago Press.

Part III

Contested Identities/ Contested Displays

12 Exotics to erotics

Exploring new frontiers of desire within Parisian department store décors

Kevin C. Robbins

The publication of Émile Zola's masterwork *Au Bonheur des Dames* (*The Ladies' Paradise*) in March 1883 unleashed a wave of scandals in metropolitan French culture and society. This was the first great European or French novel to feature a department store and its ceaselessly redecorated interior designed for commercial display as the main protagonists. Zola's entrepreneurial exposé shocked the reading public with frank descriptions of inspired but duplicitous retail merchandizing techniques, wretched living and working conditions for store staff, rampant sexual abuse of vulnerable female employees by male store managers, and sales décors capable of inciting female shoppers into shameless public frenzies of desire, mad buying, and almost orgasmic kleptomania (Tiersten 2001, 15–18; Uzanne 1892). Predicated on Zola's interviews with the architects of these new stores and on his meticulous observations of department store displays and operations recorded in his personal notebooks, *The Ladies' Paradise* featured a central male character, the store owner Octave Mouret, renowned as "the best window-dresser in Paris, a revolutionary window-dresser in fact who had founded the school of the brutal and gigantic in the art of display" (Zola 1995, 48). Zola lavished attention on the interior designs and constantly redecorated shop windows and sales floors of one great Parisian department store. To Octave Mouret, heroic owner of The Ladies' Paradise, Zola ascribed "a stroke of genius for display" (Zola 1995, 398). Such descriptions are of major sociocultural and socio-psychological importance since Zola denoted an entirely new, ever-shifting environment of intensifying indoor commercial activity. The author also emphasized the effects such cleverly built and constantly redecorated commercial zones exerted on the psyches and social behaviors of urban consumers, especially women. He observed that new urban entrepreneurs amassed and cheapened public access to formerly exotic commodities. In the process, they capitalized on the mass allure of these goods to stoke consumer desires via sensually stimulating store displays that eroticized consumption itself, yielding ever higher profits. For Zola, to comprehend such fusions of economics and emotions that were radically modernizing urban life required the closest possible scrutiny of commercial interior design.

First published serially in the Parisian daily *Le Gil Blas* (December 1882 to March 1883), *The Ladies' Paradise* went rapidly into book production at the great Parisian publisher Charpentier, with an initial printing of 60,000 copies (Zola 1998, 40–41). Nearly unanimous critical acclaim drove the new novel through at least three later editions, assuring a wide readership. Zola's text gained exceptional multimedia cultural impact in Paris and abroad. Foreign editions appeared instantly in Budapest (1883), two editions in England by 1886, an Italian version in 1900, and a Russian edition in 1903. This influence was sustained over decades by projects such as a successful and spectacular staged version of the story mounted as the grand finale to the 1896 theater season at the Parisian Théatre du Gymnase (*Annales du Théatre* 1896, 172–176).

These literary, dramatic, intensely visual, and seductive representations of innovative commercial spaces took place amidst and catalyzed a broader vogue for provocative new images of department store interiors produced especially by contemporary French and émigré graphic artists active in Paris. Exterior and interior views of elegant shops and huge emporia now gained unprecedented prominence in the work of visual artists active in France. In oils and graphic works, artists such as Jean Béraud, Theodore Roussel, and James Tissot examined commercial sites in greater detail. But the curious standout here is the Swiss migrant painter, woodblock carver, and engraver Félix Vallotton. Vallotton first moved to Paris in 1882 at exactly the moment when the novel *The Ladies' Paradise* intensified public debate over department stores and the effects of their displays on urban society. Vallotton's largest and most ambitious early painting, *Le Bon Marché* (1898), a huge triptych in oils depicting multiple acerbic scenes set in a packed, ominous department store interior, contributed to the spectacularizaton of innovative mass-market retail venues encouraged by popular and impressive staged settings of Zola's novel (Cogeval et al. 2013). Long captivated by the symbolic power and moral ambiguity of the big stores, Vallotton went on to include them in his visual surveys of what he called "Paris Intense." He executed both huge, brilliantly colored oil paintings and stark, disturbing black and white graphic pieces, often reworked for more suggestive visual effects and powerfully evoking the exotic, kinetic, visually impressive, and promiscuous interiors of great Parisian emporia. These were the same stores whose attractive lore Zola capitalized on to make *The Ladies' Paradise* a compelling social-realist, critical commentary on his times. Vallotton's images also problematically displayed women as both conspicuous, predatory consumers on the hunt and emotionally vulnerable while alone amidst the constantly seductive environments of major department stores.

The analytical habits and visual politics of Zola and Vallotton are highly complementary. Both men sought to map and look beneath urban façades of propriety to lay bare what they saw as the moral challenges and failures of bourgeois urban society (Stock 2015, 95–96). Zola and Vallotton are but two of the more virtuoso, symbiotically linked French artists inspired by a long-running public debate over the moral and political impact of great French department stores. Zola's writings and Vallotton's images circulated as other critics of rampant commercialism in the French Third Republic alleged that unscrupulous, profit-maximizing store owners and their guileful salesmen enticed consumers, especially vulnerable women, into dangerously self-indulgent and irrational purchases. More impassioned and hyperbolic conservative critics claimed that such immodest spending, fueled by unbridled feminine desire stoked by commercial advertising, threatened the financial integrity of the crazed shoppers' own households, the stability of bourgeois families, and the security of the nation as identified with prudent domestic economy and female self-sacrifice (Tiersten 2001, 15–54).

These various artful, late nineteenth-century French perspectives on novel commercial environments inspire and inform this chapter, which shows that modern interior and exterior architectures of commercial display deeply shaped and resonated through other contemporary French media of creative expression and cultural commentary at the time. New Parisian-built marketing and consumer excitement manifest themselves via innovative print and artful imagery. Both Zola and Vallotton celebrated, criticized, and exploited the innovative interior designs of Paris' vast department stores. Such graphic tales of conspicuous consumption, animated by meticulous descriptions of built commercial displays, assumed new dimensions of influence as entertainment spectacle and middle-class drama in modern Paris.

One need not look far to find the innovative Parisian mass-market and mass-retail institutions catalyzing Zola's path-breaking novel. By 1883, Paris was home to at least six great department stores, all generating vast amounts of print and pictorial publicity that drove intense competition between the emporia and stoked material desires and imaginations. By the debut of Zola's *Paradise*, the city's first great department store, the Bon Marché (Fig. 12.1), had been in operation for more than 50 years (Miller 1981, 19–47).

This innovative enterprise served as the model and competitive target for new, rival department stores, including Les Grands Magasins du Louvre (opened 1855), À la Belle Jardinière (opened 1856), Le Bazar de l'Hôtel de Ville (also 1856), La Samaritaine (1865), and Les Grands Magasins du Printemps (1865) (Williams 1982). In preparation for writing *Au Bonheur de Dames*, Zola visited several of these great department stores and scrutinized how they actually operated. He noted founders' quirks, store managerial structures, personnel recruitment procedures, employee regulations, and the actual job descriptions and daily working experiences of staff at all levels of buying and selling (Zola 1986, 147–233). Zola gave special attention to the publicity campaigns waged ruthlessly by the big stores, noting with astonishment the 800,000 illustrated Christmas catalogs sent out by Les Grands Magasins du Louvre alone in the early 1880s.

Zola also studied closely where and how highly attractive and profitable goods were actually put on display. He compiled his own lexicons of modern marketing lingo derived from publicity catalogs of the great stores' merchandize (Zola 1986, 191–203). Zola's own novel vocabulary reflects these practical, self-taught observations. He repeatedly calls Mouret, his heroic entrepreneur, "the best window-dresser in Paris, a revolutionary window-dresser" (*le premier étalagiste de Paris, un étalagiste révolutionnaire*) (Zola 1995, 48; Zola 1964, 434). That denomination itself reflects and intensifies a very recent French linguistic innovation. A respected French etymological dictionary shows that, circa 1801, *étalagiste* simply designated anyone who exposed objects for public sale, often by arraying them in a common stall (*étal*) or on make-shift tables adjoining city thoroughfares (*Larousse* 1992, s.v. "étaler," 680). However, by 1846, that term now also denoted a *décorateur* (that is, a designer or artful arranger) who specialized in the attractive, impressive contrivance of store displays – more like a stage designer or set decorator (*Larousse* 1992, 680). In this regard, frequent British and American English translations of *étalagiste* as "window-dresser" miss the mark since Zola plainly means that Mouret is a gifted, adroit, and audacious designer. Mouret becomes a virtuoso and revolutionary artist creating enticing displays of goods for sale not only in the store's windows facing the street

Figure 12.1 Albert Chevojon, Interior, the Central Hall and Grand Staircase, Le Bon
Marché, Paris, photograph, c. 1900.
Source: Archives Moisant-Savey, Tours

but also – and much more often – inside the store itself, drawing throngs of avid consumers from one great, buyable scene to another. This emergent meaning of the term
étalagiste resonates better with another modern connotation of the cognate French
verb *étalager*: "to show off" (*Larousse* 1992, s.v. "étaler," 680). A proliferation in

Paris of grandiose, ultra-competitive department stores showing off their wares enabled the development of commercial artists and artistries reflected in new meanings for terms like *étalagiste*.

Zola fixed his comprehension of these new commercial spaces and heroic professional opportunities by drawing his own highly detailed maps of the first three floors of the Bon Marché department store. He paid particular attention to building's infrastructures, including entryways, grand staircases, and communicating galleries now embellished with intricate wrought-iron frameworks and glazed, glowing ceilings. But he also visually noted the precise distribution of departments, the comparative size of store displays for certain articles, and the construction materials employed in the cabinets, cupboards, mirrored panels, shelves, and display tables that shaped customer behaviors and enticed unprecedented and controversial waves of female conspicuous consumption (Zola 1986, 171–174).

In Zola's estimation, the virtuosity of an innovative merchandizer like Mouret was akin to that of a gifted interior designer. Mouret created commercial rooms with an elegance and sophistication that sold the goods on display while successfully marketing his own brand, the store itself: "But it was in the interior arrangement of the shops that Mouret revealed himself to be an unrivalled master" (Zola 1995, 235; Zola 1964, 613). Drawing his inspiration from tours of the Bon Marché and the Grands Magasins du Louvre, Zola described the silk hall of The Ladies' Paradise as "the most elegant of all the departments, a veritable drawing room in which the goods were so ethereal that they seemed to be a kind of luxurious furnishing" (Zola 1995, 96). Indeed, Zola fastidiously inventorized exactly how the mercantile spaces of The Ladies' Paradise had been put together. His roving eye never missed even the smallest detail of innovative commercial design. The salesrooms he imagined are lined by sober but naturally rich, deep, carved-oak cupboards (Zola 1995, 50). Only long and imposing, multi-tiered, and highly polished natural oak tables could provide suitably impressive supports for the textiles and other sale goods artfully arranged across every square inch of their surfaces (Zola 1995, 93). Cleverly arranged in serried ranks, such tables, covered in brightly-hued articles, evoked impressive aristocratic gardens and mimicked a fertile, floral profusion that proved irresistible to avid female clients:

> The counters, symmetrically arranged, looked like flower beds, transforming the hall into a formal garden, smiling with a range of soft flower tones. Spread out on the wooden counter, falling from overflowing shelves, and in boxes which had been torn open, a harvest of silk scarves displayed the brilliant red of geraniums, the milky white of petunias, the golden yellow of chrysanthemums, the sky blue of verbena; and higher up, entwined on brass stems, there was another mass of blossom – fichus strewn about, ribbons unrolled, a dazzling strand extending and twisting up round the pillars, and multiplying in mirrors.
>
> (Zola 1995, 243–244)

Mouret constantly patrolled these enticing displays and superintended their frequent relocation and redecoration. Such incessant transformations worked to disorient regular customers, increasing their time in the store, augmenting their impulse acquisitions, and enriching the master's profits. Fashion here gained its vogue not simply from continual alterations in the seasonal clothing on offer but also from ceaseless and cunning changes in the décor and interior design of the store itself.

Zola credited Mouret with an exquisite sensitivity to just the right ensemble of elegant design and display elements to yield maximum customer attraction, seduction, and payout in various sections of his expanding shop. In the glove department, the boss fitted a "narrow counter covered with green velvet with nickel-plated corners" (Zola 1995, 100). Such furnishings showed off the merchandize to best advantage and strategically enabled the salesmen to take the hands of female customers while seductively intimating advice on the best purchase. In the new perfume department, Mouret opted for even greater refinement: "Inside the display counters and on small crystal shelves of the showcases pots of pomades and creams were lined up, boxes of powder and rouge, phials of oils and toilet waters; while the fine brushes, combs, scissors, and pocket flasks occupied a special cupboard" (Zola 1995, 418). To demonstrate even more ingratiating solicitude towards his predominately female customer targets, Mouret installed the very latest elevators in his store. He equipped the lifts with opulent mirrored walls, plush velvet seats, and richly decorated, polished brass doors. These elegant conveyances proved irresistible to mothers who visited the shop with children in tow and whose now easy, luxurious movement from floor to floor upped Mouret's profits almost instantly (Zola 1995, 234 and 245).

Although Zola's penchant for piling up a mass of facts about modern store furnishings wearied and even numbed some readers, contemporary literary critics, especially among the Parisian avant-garde, found such architectural details unprecedented and captivating. Arguably Zola's most sympathetic follower at the time, the progressive and inventive literary star Joris-Karl Huysmans, found *Au Bonheur des Dames* "stupefying." Huysmans singled out for special praise Zola's masterly descriptions of the store's constantly changing fixtures and displays (*les étalages*) (Huysmans 1953, 93–95). There, he claimed, Zola captured in bravura prose a "shape-shifting monster" dazzling and seducing customers. Embracing Zola's innovative attention to these vital details of built city environments, Huysmans wondered at how such potent armatures of modernity could have been so long neglected by other urbane authors.

Writing in the Parisian daily *Le Radical*, the usually sharp-tongued arbiter Albert Cim lauded "the very beautiful descriptions" Zola produced of the extravagant "white sales" and their specially contrived store displays (Cim 1883, n.p.). For readers of the respected *Revue politique et littéraire*, the critic Maxime Gaucher extolled Zola's account of "this immense department store, so richly ornamented, so splendidly illuminated with its inviting, thickly carpeted grand staircase [...] what beautiful rooms!, what glittering details!" (Gaucher 1883, 343–344). In the Parisian daily *Le Soleil* for 31 March 1883, the reviewer Jean de Nivelle confirmed Zola's stature as the primary force of French literary modernity unrivalled in his ability to "reveal the actual mechanics of these vast enterprises that today we call Great Department Stores" (Nivelle 1883, n.p.). Thus a chorus of critical praise for *The Ladies' Paradise* in the booming Parisian daily press made revelatory details about commercial interior design appear as essential components in any real comprehension or consciousness of modern urban life. This is also the tenor of a laudatory critique of *Au Bonheur des Dames* appearing in the annual compendium *Le Livre: Revue du monde littéraire* (*Le Livre* 1883, 242–244).

Among the deft merchandizing schemes and "theatrical effects" Zola ascribed to Octave Mouret, few were as profitable as the traffic in exotic foreign commodities championed by this captain of self-serving global commerce (Zola 1995, 238). This reiterated theme enabled Zola to explore not only the international reach of Mouret's resources, but also the erotic charges of modern mass-retail environments. Here, as Zola reported in his novel, a profusion of sensually alluring products was displayed openly, inviting the direct touch of consumers. Fervid customers now spent more freely and exhausted themselves as their material desires rose to almost insatiable levels. To maximize enticements for a public rush towards a great fall sale at The Ladies' Paradise, Mouret redecorated the main entryway of his store as an "oriental hall" (Zola 1995, 470). He achieved this ravishing transformation with material from the distant and mysterious Levant. He lavishly displayed hundreds of richly patterned and dirt cheap Turkish and Middle Eastern textiles, especially thick, perfumed oriental carpets never before offered *en masse* and at such attractive prices. Festooned from the ceiling and adorning all the walls, heaped in languorous piles, and confected into a sumptuous pasha's tent, these fabrics staged a "harem scene" at the door fevered by "an orgy of colors" (Zola 1995, 85 and 88; Zola 1964, 469 and 472). Such calculated, suggestive, almost scandalous commercial design had its intended seductive effect. Female customers were astonished and excited by what they, too, called a "harem" (Zola 1995, 116). Zola's wording here appropriated and amplified the lubricious connotations of "harem" in contemporary French. Since the 1870s, Littré's *Dictionnaire de la Langue Française* gave "harem" the figurative meaning *maison de débauche*, or "whore house" (Littré, 1863–1872, s.v. "Harem"). As reported by Zola, Mouret's audacious and risqué commercial displays entirely twisted and recast the antique meaning of "harem," once simply denoting the women's quarters throughout the Arab world. Here the manifestly erotic charge of Parisian mass-merchandizing and interior commercial design distorted and demoralized such ancient usages.

The sale went to a triumphant and profitable climax. In the aftermath, as spent customers departed, "Upstairs in the mezzanine departments the havoc was the same: furs littered the floor, ready-made clothes were heaped up [...] the lace and underclothes unfolded, crumpled, thrown about everywhere, gave the impression that an army of women had undressed there haphazardly in a wave of desire" (Zola 1995, 117). Mouret's cunning displays of previously exotic commodities here aroused ravishing erotic moments of conspicuous consumption by women.

From this early and blatant sexually charged account, Zola unveiled in ever more graphic terms Mouret's naked ambitions: "Mouret's sole passion was the conquest of Woman [...] he had built this temple for her in order to hold her at his mercy. His tactics were to intoxicate her with amorous attentions, to trade on her desires, and to exploit her excitement" (Zola 1995, 234). Indeed, as noted previously, Mouret's strategic selections of counter materials, display tables, and fitting room appointments were all calculated to maximize the seductive powers of the store and its staff, who often touched impressionable, un-chaperoned female customers. In the glove department, predatory salesmen had a particular advantage. Here, male store staff "attack" their female customers: "Half lying on the counter, he was holding her hand, taking her fingers one by one and sliding the glove on with a long, practiced, and sustained caress, and he was looking at her as if he expected to see from her face that she was swooning with voluptuous joy" (Zola 1995, 101). Such sensuous appeals built into the store's architecture across its departments often hit home. Mouret is particularly ingenious when arranging elegant, highly polished tables to display long, sinuous, irresistible strands of the finest lace: "The customers [...] were pale-faced and shiny-eyed. It seemed as if all the seductions of the shop had been leading up to this supreme temptation, that this was the hidden alcove where the customers were doomed to fall, the place of perdition where even the strongest succumbed. Hands were being plunged into the overflowing piles of lace, quivering with excitement from touching them" (Zola 1995, 263–264). Some housewives, so enamored with Mouret's commercial wiles, lost all sense of respectability and threw themselves into paroxysms of shoplifting: "Ravaged by a furious, irresistible urge, Madame de Boves had been stealing like this for a year. The attacks had been getting worse, increasing until they had become a sensual pleasure necessary to her existence, sweeping away all the reasonings of prudence and giving her enjoyment all the more keen" (Zola 1995, 422). In the aftermath of Mouret's most dazzling and lascivious sale ("a colossal orgy"), many other female customers "despoiled and violated (*violée*), were going away in disarray, their desires satisfied, and with the secret shame of having yielded to temptation in the depths of some sleazy hotel" (Zola 1995, 426–427; Zola 1964, 797; Jennings 1977; Abelson 1989; Shteir 2011). Zola's graphic equations of unrestrained female shopping with fervid sexual self-indulgence stimulated equally audacious Parisian artists to mount similarly brazen images of erotically conspicuous commercial display and consumption. The inveterate Parisian *flâneur* and painter Jean Béraud produced multiple scenes of women shopping for extravagant outerwear and intimate apparel in these emporia. Synergies between commercial displays of exotic commodities and the charged erotics of touching and consuming them had multiple textual and visual promoters in Belle-Époque Paris (Jennings 1977; Tiersten 2001).

Thirteen years after its debut in print, *Au Bonheur des Dames* seduced dramatic translators. For the grand finale of the 1896 entertainment season at the noted Paris Théatre du Gymnase, the playwrights Charles Hugot and Raoul de Saint-Arroman produced a stage version of the novel in six opulent scenes (*Annales du Théatre* 1896, 172–176). A reviewer for the *Annales du Théatre* was staggered by the grandeur and veracity of the sets, which became the highlight of the entire extravaganza. For scene two, the curtain rose to reveal a true spectacle: the "splendid" main commercial hall of the department store. Audiences received a memorable impression of its vast scale, grandiose central staircase, super-imposed galleries, exact mercantile fixtures, bustling staff, and sumptuously dressed, vivacious elite clientele (*Annales du Théatre* 1896, 174–175). This was a masterwork of set design perfectly mimicking the equally theatrical originals: the actual Bon Marché and Zola's novelization of that bazar. The entire dramatic ensemble displayed an accuracy "pushed to the outer-most limits of truth" (*Annales du Théatre* 1896, 175). Such fidelity to the mercantile model compelled the reviewer to call the production "a truly modern play" (*Annales du Théatre* 1896, 171). This document reminds us of the remarkable extent to which the actual appearance and interior design of Parisian department stores could shape and inform contemporary set work and stage management in the burgeoning theaters of the capital. How these great emporia were truly put together and operated became topics of sustained artistic investigation and comment in multiple, cross-fertilizing metropolitan media of the era: short stories, novels, stage plays, graphically illustrated serials, and fine art. The décors of city department stores energized modern artists and came to define modernity itself (Huysmans 1953, 93–95).

In early 1882, on the eve of Zola's striking success with *Au Bonheur des Dames*, the young, intrepid, and aspiring Swiss artist Félix Vallotton moved to Paris. Vallotton first enrolled in a private art school (the notable Académie Julian) and, in 1883, gained acceptance – as the fourth inductee out of 70 – to the prestigious École des Beaux Arts. With a base of operations in the newly chic Montparnasse district, Vallotton rapidly familiarized himself with the artful institutions and inspirations of Paris (Cogeval et al. 2013, 265–268; Koella and Poletti 2012, 233–237). From early prowls of city museums, Vallotton graduated to sharp-eyed patrols of annual artistic salons, temporary exhibitions, and gallery openings. He parlayed these surveys into occasional paid work (1890–1897) as the roving art critic for his home-town paper, *La Gazette de Lausanne* (Koella and Poletti 2012). During these instructive forays, Vallotton sought out the works and ateliers of noted French commercial and graphic designers deeply implicated in the promotion of serialized novels, mass-market merchandizers, and spectacular entertainment venues. For the 18 April 1891 edition of the *Gazette*, Vallotton wrote a glowing appreciation of Jules Chéret's colorful posters touting the department stores, theaters, dance-halls, stage plays, and exhibitions that animated Parisian entertainment of the era (Koella and Poletti 2012, 34–37). Since 1889, Chéret had been doing promotional images for Zola's novels and had just finished a poster for *Gil Blas* announcing a new serial version of Zola's *L'Argent* (Broido 1992, 29 and 32, Figures 143 and 149). Chéret's other regular clients included a multitude of great Paris stores such as Les Grands Magasins du Louvre and Printemps. Deeply touched by another artist's high praise, Chéret sent a letter of acknowledgment to Vallotton (30 April 1891) thanking him, inviting him back to his workshop, and promising as a gift in recompense artist proof copies of new commercial posters (Guisan and Jakubec 1973, 76).

Although Vallotton's early oil paintings were winning him admission to juried expositions and public honors, he took up wood-block carving and print making in 1891. His print production doubled in 1892. Amazed by Vallotton's striking creations, Zola's champion and confidant, Octave Uzanne, devoted a laudatory article to Vallotton's new graphic work and published it in the progressive Paris monthly *L'Art et l'idée* (February 1892). Energized by this encouragement, Vallotton produced multiple new suites of drawings and complementary, more complex wood-block prints depicting notable aspects of Parisian civic, commercial, and street life. During 1893, he first executed a richly worked graphite, ink, and gouache drawing that shows a packed "white sale" inside a huge department store. This image bore the simple title *Le Bon Marché*, taking the name of the oldest *grand magasin* in Paris – and mimicking Zola's earlier inspiration for *The Ladies' Paradise* (Marin et al. 2010, 13–26 and Illustrations 29–30). Shortly thereafter, Vallotton used this drawing as inspiration for a new, more detailed wood-block print also entitled *Le Bon Marché*. The images inscribed in both drawing and block print bear an uncanny resemblance to the physical spaces and gender tensions manifest in Zola's salacious narrative of modern merchandizing techniques and the erotics of material consumption generated by the big stores. Vallotton's graphic images, I would argue, became yet another medium circulating artful critiques of the human dimensions and implications of modern retail design and display.

In Vallotton's graphite, ink, and gouache piece (Fig. 12.2), the viewer is confronted by a mass of exclusively female customers attended to by a host of salesmen in dark formal jackets. The setting is clearly a brightly illuminated and opulently decorated,

Figure 12.2 Félix Vallotton, *Le Bon Marché*, 25 × 32 cm, graphite, ink, white gouache, blue pencil on wove paper, 1893.
Source: Graphic Arts Collection, Musée d'Art et d'Histoire, Geneva

columned sales hall of a *grand magasin* framed by huge plate-glass windows that form the distant façade. "White sale" goods are draped over stanchions processing at an oblique angle and growing in height across the background. The sales pit is delimited by vertical textile cascades and horizontal bands of bright white fabric that flow in undulating waves from the left and pillow up on the right. Apparently closely following Zola's literary account, Vallotton shows one salesman in the left foreground actually leaning over and nearly lying upon the immaculate white sheets to show off their delicate, supple surface. He has engaged his female customer in an intimate tête-à-tête. She obligingly bends over, her bosom in the sheets and her bustled hips in the air. Another salesman, just behind this pair, cocks an arm and lets a bolt of fabric snake down before a primmer shopper, whose narrowed eyes and pointed, gloved fingers show her sharp judgment of the goods on offer. Literally and figuratively drawing upon Zola's sexually charged shop décors, Vallotton espies how men and women newly interacted within them.

Vallotton then almost immediately used his drawing as inspiration for a more curiously detailed wood-block carving and print (Fig. 12.3). Dated to the same year (1893), this new take on the Bon Marché has been very subtly reworked to intensify

Figure 12.3 Félix Vallotton, *Le Bon Marché*, 26.2 × 33.7 cm, woodcut, 1893.
Source: The Cleveland Museum of Art, John L. Severance Fund 1998.36

the unfolding commercial courtship rituals and to heighten the tactile sexual and visual politics of the scene. In the block print, the artist has added gently curving stream-
ers and festoons of fabric topping the stanchions and splaying open-legged across
the top right background. One effect of this alteration is to channel and frame more
closely the pool of available female customers. Vallotton has given the formerly prim
and no-nonsense woman confronted by an inviting coil of fabric an entirely new and
much more receptive face. Now she turns her head, in three-quarter view, away from
her salesman-suitor, arches her eyebrows, and demurely bats or closes her eyes. She
has become a coquette and her left hand now plunges more deeply into the yielding
fabric – Vallotton has tripled the incised folds – whereas her left hand makes contact
with the cloth. The same woman's right hand and bust are now approached by new
wrinkles in the fabric that appear as slim, probing fingers or skeletal hands reaching
out to fondle her. The block print displays more lines of force on the sheets beneath
the nearly prone, well-coiffed woman in the center foreground. These indentations
accentuate her weight and draw attention to her hands nearly grasping the fingers
of her mustachioed store clerk. Vallotton has also redone the female customer in the
diamond-print blouse at lower right, foreshortening her right arm, and showing off

her delicately poised, smooth, white right hand against the black waistcoat of her consort. And his right hand, fingers open, now appears to caress the sheets over which the woman's companion or rival hovers in expectation of a consummate deal. The interplay of gestures here has become more explicitly eroticized over the earlier drawn version of *Le Bon Marché*. Frontiers of touching and desire have grown closer in the block print and Vallotton accumulates more novel indications in his graphic art that consumption and concupiscence go hand-in-hand amidst the charged and provocative built venues of modern retail commerce. These intricately designed and decorated retail spaces have become suitable, even essential settings for the most revelatory pictorial investigations of what modern urban life was and what its mores had become. Vallotton, like Zola, appears captivated by the novel expressive capacities that richly decorated department store interiors offered to artists prepared to appropriate and dramatize these built environments of mass-marketing and seductive sales rituals. Here, commercial assignations between male sellers and female buyers manifested an unprecedented and public frisson between the sexes, swelling the spectacular element in these exchanges.

As Zola's novel morphed into stage performances, Vallotton set to work on a far more imposing, unprecedentedly large and equally dramatic visual representation of the modern department store and its material fixtures/human fixations. This piece became a triptych in oils, nearly seven feet in width, also entitled *Le Bon Marché* (1898). The details here are even more provocative, and clearly indicative of how the interior appointments of great stores became known as painterly sets for the staging and moral critique of modern and promiscuous urban life. The left panel of this huge masterwork (Fig. 12.4) shows an elegantly dressed woman in close consultation with a perfectly attired salesman in cravat, cutaway coat, and fashionably striped trousers. This shadowed, negotiating, up-scale couple enveloped in the scent of seduction is juxtaposed with a brilliantly illuminated array of carefully wrapped, boxed, and highly priced soaps, perfumes, and toiletry articles. Delicate but refulgent, mirrored glass shelves at the rear sparkle with liquid attractants and their crystalline reflections. Male seller and female buyer mutually incline their heads and noses to capture together a whiff of some essential and beguiling fragrance. Vallotton's luxurious and suggestive imagery here almost perfectly corresponds to and connives with Zola's prior description of the perfume department in *The Ladies' Paradise* (Zola 1995, 418).

The right panel of Vallotton's early masterwork qualifies as an iconic "Three Ages of Woman." This history is set against multi-tiered wooden tables displaying box after box of shop-worn items on deep-discount, close-out sale, and a gaudy parade of pastel umbrellas (Fig. 12.5). A dowdy crone and stiff-collared girl march toward us with nothing to show for their shopping. Their hands are empty. They are partially eclipsed by a sauntering lady in red and black. This perfectly coiffed fashion plate in a rakish hat and with her decorated back to us sports a high-waist red jacket in black appliqué with an undulating peplum accentuating the sway of her hips. A fluted, bell-like collar emphasizes her long, elegant neck, while bouffant sleeves highlight her shoulders. The bizarre jacket pattern in black might evoke Art Nouveau tendrils but here more closely resembles insect antennae, giving its wearer the appearance of some roving female mantis dressed to kill. Zola's shop-walking sources in real Parisian department stores apprised him of the many prostitutes and adulterous women frequenting the *grands magasins* in search of male prey or simply

Figure 12.4 Félix Vallotton, *Le Bon Marché*, 1898 (detail, left panel), oil on cardboard, 70 x 50 cm.
Source: Private Collection, Photo Credit and image reproduced with the permission of the Fondation Félix Vallotton, Lausanne, Switzerland

their next illicit assignation. Such scandalous behavior in the great stores became known to the Parisian police (Bertrand Jennings 1977, 37–81). Zola deliciously spins out several such subplots of adulterous men and women cruising The Ladies' Paradise. Vallotton strikes one as entirely au-courant with such modern mating rituals now so often conducted against the transient and promiscuous backdrop of unpopular or damaged goods set for immediate liquidation. These can also mark the life stages of modern city women. Such ominous lessons haunt, I think, the pictures Vallotton conjures out of the instructive aisles and displays of contemporary department stores.

The central and largest panel of Vallotton's disturbing triptych (Fig. 12.6) shows the vaunted, grand main staircase so coveted amidst the interior designs of the Parisian monster shops. Exhausted, black-clad consumers encased in expressionless faces troop for the exit. Clutching pupa-like parcels, these city drones apparently derive no excitement or delight from their acquisitions amidst this crowded hive of activity. Garishly colored, intertwined swags of material creep across the ceilings, isolating the public

Figure 12.5 Félix Vallotton, *Le Bon Marché*, 1898 (detail, right panel), oil on cardboard, 70 x 50 cm.
Source: Private Collection, Photo Credit and image reproduced with the permission of the Fondation Félix Vallotton, Lausanne, Switzerland

choke point on the curving steps. Globular electric lamps, also intensely fashionable amidst the interior designs of new Parisian emporia, cast a very unflattering light over everything they harshly illuminate. Ubiquitous department markers and picket-like "Sale" signs truncate all sight lines, intensifying the ironically claustrophobic dimensions of this multistorey but tightly packed space. Forlorn, apparently drained or fatigued customers are impervious to the bright decorations and can reflect only a dark, grim determination to leave with what little money they still have left. Enclosed in a commercially viable, colossal art work expressly designed to stimulate productive exchange, these veterans of merchandizing on an industrial scale seem more the victims than the beneficiaries of their acquisitions.

In the most recently published critical scholarship on Vallotton, the art historian Bridget Alsdorf argues persuasively that an "attention to the ethics of vision structures a significant portion of Valloton's *fin-de-siècle* drawings and prints, in which the physical and psychological pressure of human proximity is a primary

Figure 12.6 Félix Vallotton, *Le Bon Marché*, 1898 (detail, center panel), oil on cardboard, 70 x 100 cm.
Source: Private Collection, Photo Credit and image reproduced with the permission of the Fondation Félix Vallotton, Lausanne, Switzerland

theme" (Alsdorf 2015, 210). Alsdorf surmises that similar inquiries by the literary ethicist Zola probably encouraged Vallotton to pursue this line of urbane, charged pictorial investigation (Alsdorf 2015, 213). Vallotton here excelled in deploying compositional devices that implicated viewers, putting them "in uncomfortable positions [...] forcing reflection on the ethical stakes of vision" (Alsdorf 2015, 217). Close scrutiny of Vallotton's overtly commercial scenes set in one great Parisian department store, rendered in panoramic sweep and suggestive detail, amply confirm, I believe, the moral grounding of these images. Resolutely taking up Zola's charge to scrutinize the great emporia of modern Paris in order to uncover information on how these colossal mercantile organizations were forever altering lifestyles, Vallotton plunged his viewers into the jostling aisles and fraught negotiations customers waged in these carefully and tellingly constructed engines of mass commerce. Such stores and the ways in which they were actually put together formed ravishing and instructive pressure points in modern urban life, capable of revealing how citizens – men and women, rich, middling, and poor – responded to the mass-mercantile stratagems now integral to acquisitive and more inherently unstable civic lives and economies. Neither Zola nor the French playwrights and Swiss artists he inspired ever shied away from the brutal, vicious and rapacious human relations and fixations these leviathan stores could promote amidst their gilded profusion. That was part of the "relations between guilt, responsibility, and vision" that

Alsdorf claims Vallotton investigated graphically (Alsdorf 2015, 210). Predicated on crowd access and confusion, designed to seduce and enthrall, these vast retail establishments became accessible but deeply problematic venues. They formed new frontiers where exoticism and eroticism intermingled promiscuously and were enshrined at a price both material and moral. Struggling to sum up his painterly ethos, Vallotton once confided to his diary: "It strikes me that I paint for well-balanced people but also for those who, deep inside, harbor a bit of unacknowledged vice" (Guisan and Jakubec 1975, 245). Encouraging self-revelatory introspection for such wayward urbanites must rank high among the motivations prompting French literary, dramatic, and graphic artists to ply their audiences with new depictions of great department stores and their interior designs. From such exposures, avid viewers gained new perspectives on the dangerous inner passions that contemporary commercial displays could engender.

References

Abelson, Elaine S. 1989. *When Ladies Go A-Thieving: Middle-Class Shoplifters in the Victorian Department Store*. Oxford: Oxford University Press.

Alsdorf, Bridget. 2015. "Félix Vallotton's *Murderous Life*." *Art Bulletin* XCVII, 2: 210–228.

Broido, Lucy. 1992. *The Posters of Jules Chéret*, 2nd ed. New York: Dover Publications.

Cim, Albert. 1883. "Les Livres." *Le Radical* 3e Année, 73.

Cogeval, Guy, Isabelle Cahn, Marina Durcey, and Katia Poletti. 2013. *Félix Vallotton: Le feu sous la glace*. Paris: Réunion des Musées Nationaux, Grand Palais, Musée d'Orsay.

Gaucher, Maxime. 1883. *Revue Politique et Littéraire* 3, 11: 343–344.

Guisan, Gilbert and Doris Jakubec. 1973. *Félix Valloton. Documents pour une Biographie et pour L'Histoire d'une Oeuvre I*. Paris: La Bibliothèque des Arts.

Guisan, Gilbert and Doris Jakubec. 1975. *Félix Vallotton. Documents pour une Biographie et pour L'Histoire d'une Oeuvre III "Le Journal."* Paris: La Bibliothèque des Arts.

Huysmans, Joris-Karl. 1953. *Lettres inédites à Émile Zola*. Geneva: Droz.

Jennings, Chantal Bertrand. 1977. *L'Eros et la femme chez Zola*. Paris: Klincksieck.

Koella, Rudolf and Katia Poletti. 2012. *Félix Vallotton Critique d'art*. Milan: 5 Continents Editions.

Larousse Dictionnaire de la Langue Française Lexis. 1992. Paris: Larousse.

Le Livre: Revue du Monde Littéraire. 1883. Tome V, "Bibliographie Moderne:" 240–242.

Littré, Emile. 1863–1872. *Dictionnaire de la langue française*. Paris: Hachette.

Marin, Jean-Yves, Christian Rumelin, and Caroline Guignard. 2010. *Félix Vallotton: De la gravure à la peinture*. Berne: Benteli.

Miller, Michael B. 1981. *The Bon Marché: Bourgeois Culture and the Department Store 1869–1920*. Princeton: Princeton University Press.

Nivelle, Jean de. 1883. "Livres Nouveaux." *Le Soleil*, 31 March n.p.

Shteir, Rachel. 2011. *The Steal: A Cultural History of Shoplifting*. New York: Penguin Books.

Stock, Karen. 2015. "A Portable Keyhole into the Fictional Apartment Building: The Interiors of Félix Vallotton and Émile Zola." In *Designing the French Interior: The Modern Home and Mass Media*, edited by Anca I. Lasc, Georgina Downey, and Mark Taylor, 95–105. London: Bloomsbury Academic.

"Théâtre du Gymnase." 1896. *Annales du Théâtre*: 171–176.

Tiersten, Lisa. 2001. *Marianne in the Market: Envisioning Consumer Culture in Fin-de-Siècle France*. Berkeley: University of California Press.

Uzanne, Octave. 1892. *La Femme et la mode: Métamorphoses de la Parisienne de 1792 à 1892*. Paris: May et Motterez.

Williams, Rosalind H. 1982. *Dream Worlds: Mass Consumption in Late Nineteenth-Century France*. Berkeley: University of California Press.

Zola, Émile. 1964. *Au Bonheur des Dames*. In *Les Rougon-Macquart. Histoire naturelle et sociale d'une famille sous le Second Empire*, III. Edited by Armand Lanoux. Paris: Bibliothèque de la Pléiade.

Zola, Émile. 1986. *Carnets d'Enquêtes. Une ethnographie inédite de la France*. Edited by Henri Mitterand. Paris: Librairie Plon.

Zola, Émile. 1995. *The Ladies' Paradise*. Translated by Brian Nelson. Oxford: Oxford University Press.

Zola, Émile. 1998. *Au Bonheur des Dames*. Edited by Sophie Guermès. Paris: Librairie Générale Françiase.

13 Dovetailed displays

Show windows, habitat dioramas, and bird hats

Emily Gephart and Michael Rossi

Exquisite specimens

In a brief editorial published in November 1883, *Frank Leslie's Illustrated Newspaper* decried "The Cruelties of Fashion" that "doom[ed] to destruction thousands and thousands of beautifully feathered choristers" (birds, that is) at the hands of those who would dismember them in order to use their colorful feathers for the adornment of ladies' hats. Yet, in an apparent contradiction, the writer also praised the artistry capable of transforming the inert matter of a dead bird into "an exquisite specimen of ornithology which, thanks to the skill of the hunter and taxidermist, looks as though it were yet alive, and reveling in its native grove."

The image accompanying the article (Fig. 13.1) reinforced this ostensibly obvious schism between two seemingly distinct activities: the collection and preservation of living things for natural history display, and the predation of birds for the manufacture of elaborate headwear. In the illustration's upper register, two vignettes read in sequence. First, a skilled hunter on the left brings down one of the "gorgeously-feathered songsters," leaving its nest-bound offspring to an uncertain fate. On the right, a taxidermist prepares the bird for ornithological study. The crocodile and bull's horns in his studio suggest that he is not a milliner subject to editorial censure, but rather a natural scientist, his activities authorized under the banner of legitimate scientific inquiry. In the print's lower half, meanwhile, the caption "fine feathers make fine birds" calls attention to the habitués of a fashionable urban shopping street: a bevy of women showing off their plumed hats before the approving gaze of a young dandy. A lively sparrow flees from the hunter, directing our eye towards its artfully stuffed counterparts at right, who alight atop the head of a prominent, coquettish young figure – herself a specimen of "woman," "at whose door lies the destruction of millions of beautiful birds," as the article pointed out. And yet, in emphasizing both the liveliness of taxidermied birds and the equally lively presentation of fashion's conspicuous excesses, the *Leslie's* piece invited a different and deliberately orthogonal reading: one in which the notionally natural and the seemingly social commingle, an unlikely moment that, following historian of science Donna Haraway, we might identify as natureculture, or perhaps better yet, nature*couture* (Haraway 2003, 1).

Following a tangential flight path, this chapter examines sites and spaces where stuffed birds might be seen: the millinery shops and department stores where these staples of turn-of-the-century fashion were shown for purchase, and the museums where ornithological specimens were arrayed. Building upon recent studies of the intersection between museums and commercial enterprises, we argue for further affiliations

THE CRUELTIES OF FASHION.—"FINE FEATHERS MAKE FINE BIRDS."
See Page 182.

Figure 13.1 John N. Hyde, "The Cruelties of Fashion – Fine Feathers Make Fine Birds,"
Frank Leslie's Illustrated Newspaper (November 10, 1883): 183–184.
Source: Image courtesy Library of Congress Prints and Photographs Division

between seemingly disparate institutional aims that arose from interrelated strategies of display. For while *Leslie's* cast culpability upon "woman, lovely woman" – feather-brained driver of fashion's unstoppable "juggernaut" – the article's informative illustration perspicaciously suggests that condemnation of "woman" for loss of bird life was premature, or at least incomplete, opportunistic, and myopic.

As conservation-minded bird lovers courted the attention of the public through museum displays of "real" creatures in action, so did representatives of the booming millinery industry, while retail establishments expanded their strategies of visual enticement alongside museums. If their motives represented incompatible agendas, their methods nevertheless aligned in curious ways. Far from insisting on a distinct ontological scheme keeping "nature" rigidly separate from "commerce," these arenas of exhibition and presentation drew museum groups and show windows into an intricately dovetailed logic. Contested objects straddling the mutable boundary between art and nature, bird hats illuminate a common conceptual framework undergirding turn-of-the-century display techniques in commercial and natural history displays alike.

The plume crisis

In singling out the trade in avian headwear for censure, *Leslie's* was an early voice in an increasingly vocal public crusade. As many scholars have observed, bird hats fueled the emergence of the American conservation movement (Doughty 1975; Moore-Colyer 2000). While the showy ostrich feathers sweeping from the sides of many hats could be plucked without harm to birds, most other avian ornaments necessitated killing and dismantling them (Stein 2008). The plumes of whole birds topped one season's popular bonnets in fluttering cascades (Fig. 13.2); wings and breasts were arranged into outlandish arabesques on others. Some species suffered more than others: by the mid-1890s, egrets were nearly extinct, their airy mating quills amassed in the millions for use as millinery "aigrettes," as Jennifer Price and others have recently pointed out (Price 2000; Weidensaul 2008; Hanson 2012). Hummingbirds were also under threat for their jewel-toned heads, which were assembled on lavish bandeaux adorning brims, or in facsimiles of flowers at the crown. Along the eastern seaboard of the United States, entire nesting colonies of common terns were wiped out, their wings applied whole to the sides of "mercury hats," in emulation of the sartorial style of the fleet-footed Roman messenger god (Chapman 1899, 205).

In *The American Museum Journal* in 1916, ornithologist T. Gilbert Pearson reflected on the alarming rise of the American plume trade in the decade after 1880. "People seemed to go mad on the subject of wearing feathers [...] Never in this country have birds been worn in such numbers," he observed, worrying whether "the call for feather finery rings so loudly in the hearts of women that it must never cease to be heard" (Pearson 1916, 254, 258). Bird hats were *de rigueur* for women of all kinds and classes. As one Mrs Charles Mallet put it, mixing emergent conservationism with bourgeois entitlement, millions of American songbirds suffered the same fate as more exotic species, simply because "servant girls and factory lasses must, of course, follow the fashion set them by their leaders" – and thus set about decorating their hats with less expensive local birds, rather than with more spectacular and pricier tropical plumes (Mallet 1900, 244). Despite the concerns of Pearson and others, feathers

Figure 13.2 Bain News Service, Model wearing "Chanticleer" hat of bird feathers, c. 1912.
Source: George Grantham Bain Collection, Library of Congress Prints and Photographs Division

remained enduringly popular: in her textbook on millinery history and manufacture, Charlotte Rankin Aikin noted that, whether domestic or exotic, "feathers are suitable for all seasons as they are always attractive" (Aikin 1918, 72).

The appalling scope of avian devastation motivated the establishment of Audubon Societies. These bird protection organizations were composed chiefly, at least in their early days, of wealthy elites, many of them women, perhaps themselves reformed buyers and sellers of bird hats as suggested by Mrs. Mallet (Mitchell 1996, 3). After *Forest and Steam* editor George Bird Grinnell's 1886 attempt to establish a successful association dedicated to bird conservation, the subsequent local and state chapters founded in the 1890s ultimately unified as a national organization in 1905, their lobbying devoted to legislative restriction of the vigorous plume market (Mason 2002; Graham 1990). Among its most vociferous early members were natural historians – museum men like Frank Chapman of New York's American Museum of Natural History (AMNH), who saw in natural history displays the legitimate flip-side to the depredations visited by modern commercial appetites. Moved by one of Chapman's vivid displays, Theodore Roosevelt founded the first Federal Wildlife Refuge in 1903

(Wonders, 1993b, 433). Yet, despite the increasingly frequent outcries against the immorality of hawking bird hats, the trade in wings, heads, breasts, and plumage continued almost unabated until the First World War.

The ironies of display

As bird slaughter for commercial purposes reached soaring heights, conservationists like Chapman began spreading their message through the emerging medium of "habitat groups" – displays in natural history museums that featured carefully taxidermied animals amidst simulations of their surroundings. Arising in the late nineteenth century from a burgeoning public fascination with taxonomies of animal life, taxidermy, and artifice, the earliest of these were ornithological models in the 1880s (Webster, 1945; Wonders, 1993a). Praised for its lively drama, Chapman's 1902 display of the threatened Pelican Island, Florida habitat – the first of its kind in complexity and thoroughness – was instrumental to conservation efforts. Like windows into the natural world, these presentations exceeded arrays of collected bird specimen types displayed at many museums and World's Fairs; they enabled museum goers to imagine, even to experience, nature at its most relatable, as the posed animals fed, fought, courted, and, perhaps most often and most sympathetically, cared for their own preserved families.

Artfully arranged bird displays were as attractive to visitors who flocked to view the novelties as they were to philanthropists seeking popular outlets for public munificence. Prominent New York socialite Mrs. Robert Stuart provided the funds for a few of the earliest habitat groups, which debuted at the AMNH in 1887 – 18 small cases containing breeding pairs and preparations of branches, plants, nests, and eggs, "mounted in characteristic attitudes and surrounded by natural accessories, each group being a facsimile reproduction from nature" (AMNH 1887–1888, 14). Following the success of these modest cases, Chapman, who was distinguishing himself as an ornithologist and bird preservation advocate, was invited by the AMNH in 1888 to oversee the preparation of larger, more vivid, and more rigorously realistic ornithological dioramas, a project that occupied him for the next three decades.

The initial assemblies of avian habitats orchestrated by Chapman and museum taxidermists Jenness Richardson and John Rowley were brought together in 1909 as the Hall of North American Birds: a series of 34 large glass-fronted cases filled with representative family groups of distinctive type specimens and characteristic fauna against painted backgrounds. As Oliver Davie would later advise in his *Methods in the Art of Taxidermy*, "[w]hatever you design in mounted birds, let them be so arranged that each scene will serve as an object lesson representing some phase in the life history of the species. If you are building a museum for instruction, the best way to interest and instruct is with scenes fresh from the fields of nature" (Davie 1911, 130). Similarly, in his guide leaflet to the "Habitat Groups of North American Birds," Chapman testified to the "universal appeal" of ingenious display: "attracted primarily by its color, its atmosphere, the scene it represents, the aimless visitor involuntarily pauses. His imagination is stirred, his interest aroused, and the way is opened for him to receive the facts the exhibit is designed to convey" (Chapman 1909, 165).

For conservation-minded exhibitors, the central facts their displays were designed to convey included the plight of animals at the mercy of a greedy modern market. As Chapman wrote in the leaflet, "so effectively [...] have the plume hunters done their

Figure 13.3 The American egret in a South Carolina cypress forest, North American Bird
Hall, American Museum of Natural History, c. 1909.
Source: Image courtesy of the American Museum of Natural History Library Services

work that it was feared that this beautiful and fast-vanishing species could not be
included among the Habitat Groups" (Chapman 1909, 21). Fortunately, he continued,
the museum had discovered a small number of these birds on a "shooting preserve"
in South Carolina, which enabled the museum's collectors to kill and preserve enough
specimens (three adults and four chicks) that the public could see what the magnificent beasts looked like in full plume (Fig. 13.3).

If Chapman didn't call attention to the irony of killing birds in order to save them,
it was nevertheless apparent to others. A 1910 article in *Everybody's Magazine*
entitled "Who Killed Cock Robin?" opened with a scene in which poachers, hoping
to raid a nest of egrets, are foiled by "scientific bird-collectors," who successfully
"collect" the birds before the poachers. "'Curses!'" say the poachers, "'It's taking
bread from our mouths!' [...] 'We arrived in time [...] to save the rookery,'" say
the naturalists, with great satisfaction. From the perspective of the Audubon society, however, the author noted: "'Birds sacrificed to the need of a collection are
just as dead as those killed for plumes'" (Clarkin 1910, 3). In an inverse fashion,
a correspondent to *Forest and Stream* magazine wrote of a chance encounter at
the Museum of Comparative Zoology in Cambridge, MA, in which he overheard a
young woman observing the stuffed birds exclaim: "'What a horrid shame it is to
kill these poor little dears.'" "Glancing at her dainty hat," wrote the correspondent,

"I beheld thereto attached a bird most wonderfully constructed and composed of portions of at least two or three lovely denizens of the tropics" ("Merlin" 1884, 83). In these published anecdotes, an uneasy overlap between the work of millinery and the work of taxidermy emerges; they were more closely related, perhaps, than naturalists would have wanted to admit.

Moreover, "fresh from the fields of nature" did not necessarily mean "of nature itself." If it was important that the birds be authentic specimens of avian life – "collected" in the field – the displays were, at their best, beholden to a different standard. As Davie pointed out, "the more elaborate and costly the flower, branch, rock or ground work, the more impressive it will be." Indeed, he continued, at the best museums, "the surroundings are reproduced by natural and artificial accessories; many of the artificial plants and flowers being of a rich and costly design" (Davie 1911, 129, 132).

Oftentimes, these corollary accessories came from the very millinery industry which exhibitors criticized. Mary Akeley, wife of celebrated taxidermist and diorama creator Carl Akeley, recalled that at the Field Museum in Chicago, "taxidermists had been purchasing heavy leaves from manufacturers of millinery supplies and wiring them to the branch in order to provide atmosphere" in the creation of early habitat groups (Akeley 1940, 68). The Field's curator of ornithology, Charles Cory, took this process one step further when, in 1896, he hired Mrs. E.S. Mogridge and her brother Henry Mintorn, expert British fabricators of decorative faux flowers, to turn their creativity away from frivolous millinery and towards duplicating botanically accurate specimens. Mogridge and her extended family were profiled by *New York Times* in January 1896, in an article celebrating their artistry and innovation ("Art in Wax Flower Work" 1896).

Mogridge and Mintorn had previously worked in renowned museums: they were employed at London's British Museum of Natural History, when they were hired in 1885 by Morris Jesup, president of the AMNH, to assist Jenness Richardson in the creation of fake foliage for dioramas. After lending their talents to the AMNH, the siblings offered their closely guarded waxwork techniques to the National Museum of Natural History in Washington, DC. At the time Cory hired them, he reckoned them to be "undoubtedly the best workmen [sic] in the country," and he looked forward to their help in completing groups including a "common robbin [sic] in an apple tree" – since that was "always pretty and interesting;" a group of nesting prairie chickens, which he supposed to be of special interest to the people of Illinois; and a "Florida group showing the white heron breeding with the alligator, turtles, etc." (1896).

That natural history displays recapitulated the commercial culture that gave rise to them is well understood in scholarship tracing their complicated history. A campaign of historical scrutiny undertaken by Haraway, Victoria Cain, and Karen Wonders, among others, has elegantly exposed how the aesthetics of natural history display subtly – and not so subtly – emulate the ways in which the putatively natural and the notionally social overlap (Haraway 1984; Cain 2012; Wonders, 1993). But more than overlapping, the logic of display in natural history museums was predicated on the very sense that there was, indeed, no "natural" at all – the "natural" was always first, and at best, commercial. To put it another way, even when protecting birds against predation for modern commodity aesthetics, conservationists were still working within the architecture of commercial capitalism.

While not as visible (or as evidently rapacious) as the market for millinery, ornithologists maintained their own thriving economy in bird skins for scientific collection:

prominent advertisements sponsored by hunter/naturalist Charles H. Marsh of Silver City, New Mexico featured on the back pages of the journal *The Ornithologist* promoted his impressive offering of "First Class Bird Skins at Hard Times Prices" (1885, 40). He was merely one among several similar purveyors of skins in that 1885 volume, representing hundreds of available species. But dioramas of vitalized birds deflected any questions that might have arisen about the scale of ornithological collecting. When birds were reanimated in the glass-fronted cases that drew burgeoning numbers of visitors to museums, scientific predation could be forgiven, just as the techniques of display and fabrication became invisible.

Display sites and affiliated artifice

A similar connection between circumstances, locations, and practices also emerged in Chicago, where advances in commercial display mirrored those of museums like the Field. The dense interrelationship is perhaps not surprising, since the Field Museum was named for department store magnate Marshall Field, who had donated the impressive sum (in 1893) of one million dollars towards the museum's founding. Sophisticated display was central not only to the museum's success, but to Field's business: his show windows had legendary status among window trimming professionals. As one leading trade journal observed in September 1908, Marshall Field "is a household word all over the country [...] It is regarded in much the same light as a museum" (Tannehill 1908, 40). Another commentator reported: "Ideas introduced into the windows of this store have been adapted to the windows of other stores all over the world" (Robertson 1913, 30). Hat displays were particularly attractive: a fashion journalist writing for the *Millinery Trade Review* in 1904 speculated that during the "Grand displays of Fall and Winter millinery in the great retail establishments of State Street," 250,000 people passed Field's store during October's "Exposition Week," an annual promotion of the season's newest attractions and goods ("Chicago" 1904, 61).

Creating beautiful artifice wasn't simply the work of the invisible hand of capitalism. Just as museums were able to hire fabricators like Mogridge and Mintorn, natural history displays and bird hat makers manipulated similar materials and shared common practices. Indeed, in the early years of the rising plume trade, it was possible for an ornithologist to admire the adroit knowledge and talent of plumassiers: specialists in feather design and millinery "novelties." In March 1886, *Forest and Stream* published a surprisingly enthusiastic study of the burgeoning feather industry, praising the "feather foundry" of Mr A.H. Alexander, "a naturalist, a lover of birds," who "has studied bird science in books and watched them in their leafy homes," traveling widely in search of new species to employ as feather adornments. "To visit the manufactory is a privilege, to hear its head talk about bird lore is a pleasure to any ornithologist," reported the author ("The Feather Industry" 1886, 162).

Although ornithologists soon took pains to distance themselves from the traffic in ornamental feathers – "a depth to which the true collector or Taxidermist never falls," according to one professional – they commanded the same basic skill set. Since photography had not yet improved sufficiently to capture images of birds in the field, the *Ornithologists and Oologists Semi-Annual* of January 1889 instructed its readers in how to field-clean freshly-shot specimens to preserve the best display of species-representative feathers. Of course, the article cautioned, "[a]fter you've learned to make a skin do not prostitute your knowledge to the making of 'millinery skins.'" Moreover, the writer urged moderation in one's collecting: "The professional Ornithologist needs large series of each species; but such is not the case with the amateur," who "should be satisfied with a pair, male and female, of each species." But since "plumage varies greatly with the seasons he may have specimens enough to show the variations," and surplus could always be sold to a museum (Singley 1889, 12).

Despite the professionalization that increasingly imposed boundaries between different arenas of expertise – and the threat of moral censure from naturalists – individuals did lend their skills to complementary exchange in the marketplace. Taxidermists supplemented their incomes by working in related fields, including the feather trade, as natural history agents and supply-sellers, and even as hairdressers (Milgrom 2010, 170). Show window experts could also become milliners, as Altman's leading display man Herman Frankenthal proved in 1909: his hat arrangements proved so popular that viewers demanded his creations straight from the windows ("Mr. Herman Frankenthal" 1909, 40). And in April 1910, *Illustrated Milliner* proudly forecast that, given the unabated vogue for exotic plumes, "the modiste will soon become an ornithologist" ("Plumage a Popular Trim" 1910, 23).

This statement was not merely promotional whimsy. Plumassiers wedded taxidermy skills to ingenious artistry in the fabrication of ever-more vividly captivating hats. As bird ornaments became increasingly complex, milliners had to master bird preservation as well as feather dyeing, curling, and "willowing" – the expert weaving of individual strands of feathers. One 1909 textbook recommended that a milliner "shall make herself familiar with the various kinds of feathers," and detailed how to prevent the oils in bird breasts from staining the surrounding ribbon and velvet by using arsenical salts in the preparation of bandeaux (Ben Yusuf 1909, 177, 186). If many feather ornaments and faux flowers were created by inexperienced sweatshop laborers, skilled milliners commanded a broader range of talents (Van Kleeck 1917, 46, 112, 144). Some of these involved elaborate illusions of bird animation. In 1894, for example, one observer in *Popular Science Monthly* wrote: "A naturalist in a milliner's shop finds himself confronted with a hundred varieties of plumage never seen in Nature, but excellent in art, for which it would puzzle any one [sic] but the plumassier or the taxidermist to find a name" ("Artificial Birds for Women's Hats" 1894, 860). Again, the plume hunter and the naturalist found themselves in unlikely coordination.

And why not? For both the naturalist and the milliner were in the business of creating wonderment and surprise, as were the rising numbers of show window display specialists (Leach 1993; Iarocci 2013). In the case of feathery hats, display windows could produce a certain degree of categorical confusion, even among seasoned professionals. While few viewers would have seriously mistaken a window for a scientific diorama, one strolling reporter for L. Frank Baum's journal *The Show Window* commented wryly upon the "terrific collections of mineral, animal and vegetable matter" arrayed in millinery shops that confounded his ornithological acumen: "for the first time perhaps, you realize how futile your education has been. You find that the close study you once gave to Dr. Eliot Coues' 'Birds of North America' has not served to acquaint you with such feathered creatures as one finds perched [...] they alight airily on these bonnets, find a suitable perching place, and then stand up" (Teall 1898, 99).

In another example of praiseworthy display, initially illustrated in *The Show Window*, spring bonnets resemble exotic shore birds posed neatly on slender

Figure 13.4 Millinery display, in L. Frank Baum, *The Art of Decorating Dry Goods Windows and Interiors* (Chicago: The Show Window Publishing Co., 1900, 109).
Source: Rare Book and Manuscript Library, Columbia University

pedestals, bodies too large for their fragile legs (Fig. 13.4). Like an avian community in a fictional rookery, they show off a frilly excess of seasonal plumage. But here each one is singular, a representative of its kind among others of its genus, set out in a taxonomy of fashion's mandated color and shape. Baum invested show windows with particular agency: amid the attention-getting, mechanized novelties he recommended for window display, he also endorsed contextual arrangements akin to increasingly lively natural history dioramas (1900, 146, 225). Presenting novel objects within a staged setting – or even in a "habitat" of appropriate use – enhanced their visual and emotional appeal. Thus shown in their 'proper' surroundings, displayed as readily obtainable commodities, hats roost near wax mannequins demonstrating the favored angle for wear atop human heads.

Window dressing manuals urged mastery of natural mimicry and finely-crafted illusions. In the increasingly sophisticated displays of the 1890s, one could see the emphasis experts such as George Cole placed on techniques devoted to the "imitation of nature," which upholds "the perfection of art" in windows. "Whether we walk in the garden or street, in store or shop, the eye is gratified with some glimmerings of this noble work," he observed. Its dictates prevailed in all arenas of display: "In a peep at nature we behold [...] flowers of delicate tints, or birds of gaudy plumage," which produced "a combination of effect from an exhaustless store – a book of reference always open" to the attentive window-display man (Cole 1892, 474). Consequently, windows throughout the early 1910s – especially hat windows – displayed the season's desirable

Plate No. 7473. An Unusual Display by Walter E. Zemitzsch for the Famous and Barr Co., St. Louis.

Figure 13.5 Plate 7473, *The Merchant's Record and Show Window* 34, no. 2 (February 1914, 23).
Source: New York Public Library

items amid flowers, leafy branches, and even on occasion whole trees and abandoned nests, as one display manual recommended (*100 Easy Window Trims* 1913, 27).

Not unlike habitat displays which delivered persuasive lessons in bird ecology and behavior, windows showed off hats and their feathery accessories to exceptional advantage: "We all know that no line of merchandise affords better opportunity of display than millinery," reported *The Show Window* in February 1899, "Not because trimmed hats are the most beautiful goods on earth, but [... because ...] milliners are enterprising and untiring in their efforts to produce attractive windows and many of them succeed to such an extent that their windows become famous" ("Millinery Display" 1899, 85).

Just as bird plumage and nesting patterns naturally vary greatly from season to season, so too did shop windows appear to follow natural cycles. Few did this more conspicuously than displays of ornate headgear and bird ornaments – among the most prized modern, ready-to-wear garments – which drew crowds to gaze at the latest trends featured during regular seasonal "openings." One February 1914 display (Fig. 13.5) contained an opulent spring arrangement of plumes, hats, and foliage: "birds of paradise to the value of about four thousand dollars [...] perched upon the branches" ("An Unusual Display" 1914, 23). Even after the stringent 1913 revisions to the landmark 1900 Lacey Act – the first federal wildlife protection law restricting the distribution and sale of protected animals and plants – had curtailed the trade in wild birds, this window commanded attention for its extravagance.

As show window displays, in parallel with habitat dioramas, had seen steady growth in sophistication, complexity, and artistry, the goal of most shop windows evolved beyond merely presenting available goods to making more expansive appeals to the imagination. In 1912, the *Merchant's Record and Show Window* advised: "The advertising window must tell a story that can be read at a glance and which will be understood by all who see it. It must be simple and direct and strike the beholder [...] the display should act upon the mind in such a way that it will not be forgotten [...] It should be more than a display – it should be an argument" ("Advertising Windows" 1912, 12).

In a curious turn, this "argument" made by shop window displays – particularly the most attractive bird-hat ones – ended up being not so diametrically opposed to that of the habitat group. On the one hand, dioramas appeared to serve only timeless nature, while the shop window seemed to serve only fleeting commerce: a conventional choice between God and Mammon. On the other hand, as desirable commodities that served a thriving modern commercial network, hats in show windows occupied an entirely fitting, even "natural" place in what could roundly be articulated as an ecology of trade, complete with seasons, species, and stories to arrest viewers. There, by attracting viewers and stimulating desire for fashion's ever-changing novelties, they fulfilled their role as conspicuous emblems attesting to status and the command of shifting sartorial codes. The rhythms that propelled seasonal cycles of endlessly renewable millinery variety continued to beat on, feathers in the airstream, borne forwards ceaselessly towards modernity.

Conclusion: Object-lessons on display

For all of their *sub rosa* commonalities, by the second decade of the twentieth century the ends of museums and millinery had considerably diverged. True, as museum dioramas and millinery displays developed in the 1880s and 1890s, visitors became accustomed to seeing scientific knowledge delivered via modeled dramas. Meanwhile, similarly captivating windows at Marshall Field's and other leading establishments contributed to the rising dominance of department stores in the retail marketplace. Yet, the viewer's attention, once harnessed, was directed towards disparate paths in these respective sites. While shop windows continued to transmute visual stimulation into desire for the most luxurious artifacts, public sympathy for birds – and the combined efforts of Progressive era elites and scientists – won out in the battle over millinery, just in the nick of time for the egrets. As regulatory legislation slowly diminished the plume trade's rapacity – and wartime austerities initiated changes in fashion – featherless "Audubon hats" replaced avian excess. Elaborate bird-hat displays passed out of fashionable currency by about 1919, while museum dioramas continued to develop in intricacy, complexity, and technical sophistication.

But if hats in windows had reflected a poignant ambivalence towards "the Cruelties of Fashion" – indifferent to bird death but attuned to human affect – what did stuffed birds in museums reveal about the 'nature' they promoted? Celebrated for their "authenticity" and their efficient delivery of ecological awareness, the lively but equivocal dioramas arrested time's organic flow in the service of preservation, education, and entertainment. Museum specialists turned their fabricated habitats into exemplars of behavior and environment, even while the edifice of scientific authority obscured their techniques. The strident censure the *Frank Leslies's* editorial heaped upon "woman, lovely woman" for her vanity did not tarnish the makers of the illusions that filled museum display cases.

A century on from the heyday of ornate millinery, fanciful hats and their animal materials have once again found a place in institutional display. At the time of writing, a small cartouche showing a woman wearing a plumed hat subtends a stuffed egret at the Field Museum. Foregoing talk of "feathered choristers" or dastardly damsels, the caption to the picture simply announces: "in the late 1800s, bird plumes were in great demand for hats and dresses. To get egret plumes, hunters invaded nesting colonies, killing up to 3 million birds a year. Efforts by early conservation groups halted the trade by the 1930s" (Exhibit text, Field Museum, Chicago, 2017). The Royal Alberta Museum's more prominent and expansive exhibition, "Fashioning Feathers" (2012), was just one of a spate of recent shows presenting paradigmatic examples of fashion's excesses, exploring the troubled history of the plume trade, and illustrating the use of birds in art, in fashion, and in science.[1]

Alluring relics of a bygone fashion fetish, plumed hats captivate observers today, if for a somewhat different reason than they did in 1900. In museums of history – whether natural or social – curators of material culture bring their skills, knowledge, and persuasive displays to bear on the task of "preserving" a moment before it vanishes like an extinct species (Patchett, 2012). Many present this "history" like ornithological dioramas, mounting fragile objects in cases sequestered from the realm of the everyday for comingled enticement and edification. At the same time, shows of once-essential fashion address contemporary audiences in a manner that might strike a chord with turn-of-the-century exhibitors and retail display experts alike, turning a distant era's now-exotic cultural practices into dazzling spectacles.

When tantalizingly exhibited in museum cases, stuffed birds and plumed hats still possess strong imaginative appeal, and attest to the efficacy of vitalized display. Arrested in time behind glass, these material artifacts of nature and culture combined rehabilitate vanished species and reanimate lost historical sensibilities. Yet, in an ironic turn in a story full of ironic turns, the "Cruelties of Fashion" – fickle, fleeting, and eminently trivial – are now preserved as an enduring part of the history of timeless nature – which, as ever, is enmeshed with commerce and invested in the dynamics of display. In 1997, philosopher Erazim Kohák posited nature itself as an endangered species, threatened by the evasive narratives and willful obfuscations humans construct about the history of life on earth. He pondered which models of relationship to the surrounding world could best impart our responsibility for maintaining its fragile coherence (Kohák 1997, 153–155). As bird hats demonstrate, the relationships most fraught and difficult to grasp are those that, like the surprisingly integrated natural and cultural forces conspicuously invisible in the *Frank Leslie's* illustration, are contradictions hiding in plain sight.

Note

1 Similar exhibitions concerning feather fashion and the plume trade have been held in Pennsylvania (Everhart Museum, "Flocks and Feathers," 2008); in Minnesota (Goldstein Museum of Design, "Flights of Fancy," 2010); in Florida (Historical Society of Palm Beach, "Feather Wars," 2011); in Washington (Henry Art Gallery, University of Washington, "Plumage and Pillage," 2015); as well as in the UK (Horniman Museum, South London "Plume Boom," 2014) and Belgium (Mode Museum, Antwerp, "Birds of Paradise," 2014).

References

Archives

Charles B. Cory to Frederick J.V. Skiff. 9 Nov 1896. *Directors Papers General Correspondence Box 1893–1907, COM-CUS*; Folder: CB-Cory Ornithology, Library and Archives, Field Museum.

Published Sources

100 Easy Window Trims. 1913. Chicago: Byxbee Publishing Co.

"Advertising Windows." 1912. *Merchant's Record and Show Window* 31, 1: 11–12.

Aikin, Charlotte Rankin. 1918. *Millinery*. New York: The Ronald Press Co.

Akeley, Mary Jobe. 1940. *The Wilderness Lives Again*. New York: Dodd, Mead and Co.

American Museum of Natural History. 1887–88. *Annual Report of the Trustees*. New York: American Museum of Natural History.

"Art in Wax Flower Work: A Woman Who Has Devoted her Life to Its Perfection." 1896. *The New York Times*, January 12.

"Artificial Birds for Women's Hats." 1894. *Popular Science Monthly* 45: 860.

Ben Yusuf, Anna. 1909. *The Art of Millinery*. New York: Millinery Trade Publishing Co.

Baum, L. Frank. 1900. *The Art of Decorating Dry Goods Windows and Interiors*. Chicago: Show Window Publishing Co.

Cain, Victoria. 2012. "'Attraction, Attention, and Desire:' Consumer Culture as Pedagogical Paradigm in Museums in the United States, 1900–1930." *Paedagogica Historia* 48, 5: 745–769.

Chapman, Frank. 1899. "The Passing of the Tern." *Bird-Lore* 1, 6: 205.

———. 1909. *Habitat Groups of North America*. Guide Leaflet 28. New York: American Museum of Natural History.

"Chicago." 1904. *Millinery Trade Review* 29, 11: 61.

Clarkin, Franklin. 1910. "Who Killed Cock Robin?" *Everybody's Magazine* 22: 81–91.

Cole, George. 1892. *A Complete Dictionary of Dry Goods…With an Appendix Containing a Treatise on Window Dressing*. Chicago: W. S. Conkey and Co.

Davie, Oliver. 1911. *Methods in the Art of Taxidermy*. Philadelphia: David McKay.

Doughty, Robin W. 1975. *Feather Fashions and Bird Preservation: A Study in Nature Preservation*. Berkeley, CA: University of California Press.

"The Feather Industry." 1886. *Forest and Stream* 26, 9: 162.

Graham, Frank, Jr. 1990. *The Audubon Ark: A History of the National Audubon Society*. New York: Knopf.

Hanson, Thor. 2012. *Feathers: The Evolution of a Natural Miracle*. New York: Basic Books.

Haraway, Donna. 1984. "Teddy Bear Patriarchy: Taxidermy in the Garden of Eden." *Social Text* 1, 11: 20–64.

———. 2003. *The Companion Species Manifesto*. Chicago: Prickly Paradigm Press.

Iarocci, Louisa. 2013. "'The Art of Draping:' Window Dressing." In *Visual Merchandising: The Image of Selling*, edited by Louisa Iarocci, 137–156. Burlington, VT: Ashgate.

Kohak, Erazim. 1997. "The Varieties of Ecological Experience." *Environmental Ethics* 19, 2: 153–171.

Leach, William. 1993. *Land of Desire: Merchants, Power, and the Rise of a New American Culture*. New York: Pantheon.

Marsh, Charles H. 1885. "First Class Bird Skins at Hard Times Prices." *The Ornithologist* 1, 6: 40.

Mason, Kathy. 2002. "Out of Fashion: Harriet Hemenway and the Audubon Society, 1896–1905." *Historian* 65, 1: 1–14.

"Merlin." 1884. "Protect the Small Birds." *Forest and Stream* 22, 5: 83

Milgrom, Melissa. 2010. *Still Life: Adventures in Taxidermy*. Boston: Houghton Mifflin Harcourt.

"Millinery Display." 1899. *The Show Window* 4, 2: 85.

Mitchell, John H. 1996. "The Mothers of Conservation." *Sanctuary: The Journal of the Massachusetts Audubon Society*, January-February: 1–20.

Moore-Colyer, R. J. 2000. "Feathered Women and Persecuted Birds: The Struggle Against the Plumage Trade, c. 1860–1922." *Rural History* 11, 1: 57–73.

"Mr. Herman Frankenthal." 1909. *Merchant's Record and Show Window* 24, 6: 40.

Pearson, T. Gilbert. 1916. "The Traffic in Feathers." *The American Museum Journal* 16, 4: 253–258.

Patchett, Merle. 2011. *Fashioning Feathers*. Accessed February, 2015. http://fashioningfeathers.com/

"Plumage a Popular Trim." 1910. *Illustrated Milliner* 11, 4: 23.

Price, Jennifer. 1999. *Flight Maps: Adventures with Nature in Modern America*. New York: Basic Books.

Robertson, Frank. 1913. "Window Displays de Luxe." *Merchant's Record and Show Window* 3, 2: 30.

Stein, Sarah Abrevaya. 2008. *Plumes: Ostrich Feathers, Jews, and a Lost World of Global Commerce*. New Haven: Yale University Press.

Singley, J. A. 1899. "Brief Instructions for Collecting and Preserving Birds and Eggs. Part Second." *Ornithologists and Oologists Semi-Annual* 1, 1: 12.

Tannehill, J. E. 1908. "Address to Nat'l Association of Window Trimmers of America." *Merchant's Record and Show Window* 23, 2: 40.

Teall, Gardner. 1898. "Up the Street." *The Show Window* 2, 3: 99.

"An Unusual Display." 1914. *Merchant's Record and Show Window* 34, 2: 23.

Van Kleeck, Mary. 1917. *A Seasonal Industry: A Study of the Millinery Trade in New York*. New York: Russell Sage Foundation.

Webster, Frederick. 1945. "The Birth of Bird Habitat Groups." *The Annals of the Carnegie Museum*, September: 97–118.

Weidensaul, Scott. 2008. *Of a Feather: A Brief History of American Birding*. New York: Harcourt.

Wonders, Karen. 1993a. *Habitat Dioramas: Illusions of Wilderness in Museums of Natural History*. Uppsala: Almqvist & Wiksell.

———. 1993b "Bird Taxidermy and the Origin of Habitat Dioramas." In *Non-verbal communication of science prior to 1900*, edited by R. G. Mazzolini, 411–447. Florence: Olschki.

14 Department stores and their display windows during the prewar Third Reich

Prevailing within a hostile Nazi consumer culture

Douglas Klahr

German department stores (*Warenhäuser*) differed from their English and French counterparts not merely on account of their delayed development due to Germany's later industrialization, but also for the extent of the opposition they engendered within the lower middle class (*Mittelstand*), a societal reaction that began in late 1880s and reached its most intense expression during the Nazi period. As Tim Coles observed, "German shopkeepers were not unique in terms of their uneasy experience of modernity with associated structural and organizational changes in the retail system" – France witnessed such attitudes as well. However, he continued: "What makes the German case so remarkable is the high profile the *Mittelstand* movement attained in the process of social and cultural change in modern Germany especially through the sustained vehemence of its attacks on large-scale retail organizations" (Coles 1999, 34). This chapter follows that strand of anti-*Warenhäuser* sentiment through the prewar years of the Third Reich, examining how it interacted with the principal public faces of department stores: their display windows.

During the Third Reich, window display architecture in *Warenhäuser* existed within a complex milieu that had three salient characteristics: the Nazi party's long-standing anti-*Warenhaus* stance, the regime's desire to create a middle way between consumerism and Bolshevik socialism, and the nation's striving for autarky. Complicating matters was the reality that a significant degree of ambiguity permeated these features, often resulting in a dissonance between rhetoric and policy. A further challenge is the paucity of photographic documentation of *Warenhäuser* display windows, whether in publications from during or after the era. Concerning the lacuna of photographic evidence: it is akin to seeking a glimpse of an elusive species of animal, which causes this scholar to pause – one must be careful not to read too much into the limited supply of images that exist. Nevertheless, even though their number is small, once the three characteristics of the milieu are examined and explained, one inference can be drawn: *Warenhäuser* used their unparalleled display window sizes to create elaborate *tableaux* in which goods for sale were part of a narrative, differentiating *Warenhäuser* from the small shop owners who formed a backbone of the Nazi party. Undergirding the antagonistic milieu that *Warenhäuser* faced therefore were the literal and metaphorical roles that display windows played in Germany. This chapter pulls together these strands.

The dearth of *Warenhäuser* display window images during the Third Reich exists for two reasons. First, due to the anti-*Warenhaus* stance of the Nazi party, which frequently focused on the prominent role that Jews played in bringing the department store to Germany, photographs of department store display windows were noticeably rare in Nazi-era publications, whether trade journals or books devoted to display window techniques. Both leading journals, *Das Schaufenster* (*The Display Window*) and *Schaufenster-Kunst und Technik* (*Display Window Art and Technique*), featured design proposals largely for *Einzelhändler* (small shop owners), and the photographs of actual display windows reflected this emphasis.[1]

In contrast, there exists a wealth of department store display window photographs during the period immediately preceding Nazi rule, the years of the Weimar Republic, whether in textbooks about the profession or in publications by the stores themselves. One example of the latter is referenced by Ulrike Zitzlsperger: a 192-page commemorative volume published in 1932 by Berlin's most upscale department store, Kaufhaus des Westens (KaDeWe), to celebrate its 25th anniversary, in which some display windows were shown (Zitzlsperger 2013, 139, 147). No equivalent publication by *Warenhäuser* appeared during the Nazi years.

The second reason why documentation of Nazi-period *Warenhäuser* windows is so meager resides within the postwar histories of *Warenhäuser*, whether scholarly works or commemorative books published by the stores themselves. If photographs of *Warenhäuser* of the period are shown, they rarely include close-ups of display windows: indeed, photographs of such windows often stop precisely at 1932 and do not resume until the late 1940s or early 1950s in the numerous publications consulted (Breuss 2010; Dahms 2012; Fuchs 1990; Karstadt 2006; Ladwig-Winters 1997; Lenz 1995; Meiners 2007; Osterwold 1974; Schleif 2004; Sultano 1995; Tietz 1965; Wiesen 2011; Zitzlsperger 2013). Searches were also conducted through four major archives: the federal Bundesarchiv and the regional Landesarchiv Berlin, Bildarchiv Foto Marburg, and the Landesarchiv Baden-Württenberg. The search term "*Schaufenster*" (shop window) produced 756 entries, but only 28 of these were from 1933–39, and all were of small shops, not of department stores. The search for "*Warenhaus*" produced 1,021 entries, with only 19 from 1933–39, all either non-photographic documentation or photos that are distant exterior shots or views of display windows obscured by anti-Semitic propaganda.

Since their advent in the 1880s, *Warenhäuser* were viewed with resentment by certain segments of the public, an attitude augmented by suspicions regarding the French origins of the venues and the Jewish merchants who pioneered their entrance into Germany. Uwe Spiekermann outlined eight historical criticisms that German retailers had cited regarding *Warenhäuser* since the 1880s: unfair competition, erosion of the social order, disturbance of the patriarchal order, questionable quality of goods, large-scale employment of female personnel, Jewish ownership, the pacesetting role in transforming Germany into a consumer society, and the production of illusions (Spiekermann 2013, 42). That final criticism – the production of illusions – is the most pertinent to this essay, for display windows, more than advertising, were the principal and most consumer-direct means of creating illusions. In a 1931 Nazi publication entitled "Department Store Politics and National Socialism," Hans Buchner referenced such illusions: "Swarms of those eager to gaze and to buy, surge through the gates of the magnificent buildings that unlock the magic land of greed and buying ensnarement" (quoted in Strohmeyer 1980, 155–56).

The competitive edge that *Warenhäuser* enjoyed in terms of pricing and assortment of goods not only spawned periodic attempts by politicians from 1900 to enact legislation that would tax or limit what *Warenhäuser* could do. It also created a variety of magazines and books dedicated to teaching *Einzelhändler* how to compete with and differentiate themselves from *Warenhäuser* and *Kaufhäuser* (large speciality stores – the predecessors of *Warenhäuser* – that usually sold only clothing, dry goods, and sometimes furnishings).[2] Space limitations in this chapter preclude discussing the shifting definitions between a *Warenhaus* and a *Kaufhaus* that bedeviled German economists and politicians from the 1880s through the 1930s. The existence of branches sometimes differentiated *Warenhäuser* from *Kaufhäuser*, but, in the end, the fact that *Warenhäuser* also sold foodstuffs and groceries demarcated them definitively from *Kaufhäuser*, and also aroused the most wrath among *Einzelhändler*.

The long-standing complaints and grudges that merchants held against the *Warenhäuser* found a receptive audience very early in the Nazi party. Point 16 of the 1920 party program stated: "We demand the creation and maintenance of a healthy middle class, the immediate communalizing of big department stores, and their lease at a cheap rate to small traders, and that the utmost consideration shall be shown to all small traders in the placing of State and municipal orders" (Program of the German Worker's Party 1920). It is relevant to this chapter to note that while handworkers comprised the largest faction of the early Nazi party in 1925 (20%), *Einzelhändler* came in second at 13.6%, underscoring the political appeal of an anti-*Warenhäuser* stance (Kater 1971, 139). As the party gained strength, the rhetoric increased, resulting in the first attempted boycott of *Warenhäuser* in November 1928. The Nazi party newspaper, the *Völkischer Beobachter*, urged the public not to purchase Christmas-related items at Jewish shops, especially *Warenhäuser*. In 1932, the campaign resulted in the first instance of violence aimed at *Warenhäuser* and also at some *Kaufhäuser*, with display windows being smashed, bombs tossed, and tear gas set off inside (Uhlig 1956, 20–21, 35, 68).

It is important to briefly note that while many of Germany's *Warenhäuser* and *Kaufhäuser* were Jewish-owned, some were not. Berlin's oldest *Kaufhaus*, Rudolph Hertzog, was perhaps the most prominent example of gentile ownership, given its longevity and premier location less than one block away from the royal palace. Founded in 1839 by Rudolph Carl Hertzog, it catered to a conservative clientele and abstained from large-scale, flashy promotions. During the Nazi period, the store at times felt it necessary to remind the general public of its non-Jewish origins, as recounted by Jonas Geist: "Around 1937, after Rudolph L. Hertzog publicly announced that he had joined the Nazi Party, he exhibited his conviction in the store's windows: he let them be 'decorated' with army and party uniforms." Two years later, on the occasion of the firm's 100-year celebration, the local Nazi deputy district leader confirmed that the firm was a "true German *Kaufhaus* enterprise" (Geist 2001, 76).[3]

Despite the rhetoric and sporadic incidents of violence against *Warenhäuser*, once the Nazis came to power in 1933, leading party members quickly realized that the negative economic consequences of the communalization of *Warenhäuser* would be far greater than any boost it might provide *Einzelhändler*. This was manifested in a speech that Rudolf Hess gave on 7 April 1933, a mere nine weeks after Hitler's electoral victory, in which he not only dispensed with a general boycott of *Warenhäuser* that had occurred in March, but also enunciated the difficulties of resolving the issue. Hess stated:

> The stance of the National Socialist Democratic Workers Party regarding the 'department store question' remains unchanged in founding principles. The solution

will occur at the appropriate time in the sense of economic programs. In view of the general economic situation, this keeps the party line, for the time being, an active approach, with the goal of bringing department stores and their operations to a halt not necessary.

(quoted in Fuchs 1990, 208)

Warenhäuser, Nazi consumer culture, and autarky

This backtracking on the matter introduced the broader issue of what kind of consumer culture the party leadership envisioned for the Third Reich, and why *Warenhäuser* remained problematic within this more expansive context. The primacy that the Third Reich placed upon military and infrastructure spending might seem to make the matter of a consumer culture somewhat tangential, but in an essay about Nazi economic ideology, Albrecht Ritschl accords it a central place. He writes:

> Hitler's long-term goal was not the industrialization of East European nations: they were to serve solely as the basis for raw materials and agriculture for the later Reich [...] The end purpose of all economic activity would be consumption (*Verbrauch*), and the future of German industry would reside in the mass production of consumer goods.
>
> (Ritschl 1991, 63)

Michael Geyer provides further historical context by noting that, during the Weimar Republic, "mass consumption, although a 'mass' icon, was in fact confined to urban and industrial centers. Only with the Third Reich did the nation at large come into its own as a consuming public, due to State control of the market and the deliberate populism of Nazi propaganda" (Geyer 1997, 692).

Nazi assumption of power in 1933 called for a transformation of the mass-consumption society whose development *Warenhäuser* had spearheaded: "Ideologically, the Nazis aspired to create a new kind of consumer culture in explicit opposition to existing models: on the one side, the specter of American-style consumer capitalism, with its unabashed materialism and valorization of greed, and on the other, the threat of socialist redistribution" (Lerner 2009, 524). While the anti-Communist stance of the party on many issues was clear, the regime's complicated relationship with capitalism was defined by ambiguities. The regime strove to differentiate between what it labeled creative (*schaffendes*) versus rapacious (*raffendes*) capitalism, with excess materialism in the form of conspicuous consumption targeted as the signpost of the latter version, as Shelly Baranowski explains in her study of consumerism in the Third Reich. Yet, as Baranowski notes, Hitler left the door open for a future conception of valid luxury: "That life of luxury then is only morally justified when it has its deepest roots in a moral conception of lordship" (2004, 26, 34, 39).

This ambiguity – condemning conspicuous consumption yet suggesting that it might ultimately be redeemed – was reflected in two broad concepts that undergirded not only Nazi economic but also geopolitical policy. The quest for *Lebensraum* (living space) that drove Nazi territorial expansion eastward was cited as the prerequisite toward achieving the *Lebenshöhe* or standard of living that the Aryan race deserved. The challenge was to chart a path towards achieving such a standard that did not encourage excessive consumption. The emphasis therefore was placed upon the important concept of *Volksgemeinschaft*, the racially-defined community of German people. This indicated a desired shift away from individualistic consumption to purchasing goods framed within the context of the collective's well-being: "In the National Socialist ideal world, elevated consumption corresponded to a worthy race, as well as owing a 'living standard' to the collective German people" (König 2003, 153, 163).

A short and pithy slogan was needed to connect these matters with the all-embracing concept of *Volksgemeinschaft*. One, therefore, was created: *Gemeinnutz vor Eigennutz*, or "common good before self-interest." One of Nazism's premier economists, Werner Daitz, explained that National Socialism differentiated itself from liberalism and Marxism by striving for "organic unity." This would be accomplished by placing "common good above self-interest" so that the ethic of "mechanical profits does not again infiltrate and corrode the organic, higher production ethic of the national economy" (Daitz 1943; Part 1, 23). In a 2003 essay, Wolfgang König characterized the concept *Geminnutz vor Eigennutz* as an attempt to frame the yearning for consumer goods in a conflict-free manner that would differentiate the system from parliamentarianism, individualism, liberalism, and Marxism (2003, 139). Buying from *Einzelhändler* instead of *Warenhäuser* was helping the common good of a neighborhood, supporting local merchants instead of large, anonymous corporations.

Concurrent with this endeavor to create a new consumer society was the regime's loudly proclaimed quest for autarky. This impacted the textile and fashion industries, which formed the backbone of business for *Warenhäuser*, especially after they were prohibited from selling goods such as groceries. As Gloria Sultano relates in her study about fashion during the regime, the Reich Ministry of Economy established early on – in summer 1934 – a "Textile Raw Materials Program" that focused upon creating large-scale manufacturing capabilities to produce rayon and viscose (synthetic) silk. In that first year of Nazi rule, 3.5 billion Reichsmarks were invested in viscose silk factories, and the assortment of articles composed of rayon increased from six in 1929 to 200 in 1939 (Sultano 1995, 81).

Yet Germany's synthetic textile industry had a paradoxical effect upon *Warenhäuser* and *Kaufhäuser*, since a majority of the textiles were destined for export, the proceeds being seen as yet another step toward autarky. The figures were impressive: in 1936, bulk textiles, the majority being synthetics on account of Germany's limited capacity to grow natural fibers, brought in 450 million Reichsmarks, making them the third largest export sector. Another 70 million Reichsmarks were pulled in from the export of German clothing (Dahms 2012, 78). The result was a shortage of both textiles and garments at various times during the prewar years. For example, at the *Kaufhaus* Schocken during the 1936–37 winter, "in almost all of the textile departments certain wool and cotton articles either were no longer there or in small amounts, in part obtained with lesser quality as well" (Fuchs 1990, 237). National policies aimed at attaining autarky resulted in periodic shortages of consumer goods, with the exception of foodstuffs, which the government ensured were in plentiful supply until the onset of war (even if some foodstuff categories were of arguable quality, such as *Ersatzkaffee*, or coffee substitutes).

Wolfgang König provides a succinct overview of the situation, stating that the greatest obstacles for consumers were not only the priority of military spending and the restrictions created by events such as textile shortages. It was also the government's sharp restrictions on importing the global brands to which Germans had become accustomed in the prior decades (König 2003, 157). Nazi consumption policy was therefore, as Hartmut Berghoff wrote, a combination of "enticement and deprivation." He noted that this generated increased consumption in some sectors and suppressed consumption in others, creating what he termed *virtual* consumption: "The regime cunningly offered mouth-watering examples of mass consumption and promised more satisfaction later. In order to reach this stage by placing Europe under German rule, consumers were asked to put up with 'temporary' restrictions" (Berghoff 2001, 173).

Victoria de Grazia explains how this aspect of virtual consumption manifested itself in *Warenhäuser*. Although she is referring to the spring of 1940, customers had similar experiences during the prewar period, especially regarding clothing shortages. She writes: "In department stores, floor articles were displayed, but no stock was available for sale. To avoid accusations of fraud, law-abiding store managers attached inconspicuous signs to the effect that the 'exhibited articles are not for sale'" (de Grazia 2006, 182). Although the Nazi regime castigated department stores as Jewish enterprises that "fostered self-indulgent and materialist fantasies [...] the Nazis' utopian visions could be realized only by sustaining these institutions of consumer capitalism" (Wiesen 2011, 60).

This raises the question of precisely what sort of consumer culture the regime envisioned, and what role *Warenhäuser* would play in it. S. Jonathan Wiesen delivers what is perhaps the crispest assessment. He writes:

> National Socialist economists felt that, in and of themselves, buying and selling were soulless, even inhuman, exercises. But by sanitizing commercial relations and binding them to the fate of the Aryan race, the Nazis hoped to dissociate consumption and marketing from crude materialism [...] the Nazis defended the right of biologically acceptable individuals to buy and sell freely and to exercise their creativity in the marketplace, but they also demanded that production and consumption speak to the higher goals of the community, the nation, and the Volk.
>
> (Wiesen 2011, 6, 23)

The Aryan racial component that underscored this sanitizing of commercial relations was the end point of a decades-long discussion within German society about consumerism and materialism. Although the process of sanitization reached an extreme with Aryanization – "purifying" department stores of their largely Jewish ownership – the process began earlier within the regime, in a broader context that was only partially anti-Semitic: cleansing German advertising of undesired features.

Sanitizing commercial relations and *Warenhäuser*

A discourse had occurred within German society since 1900 concerning two words used to signify advertising: *Werbung* and *Reklame*. As Nina Schleif notes, "In the first decade of that century there arose a careful distinction between morally defensible, unobtrusive advertising (*Werbung*) and immoral, very flashy advertising (*Reklame*)." She recounts the 1908 distinction that the German economist and sociologist Werner Sombart made between the two terms, wherein he claimed that "the *Reklame* imposes upon us its subject matter, whereas the *Anzeige* [a synonym for *Werbung*] already assumes our interest in its content" (Schleif 2004, 65). The design of some department stores during this period – such as Hermann Tietz – was criticized for being the architectural equivalent of a *Reklame,* with windows of unprecedented size that many felt intruded upon the streetscape, especially when brightly illuminated at night. Other

Figure 14.1 Weisse Woche window display at Hermann Tietz, Leipzigerstrasse, Berlin, and interior display at Julius Tietz, Postplatz, Plauen, mid-1920s.
Source: Stephanie-Hahn 1926, 138, 151

stores, such as Wertheim, were praised for their restrained architectural style. But all *Warenhäuser* were criticized for the flashy in-store promotions that they ran – such as White Week (*Weisse Woche*), in January, for linens.

By 1933, Germany's *Warenhäuser* had accrued three decades of display and marketing acumen, and events such as *Weisse Woche* had assumed gargantuan proportions, encouraging the increasing levels of conspicuous consumption for which they were blamed. Figure 14.1 demonstrates how *Weisse Woche* was promoted in two of the Tietz department stores: worlds of illusion were presented to the public, whether crafting miniature "trees" out of white goods or constructing monumental towers, to provide a stimulating environment that encouraged spending. At Tietz's flagship store in Berlin (Fig. 14.2), the display space and talent that *Warenhäuser* utilized presented a powerfully immersive scene with which no *Einzelhandler* could compete: a lavish home library had been created, suggesting to the public not only the extent of personal wealth that was possible, but also what that wealth could purchase. Figures 14.1 and 14.2 are from the mid-1920s and were featured in the third edition of a textbook written by the Weimar era's leading educator of window display, Elisabeth von Stephanie-Hahn (1926).

Upon assuming power in 1933, the Nazi regime outlawed promotions such as *Weisse Woche* and also enacted measures against *Warenhäuser* regarding advertising in general. Nazi newspapers were prohibited from posting any ads from *Warenhäuser*, and neutral or civic newspapers often refused to carry such ads for fear of undesired consequences. Deprived of advertising in print and even on radio, *Warenhäuser* faced further restrictions. They were prohibited from selling foodstuffs, groceries, and Christmas-related items, the last due to their largely Jewish ownership. They also were required to close their cafés and restaurants, which, akin to their grocery departments, had been seen by café owners as major transgressors concerning unfair competition. The ultimate manifestation of this competitive advantage was

Figure 14.2 Window display at Hermann Tietz, Leipzigerstrasse, Berlin, mid-1920s.
Source: Stephanie-Hahn 1926, 179

the cut-price *Lebensmittel Freitag* (grocery Friday) policy that *Warenhäuser* had previously heavily advertised.[4] As the Nazi regime began its quest to establish a consumer culture distinct from that of capitalism, a recasting of advertising became a
major focus. Pamela Swett notes: "On 12 September 1933 the Law on Commercial
Advertising was announced. The legislation placed the uniform and effective design of
all public and private advertisement, classified, exhibitions, fairs and other ads-related
issues under the oversight of the Reich" (Swett 2007, 55).[5]

In a decree issued by Martin Bormann in February 1934, with the exception of fly-
ing the Nazi flag, *Warenhäuser* were prohibited from displaying or selling all symbols,
images, uniforms, and anything to do with the Nazi movement, including "children's
uniforms, SA dolls, and the like." Furthermore, all members of the party were forbidden to enter *Warenhäuser* in uniform (Uhlig 1956, 133). Bormann's decree was
ambiguous on whether party members could enter such venues *out* of uniform – a
tacit acknowledgment of the important economic role that *Warenhäuser* played
within the fashion industry.

Forbidding *Warenhäuser* to display or sell Nazi paraphernalia might seem incon-
sequential, but the contents of a 1937 catalog by the firm Heinz & Kühn give an
inkling of the variety of swastika-bedecked items available for display purposes:
posters, wax candles, miniature paper flags, paper escutcheons, hanging paper lanterns, floor lanterns, balloon lanterns, victory garlands, and bunting (Heinz & Kühn
1937). While a law was passed in December 1933 regulating the use of the swastika
in window displays (to prevent its overuse in the eyes of the party), its presence was
widespread on official holidays. In his 1939 book about how to design display windows, Fritz Ackermann offered an example of how a swastika could be integrated
into a display celebrating 1 May, a holiday that the Nazi regime labeled "National
Holiday of the German People" (1939, 146). Likewise, issues of a trade journal

from 1936 and 1937 offered window displays celebrating Harvest Day and the Day of Work that featured swastikas (Osterwold 1974, 131–32). In a sense, *Warenhäuser* were deprived of sanitizing their commercial relations with the public, being unable to claim their racial purity and become members of the *Volksgemeinschaft* by using symbols of the Nazi party.

The display window

The communications medium of the display window often presented seductive visions of a world of consumer goods. Janet Ward noted how pivotal the display window became during the Weimar period. For *Warenhäuser*, dealing with all the restrictions placed upon them in the subsequent Nazi years, her words assume even greater relevancy: "The display window became recognized as a major direct-marketing lure, in many ways outdoing even the print medium; city workers window-shopped when they could – in the evening – and most purchases made by women occurred after work" (Ward 2001, 197). The potency of illusion increased at nighttime, when the contrast between the giant buildings' dark stone cladding and brilliantly illuminated windows was at its greatest.

The negative societal and urban impacts of such windows upon Germany's cities were noted by critics who opined that, in addition to presenting visions of excess consumption to a gullible public, the light pollution of such vast spans of brightly lit windows disrupted the natural order of night, far more so than the giant neon signs high atop buildings that already punctuated Germany's largest cities. The fact that the large display windows of *Warenhäuser* cast so much artificial light *at the street level* – in essence, violating the personal space of pedestrians – was the crux of the matter. Figure 14.3 illustrates the staggering array of goods thrust into the civic realm without respite. It was during these nighttime hours that critics felt *Warenhäuser*'s worlds of illusion to be the most toxic to society, as voiced in 1927 by Rudolf Scherer: "Whoever goes through popular large city streets at night sees a wonder transpire: 'disdainful merchants of avarice' ensnare one in a fairy tale of splendor of which the virtuosos of the Arabian nights could not dream" (quoted in Breuss 2010, 19).

The intrusive nighttime presence of department stores fueled Nazi condemnation of this retail venue type. In 1930, Hermann Göring summarized the urban and societal impacts in a speech at Berlin's Sportpalast: "An impoverished small business class dies in empty shops, but along the main streets, the defying fortresses of capital, the department stores, shoot up high" (Uhlig 1956, 65). Nina Schleif notes that "Hitler had already indicated in the 1920s that he intended to radically devalue, if not abolish, the display window for department stores to protect small traders against the alleged superiority of the big competition" (2004, 121, 61). In line with this, during the Nazi regime, in addition to journals such as *Das Schaufenster*, books were written that instructed small shop owners how to decorate their display windows. Since *Warenhäuser* had large staffs of professionally educated display artists who did not need instruction manuals, these books offered a distillation of *Warenhaus* techniques for the small shop owner; hence their relevance to this paper and the following example.

The title of Hans Geiger's 1934 book challenged small shop owners: *Advertising Ideas Make the Display Window! Behind the Scenes of Thought-Driven Display*

Figure 14.3 Nighttime view of Leonhard Tietz, Obere Königsstrasse, Kassel, in *Schaufenster-Kunst und Technik* (January 1927), 30.

Window Work. It is striking how often Geiger forces his readers to examine the urban context of their stores. First, he states that the display window is the most expensive form of advertising, alluding to the monthly rent that buys the shop owner linear footage along a street. Next he claims that display windows influence the street and not the other way around, reflecting a cultural awareness of the visual impact that display windows have upon the street-level urban fabric. Finally, he pulls these strands together by reminding his readers that a street will be lively when the businesses along it are (Geiger 1934, 5, 56, 64). The remainder of Geiger's advice is on how to display goods so that they are not merely stacked but rather arranged either around a theme or in a manner that will catch the passer-by's eye. He reminds the reader that an advertising idea in the window must create the fastest and easiest contact with the viewer. This last point was a tacit acknowledgment that, in a fast-paced urban environment, the limited linear footage that small shops possessed placed a premium upon establishing visual contact with pedestrians in a rapid and facile manner. *Warenhäuser*, by comparison, had the luxury of making contact with pedestrians over a longer period of time due to the vast buildings they occupied.

Figure 14.4 illustrates exterior and interior views of a typical small shop that was running a promotion on preserves. These photos are from an album identified at auction only as "Passau 1936–39" that was purchased by the author, and within it were 92 photos of a small shop in the city of Passau: 89 of the shop's window displays and three of the shop's interior. The stacking of goods – called a *Stapelfenster* – had been the standard of window display for merchants in Germany since 1900. Despite

Figure 14.4 Window and interior displays at an unidentified small shop, Passau, 1936–1939.
Source: Collection of author

educators urging retailers to introduce elements of asymmetry and curvature to relieve the visual monotony of stacking, *Einzelhändler* such as the one in Passau continued to rely upon the *Stapelfenster* model: only 33 of the 89 window displays had a dominant note of asymmetry or curvature and, even then, the stacking of goods continued. What Figure 14.4 illustrates, however, is a feature *Einzelhändler* had that

Figure 14.5 Maypole window display at Wertheim, Leipzigerstrasse, Berlin, 1938.
Source: Ladwig-Winters 1997, 108, used with permission of the author

Warenhäuser sometimes did not: the ability to have *seamless continuity* between exterior and interior displays. Upon entering the shop, a customer would immediately see a similar stacking of goods on promotion, enabling one to make a quick purchase, as opposed to the entire interior world of illusion that one would have to traverse within a *Warenhaus* to locate the item sought. While the *Einzelhändler* model could work as an advantage to the customer, it could be a disadvantage to the retailer in terms of the number of items purchased.

In contrast to this *Einzenhandler*, Germany's *Warenhäuser* had much larger windows in which to build displays, and they often used this space to create not merely a theme but a complete *mise-en-scène* in which the goods were incorporated into some sort of narrative. The ability to create a lavish stage set was perhaps the best maneuver that *Warenhäuser* possessed during these years, and the use of it is underscored by a photo used in a 1997 history about Wertheim (Ladwig-Winters 1997, 108). In what author Simone Ladwig-Winters terms a "folksy" scene that reflected general political circumstances (Fig. 14.5), a mother figure and children play in an idyllic outdoor springtime scene. Although the display might not appear impressive to contemporary audiences, it exemplifies the wealth of props and display talent that *Warenhäuser* could still summon forth.

An entire artificial topography has been created, consisting of a gently rising hillside of artificial grass, augmented by lifesize trees, saplings, rocks and flowers. Such a complex undertaking, involving a support system hidden beneath the hillside, was beyond the scope of an *Einzelhandler*. Twelve mannequins of children, some partially obscured in the photograph, frolic around a maypole, with two of them sitting on the ground in the center of the scene: one plays the accordion while another strums a guitar. A thirteenth child is depicted in a playful embrace with an adult female figure who is seated on a large rock. All the figures are attired in variations of traditional German clothing, or *Trachten*, which underscores two themes: the regime's consistent attempts to promote permutations of *Trachten* as suitable for modern life, and the timelessness that such attire embodies. The space that such a *Warenhaus* window provided permitted the display staff to create a complete and compelling scene, something that could not be accomplished within the much smaller window of an *Einzelhandler*.

Similar display window scenes in *Warenhäuser* have been referenced by contemporary authors. In the 2007 book celebrating the Kaufhaus des Westens' 100th anniversary, a distant shot taken across the street provides some clues of a 1935 advertising campaign encouraging travel throughout the Reich that sprawled across the façade for several levels (Meiners 2007, 86). Paul Lerner uses the same photo in a 2013 essay and provides a close-up of one of the display windows. He describes the travel theme "in which mock railway tracks were affixed to the storefront" (Lerner 2013, 104–5). In the close-up, one display window shows the inside of a train department with four adult mannequins seated as two couples facing one another. Everything that the couples are wearing and have brought with them in terms of luggage and handbags was ostensibly available in the store.

The size of their display windows permitted *Warenhäuser* to continue practicing during the Nazi era what had differentiated them from small shop owners during the Weimar period: creating elaborate scenes in which the goods for sale were placed within a broader narrative. Promotions such as *Weisse Woche*, which had offered massive amounts of simple consumer goods at prices below those of *Einzelhändler*, were no longer permitted. Yet it appears that large advertising displays that promoted a regime-approved theme – such as encouraging travel throughout the Reich in the 1935 campaign at KaDeWe – were allowed at times. A 2006 book commemorating the 125th anniversary of Karstadt alludes to *Warenhäuser* also using their display windows to send public messages during the Third Reich, noting that display windows at Karstadt "were a forum of practical help to customers, e.g., how to put on a gas mask, how to care for stockings. The display window, an advisor" (Karstadt 2006, 63).

In summation, it was something very simple and basic that helped *Warenhäuser* prevail despite a regime whose rhetoric and regulations had diminished some of their activities: their prominent architectural presence within every German city. It was difficult to shut, communalize, or convert to other uses such massive buildings, those "defying fortresses of capital" against which Hermann Göring had railed in 1930. As Jonathan Wiesen noted, "the Nazis' utopian visions could be realized only by sustaining these institutions of consumer capitalism [...] Indeed, they were called upon to translate the vision of a Nazi consumer society into reality" (2011, 60–61). This economic reality, along with their inescapable mortar-and-brick presence as urban landmarks, enabled *Warenhäuser* to maintain a place within Nazi consumer culture. Proscribed from advertising in newspapers and on the radio, *Warenhäuser* still maintained their principal asset: unparalleled linear footage within German cities that no amount of regulation could diminish. The sheer amount of their street-level display windows contributed in large part to the image of a prosperous Third Reich, its cities aglow with light.

Notes

1 In 1934, the journal *Schaufenster-Kunst und Technik* was renamed *Die Gebrauchswerbekunst* and was advertised as the "Official Organ of the German Display Managers Association." This was a manifestation of the Nazi policy of *Gleichschaltung*, the consolidation and unification of all aspects of professional, economic, social, cultural and political life in Germany into organizations loyal to the Nazi party.

2 Journals devoted to window displays largely for *Einzelhändler* included *Das Schaufenster* and *Schaufenster-Kunst und Technik* (*Gebrauchswerbekunst* after mid-1934). Books addressing *Einzelhändler* included Fritz Ackermann, *Schaufenster-Praxis. Das Buch der Beispiele* (Berlin: Walter Detlof Verlag, 1939); Hans M. Geiger, *Werbe Ideen Machen das Schaufenster! Hinter den Kulissen der geistigen Schaufenster-Arbeit* (Stuttgart: Verlag für Wirtschaft und Verkehr, 1934); and Joseph Zimmermann, *Kampf dem Warenhaus!* (Zurich: J. Zimmermann, 1943). Anti-*Warenhaus* rhetoric apparently still resonated with Swiss and German *Einzelhändler* as late as 1943, as manifested in Zimmermann's title, in translation: *Struggle against the Department Store!*

3 The issue of what constituted a firm's founding date was complicated during the Nazi era, as S. Jonthan Wiesen addressed in his book. He noted that until the late 1930s, Aryanized businesses often acknowledged their founding anniversaries by including the "Jewish years," for this was an "opportunity to highlight the longevity and reliability of their newly acquired company and also to rejoice in the ridding of its Jewish influence." But, as Wiesen also notes, the Advertising Council declared that a firm's "Jewish years" could not be counted: "it had to measure its age from the year it became 'Jew free.'" Likewise, phrases such as "Aryan since Founding" were forbidden in 1938 "on the grounds that they put Aryanized firms at a commercial disadvantage as such firms could not claim the same thing" (Wiesen 2011, 50). The proclamation in 1939 by a Nazi official confirming Rudolph Hertzog as a "true German *Kaufhaus* enterprise" therefore was an indirect way of publicizing the firm's Aryan lineage without stating so explicitly.

4 For *Lebensmittel Freitag* see Tietz (1965, 69). For definitions for *Warenhaus* and *Kaufhaus* see Ladwig-Winters (1997, 32, 97); Lenz (1995, 21–4); and Uhlig (1956, 10, 97, 100, 154).

5 See also Sultano (1995, 141–42) and Westphal (1989, 25).

References

Ackermann, Fritz. 1939. *Schaufenster-Praxis. Das Buch der Beispiele*. Berlin: Walter Detlof Verlag.

Baranowski, Shelley. 2004. *Strength through Joy: Consumerism and Mass Tourism in the Third Reich*. New York: Cambridge University Press.

Berghoff, Hartmut. 2001. "Enticement and Deprivation: The Regulation of Consumption in Pre-War Nazi Germany." In *The Politics of Consumption: Material Culture and Citizenship in Europe and America*, edited by Martin Daunton and Matthew Hilton, 165–184. New York: Berg.

Breuss, Susanne. 2010. *Window Shopping. Eine Fotogeschichte des Schaufensters*. Vienna: Wien Museum und Metroverlag.

Coles, Tim. 1999. "Department Stores as Innovations in Retail Marketing: Some Observations on Marketing Practice and Perception in Wilhelmine Germany." *Journal of Macromarketing* 19, 1: 34–47.

Dahms, Paul. 2012. *Mode im Nationalsozialismus: zwischen Ideologie und Verwaltung des Mangels*. Norderstedt: Books on Demand GmbH.

Daitz, Werner. 1943. *Der Weg zur Volkswirtschaft Grossraumwirtschaft und Grossraumpolitik*. Dresden: Meinhold Verlagsgesellschaft.

de Grazia, Victoria. 2006. *Irresistible Empire: America's Advance through Twentieth-Century Europe*. Cambridge: Belknap Press.

"Der Reichsberufswettkampf der deutschen Jugend in der Schaufensterwerbung." 1936. *Das Schaufenster* 17, 4: 87–91.

Geist, Jonas. 2001. "Die Breite Strasse – Hausgeschichte Hausnummer für Hausnummer." In *Vom Mühlendamm zum Schlossplatz. Die Breite Strasse in Berlin-Mitte*, edited by Laurenz Demps, 37–152. Berlin: Parthas Verlag.

Fuchs, Konrad. 1990. *Ein Konzern aus Sachsen. Das Kaufhaus Schocken als Spiegelbild deutscher Wirtschaft und Politik 1901 bis 1953*. Stuttgart: Deutsche Verlags-Anstalt.

Geiger, Hans M. 1934. *Werbe Ideen Machen das Schaufenster! Hinter den Kulissen der geistigen Schaufenster-Arbeit*. Stuttgart: Verlag für Wirtschaft und Verkehr.

Geyer, Michael. 1997. "Germany, or, The Twentieth Century as History." *The South Atlantic Quarterly* 96: 663–702.

Heinz & Kühn Maskenfabrik. 1937. *Katalog Sommer 1937. Laternen, Drachen, Festabzeichen, Fahnen, Dekorationsartikel*. Manebach: Heinz & Kühn.

Karstadt. 2006, *Schaufenster Karstadt. Einblick in 125 Jahre*. Essen: Karstadt.

Kater, Michael H. 1971. "Zur Soziographie der frühen NSDAP." *Vierteljahrshefte für Zeitgeschichte* 19, 2: 124–159.

König Wolfgang. 2003. "Das Scheitern einer nationalsozialistischen Konsumgesellschat 'Volksprodukte' in Politik, Propaganda und Gesellschaft des 'Dritten Reiches.'" *Zeitschrift für Unternehmensgeschichte/Journal of Business History* 48, 2: 131–163.

Ladwig-Winters, Simone. 1997. *Wertheim. Geschichte eines Warenhauses*. Berlin: be.bra Verlag.

Lenz, Rudolf. 1995. *Karstadt. Ein deutscher Warenhauskonzern, 1920–1950*. Stuttgart: Deutsche Verlags-Anstalt.

Lerner, Paul. 2009. "An All-Consuming History? Recent Works on Consumer Culture in Modern Germany." *Central European History* 42, 3: 509–543.

Meiners, Antonia. 2007. *100 Jahre KaDeWe*. Berlin: Nicolaische Verlagsbuchhandlung.

Osterwold, Tilman. 1974. *Schaufenster: Die Kulturgeschichte eines Mediums*. Stuttgart: Württembergischer Kunstverein.

Program of the German Workers' Party. 1920. *German History in Documents and Images*. Accessed August 28, 2015. http://germanhistorydocs.ghi-dc.org/sub_document.cfm?document_id=3910.

Ritschl, Albrecht. 1991. "Die NS-Wirtschaftsideologie – Modernisierungsprogramm oder reaktionäre Utopie?" In *Nationalsozialismus und Modernisierung*, edited by Michael Prinz and Rainer Zitelman, 48–70. Darmstadt: Wissenschaftliche Buchgesellschaft.

Schleif, Nina. 2004. *Schaufensterkunst*. Weimar: Böhlau Verlag.

von Stephani-Hahn, Elisabeth. 1926. *Schaufenster Kunst. Lehrsätze und Erläuterungen*, 3rd edition. Berlin: Verlag "Der Konfektionär" L. Schottlaender & Co.

Sultano, Gloria. 1995. *Wie Geistiges Kokain…Mode unterm Hakenkreuz*. Vienna: Verlag für Gesellschaftskritik.

Swett, Pamela E. 2007. *Selling under the Swastika: Advertising and Commercial Culture in Nazi Germany*. Stanford: Stanford University Press.

Spiekermann, Uwe. 2013. "'Der Mittelstand stirbt!' Der Kampf zwischen Einzelhandel und Warenhäusern in Deutschland 1890–1933." In *Das Berliner Warenhaus/The Berlin Department Store. Geschichte und Diskurse/History and Discourse*, edited by Godela Weiss-Sussex and Ulrike Zitlsperger, 33–52. Frankfurt: Peter Lang GmbH.

Tietz, Georg. 1965. *Hermann Tietz. Geschichte einer Familie und ihrer Warenhäuser*. Stuttgart: Deutsche Verlags-Anstalt.

Uhlig, Heinrich. 1956. *Die Warenhäuser im Dritten Reich*. Cologne: Westdeutscher Verlag.

Ward, Janet. 2001. *Weimar Surfaces: Urban Visual Culture in 1920 Germany. Weimar and Now: German Cultural Criticism 27*. Berkeley: University of California Press.

Westphal, Uwe. 1989. *Werbung im Dritten Reich*. Berlin: Transit Buchverlag.

Wiesen, S. Jonathan. 2011. *Creating the Nazi Marketplace: Commerce and Consumption in the Third Reich*. New York: Cambridge University Press.

Zimmermann, Joseph. 1943. *Kampf dem Warenhaus!* Zurich: J. Zimmermann.

Zitzlsperger, Ulrike. 2013. "'Vornehme Reklame.' Advertising Berlin Department Stores." In *Das Berliner Warenhaus/The Berlin Department Store. Geschichte und Diskurse/History and Discourse*, edited by Godela Weiss-Sussex and Ulrike Zitlsperger, 139–151. Frankfurt: Peter Lang GmbH.

15 The cultured corporation

Art, architecture and the postwar office building

Alice Friedman

For C.M.

From the late nineteenth century on, the twin notions of "corporate identity" and "corporate culture" evolved and expanded, becoming core tenets not only of capitalist economic theory but also of popular ideology within the industrialized societies of the United States and Western Europe. The latter phenomenon is especially significant for the history of architecture and design as it gave rise to a host of significant projects, including such well-known early examples as the AEG electric company in Germany – in which all buildings, electrical products, and advertising copy were required to conform to a shared design identity, overseen from 1907 by Peter Behrens – and the Larkin Company (with its Buffalo headquarters designed by Frank Lloyd Wright, 1904), and a host of later buildings, including Capital Records, General Motors, and Seagram, to name only the most familiar. Beloved by historians of architecture for their design excellence and stylistic innovations, these projects also serve as significant examples of corporate display, and as part of complex merchandizing strategies designed to reach ever-wider audiences and consumer markets by associating consumer practices with positive values such as artistic excellence and elite art patronage (Marchand 1998; Douberly 2015).[1]

Thanks to the evolving technologies of print advertising and mass media, and in particular to the evolution of illuminated street signage from the 1920s on, the reach of these messages expanded not only to the public spaces of large cities like Berlin and New York, but also to the high streets of small towns. The distinction between civic and corporate space blurred – just as domestic space had been transformed in the nineteenth century from a private, family-focused realm to a site of consumption and compelled efficiency. With the improvement and spread of radio and television, the techniques of corporate display expanded still further: no longer fixed in either the spatial or temporal realm, corporate messages, laced with psychological and emotional content, were broadly – and constantly – disseminated. Experts in the emerging field of public relations grew increasingly adept at manipulating consumers' identification with businesses and their products, imbricating material desire with the desire for health, prestige, glamour, love, or social status. Corporate display was both everywhere and nowhere at the same time, both material and immaterial.

Many architects, designers, and artists readily accepted the challenges (and the financial rewards) of corporate patronage: as the focus of business strategy shifted, particularly in the post World War II era, from products to personalities, designers contributed to the creation and display of corporate identities in myriad ways, lending the prestige and social status of the art world to new buildings, entrance lobbies, furniture, and signage, decorating office walls with murals, tapestries, and paintings, creating sculpture for plazas, corridor walls, and lobby spaces, and – in some cases – by associating their own celebrity with the corporate image of their sponsors. This essay examines key examples of such projects from the 1950s and 1960s and the uneasy partnerships of art and commerce that resulted from them.

In a review published in *The New York Times* in January 1968, the newspaper's senior critic, Hilton Kramer, lambasted the work of the American sculptor Richard Lippold then on view in a retrospective exhibition at the Marion Willard Gallery in New York City (1968, D23). Calling the artist "our foremost public decorator," Kramer noted that, for him, the show was significant because it cast new light on "the way that art is conceived and consumed at the higher altitudes of corporate and cultural affluence." In Kramer's view, Lippold's many public and private installations demanded attention not as art *per se*, but because they "loomed astonishingly large at that intersection where art, money (big money), and taste (wretched, misinformed, but surpassingly elegant taste) meet to congratulate themselves on their robust power and influence." Pulling out all the stops, Kramer declared that the show was "not so much an art exhibition as a case of samples" consisting of models, drawings, and photographs documenting the high-profile commissions that the artist had received since 1962. Thus, as he reflected on Lippold's most recent works – including *Flight*, in the lobby of the Pan Am Building in New York (1963) (Fig. 15.1); *Orpheus and Apollo*, in the lobby of Lincoln's Center's Philharmonic (now Avery Fisher) Hall (1962); and the shimmering *baldacchino* over the altar at the Cathedral of St Mary in San Francisco by Pietro Belluschi (1967) – Kramer could not help noting that whatever the show might lack in aesthetic substance, it was certainly "rich in a melancholy sociology," revealing the many ways in which fine art had become debased in recent years (Foster 1994). In Lippold's success, he added, one could see the familiar circumstance in which "artistic ideas that are rewarded to the exact degree that they are betrayed:" thus was fine art turned into ornament, and the work of sculpture debased until it became "mere decoration."

Whatever its strengths or weaknesses as critical journalism, Hilton Kramer's acerbic review offers us a starting point from which to examine the relatively short-lived phenomenon of American corporate patronage of the arts in the decades following World War II, implemented not *indirectly* through the time-honored tradition of funding cultural events or organizations, but *directly* through commissions to architects and artists hired to create lobbies, offices, meeting rooms, restaurants, and other spaces in new, purpose-built office buildings. Through a handful of projects produced over the period between the mid-1930s and the late-1960s, we can track the unlikely love triangle that resulted from the marriage of what we might call the "cultured corporation" and the elite "art" of the architects and artists they entrusted with their projects. Feeling spurned by this alliance, and disconcerted by the notion that art could be made accessible to the uninitiated – the "man in the street" (even if that man spent most of his time in the boardroom or the office) – high-brow critics like Hilton Kramer obsessed over the image of their beloveds wrapped in the arms of fat-cat industrialists or plying the hallways of soaring shrines to capitalism. For others, including some popular journalists and public commentators, these works still remained far out of reach and were satirized as incomprehensible abstractions or as angst-filled autobiography (Kepes 1960, 10; Varnedoe 1990). Clearly, while the ideals

Figure 15.1 Richard Lippold, *Flight*, Pan Am (now Met Life) Building, New York, 1963.
Source: Photograph by author

of commercial patronage and collaboration had been championed since the founding of the Deutscher Werkbund (1907) and the Bauhaus (1919), these partnerships were far more difficult to carry out in practice than they were in theory.

In the United States, the many contentious issues that lay at the heart of art patronage had been made public with a loud bang in 1934 by the rift between the owners of Rockefeller Center, in New York City, and the artist Diego Rivera (Krinsky 1978; Cross 1932, 1–3). The Rockefeller family had always wanted a prominent artist – a Picasso or Matisse – to paint the wall mural that would grace the lobby of the RCA building, the central skyscraper in the new complex of office buildings and public spaces that they were building in Manhattan. They also planned an extensive program of art patronage that would highlight the work of American artists. This was a novel idea: in buildings such as Cass Gilbert's 1913 Woolworth Building, or the recently completed Empire State and Chrysler Buildings, paintings and sculpture by decorative artists were treated as background pieces rather than fine art: highly ornamented lobbies simply created an elegant entry sequence from the street to elevators that would whisk visitors up to the offices on the floors above.

Not so the Rockefeller Center project: by commissioning the well-known avant-garde artist Diego Rivera to create a work of art specifically for their new building, the Rockefellers and their architects – Raymond Hood, Harvey Wiley Corbett, and Wallace K. Harrison foremost among them – were reaching for a different sort of patronage entirely. And therein lay the fundamental contradiction that ultimately destroyed the relationship: as is well known, the artist, commissioned to paint a mural expressing the theme of "Man at the Crossroads: Looking with Hope and High Vision to the Choosing of a New and Better Future" included in his composition not only legions of workers, soldiers, and modern machinery, but also the figure of Lenin, whom Rivera, himself a Communist, admired and respected. Not surprisingly, the newspapers got hold of the story and reacted with horror. The Rockefellers demanded that the offending figure be removed, and the entire mural was painted over – we only know the work from the version that Rivera created at the Palacio de las Bellas Artes in Mexico City – and replaced by a large-scale work by the well-known Spanish artist Josep Maria Sert that celebrated "American Progress." These were soon joined at Rockefeller Center by other commissioned works, including *Prometheus* by Paul Manship, *Atlas* by Lee Lawrie and Rene Chambellan, *Eve* by Gwen Lux, *Song*, *Drama* and *Dance* by Hildreth Meière, and a small aluminum relief entitled *News* by the young Isamu Noguchi.

Despite the notoriety of these high profile breakups – another case that comes to mind is the battle between the artist Mark Rothko and his clients at the Four Seasons Restaurant in the Seagram Building (1958) – the middle decades of the 20th century were marked by a number of collaborative successes in the corporate, institutional, and civic realms. At Seagram, for example, many living artists, including Picasso – whose large painted curtain entitled *Tricorne*, created for Diaghilev's Ballets Russes in 1919, was installed in the back of the main lobby and thus clearly visible from the street – Joan Miro, Jackson Pollock, and others, contributed to what its builders hoped would be a shining example of the "art" of architecture (Scott 2011) and a new "synthesis of the arts" (Lambert 2005, 38–39).[2] These prominent painters jettisoned whatever doubts they had about serving the needs of captains of industry or having their work displayed in offices, conference rooms and restaurants frequented by "ordinary" men and women. Indeed, for a number of European and American Modernists, such commissions were particularly appealing not only for financial or professional reasons but because they offered the possibility of fulfilling shared ambitions for new modes of expression and reaching new audiences for modern art.

It was thus to this select group that many architects and developers working in the service of corporate clients often turned: for Philip Johnson, perhaps the most powerful designer and deal-maker of the postwar period, an artist like Lippold – who completed a pair of shimmering installations, composed of hundreds of suspended bronze rods, over the bar and in the far corner of the Four Seasons Restaurant's Grill Room – represented an ideal partner. In 1963, Johnson commented in the widely-read pages of *The New Yorker* that he considered Lippold "the best sculptor in the world to work with" because he understood the "architectural requirements of the space [...] and does not set out to build a monument" (Tompkins 1963, 48). Other influential theorists like Walter Gropius, founder of the Bauhaus and chairman of the architecture department at Harvard, concurred, noting that in the case of Lippold's installation at the Pan Am Building (which Gropius had designed with Pietro Belluschi in the early 1960s) "art is not added on; rather, space and sculpture become an intrinsic, inseparable, artistic whole" (Ibid.).

Gropius spoke from considerable experience, having been at the center of a sustained debate about the possibility of creating such synthetic artistic collaborations since the 1910s. After World War II, many former Bauhaus professors and members of CIAM (Congrès Internationaux d'Architecture Moderne) such as Gropius (at Harvard University), Josef Albers (at Black Mountain College) and Eliel Saarinen (at Cranbrook Academy) kept these ideas alive in the U.S. (Johnson 1951; Giedion 1958; Kepes 1960; Mumford 2004). Calling upon their colleagues not only to come to terms with the new social, economic, and psychological realities of the postwar period, these architects spoke of the need to "humanize" the new technologies with which they themselves had been, in prewar days, so uncritically enamored (Sert 1944).

For example, at the 6th CIAM conference, held in England in 1947, Sigfried Giedion, the organization's secretary general and one of the most respected advocates for the Modern movement, spoke about the need for modern architects to recognize that the "emotional world co-exists with the rational world," and thus to concern themselves with the "emotional reactions of the common man to modern art, and especially to architecture" (Giedion 1958, 131, 70–78). Seeking to understand the reasons for widespread resistance to collaboration among architects, Giedion even distributed a questionnaire, asking his colleagues for their views on modern art: among the recorded responses were comments from the artist Barbara Hepworth, who criticized architects for turning their backs on works of modern sculpture, and Le Corbusier, who called for the creation of a new "poetic phenomenon" to address the experience of "strangers on the street" (Giedion 1958, 74–76). With a characteristic combination of brilliance and self-promotion, Corbusier grasped both the significance of the professional opportunities that such projects would bring: "these strangers, in our modern society," he wrote, "may well be those in important positions, people here and there in charge of the essential machinery of the state, those who by their decisions and administration, can guide the country toward a future that is ugly or beautiful. Some among them cannot help but be susceptible to poetry." Corbusier concluded by calling for a new "collective enterprise" designed to bring "security, abundance and a delight in living, and to save the world from imbecile catastrophe" (Le Corbusier 1948; Ockman 2007; Von Moos 2009).

In Europe, the earliest products of this new approach were in the realm of church building. Thanks to the commitment of a number of hardworking individuals, such as the Dominican cleric Marie-Alain Couturier, artists like Chagall, Matisse, Léger, Braque, Roualt, and Lipchitz contributed to the creation of new, artistically rich spiritual environments at Notre-Dame de Toute Grâce at Assy (1937–1946) and Sacré-Coeur at Audincourt (1952) by Maurice Novarina; better known examples include the chapels at Ronchamp by Le Corbusier, and at Vence (1948–1952), with murals and stained glass by Matisse (1949–1951) (Pauly 1997; Pearson 2010, 76, 82).[3]

Similarly, prominent institutions like the United Nations in New York (designed by a multinational coalition of architects, including Le Corbusier, Wallace K. Harrison, and Oscar Niemeyer; 1948–1952), UNESCO in Paris (Marcel Breuer; 1951–1958) and the University of Caracas in Venezuela (Carlos Raul Villanueva; 1940–1960) sought to highlight collaborative efforts of modern architecture, painting and sculpture in the hope that high-minded principles of international cooperation might be communicated to broad audiences (Gomez 2010). All of these projects rested on the belief that modern architects and artists had a special responsibility to transcend class divisions and political boundaries by creating a transformative yet accessible language of abstract form. As Walter Gropius wrote in 1959:

> As long as our cultured elite insist that undiscriminating popular taste is beyond repair, that salvation lies in imposing on an uncomprehending public an authoritative aesthetic formula, they will sidestep the particular obligation of a democratic society – to work from the ground up rather than from the top down [...] The next generation may witness a unification of society. The role of the artist will then be to find the humanized image for society's aspirations and ideals. By virtue of his ability to give visible symbols to significant order, he may once again become society's seer and mentor, and as custodian of its conscience solve the American paradox.
>
> (Gropius 1960, 273)

In the United States, a number of examples of this new "synthesis of the arts" in institutional architecture appeared after the war. Gropius himself completed a foundational project at the Harvard Graduate Center, including works by Albers, Arp, and Lippold, in 1951. Remarkably, however, such collaborations are more numerous in the realm of commercial patronage (Prudhon 2007). The best known and most far-reaching of these was the new General Motors Technical Center (Fig. 15.2), designed and built between 1946 and 1956 in Warren, Michigan, some ten miles outside of Detroit and thus quite distant from the cultural and economic maelstrom of New York City.[4] Eliel Saarinen, then director of the nearby Cranbook Academy of Art, and his son Eero had been commissioned in 1947 to build a large complex of research buildings, laboratories, offices, meeting rooms, and extensive outdoor spaces for both cars and people. The project would ultimately include a large reflecting pool and water tower, buildings incorporating the latest new technologies and engineering, and a handful of significant works of art by American and European artists, including Alexander Calder, Antoine Pevsner (Fig. 15.3), and Harry Bertoia (Fig. 15.4) (Friedman 2010; Pelkonen 2006; Bertoia 1972; Nelson 1970; Coir 2006). The complex was equally effective as a research laboratory, an office building, a setting for advertising images, and a high brow "accessory" for the corporation. Thanks to the commitment to modern architecture and design by its clients, particularly Harley Earl, the director of design at General Motors, and Alfred P. Sloan, the CEO – and also to their understanding that such luxurious "conspicuous consumption" could only enhance the prestige of their

Figure 15.2 Alexander Calder, Fountain, General Motors Technical Center, Warren, Michigan, 1956.
Source: Balthazar Korab, Library of Congress Prints and Photographs Division

products – this innovative project was completed and celebrated by its users and by many artists and critics as well.

Indeed, Harry Bertoia's experiments in gilded metal at GM captured the attention of the eminent architect Gordon Bunshaft, who commissioned him to create a monumental screen (Fig. 15.5) for the new Manufacturers Trust Company Building at the corner of Fifth Avenue and 45th Street, completed in 1954 ("Modern Architecture" 1954). The building, a minimalist glass box characteristic of Bunshaft and of Skidmore, Owings, and Merrill in those years, was – like Seagram – most notable

Figure 15.3 Antoine Pevsner, *Flight of the Bird*, 1955, G.M. Technical Center.
Source: Balthazar Korab, Library of Congress Prints and Photographs Division

for its transparency, and for the theatrical effects of its lighting design, particularly at night. From the street, passers-by could see not only the huge stainless steel safe on the ground floor, but also the radiant gilt screen by Bertoia on the upper level and the brightly lit ceiling panels above it. Lewis Mumford described the building as a "crystal lantern" (Petty 2007, 205–211 and n.71; Dunlap 2012).

Now occupied by a clothing store, the former banking hall retains both its impressive proportions and the Bertoia screen, which confer an unlikely dignity on the racks of merchandize and cash desks installed in the space. Stretching across the full expanse of the room, and rising to over 15 feet, the screen – composed of gilt-metal rectangles, rods and abstract shapes welded together – strongly alludes to the conventional decoration of sacred spaces. Paired with a delicate wire ceiling sculpture that hangs over the front of the hall, Bertoia's screen reflected both the cultural aspirations of the client and the aesthetic goals of architects and designers like Bunshaft and Florence Knoll, who were among the period's most highly respected creators of corporate interiors (Tigerman 2007). Given the success of this project, it is not surprising that Bertoia would be commissioned some three years later to complete a large screen for the First National Bank of Miami, or that he would work in other corporate and public contexts throughout the 1960s (Schiffer 2003). His work was even used to bring a new "synthesis of the arts" to Victor Gruen's Southdale

Figure 15.4 Harry Bertoia, Screen, Employee Cafeteria, 1956, G.M Technical Center.
Source: Balthazar Korab, Library of Congress Prints and Photographs Division

Shopping Mall in Edina, Minnesota, where he completed a large hanging sculpture in 1956 (Smiley 2013).

As well as being lauded by Philip Johnson, as noted previously, Richard Lippold was also much in demand among such influential figures as Gropius and Josef Albers, whose support would carry him from the late 1940s through to the 1960s. Born in Milwaukee in 1915 and educated at the Art Institute of Chicago, Lippold was invited to teach at Black Mountain College in the summer of 1948 (Harris 1987). The artist was deeply affected by this experience and by his life-long association with people he met there, such as John Cage, Ray Johnson, Merce Cunningham, Robert Rauschenberg, and Buckminster Fuller (Anon 1952; Carter 1991; Jones 1993; Katz 2002). Shortly thereafter, his national reputation was sealed by a commission from Walter Gropius, who – on Albers's recommendation and on the strength of a work recently installed at MoMA – asked him to create the large-scale *World Tree* of stainless steel rods for the Harvard Graduate Center in 1950 (Lippold 1971, 88–92).

Thus Lippold began to receive commissions for larger architectural pieces. Among the most important was an installation entitled *Radiant I* in the lobby of the Inland Steel Building by Skidmore Owings and Merrill in 1958 (Tomkins 1963, 75) (Fig. 15.6). Created under the auspices of Leigh Block, the CEO of the corporation and a collector of contemporary art, the project began with an accommodation from the architect, who moved the wall back a number of feet – with the blessings of the client – to provide a more prominent site for the sculpture, a brightly-lit, large-scale wire installation that hangs above a pool of water (Tomkins 1963). With its jewel-like form, Lippold's

Figure 15.5 Harry Bertoia, Screen, Manufacturers Trust Company Building, New York, 1954.
Source: Photograph by author

installation added a touch of corporate glamour to the glass-curtain-walled building. The combination of sleek and orderly modern architecture and the celestial forms of Lippold's minimalist installation helped to create a new workplace environment for managers whose feet were firmly placed on the ground but whose heads were filled with American dreams (Abercrombie 2000).

The motivations behind such projects varied widely. In the case of another Lippold work, *Homage to Our Age*, installed in the headquarters of the J. Walter Thompson Company in 1961, the reasons were made explicit by the company itself. According to the company's public announcement of the Lippold acquisition, the shared values of modern art, architecture, and advertising were mutually reinforcing:

> While it does not follow that an interest in the fine arts will lead automatically to production of brilliant, persuasive advertising, it is our strong abiding interest in producing *quality* work for our clients that is fortified by our interest in art [...] We are totally involved in communication – and the raw materials of our work are creative art and creative writing. It is for this reason that it is important for our staff members to be immediately aware of the major cultural trends of our times and especially the visual arts. It is to the point that the works we have collected are mainly those done by modern artists. This goes to the heart of our business, because we are innovators on behalf of our clients. But one can't be an

Figure 15.6 Richard Lippold, *Radiant 1*, Inland Steel Building, Chicago, 1958.
Source: Photograph by author

innovator without bringing to the problems that have to be solved the qualities of mind that make for innovation – awareness of new ways of looking at reality, new ways of depicting reality.

(Thompson 1965)

These sentiments were echoed by Lippold himself (Lippold, 1978). Writing in *Balance* magazine in 1957, he made his approach clear:

Let us assume that we are concerned with the creation of great architecture. This means that we wish to make not a working shelter, but something much more: a work of art whose primary function is to provide an aesthetic experience transcending the material form of the building. (Ultimately architecture has no other purpose.) To accomplish this, the user must first be seduced into the experience, and this means that he must find a place in it that is respectful to him [...] It is the artist's responsibility in this affair to hold the building by one hand, so to speak, and the user by the other. To many artists this seems a thankless task. I can assure them that it is no more thankless than the task with which any true artist is familiar: that of being responsible to both a spiritual and material world.

(Lippold 1957, 19)

Like his corporate clients, Lippold was serious about the role played by art in collaboration with modern architecture: indeed, he saw the broad themes of his work – "space-yearning," "dematerialization," and the celebration of new materials and technologies – as deeply spiritual, regardless of the contexts for which specific pieces were made (Neumann 2011). This signal tenet of artistic faith, which belies the claim that he was a mere salesman or "decorator," is illustrated by a charming anecdote that Lippold recounts in his unpublished essay "Basic Commitments." There he describes how, as a prelude to the commission for the *baldacchino* at St Mary's Cathedral in the mid-1960s, the Archbishop of San Francisco visited him in New York and accompanied him on a tour of his many installations in the city. Later, over "coffee and brandy" at the Four Seasons, the Archbishop studied Lippold's works in the Grill Room, finally turning to the artist, "with a mixture of admiration and bewilderment," to ask a question: "Tell me, Mr. Lippold," he queried,

Why do you make such a spiritual fixture over a bar? Returning his gaze with a look of equally mixed admiration and bewilderment, I replied, 'Well, as your excellency must remember from the lives of the saints, one can have a revelation anywhere.'

This was, of course, a very serious joke. As an artist who has produced works for many public places, from churches to restaurants, with office buildings and concert halls in between, as well as residential stairwells and mantelpieces, and quiet as well as noisy museum galleries, I have known a similar excitement in the making of all of these works. There seems to have been no hierarchy of 'spiritual values' dependent on the situation within which my creative apparatus has had to function.

(Lippold c.1968, 0059)

In the 1960s, Lippold brought these convictions to his most complex corporate endeavor: an enormous wire installation for Pietro Belluschi and Walter Gropius' Pan Am Building – now Met Life – adjacent to Grand Central Terminal in New York (Clausen 2005). The piece, entitled *Flight*, covers the entire 35-foot height of the Vanderbilt Lobby and extends 80 feet across the full dimension of the room. Working with John Cage, a friend and frequent collaborator in the 1950s, and encouraged by the building's visionary developer Erwin Wilson, Lippold imagined a multimedia work that could be experienced by thousands of daily commuters who used the space as a covered passage as they moved from Grand Central Terminal onto Park Avenue. As visitors moved through the space, motion-activated sensors around the room would trigger recordings of Cage's music in overlapping zones (Vanel 2008). Together with Gropius and a committee of advisors including Museum of Modern Art director

Rene d'Harnoncourt, Ivan Chermayeff, Edward Larrabee Barnes and others, Lippold managed to win over a skeptical Juan Trippe, the Pan Am president. Although they all chimed in, it was d'Harnoncourt who clinched the deal:

> We [MoMA] were one of the first people to have one of Lippold's space designs in our lobby. I would say that *this* one would be one of the most important pieces of indoor sculpture of the twentieth century. It you want the impact of a great symbol, giving the feeling of speed through space, of expansion, and lightness, you have it in this sculpture. No one who sees it is ever going to forget it.
> (Ross 1961, 49)

For a businessman like Trippe, that sort of lasting message and the cultural cachet that it brought to his brand were priceless.

Unfortunately, the installation was completed without the planned sound effects: following Wolfson's death, the Pan Am board rejected John Cage's contribution as too costly and experimental. Yet Lippold's piece remains impressive: it is truly an oddity in corporate architecture, yet together with Josef Albers's nearby mural (since removed), it marked the Pan Am corporation as a cultured client willing to spend the extra dollars to enhance both the private space of the office building and the public space of the lobbies that connected the train station with the avenues to the north and east.

In closing, we return to the review by Hilton Kramer with which we began, to reflect again on the controversies that such public projects engendered. It is worth remembering that it was in part because Kramer recognized Lippold's debt to the high art of Constructivism that he ranted so violently, picking at that fact like a wound, and returning again and again to the ways in which the artist's work had cheated its source. "Mr. Lippold is a Constructivist of a sort," he wrote, "yet what we see in his *oeuvre* is the subversion of the Constructivist aesthetic for decorative ends." He goes on in this vein with brilliant, obsessive malice: "The technology of Constructivism," he noted, "the joining of slender masses in such a way as to use space itself as a form of sculptural mass – is maintained and indeed ingenuously elaborated, but the spirit of Constructivism is destroyed. Cogency of form is abandoned to decorative illustration. It is rather as if the followers of Cezanne had applied his principles to a revival of Bougereau." His readers – including Lippold – knew that this was the ultimate putdown (Kramer 1968, D23).

Ultimately, these comments speak volumes about the cultural and economic divide in postwar American society: artists and intellectuals had taste but no money or power; rich industrialists and newly wealthy clients aspired to cultural prominence but were continually slapped down by the critics. Thus Kramer ended his review by decrying the tricks and games that artists like Lippold resorted to: in his view, these were simply the repurposed tactics of the advertising men and the crass peddlers of the American dream. Thus it was clear why clients turned to artists like Lippold rather than to men like Pevsner or Gabo, whom he termed "authentic and original exponents of Constructivism." "The glittery superficialities of Mr. Lippold's constructions," Kramer sneered, "with their pretentions to cosmic 'meaning' and their costume jewelry effects, are the exact visual equivalent of the glittery cultural aspirations so fondly harbored by these patrons" (Kramer 1968, D23). Commentary such as this, though perhaps surprising to recall in our own postmodern world of irony and cultural populism, was hardly new: it represented simply one more battle in the war between the guardians of high art and their wealthy rivals, in a period when such things not only mattered but had a place in public discourse.

Notes

1 I am grateful to Amanda Douberly for generously sharing her unpublished dissertation with me; her work on public and corporate patronage of modern sculpture breaks new ground in the study of postwar Modernism in the U.S.
2 The Picasso painting was recently removed after 55 years by the building's current owner.
3 Also of note is the synagogue designed by Percival Goodman for Congregation B'nai Israel in Millburn, N.J. (1951), including newly commissioned works by Robert Motherwell, Adolph Gottlieb, and Herbert Ferber. For modern synagogue design, see Peter Blake, *An American Synagogue for Today and Tomorrow: A Guide Book to Synagogue Design and Construction* (New York: Union of American Hebrew Congregations, 1954).
4 The earliest such project is Isamu Noguchi's ceiling for Harris Armstong's American Stove Building in St. Louis (Mumford 2004, 46–47).

References

Abercrombie, Stanley, 2000. "Office Supplies: Evolving Furniture for the Evolving Workplace." In *On the Job: Design and the American Office*, edited by Donald Albrecht and Chrysanthe Broikos, 81–97. New York: Princeton Architectural Press.

Anon. 1952. "Four Artists in a 'Mansion.'" *Harper's Bazaar*, July: 78–79.

Architectural Forum. 1954. "Modern Architecture Breaks Through the Glass Barrier: Manufacturers Trust Company, New York" 101, December: 104–111.

Belluschi, Pietro, Harry Bertoia, et al. 1952. "Views on Art and Architecture: A Conversation." In *The Visual Arts Today*, edited by Gyorgy Kepes, special issue of *Daedalus: Journal of the American Academy of Arts and Sciences* 898, 1, Winter: 62–73.

Bertoia, Harry. 1952. "Oral History Interview." Archives of American Art, June 20.

Carter, Curtis L., Jack W. Burnham, and Edward Lucie-Smith. 1991. *Richard Lippold: Sculpture*. Milwaukee: Haggerty Museum of Art, Marquette University.

Clausen, Meredith. 2005. *The Pan Am Building and the Shattering of the Modernist Dream*. Cambridge: MIT Press.

———. 1992. *Spiritual Space: The Religious Architecture of Pietro Belluschi*, Seattle: University of Washington Press.

Coir, Mark. 2006. *In Nature's Embrace: The World of Harry Bertoia*. Reading, PA: Reading Public Museum.

Cross, Louise. 1932. "The Sculpture for Rockefeller Center." *Parnassus*, 4, 5, October: 1–3.

Douberly, Amanda Ann. 2015. *The Corporate Model: Sculpture, Architecture, and the American City 1946–75*. PhD Dissertation, University of Texas, Austin.

Dunlap, David W. 2012. "Behind the Low-Priced Clothing, a Priceless Midcentury Sculpture." *New York Times*, May 31.

Foster, Anne T. 1994. "Richard Lippold and Thomas Aquinas: The 'Baldacchino' for St. Mary's Cathedral in San Francisco." *Soundings: An Interdisciplinary Journal* 77, 1/2, Spring-Summer: 81–97.

Friedman, Alice T. 2010. *American Glamour and the Evolution of Modern Architecture*. New Haven: Yale University Press.

Giedion, Siegfried. 1958. *Architecture You and Me*. Cambridge: HUP.

Gomez, Hannia. 2010. "The Dwellers: The Integration of Art and Architecture in the Ciudad Universitaria de Caracas." *Docomomo 42, Art and Architecture*, Summer: 46–55.

Gropius, Walter. 1960. "The Curse of Conformity." In *Adventures of the Mind from the Saturday Evening Post*, edited by Mark van Doren, 263–274. New York: Knopf.

Harris, Mary Emma. 1987. *The Arts and Black Mountain College*. MIT Press.

Johnson, Philip. 1951. "Symposium on How to Combine Architecture, Painting and Sculpture." *Interiors* 110, 10: 100–105.

Jones, Caroline. 1993. "Finishing School: John Cage and the Abstract Expressionist Ego." *Critical Inquiry*, Summer: 643–647.

Katz, Vincent and Martin A. Brody. 2002. *Black Mountain College: Experiment in Art*. MIT Press.

Kepes, Gyorgy. 1960. "Introduction." In *The Visual Arts Today*, edited by Gyorgy Kepes, Special Issue of *Daedalus: Journal of the American Academy of Arts and Sciences*, Winter: 3–12.

Kramer, Hilton. 1968. "The Phenomenon of Richard Lippold: Our Foremost Public Decorator." *New York Times*, January 14: D23.

Krinsky, Carol Herselle. 1978. *Rockefeller Center*. New York: Oxford University Press.

Lambert, Phyllis. 2005. "Stimmung at Seagram: Philip Johnson Counters Mies Van der Rohe." *Grey Room* 20, Summer: 38–59.

Le Corbusier. 1948. *New World of Space*. New York: Reynal and Hitchcock.

Lippold, Richard. Papers 1944–1977, Archives of American Art.

———. 1978. "Art in Architecture: An Artist's Point of View." *Architectural Record* 164, 8, December: 69–71; 73.

———. c.1968. "Basic Commitments," Archives of American Art, N69–24, 0059–0065.

———. 1971. "Interview," December 1, Archives of American Art, 125pp.

———. 1957. "Three in One." *Balance* 6/7: 6–7.

Marchand, Roland. 1998. *Creating the Corporate Soul: The Rise of Public Relations and Corporate Imagery in American Big Business*. Berkeley: University of California Press.

Mumford, Eric. 2009. "The Emergence of Urban Design in the Breakup of CIAM." In *Urban Design*, edited by Alex Krieger and William S. Saunders, 15–37. Minneapolis: University of Minnesota Press.

———. 2004. "Triumph and Eclipse: Modern Architecture in St. Louis and the School of Architecture." In *Modern Architecture in St. Louis*, edited by Eric Mumford, 43–70. St. Louis: The School of Architecture.

Nelson, June Kompass. 1970. *Harry Bertoia: Sculptor*. Detroit: Wayne State University Press.

Neumann, Dietrich, ed. 2011. *The Structure of Light: Richard Kelly and the Illumination of Modern Architecture*. New Haven: Yale University Press.

Ockman, Joan, 2007. "A Plastic Epic: Synthesis of the Arts Discourse in France in the Mid-20th century." In *Architecture + Art: New Visions, New Strategies*, edited by Eeva Liisa Pelkonen and Esa Laaksonen, 30–61. Helsinki: Alvar Aalto Academy.

Pauly, Daniele. 2009. *Le Corbusier: La Chapelle de Ronchamp*. Paris: Fondation Le Corbusier.

Pearson, Christopher E. M. 2010. *Designing UNESCO: Art, Architecture and International Politics at Mid-Century*. Farnham: Ashgate.

Pelkonen, Eeva-Liisa, ed. 2006. *Eero Saarinen: Shaping the Future*. New Haven: Yale University Press.

Petty, Margaret Maile. 2007. "Illuminating the Glass Box: The Lighting Designs of Richard Kelly." *Journal of the Society of Architectural Historians* 66, 2, June: 194–219.

Prudhon, Theodore. 2007. "Art, Architecture and Public Space in New York." *Docomomo* 42, *Art and Architecture*, Summer: 78–89.

Scott, Felicity. 2011. "An Army of Soldiers or a Meadow: The Seagram Buildings and the 'Art' of Architecture." *Journal of the Society of Architectural Historians*, 70, 3, September: 330–353.

Sert, José Luis and Fernand Leger. 1944. "Nine Points on Monumentality," and "The Human Scale in Planning." In *New Architecture and City Planning*, edited by Paul Zucker, 392–412. New York: Philosophical Library.

Shiffer, Nancy N. and Val Bertoia. 2003. *The World of Bertoia*. Atglen, PA: Shiffer Publishing.

Smiley, David. 2013. *Pedestrian Modern: Shopping and American Architecture, 1925–1956.* Minneapolis: University of Minnesota Press.

Time Magazine. 2007. "Orpheus and Apollo," January 4.

Thompson, J. Walter Corp. 1965. "Art and Advertising." *Chicago Tribune Magazine*, September 12: 82.

Tigerman, Bobbye. 2007. "'I Am Not an Interior Decorator:' Florence Knoll, the Knoll Planning Unit, and the Making of the Modern Office." *Journal of Design History* 20: 161–174.

Tomkins, Calvin. 1963. "Thing Among Things: Richard Lippold." *New Yorker*, March 30: 47–107.

Varendoe, Kirk and Adam Gopnik. 1990. *High and Low: Modern Art and Popular Culture.* New York: Abrams.

Vanel, Hervé. 2008. "John Cage's Muzak-Plus: The Fu(rni)ture of Music." *Representations* 102, 1, Spring: 94–128.

Von Moos, Stanislaus. 2009. *Le Corbusier: Elements of a Synthesis*, Revised and Expanded Edition. Rotterdam: 010 Publishers.

16 "Knife/Fork/Spoon"

The Walker Art Center and the design and display of "Contour" sterling flatware service, 1949–1951

Alexa Griffith Winton

In late December 1948, John Van Koert, the newly appointed design director of the venerable New England silver manufacturer Towle Manufacturing, wrote to Dan Defenbacher, the director of the Walker Art Center in Minneapolis, Minnesota, seeking the museum's assistance in a highly unusual project. In collaboration with the Walker, Towle's design department would create a new sterling flatware pattern more appropriate to the increasingly informal lifestyle of postwar America. A key component of this project was the convening of Silver Design Clinics, which were essentially focus groups of "forward-thinking" women who would respond to a display of both conventional and prototype designs in order to assist Towle in creating a pattern that was both modern and commercially viable. Another critical aspect of the project was the creation of a modular and compact traveling exhibition in which the new design would be highlighted.

Van Koert was astute in singling out Defenbacher for partnership in this project. An architect by training and veteran of the Works Progress Administration, Defenbacher believed strongly in the educational mandate of the art institution, and constantly sought innovative ways to subvert the conception of the museum as for the display of the material possessions of the deceased "great and good," which he believed alienated many potential visitors. A populist at heart, who favored interactivity over pedantry, he had organized two highly influential exhibitions called "Idea Houses" in 1941 and 1947. These were participatory spectacles showcasing the possibilities of modern design, specifically tailored to the middle-class consumer. Additionally, under Defenbacher, the Walker initiated the Everyday Art Gallery, which organized a series of rotating exhibitions that attempted to introduce modern design in innovative and inspiring ways. Defenbacher immediately perceived the potential of a collaboration with Towle, and developed a coordinated plan of execution that included a traveling exhibition organized by the Walker, and a national publicity campaign to introduce the new pattern, subsequently named "Contour."

This chapter considers both the design and the exhibition of "Contour" as essential components of the same project, and as contributors to the larger efforts of modern art museums to define and promote taste to the American public via design exhibitions, effectively inserting previously avant-garde notions of domestic designs into their curatorial agendas. As Tony Bennett has argued, museums were among the numerous commercial, cultural, and national institutions that comprise the "exhibitionary complex," and, as such, "they formed vehicles for inscribing and broadcasting the messages of power [...] throughout society" (Bennett 1988, 74). The chapter will also examine the social and museological implications of the evolution of "Contour," both in its unorthodox design development and its curatorial display in the accompanying traveling exhibition, "Knife/Fork/Spoon."

The "Contour" project poses many questions about conflicting impulses in the modern design movements of mid-century America, and the structural connections between government, cultural institutions, and industry that in many ways defined the postwar art museum. What was the exhibition strategy for displaying "Contour," and how did it relate to other contemporary hybrid museum and commercial projects that likewise exploited techniques of display, such as the Museum of Modern Art's "Good Design" exhibitions of the 1950s? How did this strategy reflect larger cultural and political issues in postwar America? How did techniques of display in the exhibition reinforce the message that a flatware design adhering to principles of "Good Design" was desired and even necessary?

Creating "Contour:" "Good design pays"

Van Koert felt strongly that sterling flatware design was not keeping up with the postwar American home, and was incompatible with new domestic designs for furniture, ceramics, glass, and architecture. This disparity was highlighted by the use of new materials and techniques that characterized much postwar American design, including inexpensive and modular food storage containers such as Tupperware, disposable aluminum products, such as foil and containers made for frozen dinners, and the ever-larger and more complex kitchen appliances used to store, cook and clean up after meals (Clarke 1999 and Wang 2012). In contrast, sterling flatware was seemingly inextricably entwined with the more formal, pre-war bourgeois lifestyle and its concomitant social structures.

Van Koert conceived of the project as a means of pinpointing precisely what his target consumer wanted in a modern flatware pattern. As he described to Defenbacher:

> At this point our intention is to approach people who have well-defined and forward-looking tastes for guidance in the development of an entirely new line of silver. Many of us have found that available commercial table service falls short of our needs, but unfortunately, it has been difficult to bring together in sufficiently large groups people who are dissatisfied. We believe that organizations such as yours are rallying points and we suspect that within your membership we can find exactly the informed jury that we need.
>
> (Walker Art Center Archives, Director's Office Records,
> D.S. Defenbacher, Box 19, file 12)

In other words, Towle sought the input of consumers who were already interested in and purchasing new designs in order to create a product tailor-made for their tastes. For its part, the Walker had an agenda of its own, as expressed by Defenbacher: "The Art Center wished to prove two things conclusively. First, that good design pays. And second, that a practical collaboration of industry and education could benefit industry, educator, and consumer, each in his own objectives" (Defenbacher 1952, 78). While he was aware of the potential pitfalls of collaborating with industry, Defenbacher believed the benefits outweighed the acknowledged risks and persevered with his goal of encouraging the creation and concomitant consumption of "good design."

There existed at least one precedent for art institutions and industry collaborating on the design and manufacture of a product: in 1942, the Museum of Modern Art's Department of Industrial Design, under the direction of Eliot Noyes, proposed to the Castleton China Company that they develop a new line of dinnerware reflecting modern aesthetics, recommending industrial designer Eva Zeisel – then teaching ceramics for mass-production at the Pratt Institute – for the project. The resulting service, Zeisel's "Museum," went into limited production in 1946, and was introduced to the public via an exhibition at the Museum of Modern Art (MoMA 1946).

The American silver industry, with roots stretching back into the seventeenth century, struggled during the Depression, with few consumers able to spend large sums on luxuries like sterling flatware. Sterling functioned and was marketed as material wealth that could be transferred to family members over time, conferring an air of tradition as well as functioning as a tangible record or trace of family history, with each generation contributing to the characteristically soft patina of old silver. Consequently, much of the available design in that period appealed to the well-to-do and the aspirational consumer, with patterns that tended towards historicism or which directly emulated the work of highly influential European makers such as the Danish manufacturer Georg Jensen. These services were fabricated using laborious and expensive hand-finishing techniques, aimed at the limited clientele who could still afford this type of workmanship. During the war, many sterling manufacturers were requisitioned by the military to make armaments and other machinery for the war effort. Much of their existing technology was jettisoned in favor of mass-production techniques brought in by the military. Following the war, the industry consequently emerged with new manufacturing capabilities, a vastly expanded base of potential purchasers, and, according to people like John Van Koert, a dearth of viable new ideas to match this new domestic landscape (WACA, Exhibition Files, Knife/Fork/Spoon: Towle, Box 28, File 2).

At the time "Contour" was designed, Connecticut-based Towle Manufacturing (founded in 1853) produced only sterling flatware and hollowware, and employed a workforce of approximately 800 people (Ibid.). As the Walker's in-house design researcher, and industrial designer in his own right, Don Wallance notes in his 1950 case study on Towle:

> The manufacture of sterling silver tableware in a plant like Towle's provides a meeting ground for traditional craftsmanship and mechanization [...] The scale of production and distribution definitely belong to the era of mass production. As many as 1,000,000 pieces of a single design may be sold in one year. But the sales approach is based on the appeal of individuality and hand craftsmanship.
>
> (Ibid.)

Post-war marketing techniques aimed at selling all these millions of pieces of sterling included the door-to-door salesman, a direct-marketing technique that soon outsold the traditional jewelry store or department store. This direct sales approach eliminated the need for consumers to seek out silver in its traditional retail environment, thereby sidestepping the ritual of shopping for a silver pattern in the often formal atmosphere of retail stores. There, flatware was typically displayed out of reach in glass vitrines, a strategy of display far closer to a museum exhibition than a retail experience. Conversely, the door-to-door salesman could provide immediate, tangible access to the goods in the comfort of one's own home.

As Wallance emphasized, while design – hand in hand with craftsmanship – has always been the essential component of any successful silver manufacturer, in the postwar era the industry was tradition-bound with respect to patterns, possessing little vocabulary with which to express its relevance in the new era. Towle's general manager during this time, George Withers, recognized the importance of connecting with consumers' desire for new designs. He would hire John Van Koert in 1947 with the express mandate of updating the product line. Van Koert, a painter and sculptor who trained in metalwork at the University of Wisconsin, had worked in the offices of Henry Dreyfuss immediately after the war, and consistently expressed a personal affinity for the abstract yet humanizing modern designs from Scandinavia. Internal resistance from both the business side and the design department continually stymied Van Koert's efforts to modernize, until he found cooperation with institutions such as the Walker (Ibid.).

In addition to Van Koert himself, the focus groups, termed Silver Design Clinics, were a key component in developing "Contour." Van Koert was especially impressed with the response of the Minneapolis focus group, held in 1950, writing to Defenbacher:

> I think you will be pleased to know that my entire trip worked out exactly as I had hoped it would, and I am very much indebted to you and your associates for helping me take the first step. The groups of women varied from place to place and possibly in some cities the groups represented a wider cross-section of the local populations. However, I feel that nowhere else did I see such evidence of good guidance. I think that you have basically good material to start with. I hope that we can follow this up with an operation at another stage in the development of this new product.
> (WACA, Director's Office, Daniel S. Defenbacher, Box 19, File 12)

These groups, which appear to have been comprised exclusively of women connected to leading cultural institutions, underscore the increasing importance of women – especially those belonging to the middle and upper classes – as both consumers and style-setters of the new postwar designs. In fact, Van Koert found their influence in the marketplace both unavoidable and objectionable, advising in an article on his focus groups in a local Minneapolis paper that women should take their husbands with them when shopping for silverware. "If husbands and wives shared in their expression of taste, silver patterns would be better," he said, "simply because husbands often have better taste than their wives" (Van Koert, 1949).

In soliciting the participation of the focus group, Defenbacher composed a letter stressing the importance of their input, describing the brief of the group: "[it] will handle the silverware, try it out, and discuss values in a very informal, analytical way. The manufacturer will not take names or bother you in any commercial way now or in the future. This is purely and simply a selective design clinic conducted by us in the interest of better products for the consumer" (Ibid.). The Walker Art Center invited approximately 15 women to the three-hour-long clinic, some of whom were connected to the Walker through its board, almost all of whom came from the prosperous local families whose wealth was tied to the local timber, grain, or similar industries.

Van Koert distributed a worksheet describing the material they were to evaluate: current Towle lines, Scandinavian examples together with American products in the Scandinavian style, and prototypes for the new Towle design. This design responded to the ergonomic and biomorphic styles then gaining popularity in American design. Following a demonstration and lecture by Van Koert, these women were given a worksheet titled "What Shall We Do About Sterling Silver Table Service?" and asked to rate the material they viewed in order of preference. While correspondence between Towle and the Walker indicating the helpfulness of these focus groups to the designers survives, I have been unable to locate either the actual responses of the attendees, or, with the exception of the Walker, their names. For this reason, it is difficult to know how much significance to assign the groups with respect to the final outcome of "Contour."

In 1951, after more than a year of research and design development, the Walker unveiled "Contour," a sleek, abstract biomorphic flatware pattern designed to fit comfortably in the hand. It initially comprised a service of 34 separate pieces, with a standard five-piece place setting costing $83.50. Prior to its commercial introduction, "Contour" was selected for inclusion in the 1950 "Good Design" exhibition at MoMA and the Merchandise Mart, Chicago, which undoubtedly raised awareness about the design among those who closely monitored the "Good Design" selections (*Current Design* 1951/2). The number of service pieces was down considerably from the Victorian period, when there seemed to be a separate utensil for nearly every type of food and every occasion. While Defenbacher explained this minimal service as the result of evolutionary fine-tuning on the part of the designer and manufacturer, American flatware producers had in fact already started to reduce the number of pieces per service during the Depression (Defenbacher 1951, 41).

As with much industrial design, the issue of authorship is complicated. John Van Koert, who filed the design patents, has historically been credited with the design of "Contour;" however, silver historian Jewel Stern has established that the pattern design was actually created by Robert J. King, an assistant designer at Towle, hired by Van Koert to aid in his modernizing efforts. Considering the complex design process for this project, with Van Koert working with the Walker Art Center staff, running the focusing groups, and relaying relevant information back to his design team, "Contour" is most fairly described as a collaboration between the design director and his young designer, although King's name appears nowhere in the exhibition catalog or other promotional materials for the service (Stern 2006, 197–199).

Displaying "Contour:" The "Knife/Fork/Spoon" exhibition

For many postwar consumers, there was a pervading anxiety about how to live with the fruits of their new prosperity. "How-to" books and articles proliferated, advising women on everything from how to use a refrigerator to how to plan a wedding, and model homes and museum exhibitions on domestic design provided further guidance by example. Many of these exemplars, whether in the form of print, exhibitions or

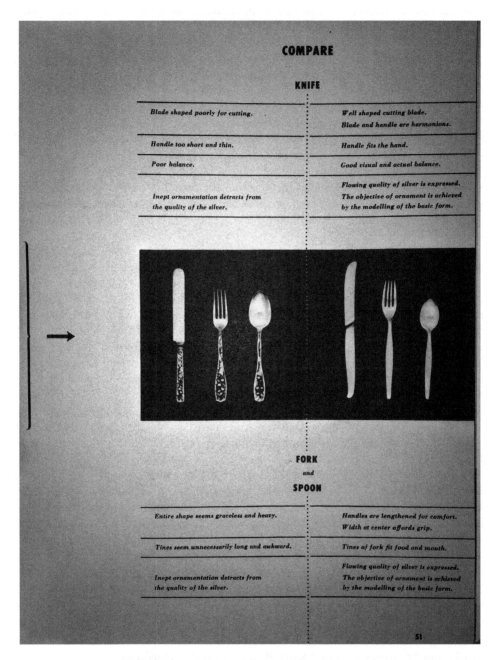

Figure 16.1 Will Hoagberg, Table set with "Contour" sterling service, Eva Zeisel's "Museum" china service, and Josef Hoffman's crystal glassware by Leerdam, image from "Knife/Fork/Spoon" exhibition catalog.

Source: John Szarkowski for the Walker Art Center. Image courtesy of the Walker Art Center Archives

model homes, stressed the multifunctional aspects of modern design. In response to this anxiety, museums sought to provide guidance to visitors as consumers, and, in so doing, to codify taste. The Walker's Everyday Art Gallery, opened in 1942, presented a curated selection of modern objects, typically grouped by object type or material. Goods were not directly sold from these exhibitions, but the museum actively sought to connect consumers with retail outlets. For example, some exhibitions of modern design included a phone in the gallery that provided an immediate connection to local retail venues carrying the goods on display.

"Idea House II," which opened to the public in 1947, took this notion of exemplary display of domestic consumer goods to its ultimate end: it was a full-scale, fully furnished and inhabitable house that allowed visitors to experience first-hand what it was like to be in a Modernist home. "Idea House I," built in 1941, had also been a fully functional single-family house, but it had stressed modern home design on a budget over the consumerism encouraged in "Idea House II" (Winton 2005). Extensive promotional materials for many of the products displayed within "Idea House II" were freely available for visitors to take home. Museum materials stressed that "Idea House II" was not meant as a conventional model home that could be recreated, but rather as a true house of ideas that homebuilders could adapt, curate, and edit to suit their own individual needs.

"Idea House II" featured a multipurpose living/dining space, with a small kitchen that could be isolated from the larger space through sliding partitions. This larger and more informal space replaced the two most important and formal spaces in traditional home layouts: the sitting/living room and the dining room. This distribution of space, favoring more casual, multipurpose areas over discrete rooms with highly particularized functions, in many ways reflected the changing social patterns that were diminishing the importance of household possessions like sterling flatware.

This hybrid exhibition model served a number of important roles for the museums that employed it. It emphasized the ways in which the realms of art (the museum) and commerce (the department store) functioned in parallel, as part of what Bennett has named the "exhibitionary complex," which itself serves to reinforce existing power structures both at the scale of government and at that of society (Bennett 1988). Connections between government and cultural institutions were commonplace, with many museum staff moving back and forth between government and museums. Like René d'Harnoncourt, who transitioned to MoMA from a cultural post in the Department of the Interior, Defenbacher had worked for the Works Progress Administration prior to becoming director of the Walker Art Center. Adding to this, the distinctions between avant-garde and popular culture were in a state of acute flux in this postwar period. As Mary Anne Staniszewski has argued, boundaries between museum, government, and industry were particularly permeable in this postwar era, allowing for "creative experimentation, provocative exhibitions and installations, and unabashed commerce and publicity" (1998, 174). Thus, museums were ideally placed to educate visitors about modern design through innovative approaches to display that often mimicked domestic environments, to codify taste during this moment of social and cultural instability, and to promote industry by giving visitors not only the reasons to acquire modern design but also the necessary connections to commercial points of purchase and examples of how to incorporate the products into their own homes.

In keeping with this sentiment, the Walker took a proactively and openly promotional stance from the beginning of the "Contour" project. In conjunction with the commercial debut of "Contour," it organized a traveling exhibition of flatware design from prehistory to the middle of the twentieth century. This exhibition was called "Knife/Fork/Spoon," and was a direct result of Defenbacher's connection with the venture (Van Koert's early descriptions of the project make no reference to an exhibition). With flatware examples from around the world and across millennia organized within an evolutionary framework, the exhibition proposed "Contour" as the necessary outcome of an inevitable progression from the least civilized to the most evolved examples. Following the exhibition's evolutionary trajectory from obsolete to essential, Defenbacher – as chief curator – identified function, both physical and social, as the constant element driving flatware development globally, from the very earliest examples to the present. The exhibition argued that the most modern, civilized and refined individuals rejected the excessive pattern and ornamentation in imitations of the courtly utensils of the past, preferring the smooth, abstract lines and functional considerations of modern design. "Contour" unsurprisingly occupied the final place in this progressive organization of eating utensils: the apogee of the modern, informal and democratic table.

While stressing the inevitable superiority of a flatware design free of historicizing ornament, the exhibition and catalog also extolled the timeless material properties of silver. The catalog explained that silver was comfortable to the touch, adjusting instantly to the temperature of the hand, and that it was durable yet visually 'soft', especially when it had acquired patina through age and use. Finally, it was luminous, able to refract and diffuse light with a subtle shine. As Nicolas Maffei and Tom Fisher have shown, the notion of shininess in the postwar era was complex, contradictory, and deeply embedded within its historical context. The introduction of numerous specular materials to the consumer market in this period, including chrome, plastics, and aluminum, created new associations with shininess. Whereas silver had traditionally connoted rarity and exclusivity, as also associated with gold, gems, and crystal, the easily degraded shininess of many new materials often signified modernity, progress, and speed (Maffei and Fisher 2013, 233). Thus, the successful design and promotion of a modern sterling pattern would need to astutely negotiate this new layer of association in order to successfully argue for the importance and relevance of modern sterling flatware.

"Knife/Fork/Spoon" had a national touring schedule, appearing at eight museums, including the American Museum of Natural History, the Dallas Museum of Fine Arts, the Cincinnati Museum of Art, and the Cleveland Museum of Art. The sole commercial venue was the JB Hudson department store in Detroit, where it was on view for one week in September 1951. According to the contract, the Walker had full creative and curatorial control of the exhibition, while Towle owned all the physical materials required to set up the exhibition.

While the Walker had already deployed innovative display techniques that provided museum-goers a direct conduit to shopping venues through both the Everyday Art Gallery and the Idea Houses, the "Contour" project and "Knife/Fork/Spoon" proposed an even more radical reinterpretation of the exhibition and display of consumer goods in a museum setting. Not only did the entire project start from a direct collaboration with a commercial entity, similar to Zeisel's "Museum," but the exhibition also directly promoted Towle's new product. This approach is

Figure 16.2 Installation view of the entrance to "Knife/Fork/Spoon" exhibition showing
display system of aluminum rods and wood panels and illuminated display
cases with glass tops.
Source: John Szarkowski for the Walker Art Center. Image courtesy of the Walker Art Center Archives

in stark contrast to the conventional museum exhibition, characterized by a sup-
posedly disinterested presentation of objects arranged with the goal of educating
visitors. "Knife/Fork/Spoon" clearly had didactic goals, but there were commercial
aspirations as well, though the Walker had no financial stake in the success or failure of "Contour."

In its conceptual structure, which was echoed in both exhibition design and the
accompanying catalog, "Knife/Fork/Spoon" was almost anthropological in its methods and encyclopedic in its approach. It attempted to articulate the complex web of
social and cultural meanings imprinted upon eating utensils, which can be among
the most prosaic and humble or the most elevated and elaborate of household items.
Borrowing objects from institutions such as the Metropolitan Museum of Art, the
American Museum of Natural History, and the Yale University Art Gallery, "Knife/
Fork/Spoon" exhibited 225 eating utensils from across the globe, stretching from prehistory to the mid-twentieth century.

Walker Art Center deputy director William Friedman, a trained architect who –
together with Hilde Reiss and Malcolm Lein – also designed "Idea House II," created
the exhibition design. Since it was conceived as a traveling exhibition, it had to be easy

Figure 16.3 Model of "Knife/Fork/Spoon" exhibition design.
Source: John Szarkowski for the Walker Art Center. Image courtesy of the Walker Art Center Archives

to assemble and to break down. To this end, Friedman created a series of aluminum panels supported by wooden platforms so that the exhibition could be mounted without the need for any interior architecture to support or organize the installation. The artist Alonzo Hauser provided illustrations for the installation in his characteristically whimsical and modern style, charting the exhibition's narrative of the progression of manners and mores alongside that of eating utensils. The accompanying catalog follows the sequence of the exhibition and includes the same text, expanded where necessary.

As illustrated in photographs of a scale model of the exhibition, the entrance to the exhibition was marked by two intersecting panels forming a cross. The principal didactic texts for the exhibition were displayed around these panels. From this point, the exhibition consisted of five modular "islands," constructed of intersecting panels and glass-covered display cases. These islands could be configured in a variety of patterns, thereby allowing them to be used for each of the eight venues to which the exhibition traveled. The scale model shows transparent panels placed horizontally over the top of some sections, but it is not clear from installation photographs if these were actually built.

Friedman's free-standing structure and free-flowing plan were in keeping with exhibition strategies at other leading modern art museums. This type of plan had been

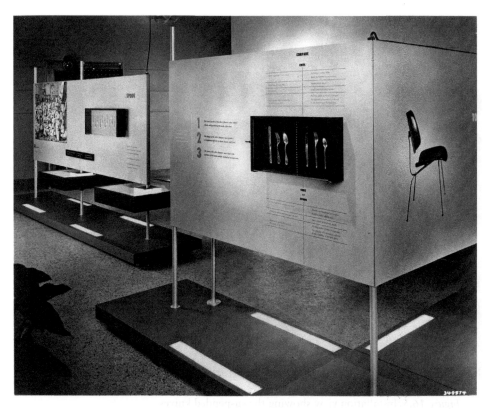

Figure 16.4 Installation view comparing a contemporary flatware design and "Contour."
Source: John Szarkowski for the Walker Art Center. Image courtesy of the Walker Art Center Archives

advocated by Herbert Bayer at the Museum of Modern Art, who was himself deeply influenced by the open-plan design of the Deutsche Werkbund Exhibition in Paris in 1930. Bayer believed that this exhibition strategy created a more exciting, dynamic experience for visitors. The independent physical structure of the exhibition also reflected recent trends in museum and department store display techniques, which de-emphasized the existing architecture of the site and focused instead on the display of exhibition materials themselves, thereby creating a more intimate scale (Staniszewski 1998, 177).

The utensils were arranged both on the vertical surfaces of the panels and within the enclosed display cases. In addition to the utensils, the panels were interspersed with didactic texts and illustrations, some from drawn historical texts and some by Arnold Hauser. The panels intersected at perpendicular points, creating nooks and corners that helped to break up the linear structure of the exhibition, and gave viewers visual access to multiple parts of the exhibition simultaneously. A palette of primary colors – perhaps in reference to the Bauhaus, De Stijl, or other early Modernist movements – was used as a way to create visual interest and to organize the exhibition. Panels were painted gray, yellow, and black, while the display cases were lined in blue, red, or black fabric. Some of the most striking examples of knives were suspended vertically from transparent strings anchored to the upper surface of the display case.

Figure 16.5 Installation view showing the suspended knives.
Source: John Szarkowski for the Walker Art Center. Image courtesy of the Walker Art Center

The case itself was transparent on both sides, creating views directly into other parts of the exhibition.

The utensils on display were organized both by type (taxonomically) and by time period (teleologically), thereby proposing a seamless, logical, and seemingly empirical progression from most primitive to the most evolved examples of eating instruments. Simple labels clearly identified each utensil, its origin, and date. Objects created by so-called primitive cultures were displayed among the earliest examples regardless of their date of creation. While there were isolated efforts in the wall texts to reference the historical context of some of the utensils, they were displayed largely without any contextual information about the cultures that created them. MoMA had employed similar exhibition strategies – highlighting formal affinities between the old and the new – under director René d'Harnoncourt in order to argue for the timeless nature of great art, whether ancient or modern (Staniszewski 1998, 128). In "Knife/Fork/Spoon," however, the de-contextualized objects were used to emphasize a relentless progression, each piece marking a distinct temporal moment. "Contour" occupied the final position in each of the three utensil displays, thereby placing the simple, biomorphic pattern created by American designers and manufactured by a historic American firm at the apogee of civilization, with the surrounding historic examples serving as evidence of its superiority. The display for knives is particularly striking, with each of the examples suspended on strings within the case; the "Contour" knife is the only utensil that has been polished, and it is placed at the center of the far right side of the cabinet. Within the exhibition's organizing structure, its central position and its glimmering form conspire to communicate its clear superiority over the surrounding, less evolved samples.

As Defenbacher wrote in the catalog, utensils combine both aesthetic and intangible values within their shiny silver bodies: "Fine knives, forks, and spoons are objects of real and psychological decoration. Their psychological decorative value is marked by their presence in the hope chest, the dowry, and the will" (1951, 7). According to the logic of the show, utensils evolved according to shifting functional requirements, with function understood as tactile, practical, and symbolic. The material properties of silver were also used to bolster the modernity of the design: functionally it conducted heat, aesthetically it was reflective and beautiful to look at. From the prospective of the designer, it offered maximum flexibility in form-making.

Looking closely at the display, we see that the changing form of the utensils was presented as an objective analysis until it reached the Victorian period, at which point Defenbacher summoned a combination of early Modernist arguments against dishonest machine decoration, Veblenian notions of conspicuous consumption, and a strong Pevsnerian progression towards functional abstraction in setting the stage for the evolutionary leap into the present that "Contour" represented. Whereas the Victorian utensils groaned under the weight of excess ornament and over-specialization, "Contour" demonstrated the notion that "the esthetic idea of our time is based on the elimination of non-essentials. Forms and arrangements tend to reflect a concern with materials and a guarded use of ornamentation. Silver flatware TODAY should reflect these factors" (Defenbacher 1951, 52). The catalog goes on to extoll the way in which the "Contour" form highlights the intrinsic, light-reflecting qualities of silver. Given that the form is predicated on the way in which it is used by the human hand, Deffenbacher equated its function directly to its aesthetic appeal:

> In *Contour* we see a sound, honest and successful effort to break the grip of a once valid but now effete tradition. In *Contour*, there is the old Greek principle – structure can be its own ornament. There is also today's version of that ancient rule – the expression of *use* can be an expression of beauty. Van Koert did not achieve this by making *Contour* plain. The play of concave and convex surfaces and the pattern of reflections in those surfaces are as ornamental as any carved silver garland.
>
> (Defenbacher 1951, 41)

Thus, evolution was employed in two parallel arguments to rationalize the "Contour" project. The first used evolution as a theoretically neutral anthropological description of how changing patterns of civilization are mirrored in shifting utensil design and use. The second, skillfully spliced into the first, used the same phenomenon of the evolving eating utensil to posit "Contour" as the logical essential utensil form to match contemporary American culture, justifying both the design and material as modern, functional, hygienic, and culturally appropriate.

Typically, exhibitions of modern design were either modeled on the showroom – grouped by object type and/or material, as in MoMA's "Good Design" program – or they mimicked the domestic environment, as in the Walker's "Idea House" program. "Knife/Fork/Spoon" is unusual in that its exhibition techniques – the display of objects to present an inevitable progression – were typically used in natural history museums, beginning in the nineteenth century. As Bennett has argued,

> If developments within history and archeology thus allowed for the emergence of new forms of classification and display through which the stories of nations could be told and related to the longer story of western civilization's development, the discursive formations of nineteenth-century geology and biology allowed these cultural series to be inserted within the longer developmental series of geological and natural time. Museums of science and technology, heirs to the rhetorics of progress developed in national and international exhibitions, completed the evolutionary picture in representing the history of industry and manufacture as a series of progressive innovations leading up to the contemporary triumphs of industrial capitalism.
>
> (1988, 90)

The techniques of display used in "Knife/Fork/Spoon" proved influential outside the realm of the museum. Industrial designer Egmont Arens cited "Knife/Fork/Spoon" in his article "The Visual Aspects of Selling" as an example of the successful display of luxury consumer products (*Craft Horizons* 1951). The article stressed the importance of clarity and restraint in the retail display of goods, particularly handmade objects, and encouraged retailers of similar wares to borrow Friedman's clean, minimal aesthetic and to avoid overcrowded, layered heaps of goods and objects in order to encourage sales. That a museum should provide inspiration for retail display exemplifies the porous boundaries between the commercial and the institutional in this period. As Mary Anne Staniszewski has argued in reference to similarities between MoMA and department stores,

> Both are institutions of modernity and modern capitalism. And both the museum and department store are created for visual delectation and display – one, traditionally for an original, timeless, aesthetic experience; the other for mass-produced, commonplace, commercial exchange. The museum and the department store are two sides of the same coin, each clarifying and defining the parameters of its 'other.'
>
> (1998, 174)

Conclusion: "If you can't beat 'em, join 'em"

Towle's collaboration with the Walker on both "Contour" and the subsequent traveling exhibition was controversial, with the Metropolitan Museum of Art declining to extend loans for the popular show on the grounds that it was overly commercial. After all, this was a self-interested business enterprise, using the reputation and resources (namely the visiting public) of the museum not only to stimulate business, but to actually devise the design. Defenbacher was aware of potential unease about the undeniable commercial aspects of the exhibition from its early planning stages, writing:

> The significance of the *Knife/Fork/Spoon* exhibition [...] represents a very advanced, and admittedly controversial, willingness on the part of education to serve industry's dollar-wise pursuits. But, by serving industry, it brought to the consumer a better product. It also narrowed the gap between a dangerously esoteric public institution and the reigning overlord of its time. 'If you can't beat 'em, join 'em' has always been a strategy of some merit.
>
> (Defenbacher 1952)

This uneasy yet unavoidable relationship between museum and corporation persists, with the exigencies of financing the modern museum forging ever-closer ties between art and commerce, and corporate sponsorship and retail tie-ins becoming the standard rather than the exception. While "Contour" is often illustrated in studies of American Modernist design, its museological roots are almost never discussed. Considering Towle maintained its traditional product line, and in fact continued to simultaneously advertise these wares along with "Contour," the uncompromising tone of the Walker catalog in favor of this new, simplified, "honest" design would seem to be at odds with the true commercial ambitions of Towle, which were naturally to appeal to as many consumers as possible.

This unique museum project was a continuation of the Walker Art Center's creative, provocative, and ultimately successful efforts to meld museum and industry for the benefit of the general public via carefully curated displays of goods. "Contour" and "Knife/Fork/Spoon" pushed the promise of the "Good Design" movement to its ultimate conclusion. Together, they went beyond the promotion of design and the policing of taste via museum exhibitions. The Walker's collaboration with Towle created a consumer product that directly engaged the rapidly expanding postwar culture of consumerism while maintaining traces of the more traditional social and material associations of sterling flatware.

The author wishes to thank Jill Vuchetich and the Walker Art Center Archives for their continued support of research into the Walker's early design exhibitions and programming.

References

"Metal Tableware." 1951/2. *Current Design* 4:12.

Arens, Edgmont, 1951. "The Visual Aspects of Selling." *Craft Horizons* 11, 2: 22–27.

Bennet, Tony. 1988. "The Exhibitionary Complex." *New Formations* 4: 73–101.

Clarke, Alison J. 1999. *Tupperware: The Promise of Plastic in 1950s America.* Washington DC: Smithsonian Institution.

Defenbacher, Daniel S. 1951. "Knife, Fork and Spoon." *Craft Horizons* 11, 2: 18–21.

Defenbacher, Daniel S. 1952. "Minneapolis' Walker Art Center and the Face of 1952." *Better Design*, February: 78.

Maffei, Nicholas and Tom Fisher. 2013. "Historicizing Shininess in Design: Finding Meaning in an Unstable Phenomenon." *Journal of Design History* 26, 3: 231–240.

Starniszewski, Mary Anne. 1998. *The Power of Display: A History of Exhibition Installations at the Museum of Modern Art.* Cambridge: MIT Press.

Stern, Jewel. 2006. *Modernism in American Silver: 20th-Century Design* (ex. catalog), edited by Kevin Tucker and Charles Venable. New Haven and London: Yale University Press.

Van Koert, John. 1949. "Let husband help you buy silver, designer urges women." *Minneapolis Star*, February 16.

Walker Art Center Archives. Director's Files (Daniel S. Defenbacher).

Walker Art Center Archives. Exhibition Files (*Knife/Fork/Spoon*).

Wang, Grace Ong. 2012. "Wrapping Aluminum at the Reynolds Metal Company, From Cold War Consumerism to the Age of Sustainability." *Design and Culture* 4, 3: 299–323.

Winton, Alexa Griffith. 2005. "A Man's House Is His Art: The Walker Art Center's Idea House Project and the Marketing of Design, 1941–47." *Journal of Design History* 17, 4: 377–396.

17 Galerías Preciados (1943–1975)

A Spanish cathedral of consumption and its display strategies during the Franco years

Ana María Fernández García

On 5th April 1943 the first Spanish postwar department store, Galerías Preciados, opened in Madrid. Hundreds of citizens milled at the doors of a business that was to mark a new departure in sales techniques and store concept. Such a venture was a real gamble in the aftermath of a four-year civil war (1936–1939) that had ended with more than 300,000 dead, and that was followed by widespread repression, shortages, and rationing. Spain was in the throes of reconstruction after its material and psychological collapse, and all this against the background of the outbreak of the Second World War affecting the rest of Europe. Despite initial difficulties, Galerías Preciados became, along with its principal competitor, El Corte Inglés, the most prominent department stores in Spain during Francisco Franco's dictatorship. Some historians have gone so far as to see in the opening of the modern Galerías Preciados building a symbol of "the slow rebirth of the Spanish economy" (Montoliú 2006, 103). During the first decades of the Franco regime, this symbol of modernity and uncritical consumption served to palliate the lack of basic goods, and the isolation of the country from the international community. Paradoxically, this occurred at a time when the governing ideology rejected the capitalist model of consumption (Alonso and Conde 1994). The stabilization plan of 1959 – based on the three fundamental factors of tourism, the economic benefits of emigration, and, above all, foreign investment – gave rise to a voracious consumption pattern in which the individual's success in life was expressed by material show, and consumerism was enthroned in the collective consciousness. In both periods of Francoism – the first marked by austerity due to the postwar crisis and the second identified with western models of consumption – Galerías Preciados was a key element in the image of Spanish society that the regime was striving to present. Shop windows full of the latest and most varied goods, aggressive advertising, and stylish, modern interior design symbolized the prosperity, modernity, and efficiency of a dictatorial regime that exalted nationalism. Franco's support for the company should therefore come as no surprise. His wife was almost always present at the opening of new branches, while the store's founder – no doubt due to his involvement with and financing of the Fascists during the civil war – was rewarded with honorific titles and medals, and was granted certain privileges by the government in such matters as business opening hours (Cuartas 1992, 278).

The introduction of modern retail methods in Spanish department stores began in the late nineteenth century, following the model of Au Bon Marché in Paris, and was concentrated in the big cities, especially Madrid and Barcelona (Pasalodos Salgado 2012, 6–21). The pioneers were El Aguila (Madrid 1850), Bazar la Unión (1868) and New England (1899), which imitated display, sales, and promotional techniques already being employed elsewhere in Europe and the Americas, includ-ing various departments organized across several floors, illustrated catalogs, mail order, fixed prices, and sales for seasonal stocks. Other stores opened in the first three decades of the twentieth century, such as Los Almacenes Alemanes (1917) and Jorba (1926) in Barcelona, and Madrid-París (1920) and El Siglo (1922) in Madrid. But most of these ventures were short-lived, did not prosper sufficiently to open branches, and rarely sold merchandize other than textiles and fashion acces-sories. By the end of the civil war most of these establishments had disappeared and were replaced by Galerías Preciados and El Corte Inglés, the latter a tailor's shop founded in 1890 and later acquired and turned into a department store by Ramón Areces in 1950.

Although there is some published work analyzing the commercial history of Galerías Preciados and El Corte Inglés (Toboso Sánchez 2000; Cuartas 1992), this chapter aims to reconstruct the process of the arrival of a department store model in Spain through the "Cuban route," which surpassed the embryonic establishments exist-ing before the civil war that had corresponded to the proto-department store model (Lancaster 1995). It was precisely during the Franco years, Spain's initial isolation from the international community notwithstanding, that a true mass-consumption society was born, and, with it, a "department-store culture" (Alonso and Fernández 1995, 212–213). In this climate, the duopoly of Galerías Preciados and El Corte Inglés developed a commercial model that had been previously tried out in Havana follow-ing North American practices. These included the separation of goods by departments, aggressive advertising, the establishment of gift days on specific dates throughout the year, and carefully designed strategies for product presentation. Although these prac-tices were common strategies in European department stores, this commercial model arrived from America through Cuba, where Spain had closer economic relations and business interactions than with the rest of Europe. Taking the example of Galerías Preciados as a paradigm for modern consumerism in Spain, this chapter will trace developments in window displays, merchandize display, and in the introduction of architectural technologies (such as escalators, air-conditioning, and external illumina-tion), which would soon be copied by its great competitor El Corte Inglés, and, on a lesser scale, by other popular stores and regional establishments.

Via Cuba: The arrival of a new department store model in Spain

Although the first Spanish department stores bore names that implied links with stores in London (New England) or Paris (Madrid-París), the modern commercial model imported into Spain came, rather curiously, from Cuba.[1] The owners or managers of these pioneering establishments had often acquired their first business experience on the island, which was a Spanish colony until 1898 (Toboso Sánchez 2010, 1–21). A sizeable Spanish community stayed on after independence, and was especially active in the retail trade. Between 1880 and 1930, of the more than 3.5 million people who emigrated from Spain to the Americas, 33% chose Cuba as their destination (Naranjo 1992, 182). Now residing in a sovereign state in the area of influence of the United States, small shopkeepers and large storeowners swiftly adjusted to the new political reality. They saluted the new order no less fervently than they had acclaimed the former (Clark 1898, 11).[2]

Of the island's urban Spanish immigrant population, the largest sector was that of shop assistants, whether working in traditional small retailer shops or in the island's first department stores such as Fin de Siglo, La Casa Blanca and La Casa Grande (Erice 1994, 92). Working conditions were very hard: shop workers usually worked 16 hours a day, with one Sunday free each fortnight, and lived at the back of the shop in precarious conditions. This was due in part to the family ties prevailing between employers and employees – the so-called "ethnic labour networks" (Vidal Rodríguez 2004, 43).[3] The bosses employed family members or people from their native district, usually teenagers used to doing as they were told and unlikely to complain, a policy that clearly discriminated against the Cuban workforce (Ibarra 1992).[4] This was the case with the future founder of Galerías Preciados, José Fernández (1891–1982), nicknamed Pepín, and his cousin Ramón Areces (1904–1989), future founder of El Corte Inglés (Cuartas 1992, 90). Both were born into humble families in the district of Grado, in the northern province of Asturias, where the best chance to improve their lot was to emigrate to the Americas. After working in Mexico for two years, José Fernández arrived in Havana in 1910 and got a job at the department store El Encanto, which was owned by the Asturian company Solís, Intrialgo and Co.

El Encanto was considered "the best shop in Cuba" (Coyula 2010, 20). It was founded as a small business in 1888 by two brothers from Asturias, José and Bernardo Solís. Encouraged by the buoyant economy of the island following independence, they travelled to the United States and Europe in 1902 to contact suppliers and to research the organisation of stores by departments. Upon their return, they implemented a thorough overhaul that put El Encanto on a par with the best on the continent. In its heyday during the late 1930s, it employed a thousand workers under a paternalistic labour structure. Workers might start at the lowest level as "cañoneros" – errand boys who had to respond quickly to any orders – but, if they proved their worth, they could be promoted. This is exactly what happened with José Fernández and Ramón Areces, who ended up as managers of the company in Havana after four years as ancillaries (Toboso Sánchez 2010, 12).

El Encanto faithfully copied the interwar North American department store model (Maixe-Altes 2009, 8). The proximity of Cuba to the United States favoured strong commercial ties between the two countries, not only in trade but also in commercial strategies and business practice. American marketing techniques, with their apparently innocuous but subliminally aggressive messages, bulk buying, organisation by departments, and attentive customer service, were quickly copied by other businesses in Havana. As a result, haggling, until then a prevalent practice, disappeared and the business became more profitable. For José Fernández and Ramón Areces, Havana was a test-bed for the new way of doing business that would be extended to their future establishments in Madrid and the rest of Spain (Rodríguez-Vigil 2015).

In 1931 José Fernández returned to Spain with the capital he had amassed in Cuba and the professional experience he had acquired both in Cuba and during his frequent visits to the United States. In 1934, together with César Rodríguez (another Asturian who had learnt the trade at El Encanto in Havana), he opened a shop, Sederías Carretas, on Preciados street in Madrid. This was a textiles shop that allowed him to try out modern business techniques. The shop did well, and expanded until it occupied the whole block. It seemed as though the owner was "toying with the idea of installing a department store in Madrid" (Toboso Sánchez 2010, 119). Sederías Carretas struggled to survive the civil war and the siege of the city, so it was with great enthusiasm that the store hailed Franco's victory. The window displays of April 1939 eloquently expressed the warmth with which the company greeted Spain's

Figure 17.1 Window display of Sederías Carretas, celebrating the end of the Spanish civil war.
Source: Galerías Preciados Collection, File 0918761/033, Archivo Regional de la Comunidad de Madrid

"*caudillo*" in the slogan "Triumph and Resurrection" (GP, File 0918761/033, ARCM) (Fig. 17.1).

Marketing and display strategies (1943–1960)

In April 1943 Galerías Preciados opened as a department store. Although in the postwar period the high cost of electricity limited its opening hours in the evenings, the citizens of Madrid were invited to visit the store at night and witness "a magical show of extraordinary beauty" (*ABC* 1943). The five-storey building had a floor space of over 3,000 square metres on the corner of Rompelanzas and Preciados streets, very close to the central Plaza del Sol. Each floor housed several departments and incorporated some of the latest features defining department stores. Customers could enter the establishment freely, wander around and examine the merchandize at their ease – a rare privilege in traditional Madrid shops, where poor interior lighting meant that the shopkeeper had to bring the goods out into the street, where they were set out in baskets or on shelves. Another fundamental change was that, instead of being kept in boxes and displayed only at the customer's request, goods were now placed in showcases, on display stands, or on counters within reach of visitors (Fig. 17.2). This marked a shift in the Spanish retail system. Although such practices had been previously introduced in the short-lived Spanish proto-department stores, it was Galerías Preciados that established them in the postwar period. The driving force behind transactions was no longer demand but supply, with the goods being offered seductively right before customers' eyes. The sales staff abandoned their old role of showing goods to the clients and became instead shopping advisers. All this meant that display strategies were carefully studied to ensure that the customer would receive an attractive and thorough impression of the product and could easily see the

Figure 17.2 Scene from the film *Me quiero casar contigo* directed by Jerónimo Mihura, starring Fernando Fernán Gómez and set in Galerías Preciados, 1951.
Source: Galerías Preciados Collection, File 0918743/051, 1951, Archivo Regional de la Comunidad de Madrid

price or any discount available. Furthermore, the stores ceased being merely places for commercial transactions and became spaces of socialization, especially among middle-class women, who would cherish the opportunity to meet their friends while shopping (Rodríguez-Vigil 2014, 110). An excellent illustration of the social vitality of the establishment is represented in the film *Las muchachas de azul* (*The Girls in Blue*) of 1957 directed by Pedro Lazaga, which featured Galerías Preciados' shop assistants wearing their blue uniforms. The shop was frequented by women, entire families, single men, and the elderly. Customers visited not only to see the latest trends in fashion, beauty products or interior decoration, but also to chat, spend a day out, or even, as the film suggests, to look for a romantic partner. The attractiveness of the department store as a socializing place was heightened by the incorporation of a cafeteria in the 1960s.

The department stores of the Franco period – Galerías Preciados and its rival El Corte Inglés – focused on attracting a middle- and upper-class clientele.[5] This was reflected in the sophisticated way in which goods were presented, and in advertising slogans which, instead of using low prices as bait, emphasised distinction, elegance, quality and good taste. For example, the department stores shunned the word "sales" in favour of "stock/post-inventory clearance" or "Christmas/Summer Offers." Similarly, newspaper and magazine advertisements did not display prices until the 1970s. To further distinguish themselves from the popular stores, they carefully spaced their special-offer periods so as not to give the impression that they were perpetually holding sales. In these years, the word *"rebajas"* (sales) was associated more with Spanish popular stores such as Simago (founded in 1960), or neighborhood retailers with a lower-class clientele. The two and only department stores, clearly addressed themselves to a better-off segment of society, at the same time giving the impression to those with less purchasing power that they offered a refinement hitherto the preserve of the bourgeoisie.

The commercial innovations adopted by Galerías Preciados, and rapidly copied by its competitor El Corte Inglés, have had a marked effect on Spanish consumer and social habits right up to the present. For example, the January sales, known as "End of Season Offers," still exist today, as do Father's Day (coinciding with Saint Joseph's day), Mother's Day (originally the day of the Immaculate Conception but now celebrated the first Sunday in May) and Saint Valentine's Day sales, all of which were introduced by Fernández (Cuartas 1992). He also promoted the habit of giving presents to name-sakes on saints' days such as Pilar, Teresa, Rafael, Felipe, etc, and even Euphrasia, to commemorate the "day of the housemaid." Galerías Preciados drew up a carefully designed commercial calendar following the American model, which Fernández had encountered during his time in Cuba (Schmidt 1991, 887–916), and which perfectly suited the slogan that the business used for many years: "communicating elegance through gifts" (*practique la elegancia social en el regalo*). In other words, Galerías Preciados, soon followed by El Corte Inglés, successfully combined the gift-consumption tradition of North America with the cultural traditions of Spanish Catholicism, exemplified in the commemoration of name days in accordance with the calendar of saints.

Since the very beginning, a hallmark of Galerías Preciados were its window and façade displays (Fig. 17.3). In 1946 Fernández hired Samuel Venero, who had previously worked as window dresser in the Cuban stores Casa Grande and El Encanto. Venero directed the store's professional window dressing, signage and decoration until

Figure 17.3 Galerías Preciados façade decorated as a castle, Madrid, 1954.
Source: Cristóbal Portillo Collection, 1/1/1954, File 97086_001-GP, Archivo Regional de la Comunidad de Madrid

he left the company at the start of the 1960s.[6] Attractive window displays took over the streets, dissolving the boundary between the interior and the world outside, and offering an elegant sample of the goods on sale. Unlike the cluttered shop windows of the past, those of Venero presented an artistic composition clearly inspired by American trends (Benson 1987, 18). He used mannequins, and direct and indirect lighting of variable intensity with coloured glass lenses. Venero followed the precepts of the *Shop Window Illumination Manual* of 1932 (Iluminación 1932), which was the only manual available in the country up to the 1960s.[7] In the mid-1950s, the store's Creative Design department incorporated photography to its window dressing activity. As a result, it became normal practice for outsized photographic work to serve as a backdrop to the mannequins and the goods on display. Initially, these photographs measured one metre by two, and several were used to cover the back of the display. As the director of the photography department declared in 1956, the aim was to make two-metre-by-four enlargements, despite the fact that paper of this size was not manufactured in Spain, and to make them part of the interior design of the different departments:

> I believe that this will give a new dimension to the display. Imagine in a window a two by four image of a landscape, a single flower, a snail, the head of a dog [...] But this will not only be for window-dressing; splendid decorations can also be created within the departments.
>
> (Boletín de Galerías 1956, 9–10)

Galerías Preciados' Internal Rules and Regulations of 1948 (GP, File 124661/ 6, ARCM) included an artistic director together with a window-dresser and sign-painter, along with various apprentices and hands. The emoluments of the window-dresser and design-sketcher were similar to those of the department director or branch manager, with generous bonuses, an indication of the importance given to these roles, following the Cuban and, above all, the American model. Venero also took charge of exterior lighting, especially at Christmas, with spectacular illuminations that shone out in the nights of postwar Madrid, which was still subject to electricity restrictions.

Another sign of the times, common to department stores worldwide, was the emphasis on technological innovation, again marking the difference from traditional retailers (Crossick and Jaumain 1999, 8). The installation of the first mechanical escalator in Galerías Preciados in 1955 was a social event without precedent, and led to long queues of visitors eager to experience being transported effortlessly from one floor to the next (Toboso Sánchez 2002).

The modernisation of display strategies in Galerías Preciados

In 1960 the architect Javier Feduchi Fernández (1929–2005) was appointed to replace Venero as artistic director.[8] His arrival was to spur a new entrepreneurial period characterized in the first place by the expansion of the company throughout Spain, starting in the suburbs of Madrid (for example, Arapiles) and subsequently spreading to the fifty-two provincial capitals. The business also went through a modernisation of its image and the development of product placement strategies. The opening of new branches both in Madrid and in other provincial capitals coincided with the second period of General Franco's dictatorial regime, known as *"Crecimiento del Franquismo"* (Francoist growth), which saw spectacular economic growth accompanied by an opening up of the regime internationally, and the arrival of foreign investment and tourists. This favoured the growth of national industry, which had until then been isolated from Europe and the international markets. *Per capita* income was rising and Spanish society was becoming increasingly urban, developing a new mass-consumption and leisure culture. There was thus a transition from the subsistence economy of the postwar period to a voracious consumerism, in which the middle classes evidenced their rise up the social ladder via ownership of material symbols (Alonso and Conde 1994, 148).

Feduchi began his work in Galerías Preciados with internal modifications to some of the existing buildings, and was also responsible for most of the architectural projects for new branches. Each local workshop followed the guidelines laid down by his team in Madrid (*Boletín de Galerías* 1973, 22), which controlled every aspect of the designs, whether window-dressing, product display, sign-painting, furniture, or the interiors. As the architect declared some years later:

> The possibility of integral design, of controlling all the components of a project, from the façade to the tables and chairs and the style of a window, was something I learned from my father, who himself had learned it from the Bauhaus. In Galerías Preciados, as we were also responsible for window-dressing, we could select items at foreign fairs and put them in a setting reflecting modern taste. There was simply nothing like it at that time in Spain.
>
> (San Vicente 1994, 60)

Among the innovations introduced by Feduchi, perhaps the most important was the replacement of counters, showcases and shelving with a different kind of furniture, the aim of which was to display rather than to store. The clients now had easier access to the merchandize, being able to handle it before making a purchase. Previously, all the goods, in their different sizes and colours, had been heaped on the counters, making it difficult to properly appreciate and compare the variety on offer. This new approach also meant that the basements had to be used for storage. The sales directors of each department made a prior selection of the sizes, colours and styles to be put on display, keeping the bulk of the merchandize stored in the basement. This gave rise to what was called the GPS and GPA lines of fittings, which could be assembled, dismantled, extended, and adapted to accommodate all kinds of merchandize. The fittings consisted of tubular metal structures, sometimes with plastic-lined wooden drawers or cupboards in the lower part, set on wheels to facilitate movement. The most famous of these models was the *gondola*, which had drawers in the lower part and shelves at either side, whose shape and size depended on the goods they were to house. In 1964 trials were carried out at the Arapiles store in Madrid with a structure of iron tubes making up a kind of *meccano*, built with angle brackets supporting the tubes (Fig. 17.4), on which sheets of metal, wood or plastic could be placed to hold the goods or for window displays. These items were manufactured in the company's own workshops, where Feduchi shared his previous experience as metal furniture designer for Rolaco (a company manufacturing rationalist furniture, founded by his father, Luis M. Feduchi in 1932). His tubular metal structures permitted flexible assemblies, depending on the type and size of the items on display, which could also be easily stacked and transported.

Another Feduchi innovation was to endow Galerías Preciados with an identifiable and coherent façade image. None of the earlier buildings conveyed a clear exterior image. Indeed, the windows of the first ones made them look more like an office block than a department store. In the new store branches, or in extensions to existing ones, the architect replaced the upper-floor windows with horizontal bands of aluminium or precast concrete, equipped for fitting lighting elements, billboards and shop signs. The aim was to standardise the image of the buildings as it appeared from the street: large display windows on the ground floor with a clean modern style, equipped with fittings that meant the company could be visually identified with ease. The façade became the platform for a continuously changing advertisement. Feduchi stipulated that a department store should offer a defined, uniform space with modern materials, be well illuminated, and integrate the escalators in the façade. Seeing the movement of people from one section to another was fundamental to the new sales strategies (Barbeito 2006, 122). Another strategic innovation was the construction of canopies to protect the shop windows' area, or even, as in the case of Zaragoza (1971), the building of arcades, which allowed potential clients to contemplate the goods while sheltered from rain or sun. The interior of the buildings, as redesigned or constructed by Feduchi, invariably had false ceilings, known as Rotterdam style since they derived from the De Bijenkorf store (1957) in that city. The electrical wiring, piping and sprinkler systems were concealed, while lighting points could be arranged at will. In Arapiles, one of the six Madrid branches, these false ceilings were hexagonal, masking the light sources and at the same time determining the shape of the floor and furnishing modules. Feduchi employed metal tubing, mirrors, plastic, and even the ultra-modern metacrylate in many of his interior design projects, all arranged so as to enhance the company's modern image. Inside the store, the mannequins were arranged in small groups on stands that customers could see from all sides. The stands determined the axes of the internal space, normally defined by metal structures emerging from the ceiling, forming hangers or modular shelves (Fig. 17.4).

Although each branch of Galerías Preciados had its own advertising department, the instructions regarding materials, colours and poster design came from Madrid. Directives were also sent out periodically concerning special campaigns such as Christmas, sales (euphemistically called "post-stocktaking offers"), or Mother's Day. During sales in the 1960s, for example, the shop windows were lined with red silk and had two rows of advertising slogans framing the upper and lower halves. Interior posters, generally suspended from the ceiling, also conformed to a corporate image emanating from head office in Madrid. During sales, it was specifically recommended that the window displays should be arranged in three sections (fabrics, clothing, and accessories), and that an impression should be given of "a large quantity of articles, but clearly displayed" (GP, File 124664, ARCM).

Competition from El Corte Inglés was constant, despite the good relationship between the respective owners due to their shared past in Cuba. Each spied on the other to discover the price at which they proposed to sell, and both competed for the introduction of new technology. Thus, in the summer of 1958, Galerías Preciados installed what were termed "curtains of air" – a technology that provided cold air just above the entrances, so that the visitor coming in would experience a fresh, cooling sensation. This technology was developed by the company's own engineers. Shortly

Figure 17.4 Stand in the ladies' fashion department of Galerías Preciados in Arapiles, Madrid, 1964.
Source: *Boletín de Galerías Preciados*, 1964, Galerías Preciados Collection, File 124661/7, Archivo Regional de la Comunidad de Madrid

afterwards, in 1961, the summer press advertisements emphasised the store's air-conditioning technology, providing interiors with a more pleasant temperature. This technology became a symbol of modernity in itself, just like the spacious lifts and escalators had done before. Galerías Preciados pioneered innovations that facilitated public access and customer comfort. In the early 1960s, the Madrid stores had their own baby- and child-care facilities to make the visit more appealing to young mothers. They also incorporated visitor parking with direct access to the different floors, as in the Callao store in Madrid, which was "the only retail establishment in Spain with a car park of this kind, such as those existing in some of the department stores abroad."[10]

Along with conventional window displays showing new merchandize for each season, Galerías Preciados also introduced "*espectáculos culturales*" – commemorative cultural displays that were artistically designed and referred to anniversaries, awards and important occasions (Rodríguez-Vigil 2015, 119). In these cases the emphasis on selling was less pronounced, and gave way instead to a show of virtuosity in the staging and symbolism of the elements employed. In 1972 the main branch in Barcelona dedicated its main window to the composer Amadeo Vives on the occasion of the centenary of his birth. On one side, several wind and string instruments, supported by transparent threads, seemed to float in space. A conductor's stand and ten white-gloved hands on the floor made up the rest of the set, at once minimalist and subtle.

Five years earlier, in 1967, the store surprised the citizens of Barcelona by incorporating "living dummies" into a floodlit display of merchandize and mannequins. These were professional models who, for an hour a day, used the exhibition as a catwalk to give a preview of women's fashions for the autumn and winter seasons, mimicking French haute couture in the early 1900s. This was a curious hybrid of static mannequins and professional models in movement, and each of the models carried a card showing the price of the outfit (Boletín de Galerías 1967, 1–2). On other occasions, the commercial strategies of Galerías Preciados were inspired by the cinema, as in 1965 when it took advantage of the success of *Doctor Zhivago* (some scenes of which were shot in Madrid, Soria and Granada). The window displays exhibited fur coats and women's accessories inspired by the film, and used the film poster as backdrop (GP, File 0918763/011, ARCM) (Fig. 17.5).

Among its advertising innovations, in the 1960s Galerías Preciados came up with the idea of displays celebrating a foreign country, such as France, Germany, Japan or Great Britain. Products representative of each country were imported and put on sale at a time when Spain was emerging from its economic isolation. These promotions achieved a remarkable echo in the media, enlisting the presence of the ambassadors of the countries on display and other outstanding personalities. Live models were

Figure 17.5 Window display themed on the film *Doctor Zhivago* in Jorba-Preciados, Barcelona, 1965.

Source: Galerías Preciados Collection, File 0918763/011 1965, Archivo Regional de la Comunidad de Madrid

employed to recreate scenes from the everyday life of each country. In April 1964 the display given to the Far East involved the installation of a Japanese garden in the Barcelona store, through which female models strolled wearing the traditional dress of the country. When Great Britain was the chosen nation, a real London double-decker bus visited the cities where Galerías Preciados had branches to publicize the campaign. This internationalization of the store's advertising efforts and display strategies was fuelled by the opening up of the Franco regime, which was slowly re-establishing contact with the rest of the world following decades of isolation. After the death of Franco, and with the adoption of democracy, Galerías Preciados continued its business activity, in strong competition not only from El Corte Inglés but also from other establishments that were supported by foreign capital. The company's aggressive expansion policy led to indebtedness, and it eventually fell into the hands of its creditors until the forceful expropriation of its last owner, the holding group Rumasa, in 1983. This marked the beginning of a legal and commercial process that culminated in the store's takeover by its lifelong competitor, El Corte Inglés, in 1995 (Cuartas 1992).

Conclusion

Galerías Preciados and El Corte Inglés were the first modern department stores in Spain. After the civil war, these stores introduced a modern business model imported from Cuba, which in turn was based on American retailing practices. From the very beginning of Galerias Preciados, interior designer Samuel Venero took display techniques and product visualisation to a new level, abandoning the convention of storing goods in boxes. Under his artistic direction the store displayed merchandize on stands, showcases and counters, granting easy access to customers. Window dressing also acquired a renewed importance, driven by an original calendar of advertising campaigns that has influenced the habits of Spanish consumers to the present day.

From the 1960s onwards, the architect Javier Feduchi worked towards the visual and corporate modernisation of the company in the context of the "Spanish economic miracle." This took place as isolationism was abandoned and Spain opened up to the rest of the world embracing a consumer society. Galerías Preciados expanded and the new premises acquired distinct personalities, expressed in their façades with a uniform, well-illuminated surface that could accommodate large-scale advertising and display windows. New shop furniture integrated modern materials and modular construction, a trend that was quickly imitated by competitors. A commitment was made to integrate the latest in modern technology in the form of mechanical escalators, air-conditioning, and modern lifts. Throughout the pre- and post-1960s periods, Galerías Preciados set the pace in Spanish retailing. The store was considered, at the time, a symbol of the country's modernisation. Today it may be seen as a paradoxical example of the economic achievements of an autocratic and nationalist regime that, on an ideological level, opposed capitalist consumption.

Notes

1 This kind of business closely resembles what, in the British context, is known as a proto-department store (Lancaster 1995).
2 In 1898 William J. Clark wrote a guide aimed at potential North American investors interested in commercial colonisation of the island after the end of Spanish rule.

3 A vivid example of the living conditions of shop workers can be seen in the news report of the fire at La Rosita in Havana in 1904. The fire broke out in a barbecue area that served as a dormitory for the employees and "a store for wreaths, flags and wickerwork" (*El Carbayón* June 27 1888).
4 Discrimination against the native workforce in favour of a Spanish labour monopoly, especially in the retail sector, fuelled the markedly nationalist socialist workers' movement.
5 In contrast to what occurred in other countries, popular stores that targeted those with low purchasing power had hardly any success, as this type of client remained faithful to the traditional neighbourhood shop and street markets.
6 Venero worked for Galerías Preciados at the same time as he directed, from 1955, the school of window-dressing in Madrid, which depended on the city's Chamber of Commerce and Industry. At the beginning of the 1960s he founded the consultancy firm Hervi, devoted to the design and distribution of fittings for shop windows, and opened offices in various Spanish cities.
7 The *Shop Window Illumination Manual* was published by the Lighting Association in Spain, founded in 1929. The association organised many conferences to promote the correct use of electricity in schools, and it managed a Shop Window Illumination competition in 1932, which received 890 proposals. The association also published other manuals, but after the civil war it stopped its editorial activity.
8 Javier Feduchi Benlliure was educated at the Madrid School of Architecture (graduated 1959). From 1962 he had a professional relationship with Galerías Preciados in the area of interior and office design.

References

ABC, April 7, 1943.
Alonso, Luis Enrique and Fernando Conde. 1994. *Historia del Consumo en España: Una Aproximación a sus Orígenes y Primer Desarrollo*. Madrid: Debate.
Barbeito, José. 2006. "In Memoriam. Javier Feduchi." *Arquitectura* 343: 122–123.
Benson, Susan Porter. 1987. *Counter Cultures. Saleswomen, Managers, and Customers in American Department Stores, 1890–1940*. Champaign: University of Illinois Press.
Boletín de Galerías, n° 63, June 1956.
Boletín de Galerías, n° 149, October 1964.
Boletín de Galerías, n° 175, November 1967.
Boletín de Galerías, n° 236, December 1973.
Clark, William J. 1898. *Commercial Cuba: A Book for Businessmen*. New York: Charles Scribner.
Cristóbal Portillo Collection. 1/1/1954, File 97086_001-GP, Archivo Regional de la Comunidad de Madrid.
Coyula, Mario. 2010. "Al Margen del Centro." *Arquitectura y Urbanismo* 31: 16–26.
Crossick, Geoffrey and Serge Jaumain. 1999. "The World of the Department Store: Distribution, Culture and Social Change." In *Cathedrals of Consumption. The European Department Store (1850–1939)*, edited by Geoffrey Crossick, and Serge Jaumain, 1–45. Aldershot: Ashgate.
Cuartas, Javier. 1992. *Biografía de El Corte Inglés: Historia de un Gigante*. Barcelona: Libros Límite.
El Carbayón, June 27, 1888.
Erice, Francisco. 1994. "Los Asturianos en Cuba y sus Vínculos con Asturias: Rasgos y Desarrollo de una Colectividad Regional en la Etapa Final del Colonialismo Español." In *De Asturias a América. Cuba (1850–1930): La Comunidad Asturiana en Cuba*, edited by Pedro Gómez, 71–152. Gijón: Archivo de Indianos.
(GP) Galerías Preciados Collection. (ARCM) Archivo Regional de la Comunidad de Madrid.
(GP) File 0918761/033 (ARCM).
(GP) File 0918743/051 (ARCM).
(GP) Internal Rules and Regulations. File 124661/6 (ARCM).

(GP) File 124664 (ARCM).

(GP) File 0918763/011 (ARCM).

(GP) File 0918763/011 (ARCM).

(GP) File 0918761/033 (ARCM).

Ibarra, Jorge. 1992. *Cuba: 1898–1921. Partidos políticos y clases sociales.* La Habana: Editorial de Ciencias Sociales.

Iluminación de Escaparates. 1932. Madrid: Asociación de Luminotecnia de Madrid.

Lancaster, Bill. 1995. *The Department Store: A Social History.* London: Leicester University Press.

Maixe-Altes, J. Carles. 2009. "Interpreting the Early Stages of the Self-service Revolution in Europe: the Modernization of Food Retailing in Spain, 1947–1972." Munich Personal RePEc Archive, MPRA paper No. 18164. Accessed December 26, 2015. http://econpapers.repec.org/RePEc:pra:mprapa:18164

Montoliú, Pedro. 2006. "Presión Aliada en medio de un Panorama de Miseria." In *1943. Franco Viste de Uniforme a las Cortes*, edited by Javier Arjona and Silvia Fernández, 98–106. Madrid: Unión Editorial.

Naranjo, Consuelo. 1992. "Análisis Cuantitativo." In *Historia General de la Emigración Española a Iberoamérica*, vol. I, edited by Pedro Vives, Pepa Vega and Jesús Oyamburu, 177–200. Madrid: Historia 16.

Pasalodos Salgado, Mercedes. 2012. "Ir de Compras por Madrid. Los Grandes Almacenes y sus Catálogos Ilustrados." *Datatèxtil* 27: 6–21.

Rodríguez-Vigil, José María. 2014. "Tradición Asturiana de Distinción: una Aproximación al Estudio de los Grandes Almacenes Botas." *Liño* 20: 109–124.

Rodríguez-Vigil, José María. 2015. "Arquitectura, Consumo y Sociedad: Galerías Preciados y otros Grandes Almacenes en la Ciudad de Oviedo." In *Otras Voces, Otros Ámbitos: los Sujetos y su Entorno. Nuevas Perspectivas de la Historia Sociocultural*, edited by Vicent Bellver Loizaga et al., 11–120. Valencia: Universitat de València.

San Vicente, Jesús. 1994. "Entrevista. Javier Feduchi." *Experimenta. Número Monográfico Diseño del Mueble en España: 1902–1998*: 20.

Schmidt, Leigh Eric. 1991. "The Commercialization of the Calendar: American Holidays and the Culture of Consumption, 1870–1930." *The Journal of American History* 7: 887–916.

Toboso Sánchez, Pilar. 2000. *Pepín Fernández (1819–1982) Galerías Preciados. El Pionero de los Grandes Almacenes.* Madrid: Lid Editorial Empresarial.

Toboso Sánchez, Pilar. 2002. "Grandes Almacenes y Almacenes Populares en España. Una Visión Histórica." *Documentos de Trabajo. Historia Económica (Fundación SEPI)*, 2.

Toboso Sánchez, Pilar. 2010. "Los Orígenes Cubanos de El Corte Inglés y de Galerías Preciados: los dos Grandes Almacenes del Comercio en España." Paper presented at 9 Encontro Internacional da Anphlac, Universidade Federal de Goiás, July 26–29.

Vidal Rodríguez, José Antonio. 2004. "La Inmigración Española a Cuba durante la Primera Ocupación Militar Norteamericana (1899–1902): El Control del Mercado Laboral." *Migraciones y Exilios* 4: 31–49.

Index